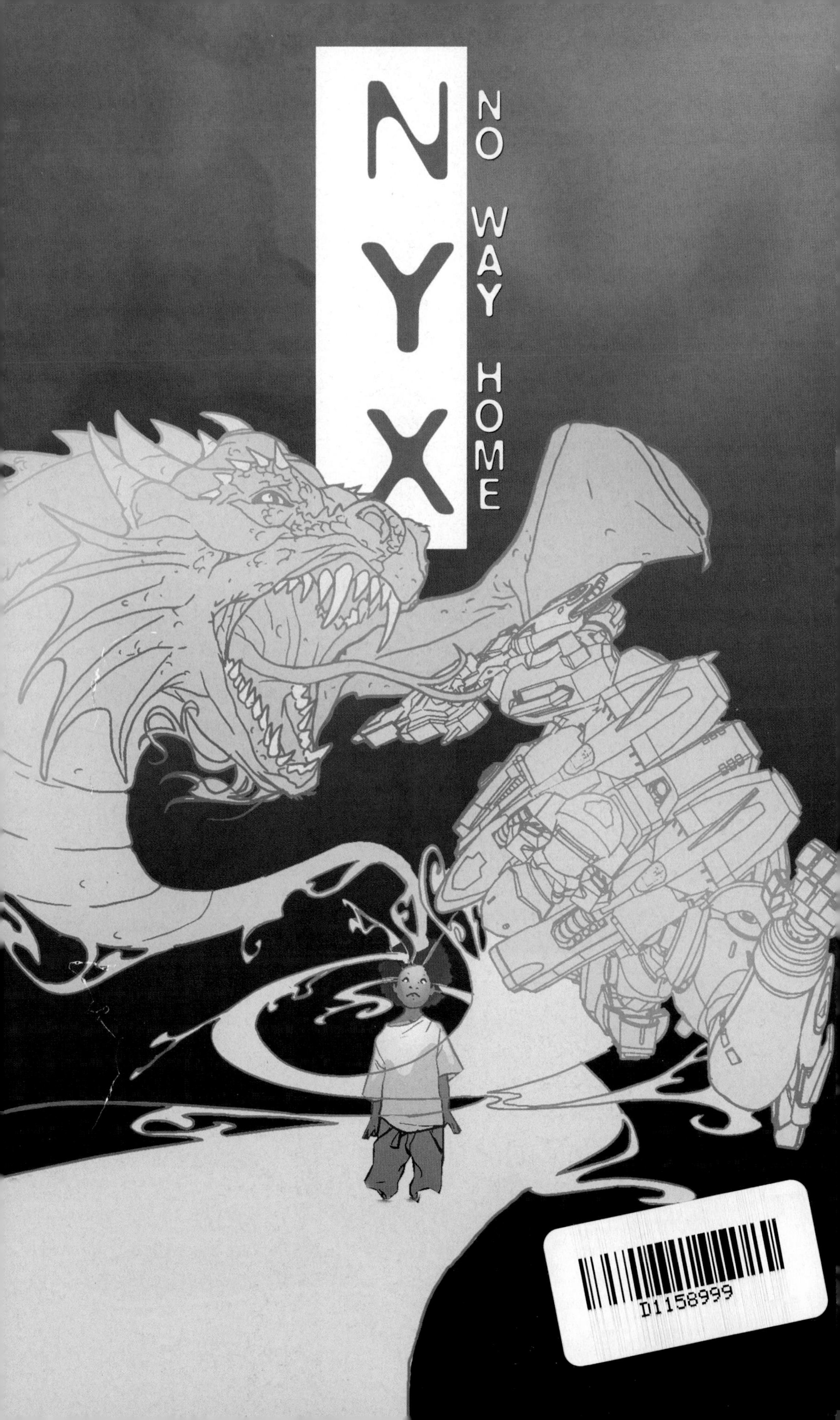
NYX
NO WAY HOME

WRITER:
MARJORIE LIU

PENCILERS:
KALMAN ANDRASOFSZKY & SARA PICHELLI

INKERS:
KALMAN ANDRASOFSZKY, RAMON PEREZ &

SARA PICHELLI

COLORS:
JOHN RAUCH

LETTERS:
VIRTUAL CALLIGRAPHY'S JOE CARAMAGNA &

CHRIS ELIOPOULOS

COVER ART:
ALINA URUSOV

ASSISTANT EDITOR:
MICHAEL HORWITZ

EDITOR:
JOHN BARBER

GROUP EDITOR:
AXEL ALONSO

NYX

NO WAY HOME

COLLECTION EDITOR:
JENNIFER GRÜNWALD

EDITORIAL ASSISTANT:
ALEX STARBUCK

ASSISTANT EDITORS:
CORY LEVINE &
JOHN DENNING

EDITOR, SPECIAL PROJECTS:
MARK D. BEAZLEY

SENIOR EDITOR, SPECIAL PROJECTS:
JEFF YOUNGQUIST

SENIOR VICE PRESIDENT OF SALES:
DAVID GABRIEL

BOOK DESIGNER:
SPRING HOTELING

BONUS MATERIALS DESIGN:
JOE SABINO

EDITOR IN CHIEF:
JOE QUESADA

PUBLISHER:
DAN BUCKLEY

EXECUTIVE PRODUCER:
ALAN FINE

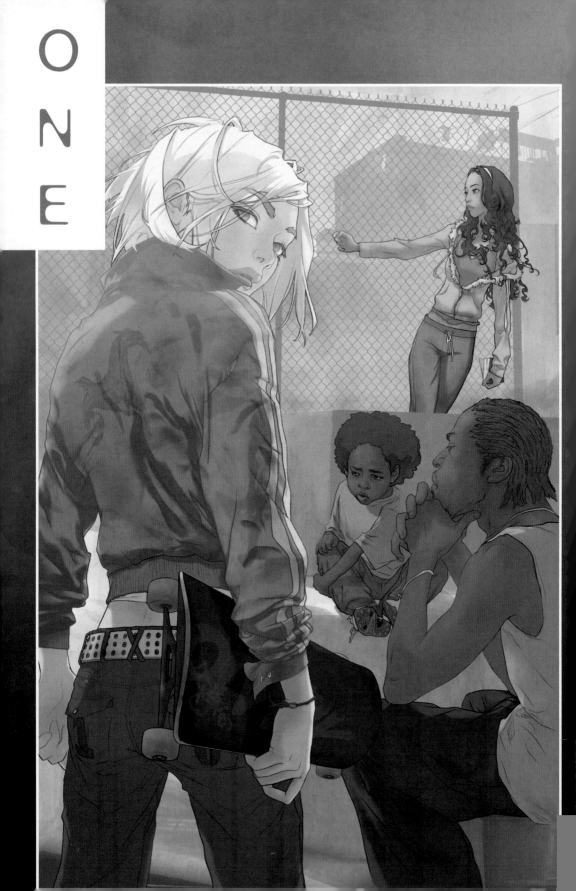

ONE

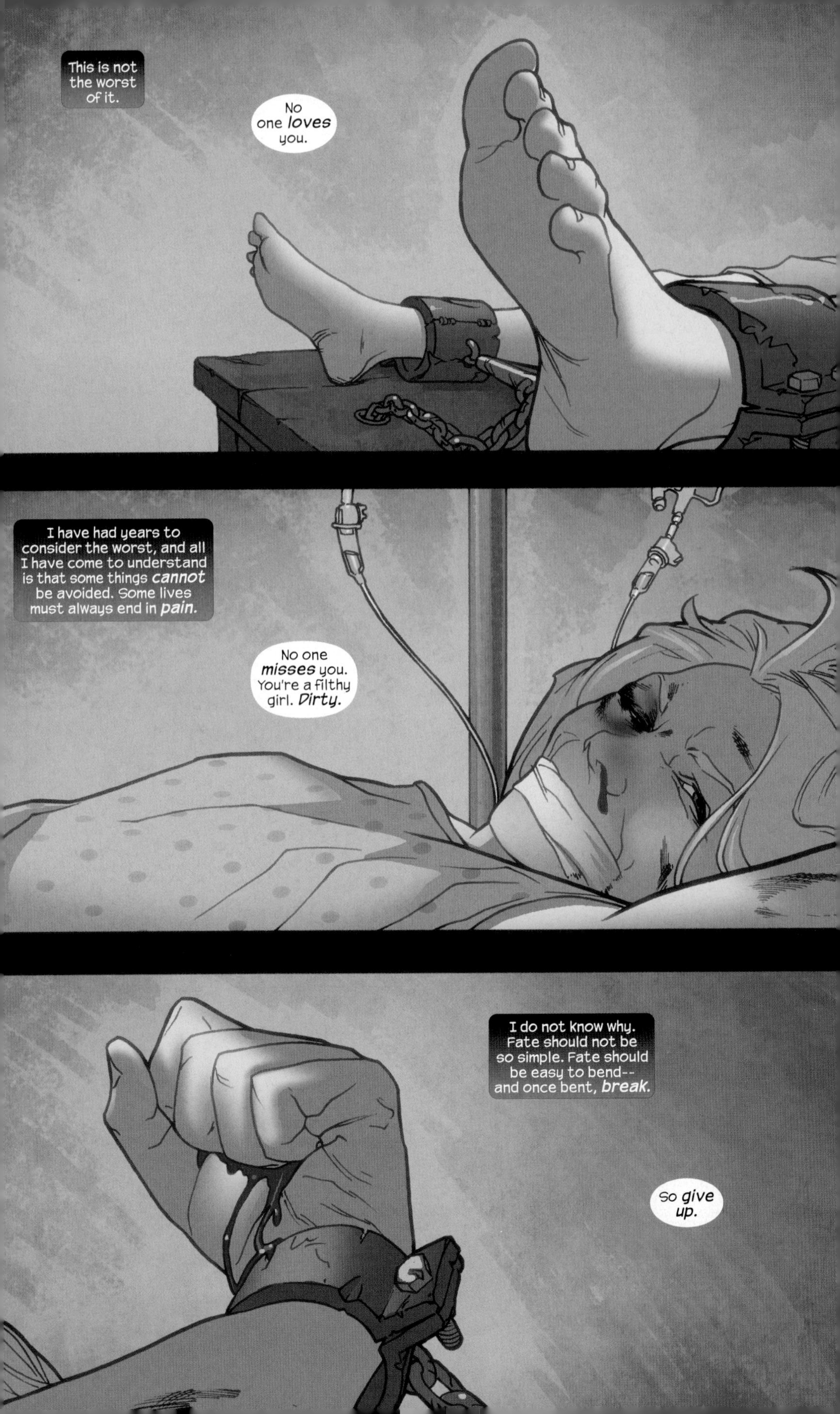
This is not the worst of it.
No one loves you.
I have had years to consider the worst, and all I have come to understand is that some things cannot be avoided. Some lives must always end in pain.
No one misses you. You're a filthy girl. Dirty.
I do not know why. Fate should not be so simple. Fate should be easy to bend-- and once bent, break.
So give up.

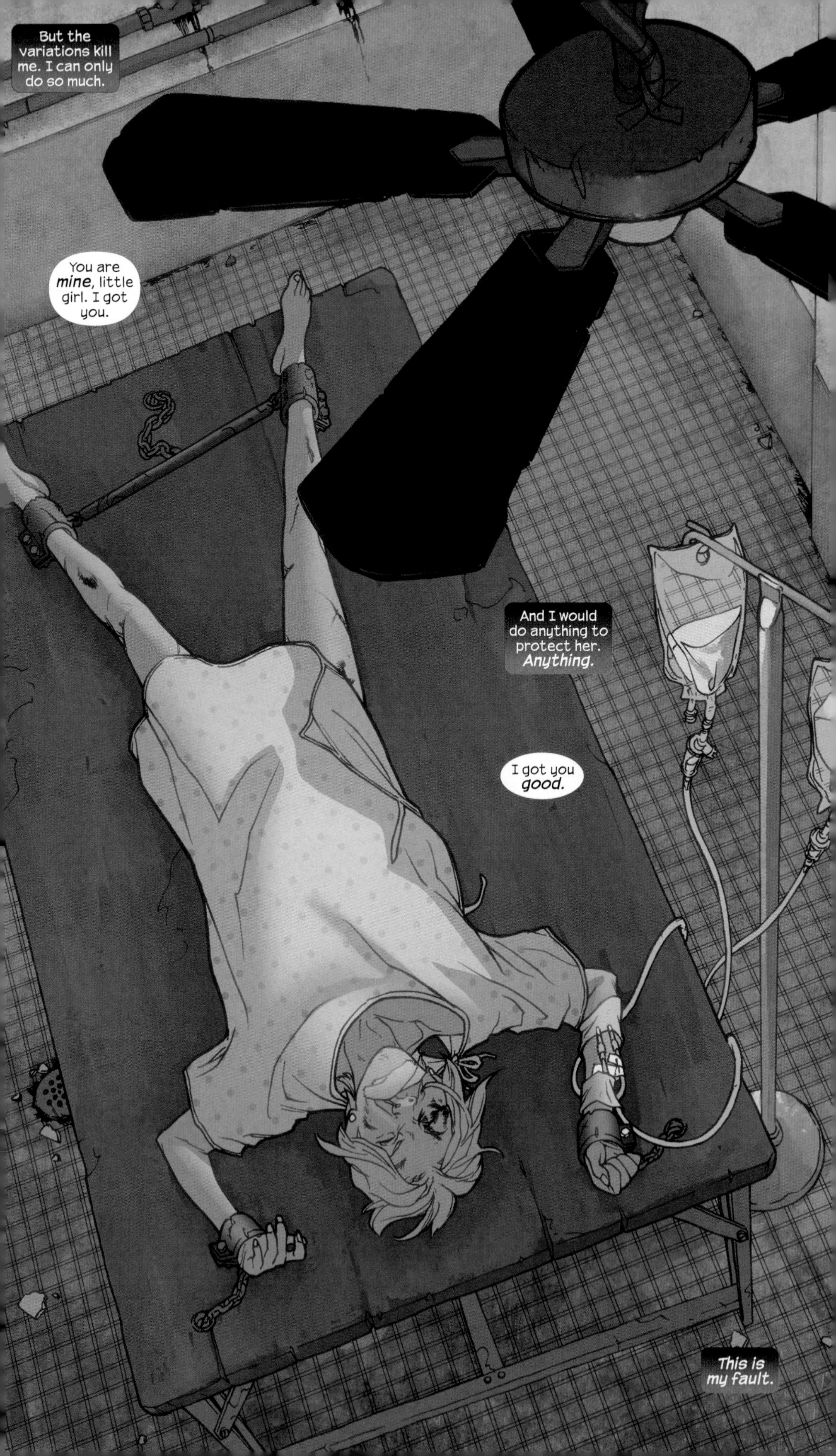

But the variations kill me. I can only do so much.
You are *mine*, little girl. I got you.
And I would do anything to protect her. *Anything.*
I got you *good.*
This is my fault.

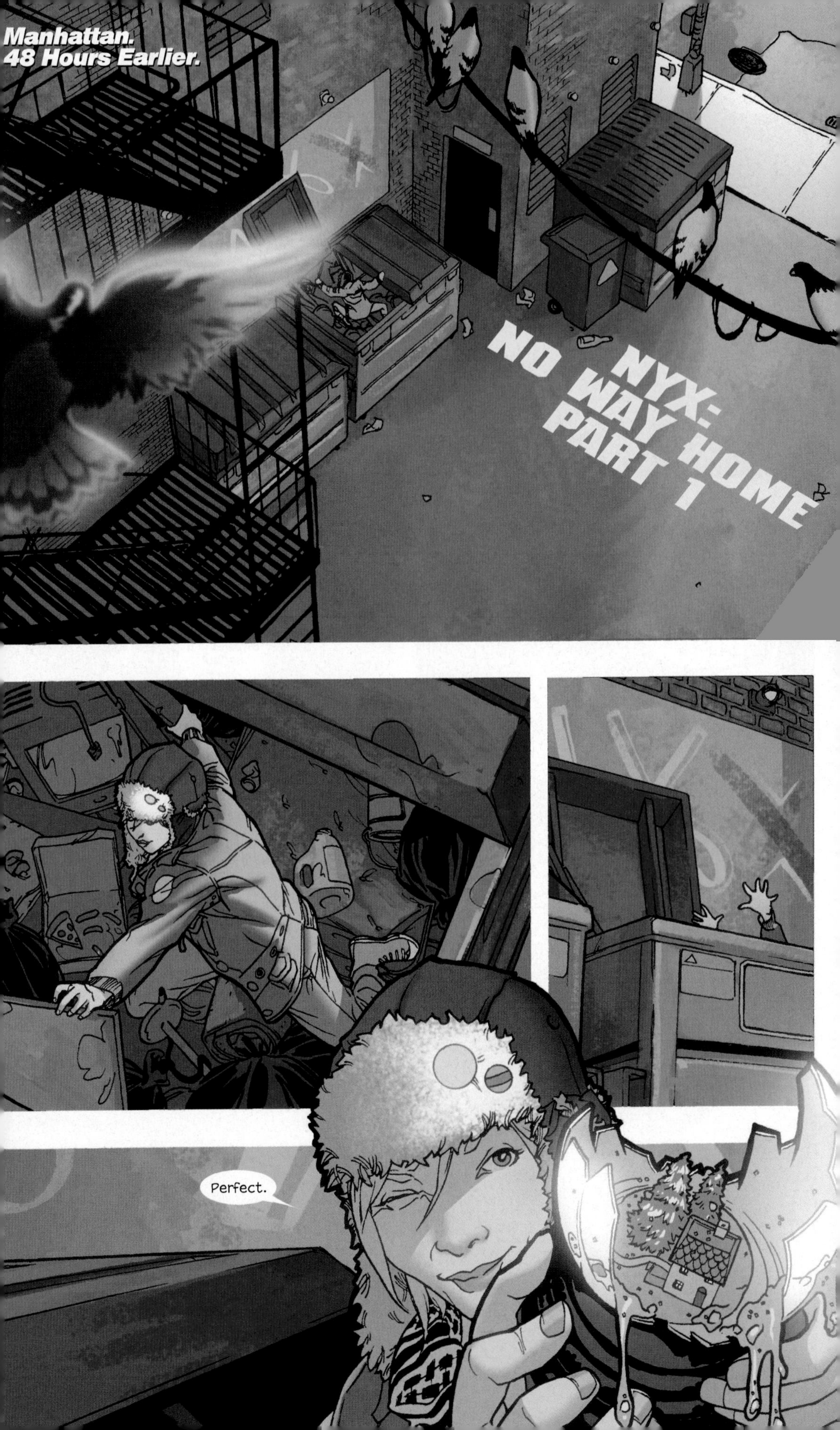
Manhattan.
48 Hours Earlier.
NYX:
NO WAY HOME
PART 1
Perfect.

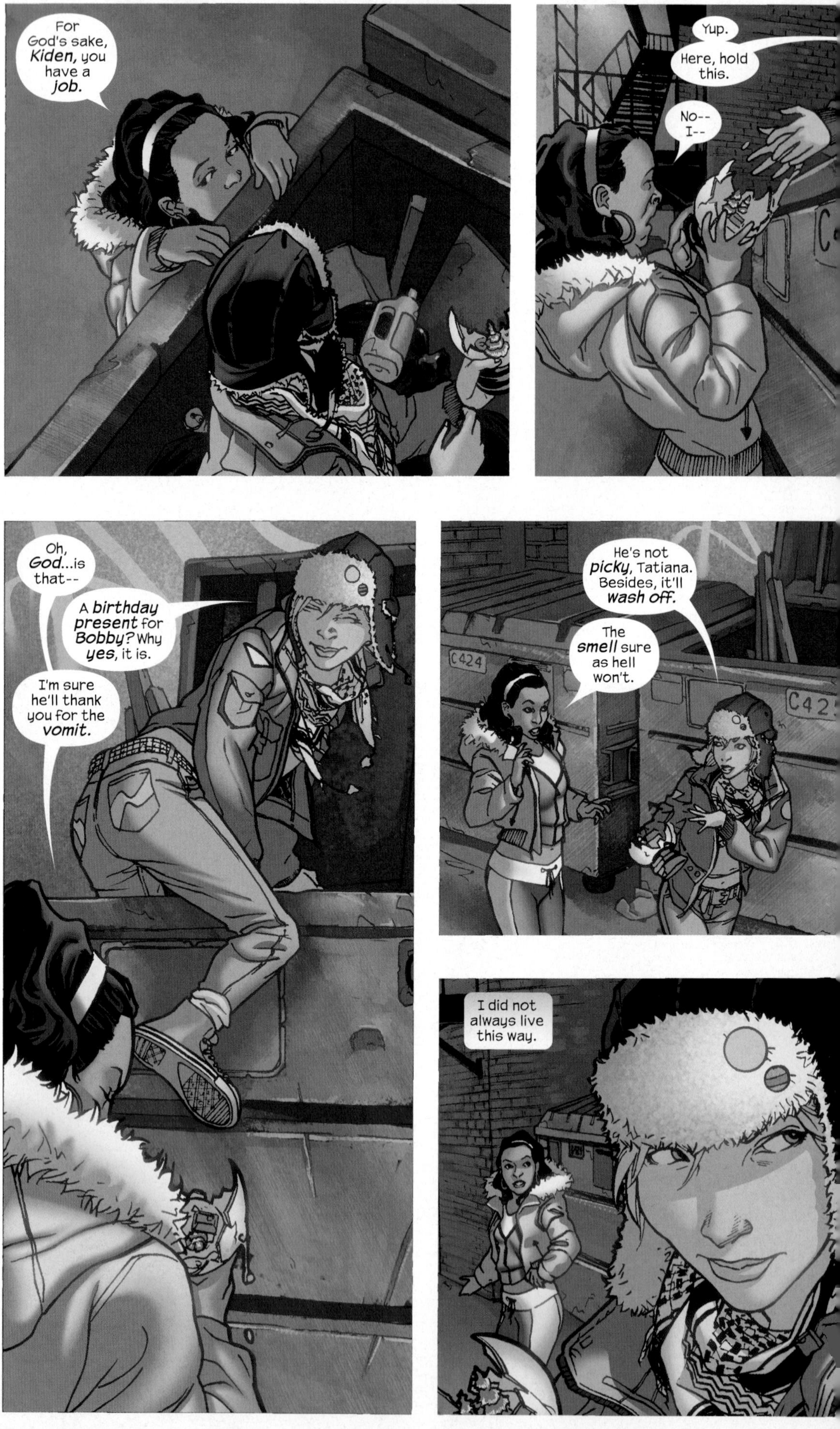
For God's sake, Kiden, you have a job.
Yup.
Here, hold this.
No-- I--
Oh, God...is that--
A birthday present for Bobby? Why yes, it is.
I'm sure he'll thank you for the vomit.
He's not picky, Tatiana. Besides, it'll wash off.
The smell sure as hell won't.
C424
C42
I did not always live this way.

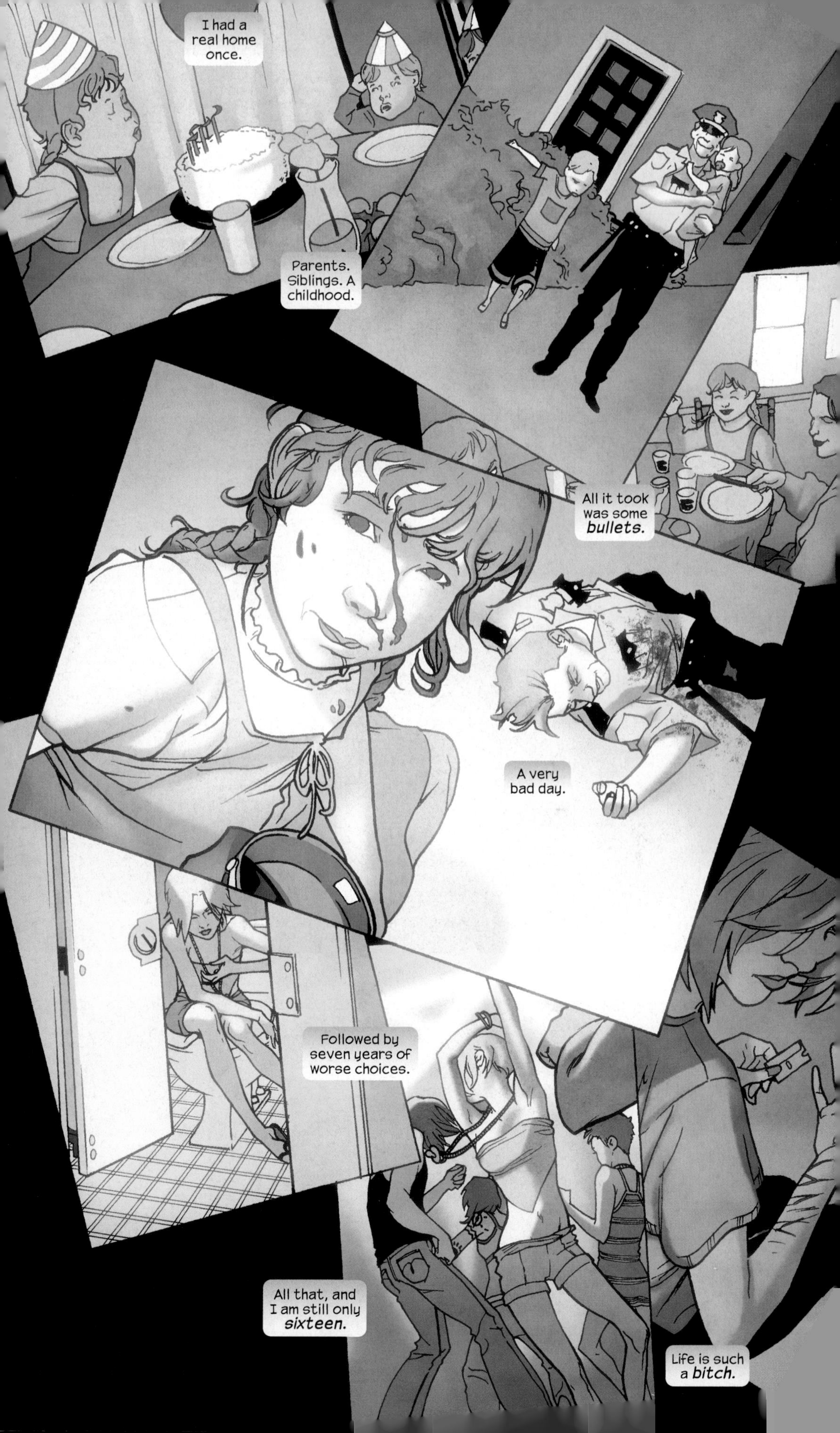
I had a real home once.
Parents. Siblings. A childhood.
All it took was some *bullets.*
A very bad day.
Followed by seven years of worse choices.
All that, and I am still only *sixteen.*
Life is such a *bitch.*

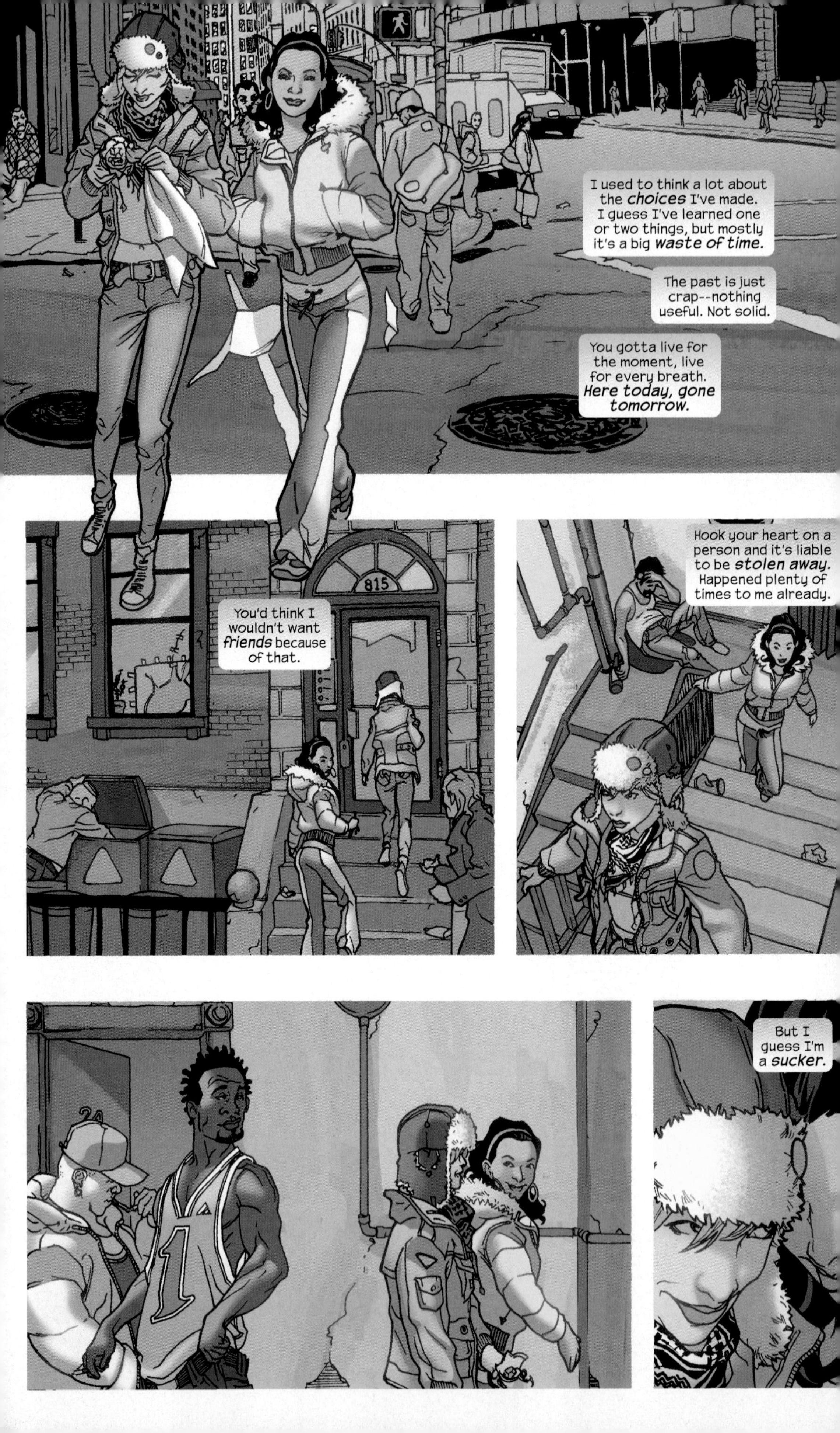
I used to think a lot about the *choices* I've made. I guess I've learned one or two things, but mostly it's a big ***waste of time.***
The past is just crap--nothing useful. Not solid.
You gotta live for the moment, live for every breath. ***Here today, gone tomorrow.***
You'd think I wouldn't want *friends* because of that.
815
Hook your heart on a person and it's liable to be ***stolen away.*** Happened plenty of times to me already.
24
1
But I guess I'm a ***sucker.***

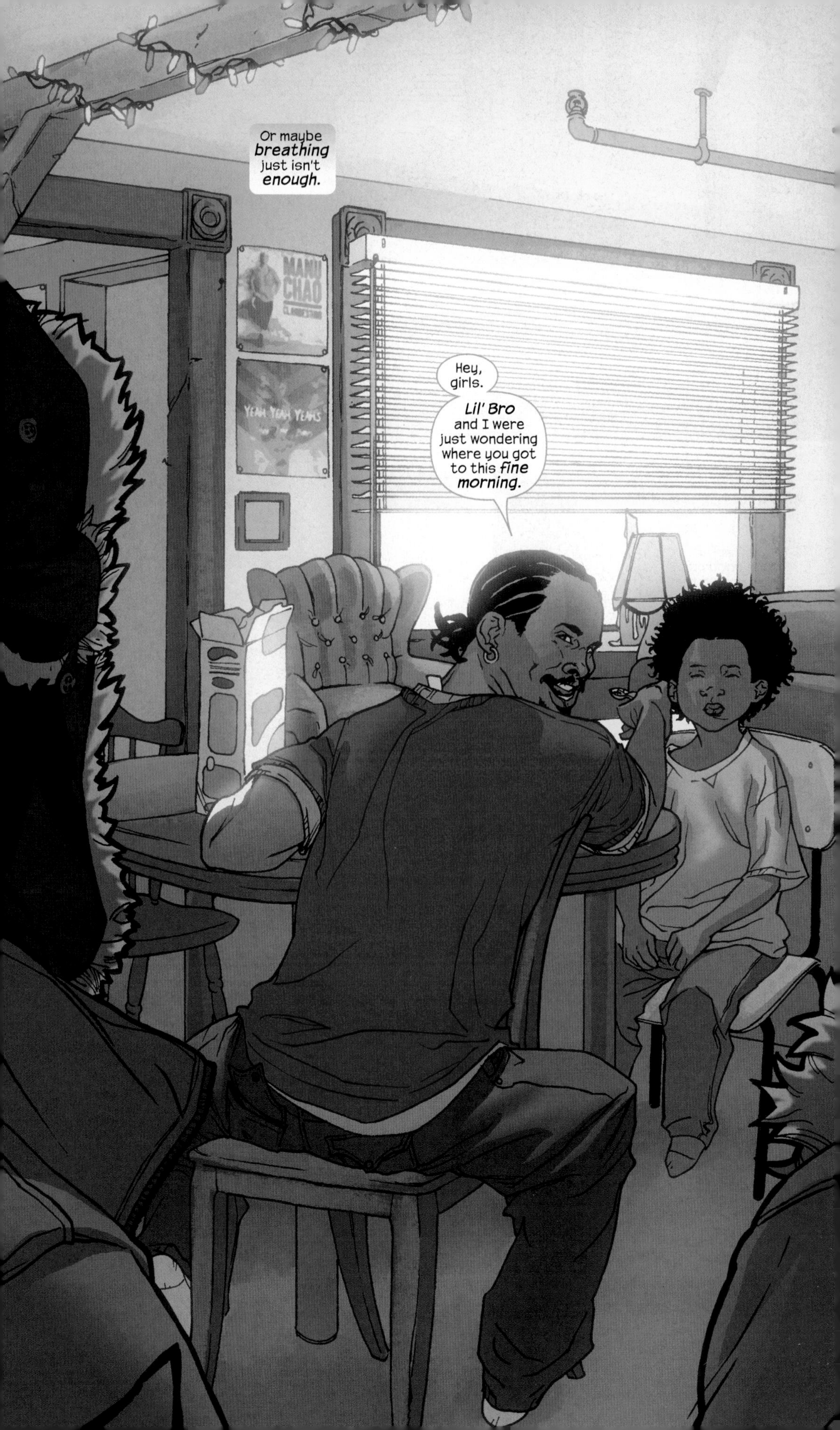
Or maybe *breathing* just isn't *enough.*
MANU CHAO
CLANDESTINO
YEAH YEAH YEAHS
Hey, girls.
Lil' Bro and I were just wondering where you got to this *fine morning.*

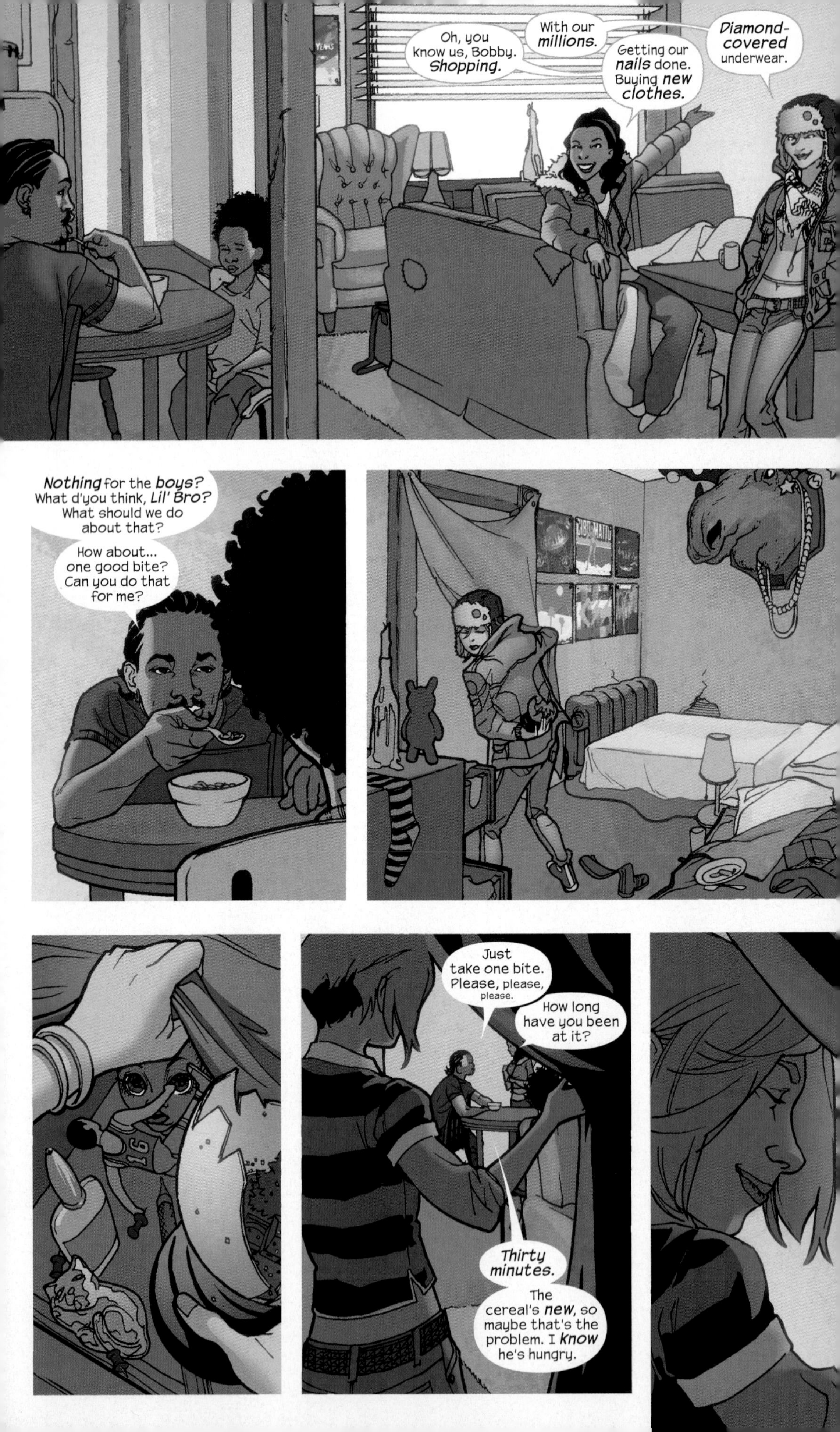
Oh, you know us, Bobby. Shopping.
With our millions.
Getting our nails done. Buying new clothes.
Diamond-covered underwear.
Nothing for the boys? What d'you think, Lil' Bro? What should we do about that?
How about... one good bite? Can you do that for me?
Just take one bite. Please, please, please.
How long have you been at it?
Thirty minutes.
The cereal's new, so maybe that's the problem. I know he's hungry.

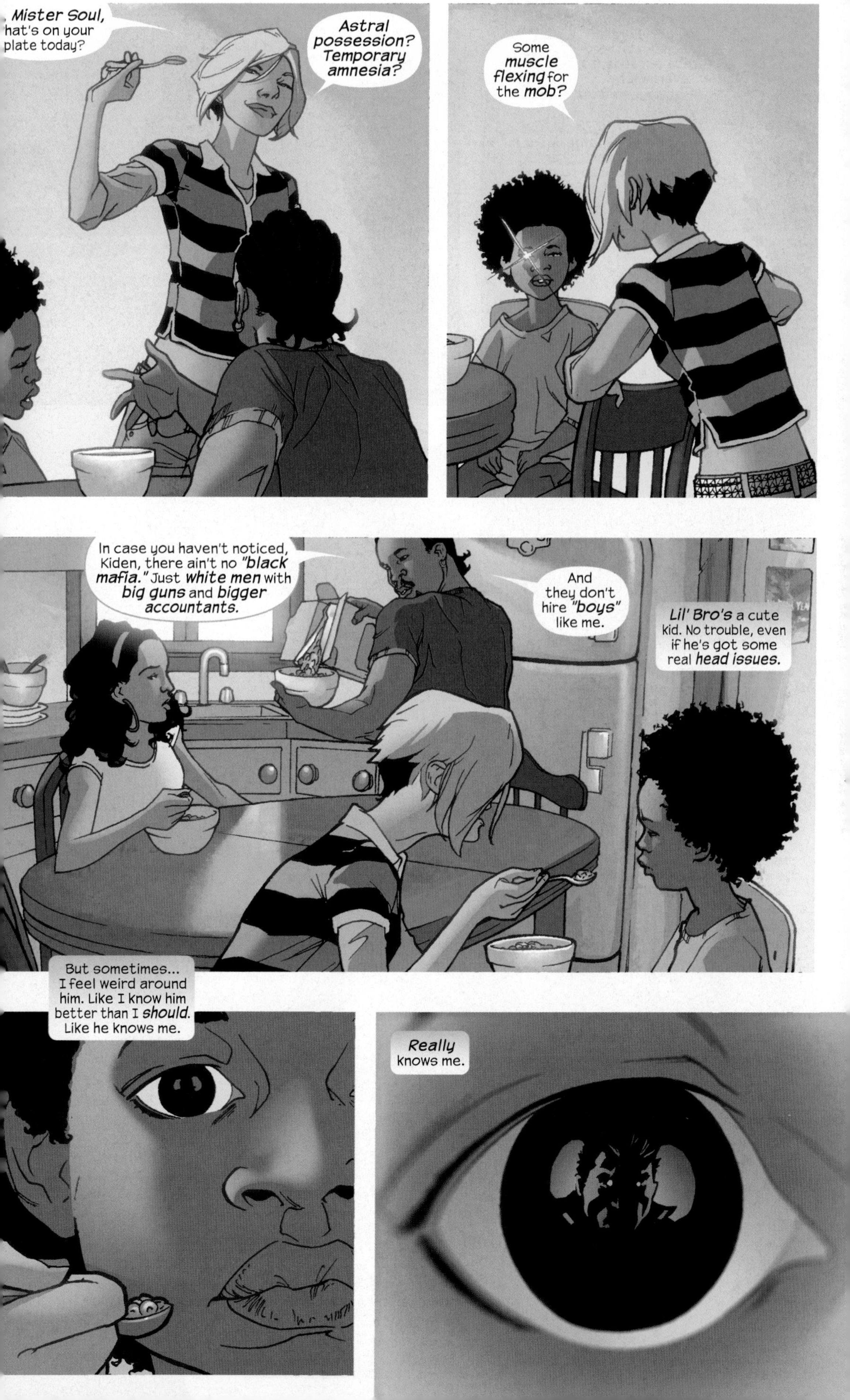

Mister Soul, hat's on your plate today?
Astral possession? Temporary amnesia?
Some muscle flexing for the mob?
In case you haven't noticed, Kiden, there ain't no "black mafia." Just white men with big guns and bigger accountants.
And they don't hire "boys" like me.
Lil' Bro's a cute kid. No trouble, even if he's got some real head issues.
But sometimes... I feel weird around him. Like I know him better than I should. Like he knows me.
Really knows me.

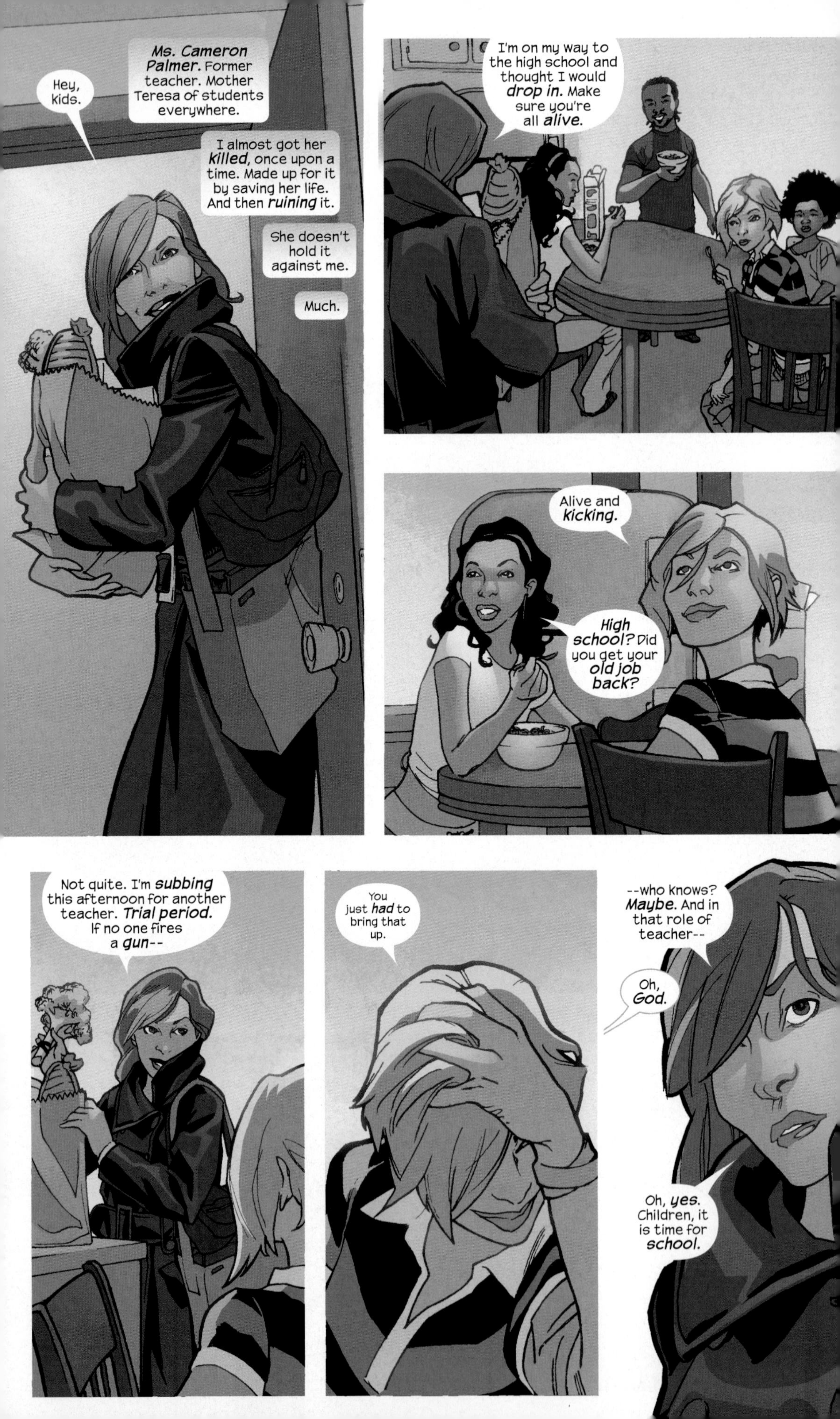
Hey, kids.
Ms. Cameron Palmer. Former teacher. Mother Teresa of students everywhere.
I almost got her killed, once upon a time. Made up for it by saving her life. And then ruining it.
She doesn't hold it against me.
Much.
I'm on my way to the high school and thought I would drop in. Make sure you're all alive.
Alive and kicking.
High school? Did you get your old job back?
Not quite. I'm subbing this afternoon for another teacher. Trial period. If no one fires a gun--
You just had to bring that up.
--who knows? Maybe. And in that role of teacher--
Oh, God.
Oh, yes. Children, it is time for school.

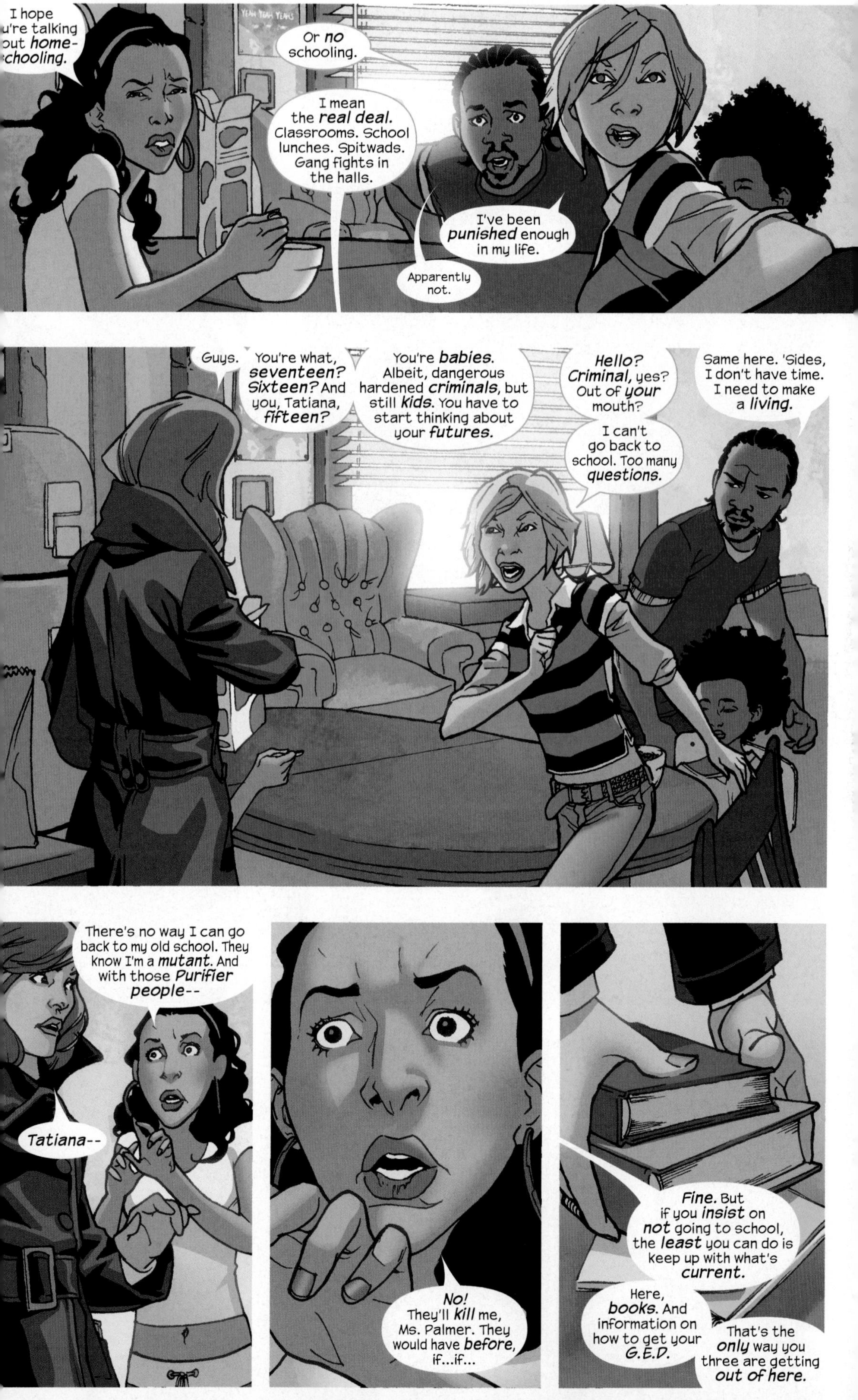

I hope
u're talking
out home-
schooling.
Or no schooling.
I mean the real deal. Classrooms. School lunches. Spitwads. Gang fights in the halls.
I've been punished enough in my life.
Apparently not.
Guys.
You're what, seventeen? Sixteen? And you, Tatiana, fifteen?
You're babies. Albeit, dangerous hardened criminals, but still kids. You have to start thinking about your futures.
Hello? Criminal, yes? Out of your mouth?
I can't go back to school. Too many questions.
Same here. 'Sides, I don't have time. I need to make a living.
There's no way I can go back to my old school. They know I'm a mutant. And with those Purifier people--
Tatiana--
No! They'll kill me, Ms. Palmer. They would have before, if...if...
Fine. But if you insist on not going to school, the least you can do is keep up with what's current.
Here, books. And information on how to get your G.E.D.
That's the only way you three are getting out of here.

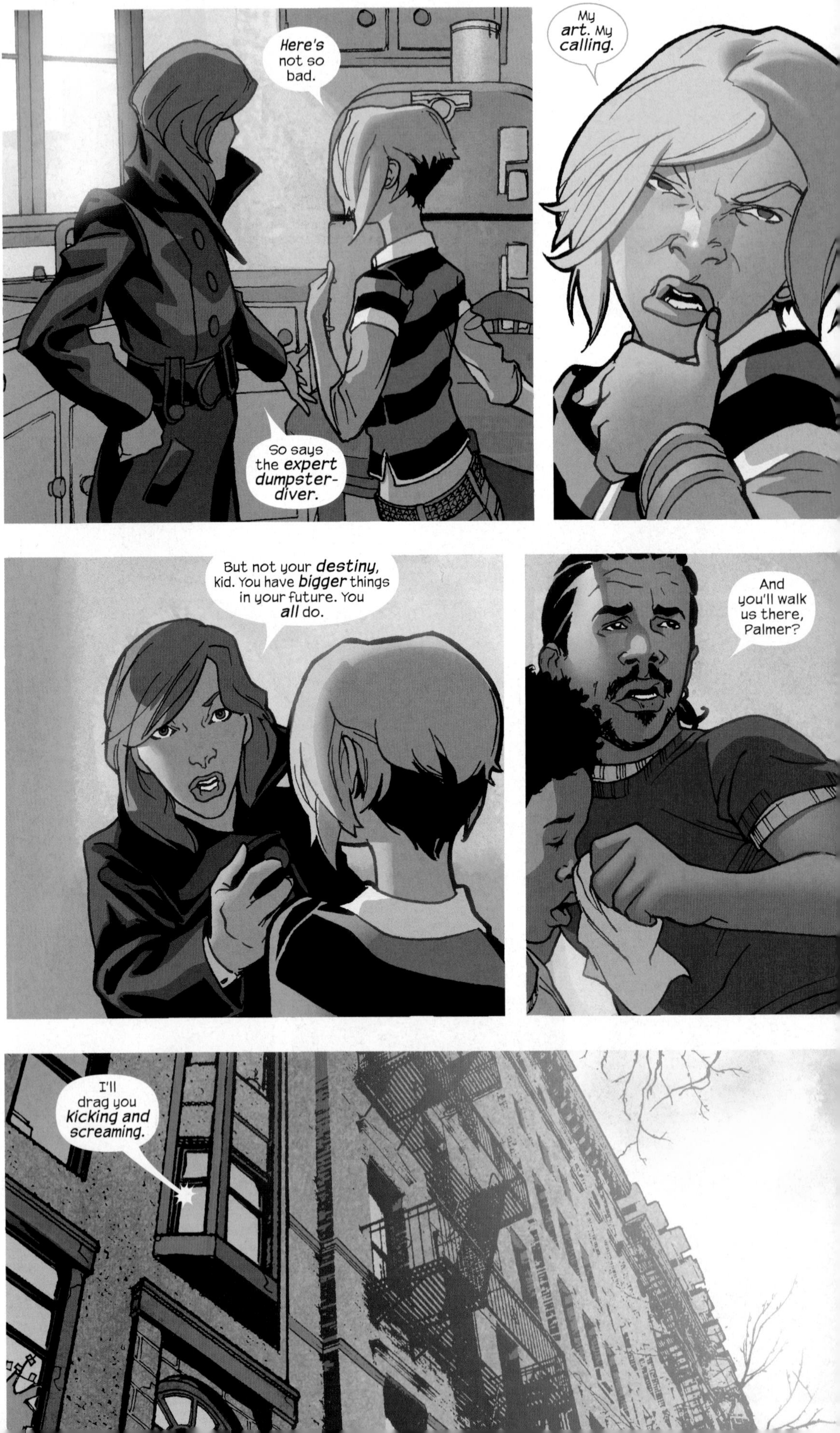
Here's not so bad.
So says the expert dumpster-diver.
My art. My calling.
But not your destiny, kid. You have bigger things in your future. You all do.
And you'll walk us there, Palmer?
I'll drag you kicking and screaming.

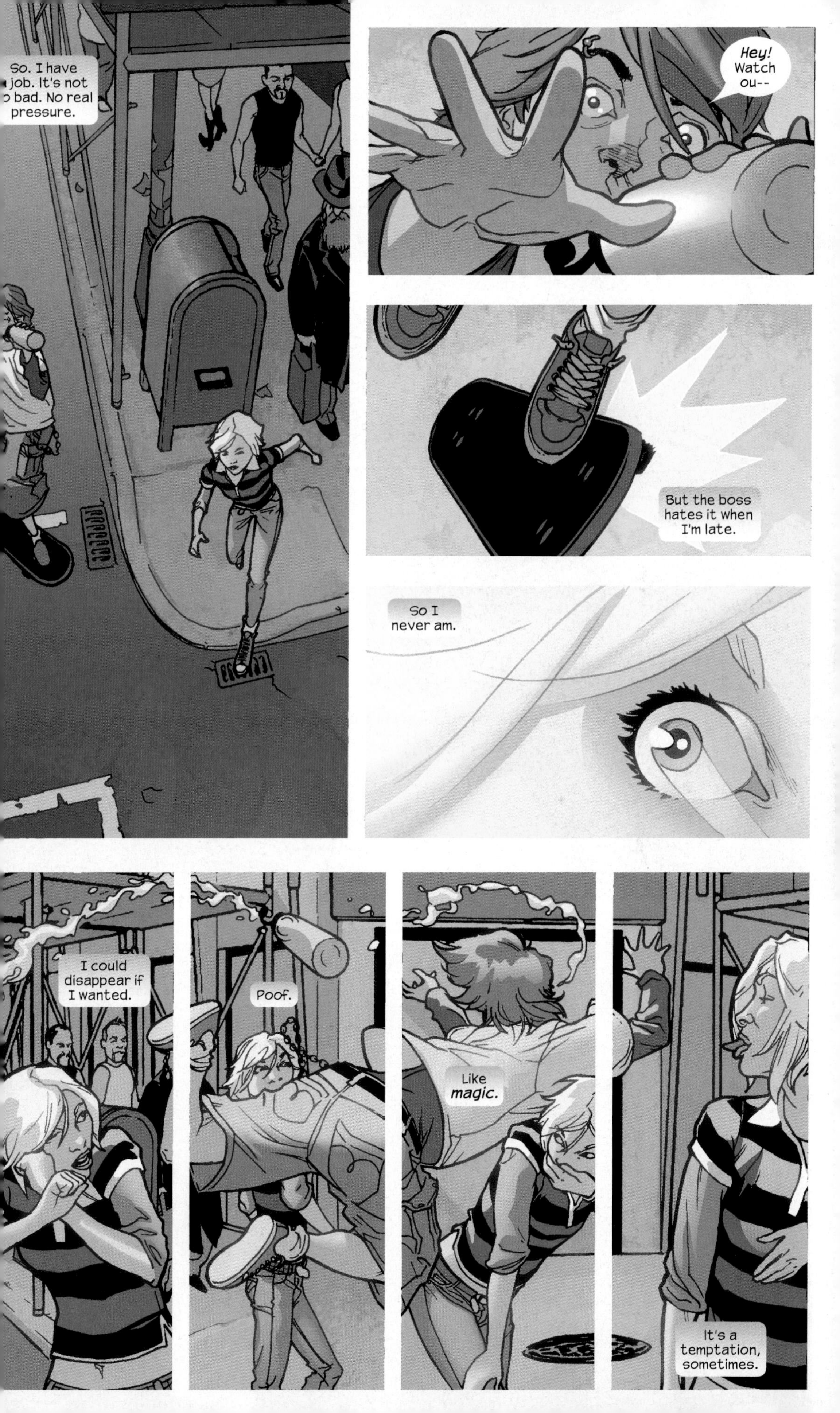
So. I have
job. It's not
bad. No real
pressure.
Hey! Watch ou--
But the boss hates it when I'm late.
So I never am.
I could disappear if I wanted.
Poof.
Like *magic.*
It's a temptation, sometimes.

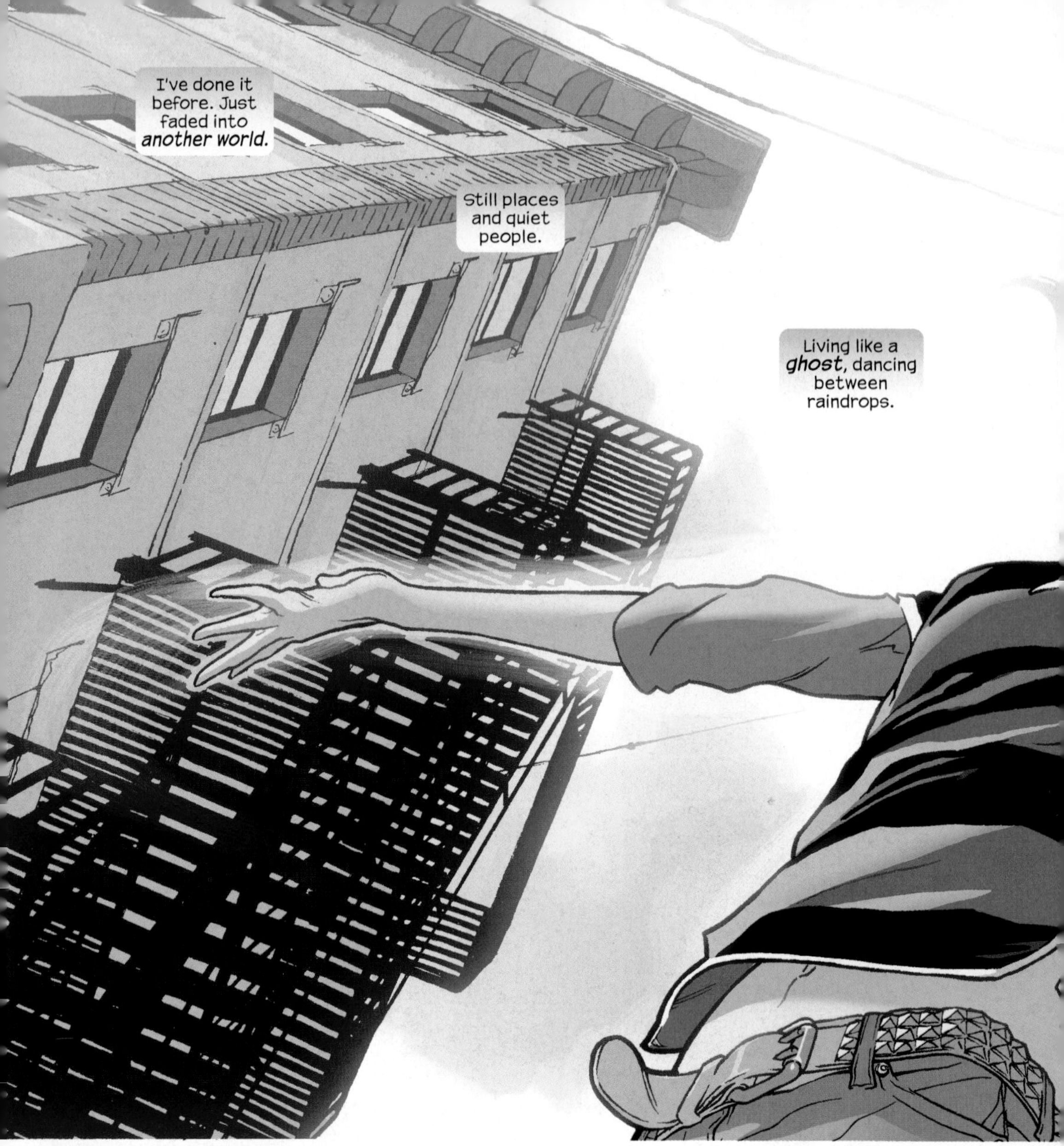
I've done it before. Just faded into *another world.*
Still places and quiet people.
Living like a *ghost*, dancing between raindrops.

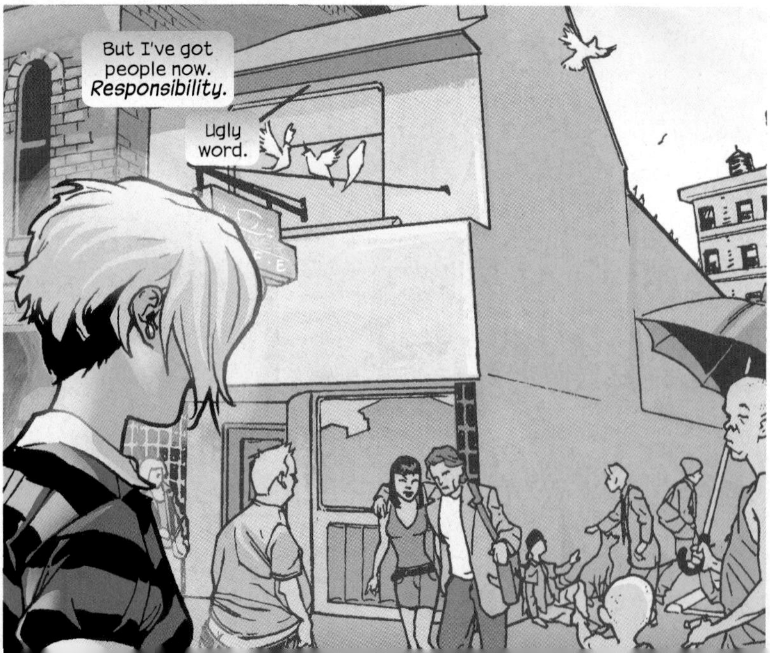
But I've got people now. *Responsibility.*
Ugly word.

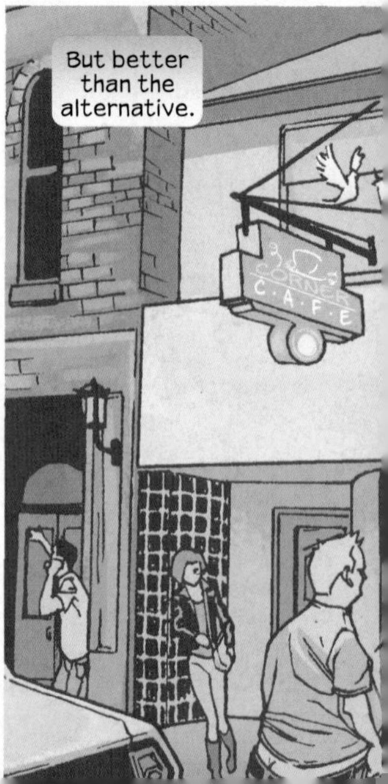
But better than the alternative.
CORNER
C·A·F·E

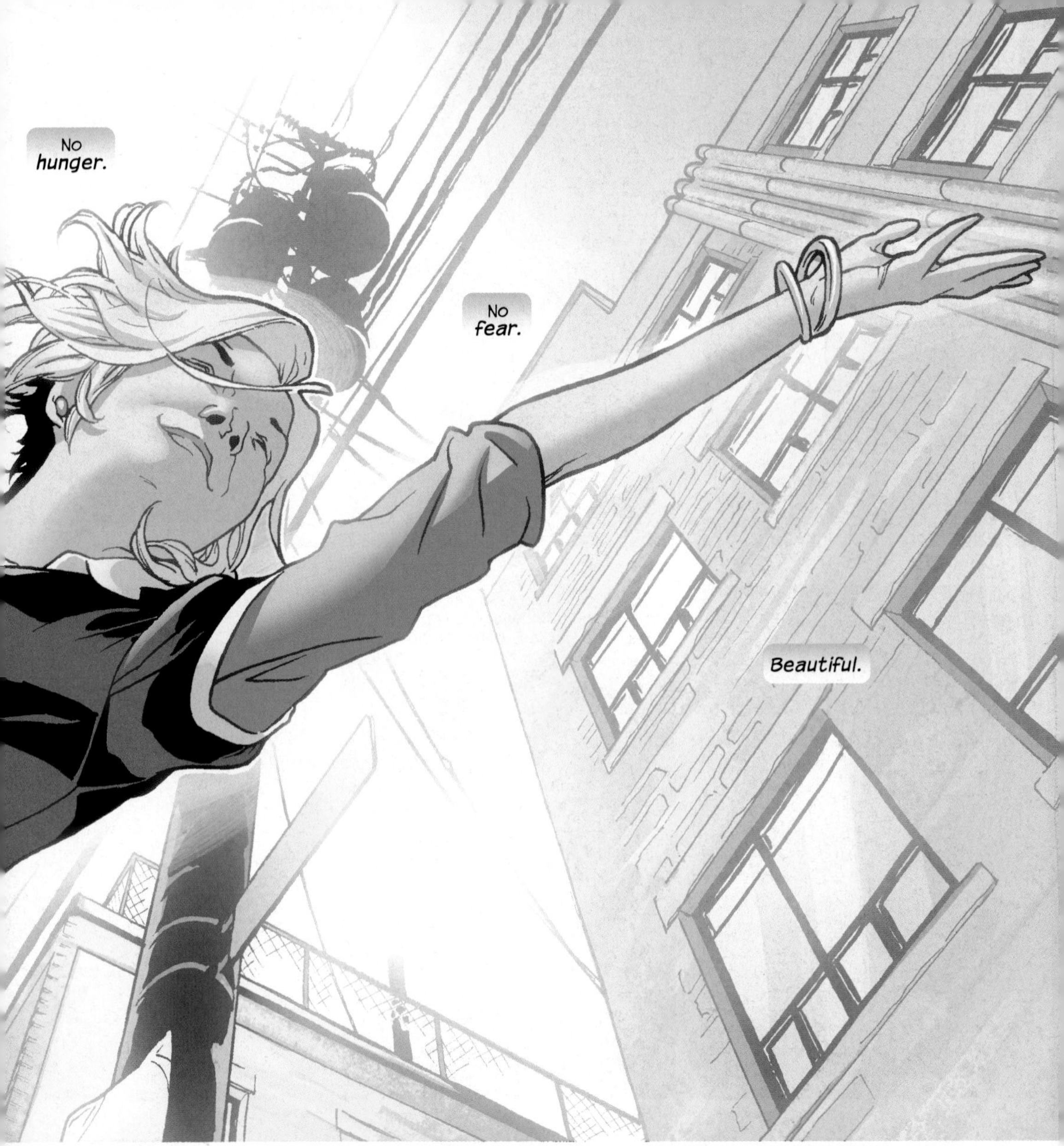
No hunger.
No fear.
Beautiful.

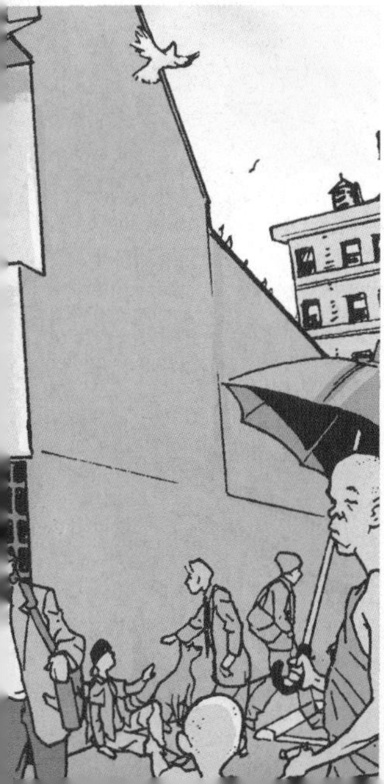

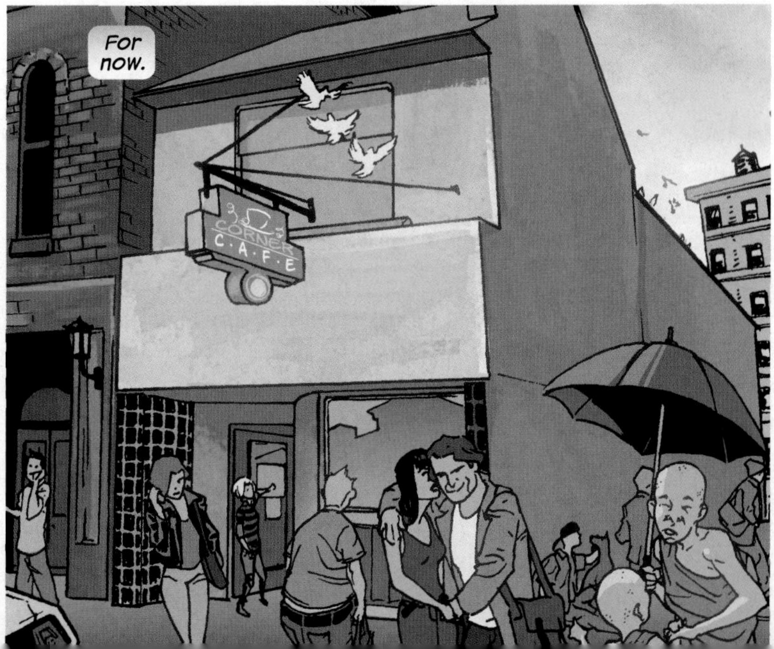
For now.
CORNER
C·A·F·E

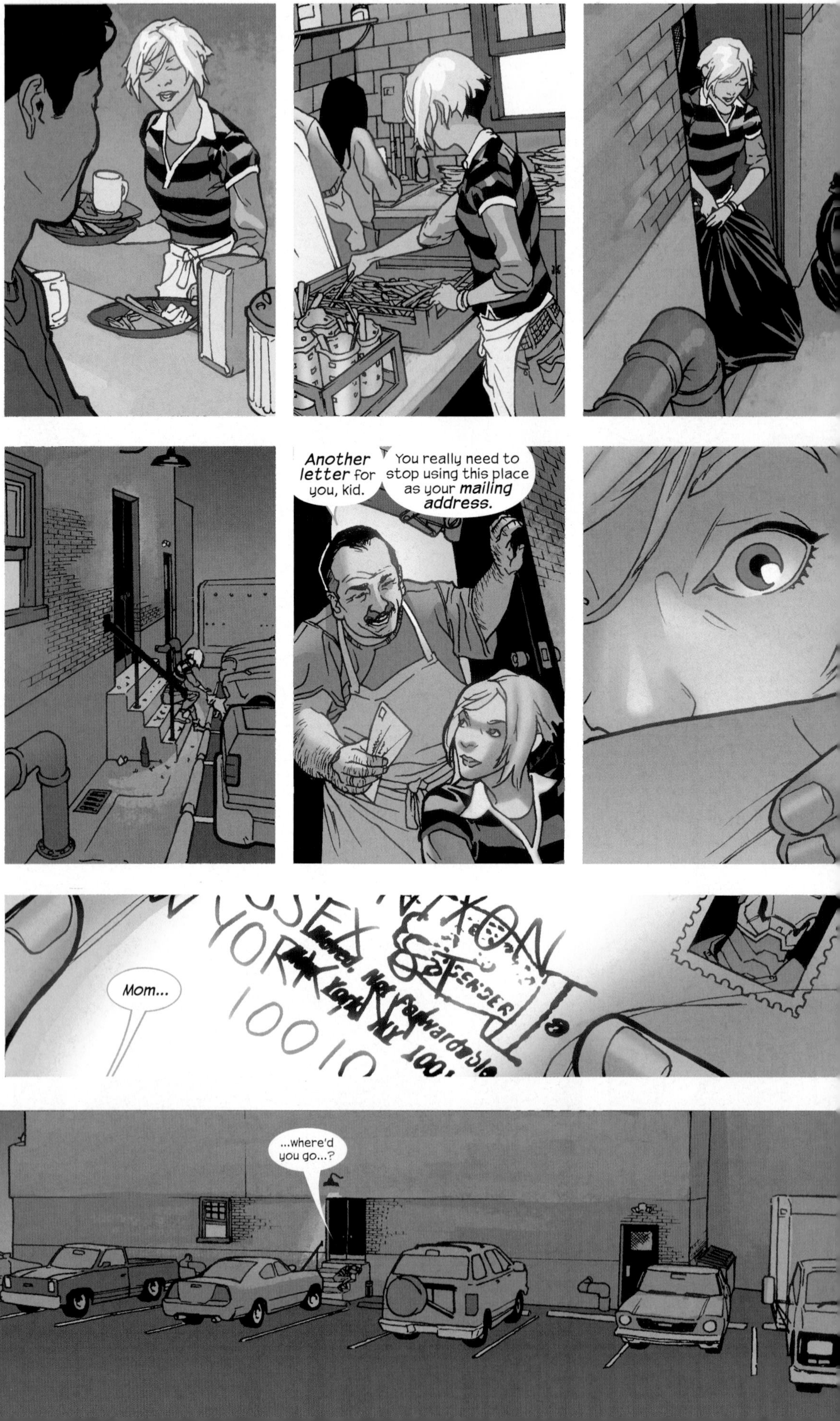
Another letter for you, kid.
You really need to stop using this place as your mailing address.
Mom...
...where'd you go...?

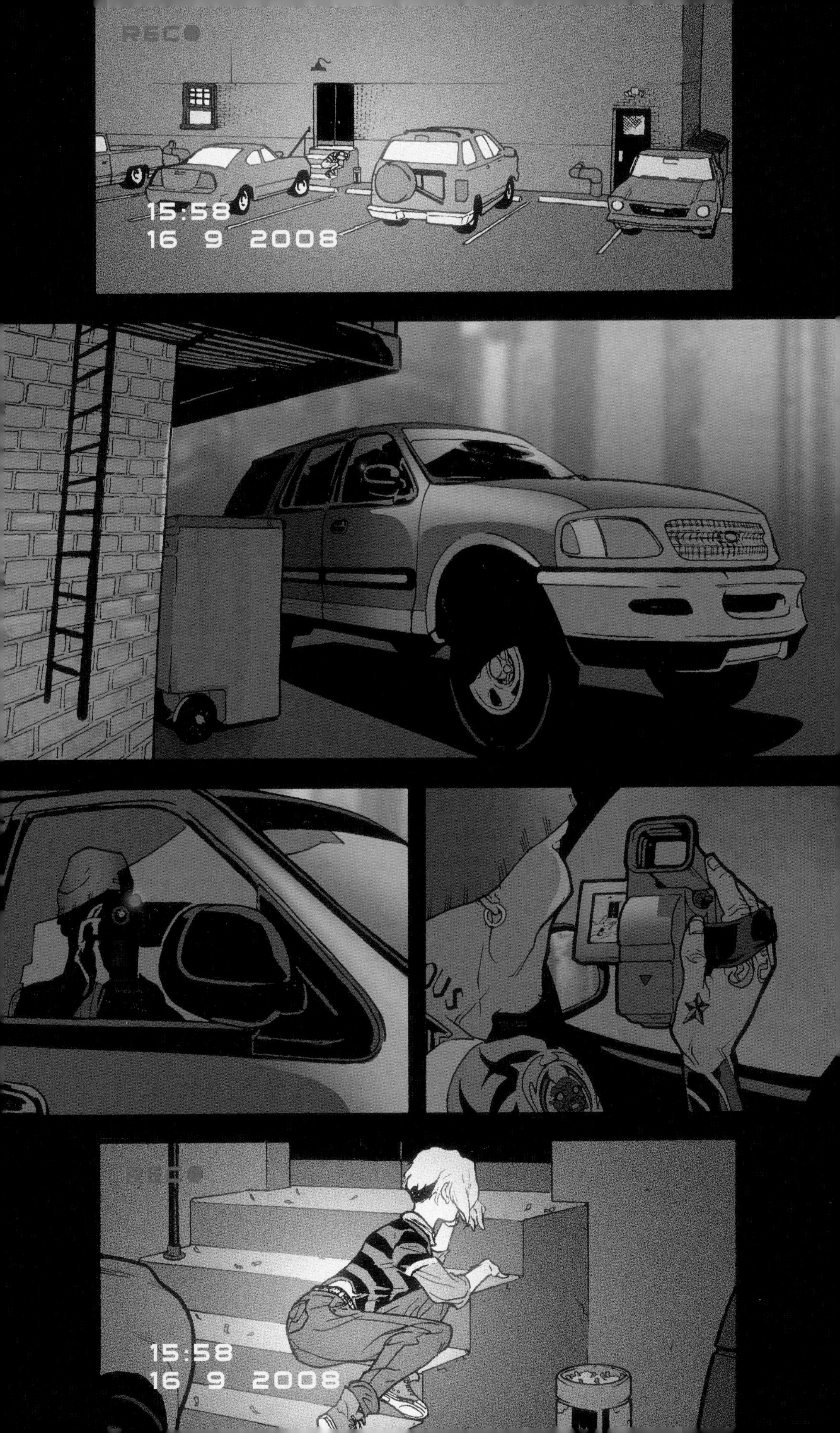
REC
15:58
16 9 2008
15:58
16 9 2008

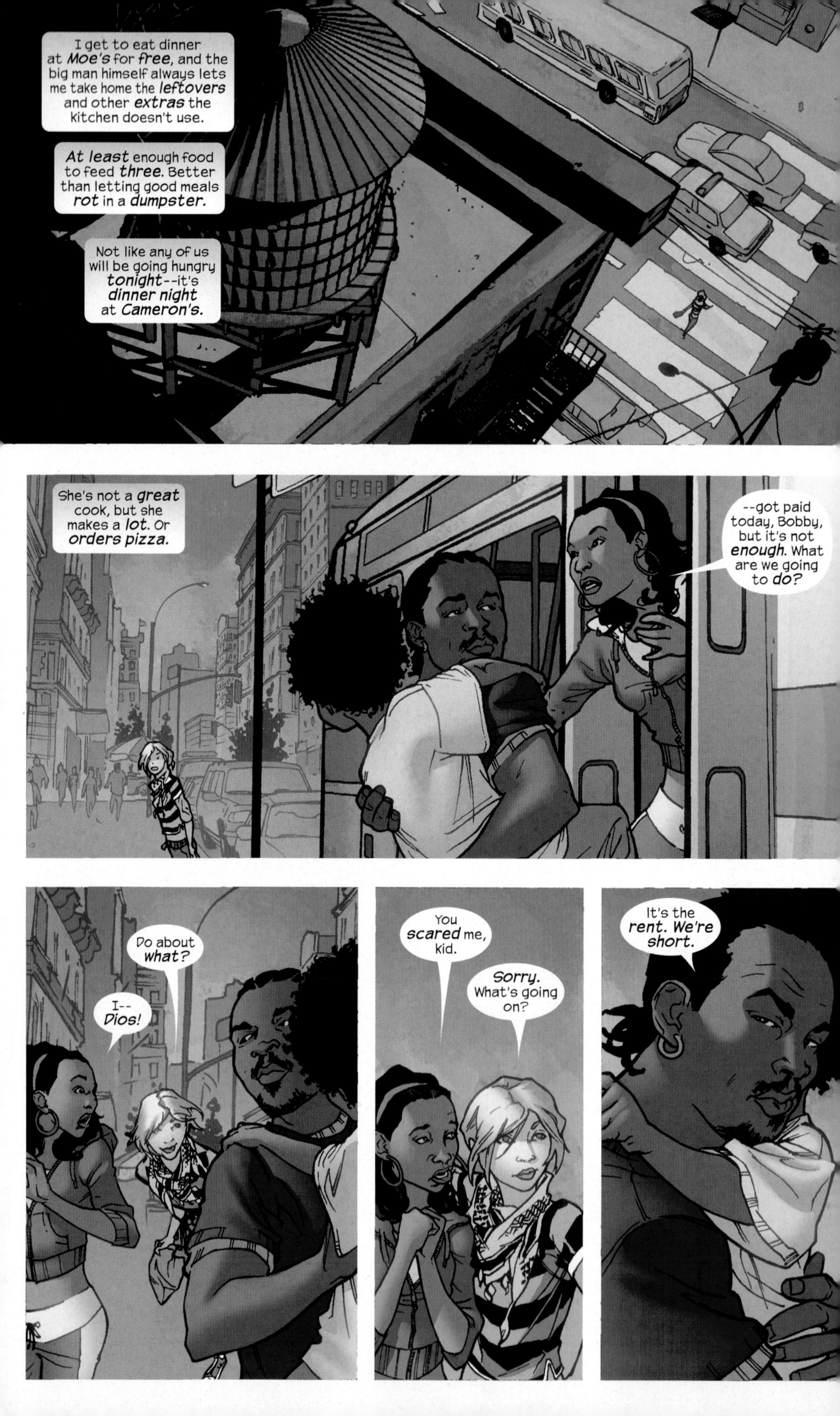
I get to eat dinner at Moe's for free, and the big man himself always lets me take home the leftovers and other extras the kitchen doesn't use.
At least enough food to feed three. Better than letting good meals rot in a dumpster.
Not like any of us will be going hungry tonight--it's dinner night at Cameron's.
She's not a great cook, but she makes a lot. Or orders pizza.
--got paid today, Bobby, but it's not enough. What are we going to do?
Do about what?
I-- Dios!
You scared me, kid.
Sorry. What's going on?
It's the rent. We're short.

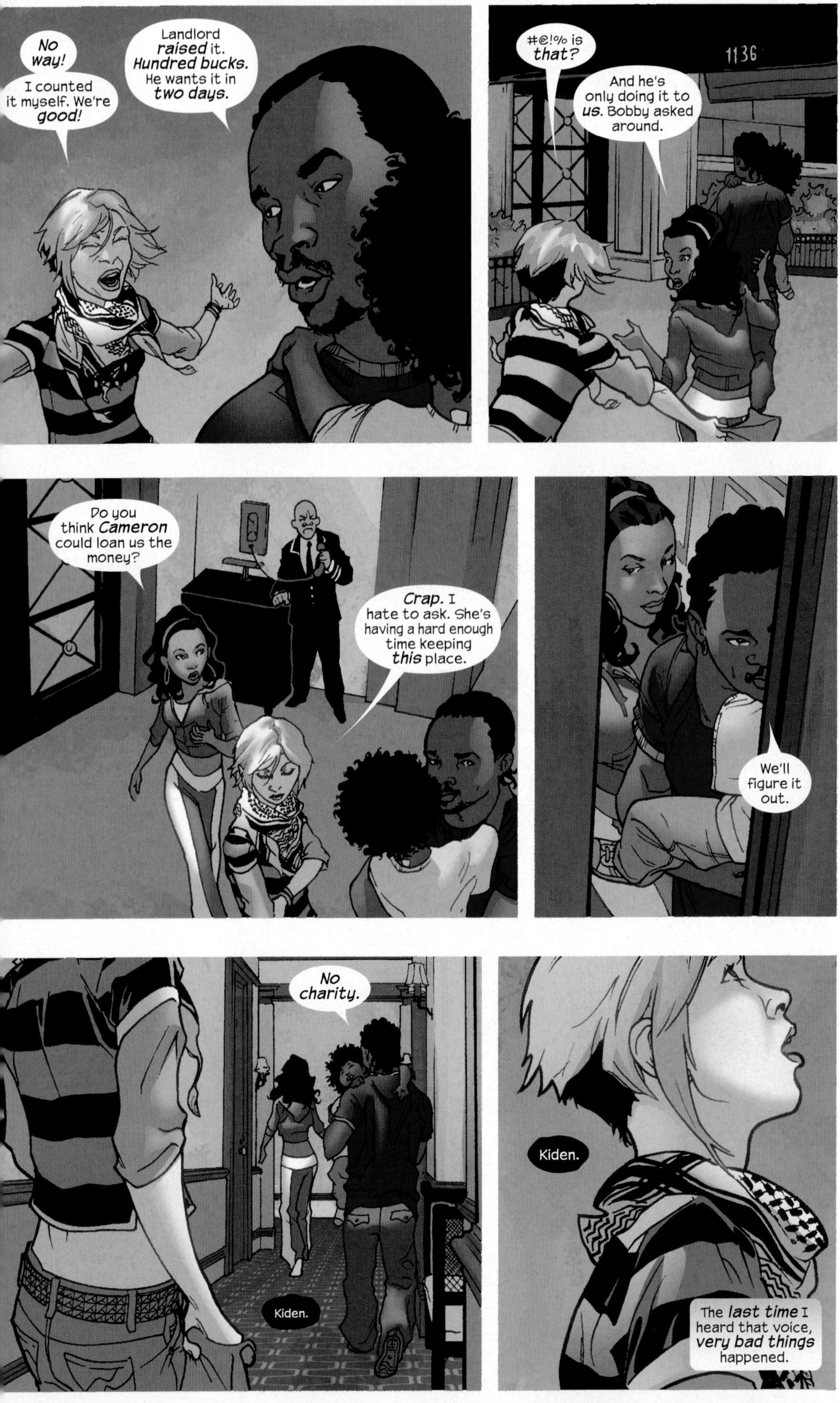
No way!
I counted it myself. We're good!
Landlord raised it. Hundred bucks. He wants it in two days.
#@!% is that?
And he's only doing it to us. Bobby asked around.
1136
Do you think Cameron could loan us the money?
Crap. I hate to ask. She's having a hard enough time keeping this place.
We'll figure it out.
No charity.
Kiden.
Kiden.
The last time I heard that voice, very bad things happened.

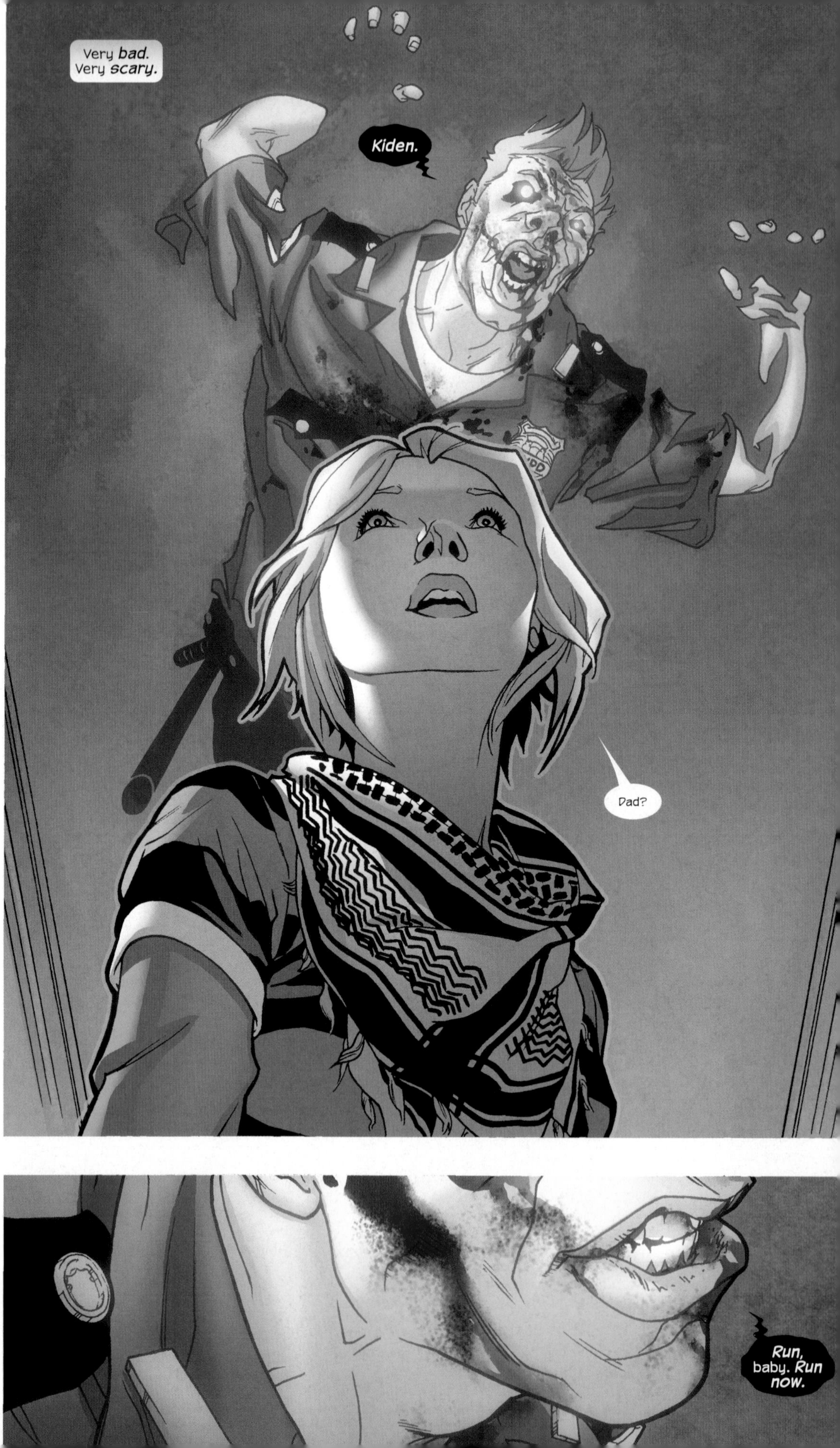
Very bad.
Very scary.
Kiden.
Dad?
Run, baby. Run now.

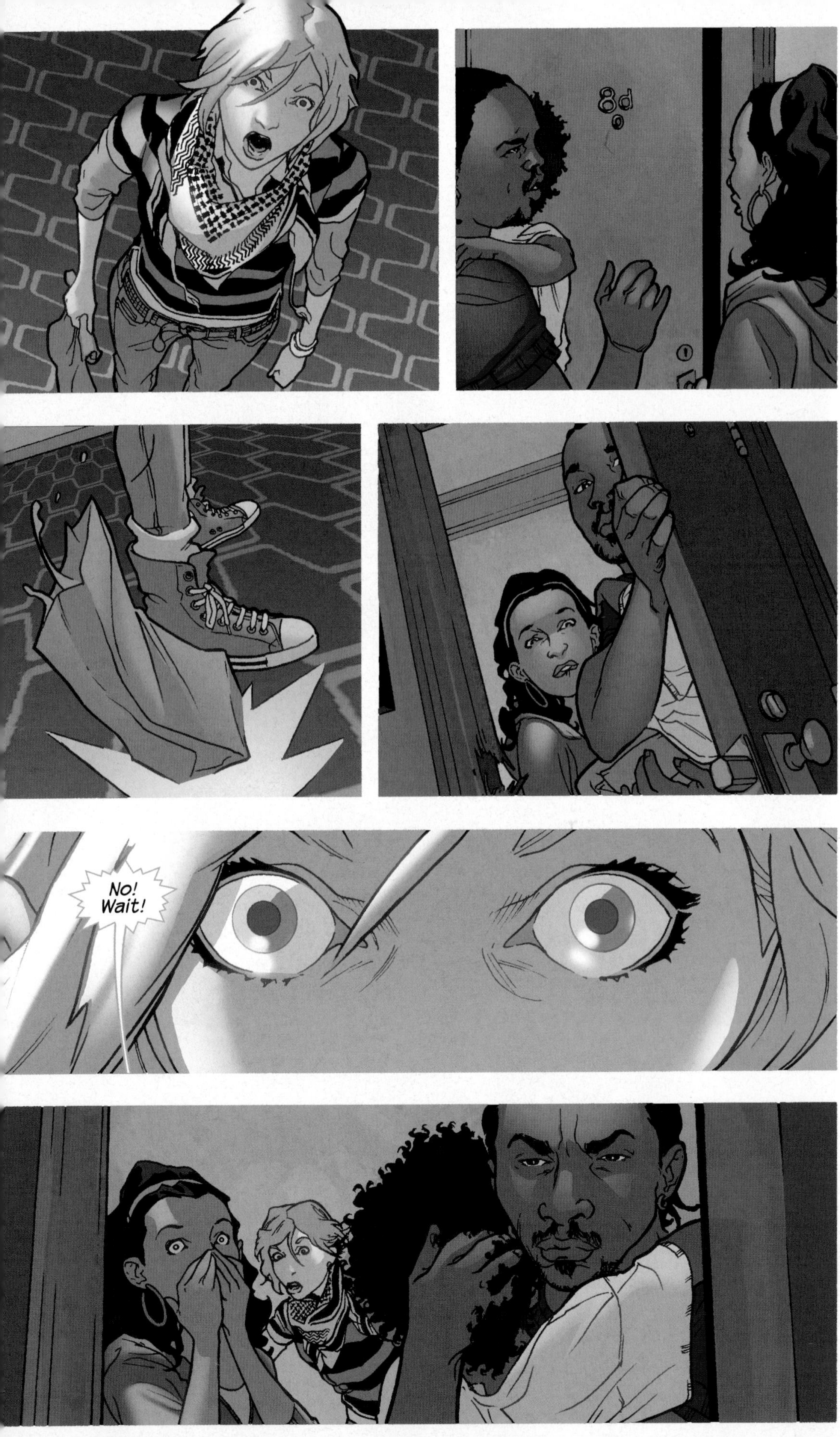
8d
No!
Wait!

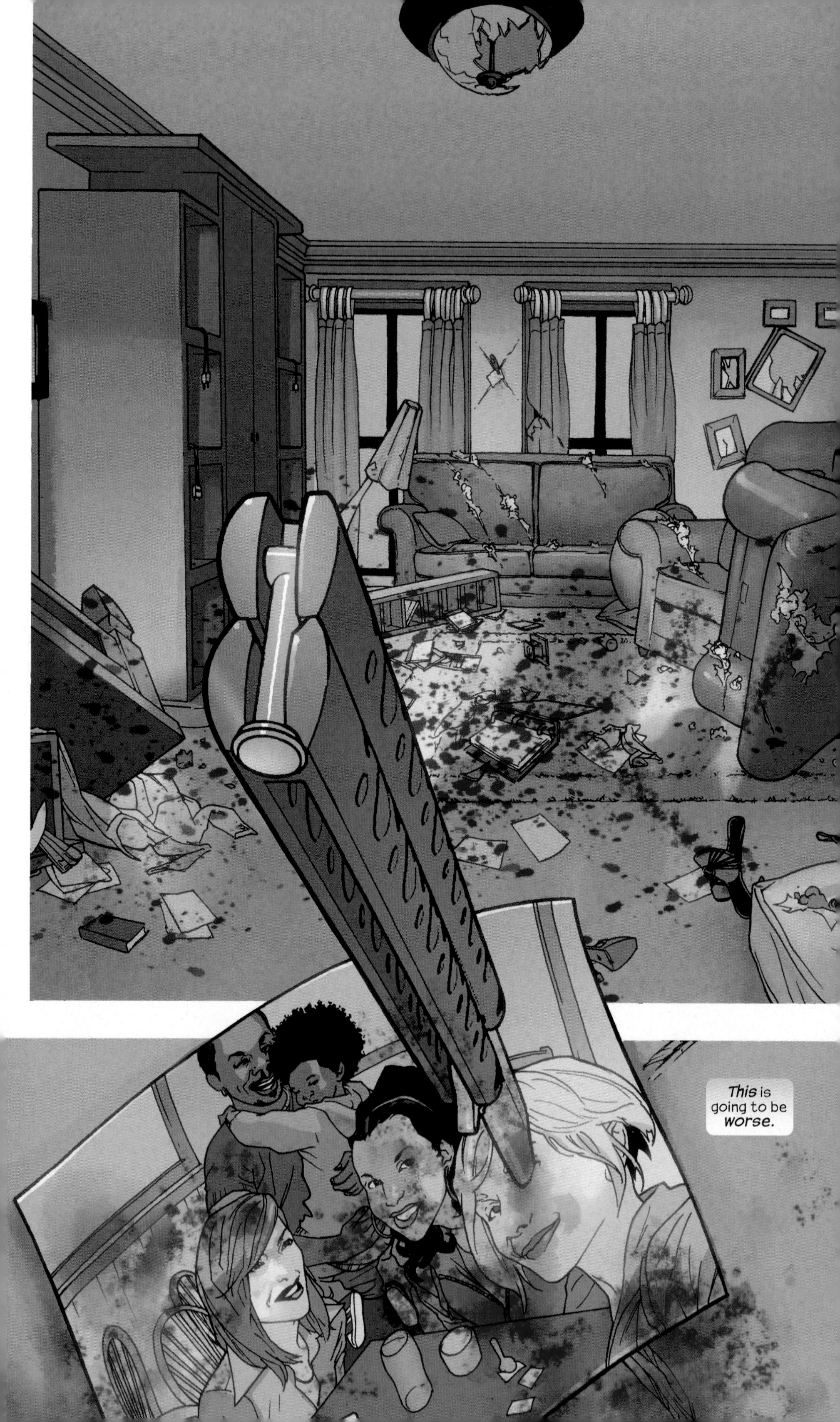
This is going to be worse.

TWO

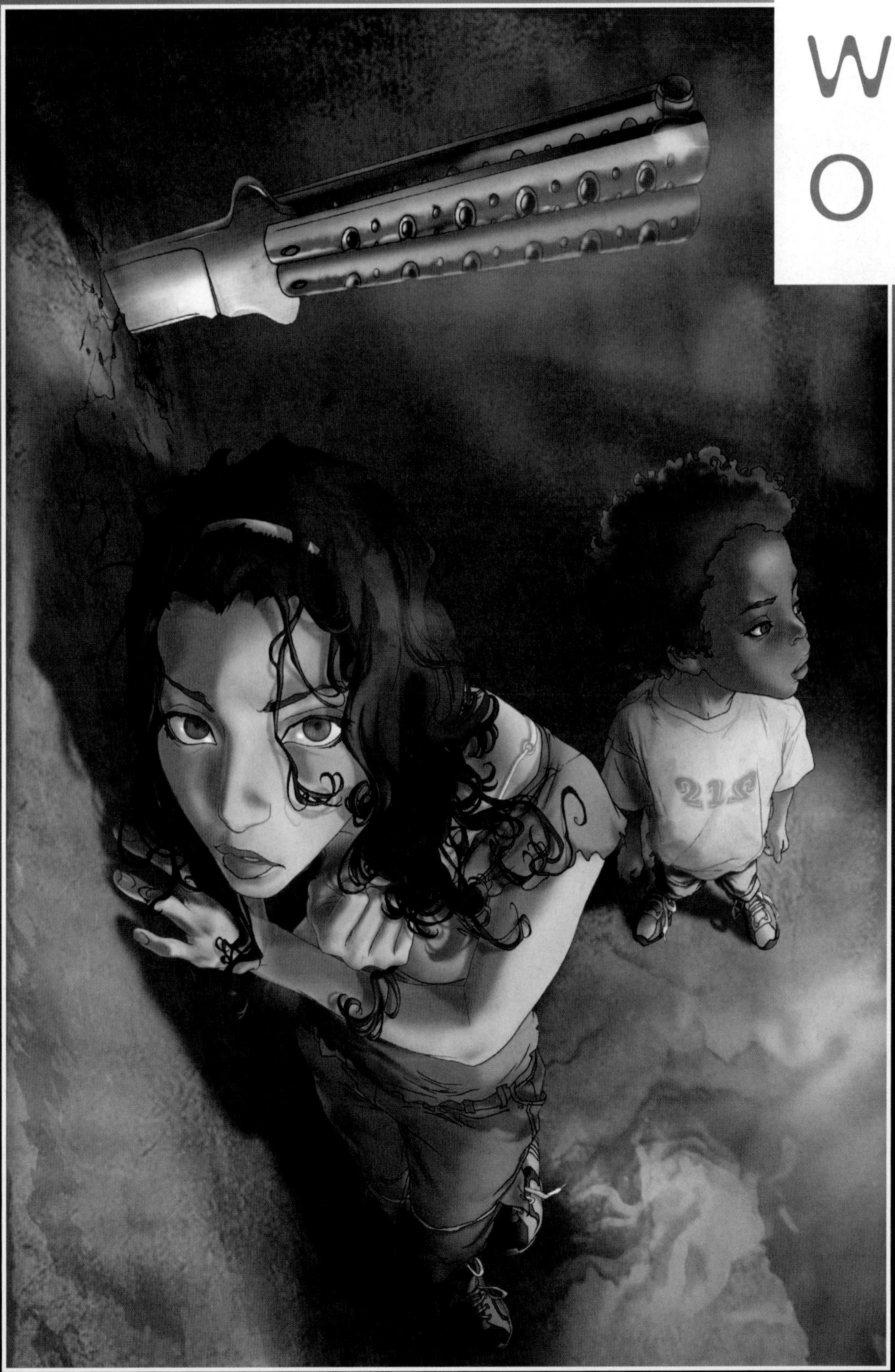
212

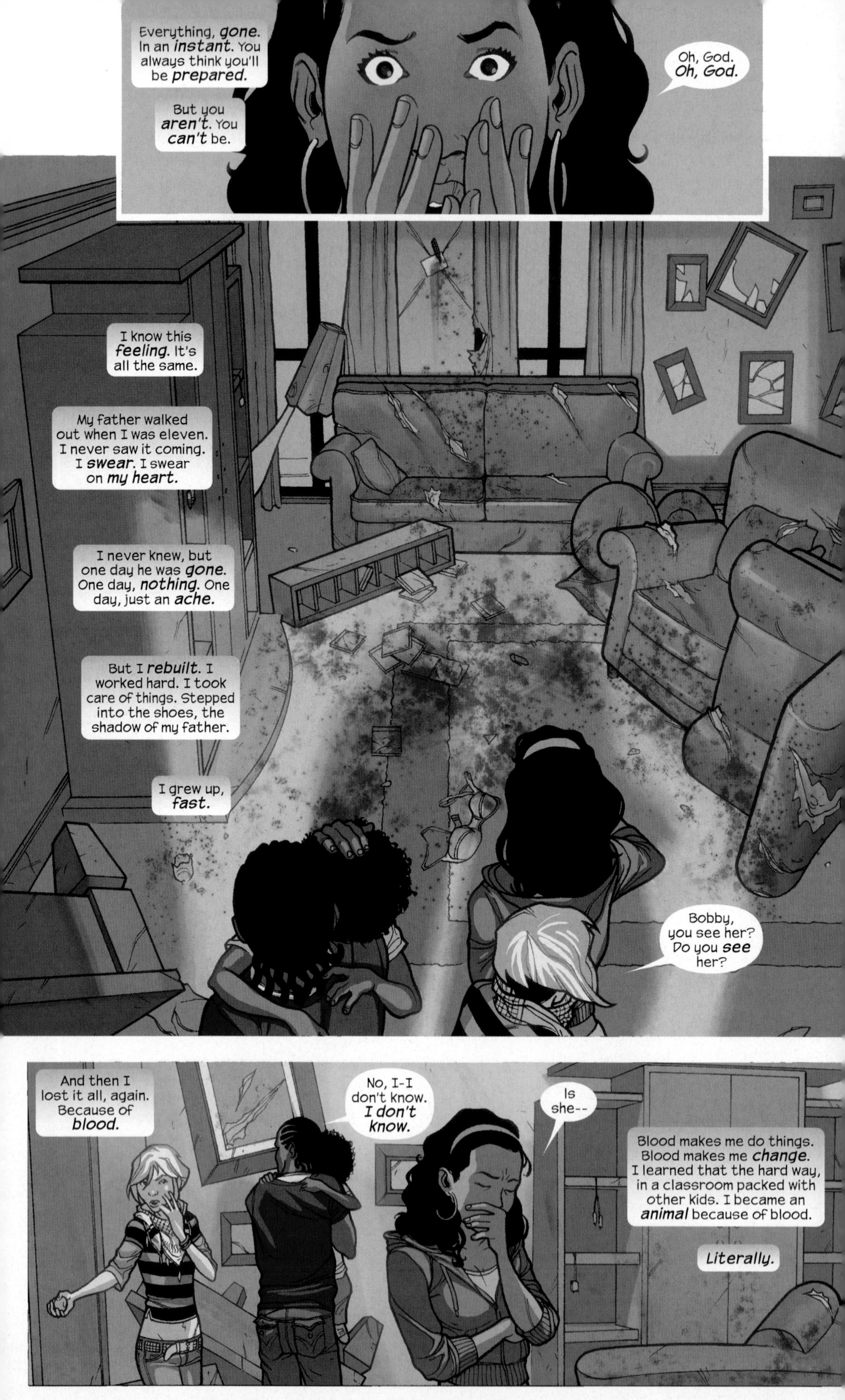

Everything, gone. In an instant. You always think you'll be prepared.
But you aren't. You can't be.
Oh, God. Oh, God.
I know this feeling. It's all the same.
My father walked out when I was eleven. I never saw it coming. I swear. I swear on my heart.
I never knew, but one day he was gone. One day, nothing. One day, just an ache.
But I rebuilt. I worked hard. I took care of things. Stepped into the shoes, the shadow of my father.
I grew up, fast.
Bobby, you see her? Do you see her?
And then I lost it all, again. Because of blood.
No, I-I don't know. I don't know.
Is she--
Blood makes me do things. Blood makes me change. I learned that the hard way, in a classroom packed with other kids. I became an animal because of blood.
Literally.

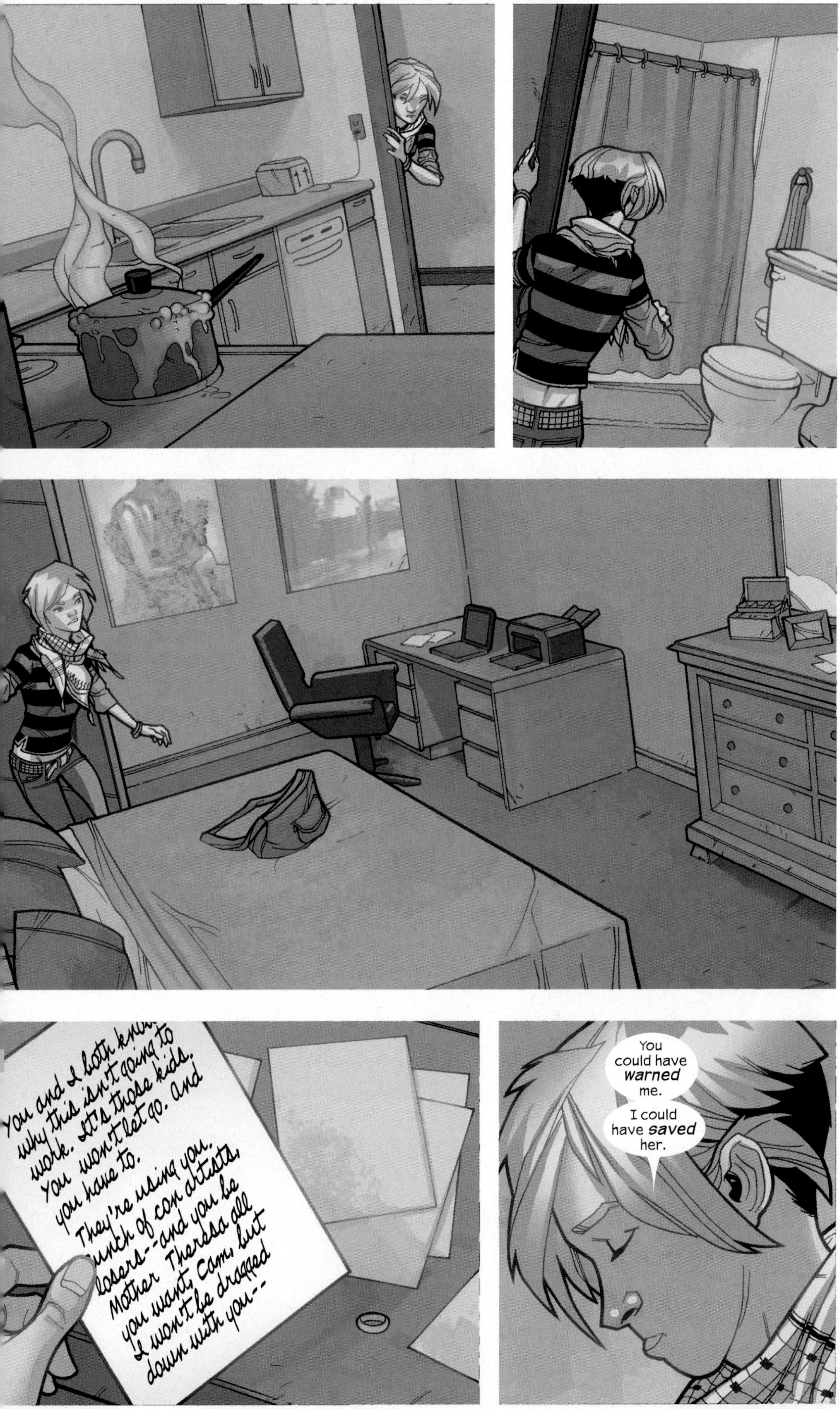
You and I both kn
why this isn't going to
work. It's those kids.
You won't let go. And
you have to.
They're using you.
unch of con artists,
losers--and you be
Mother Theresa all
you want, Cam, but
I won't be dragged
down with you--
You could have *warned* me.
I could have *saved* her.

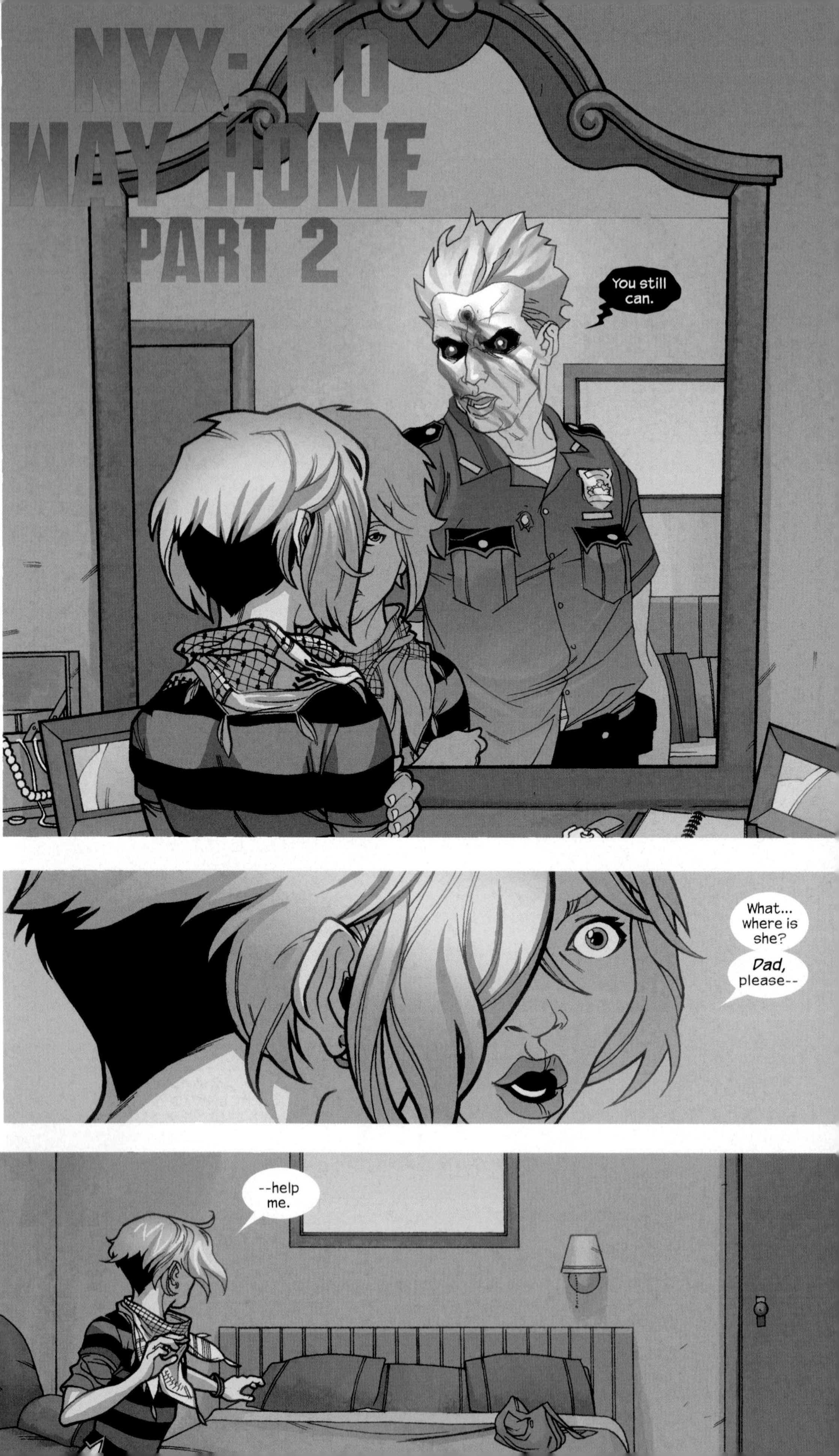
NYX: NO WAY HOME
PART 2
You still can.
What... where is she?
Dad, please--
--help me.

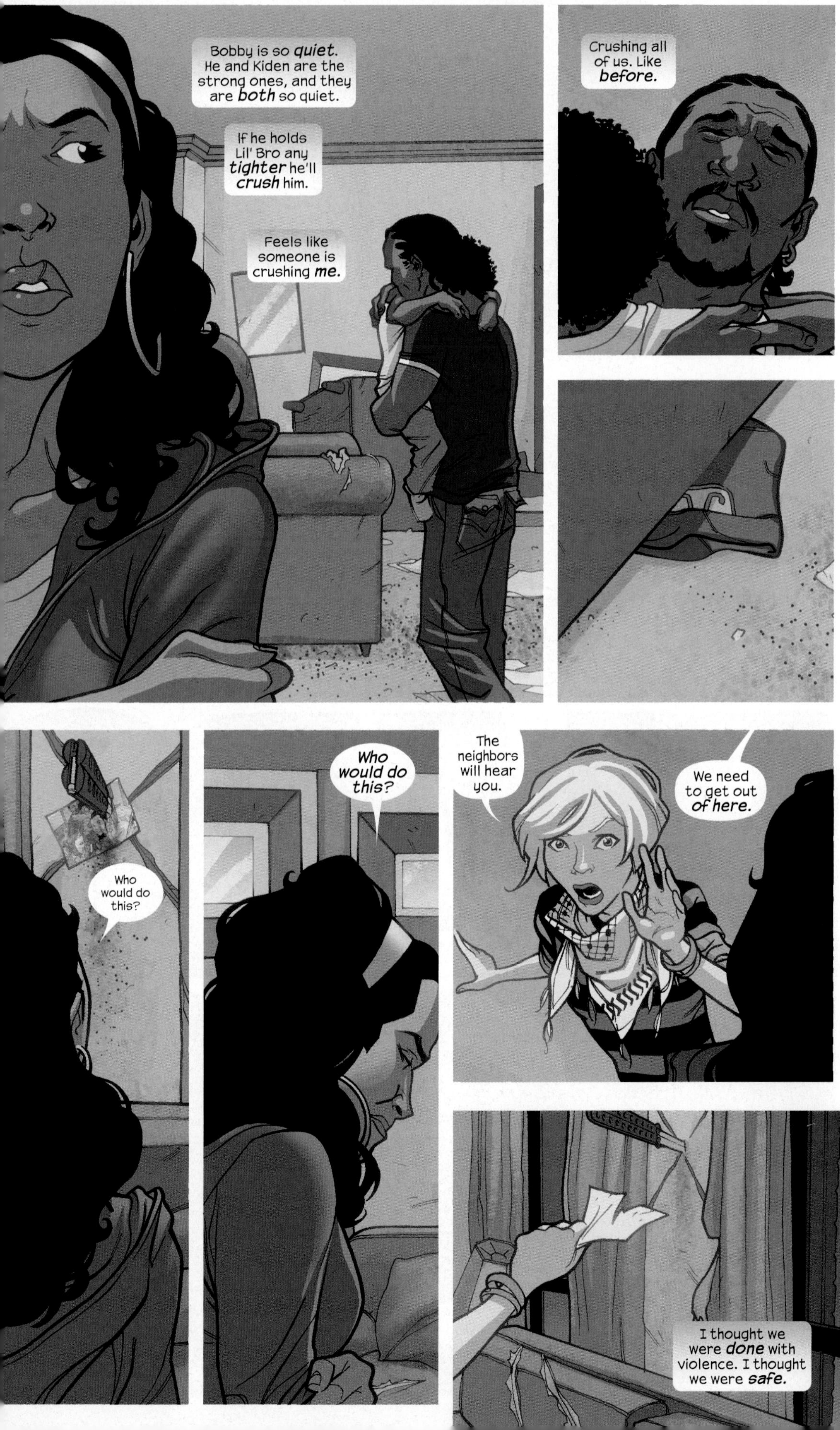

Bobby is so quiet. He and Kiden are the strong ones, and they are both so quiet.
If he holds Lil' Bro any tighter he'll crush him.
Feels like someone is crushing me.
Crushing all of us. Like before.
Who would do this?
Who would do this?
The neighbors will hear you.
We need to get out of here.
I thought we were done with violence. I thought we were safe.

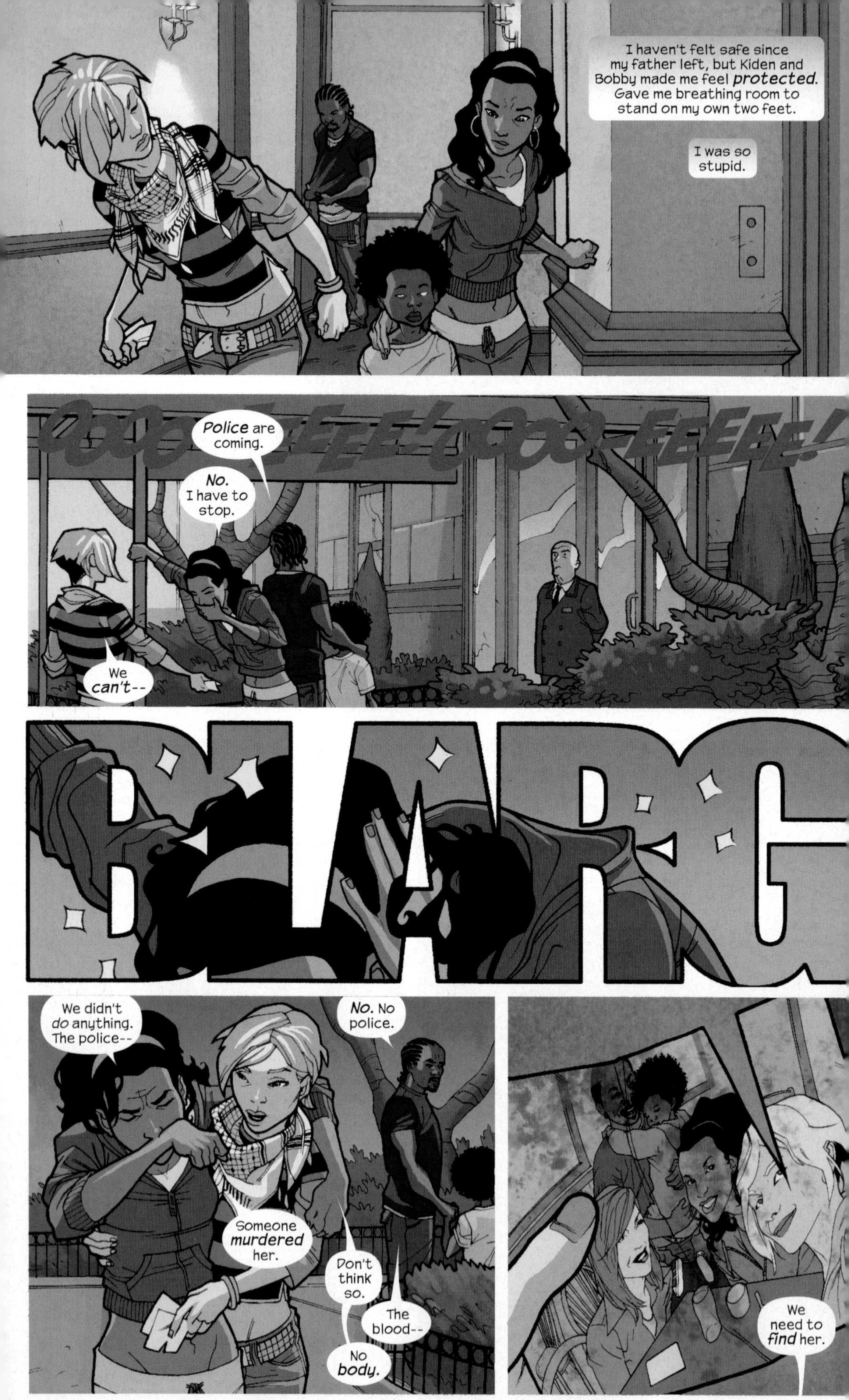
I haven't felt safe since my father left, but Kiden and Bobby made me feel *protected*. Gave me breathing room to stand on my own two feet.
I was so stupid.
OOOO-EEEE! OOOO-EEEEE!
Police are coming.
No. I have to stop.
We *can't*--
BLARG
We didn't *do* anything. The police--
No. No police.
Someone *murdered* her.
Don't think so.
The blood--
No *body*.
We need to *find* her.

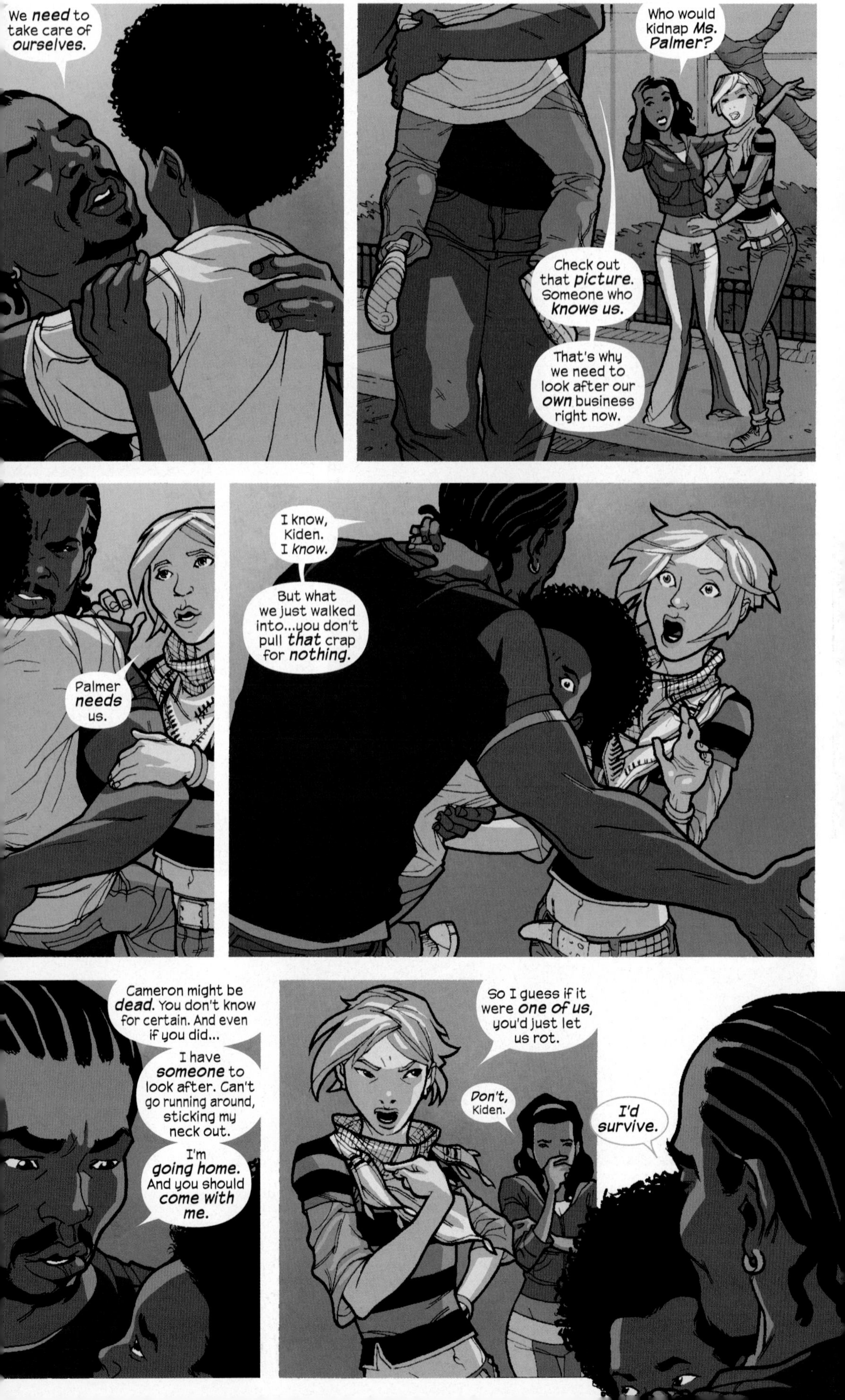
We need to take care of ourselves.
Who would kidnap Ms. Palmer?
Check out that picture. Someone who knows us.
That's why we need to look after our own business right now.
Palmer needs us.
I know, Kiden. I know.
But what we just walked into...you don't pull that crap for nothing.
Cameron might be dead. You don't know for certain. And even if you did...
I have someone to look after. Can't go running around, sticking my neck out.
I'm going home. And you should come with me.
So I guess if it were one of us, you'd just let us rot.
Don't, Kiden.
I'd survive.

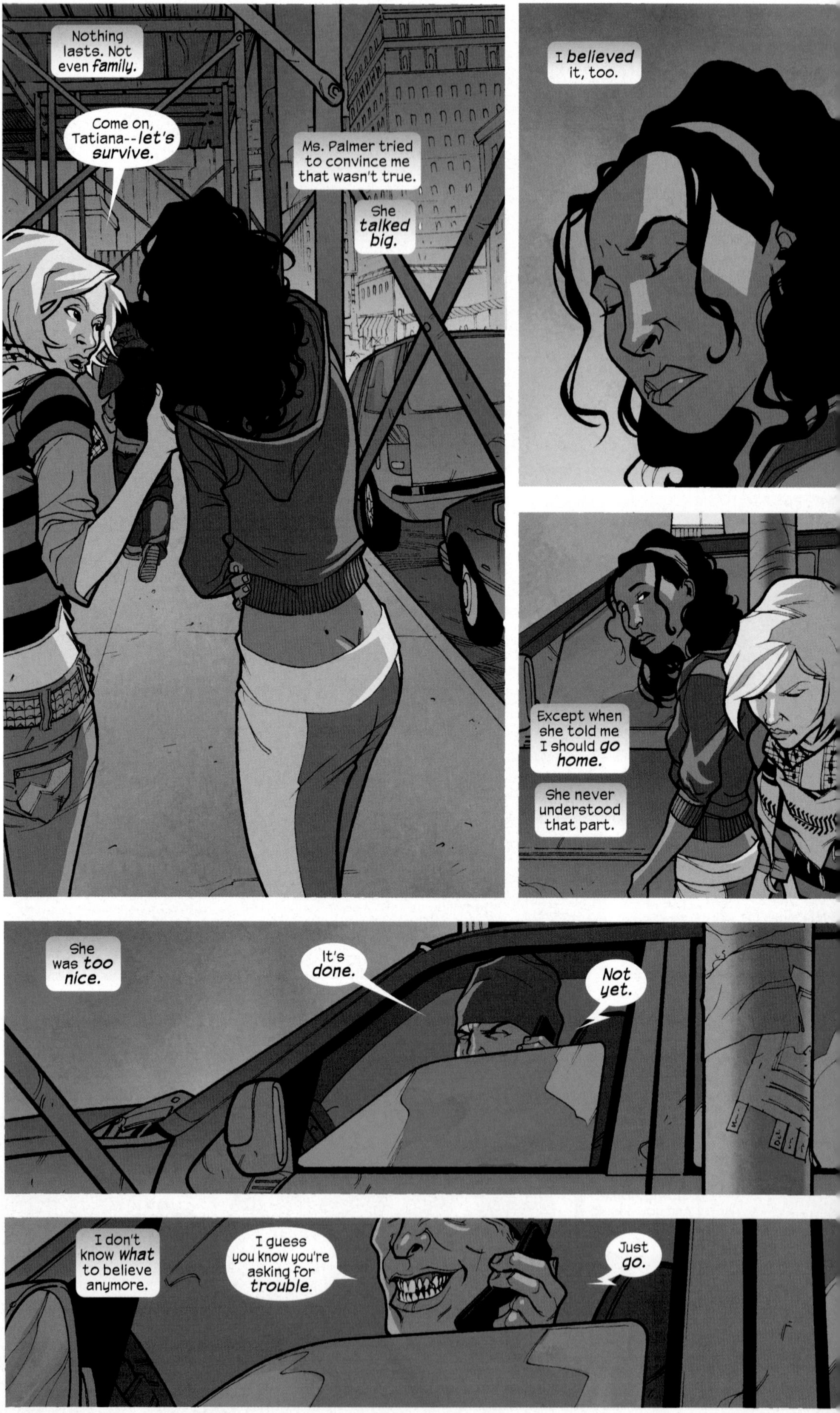
Nothing lasts. Not even family.
Come on, Tatiana--let's survive.
Ms. Palmer tried to convince me that wasn't true.
She talked big.
I believed it, too.
Except when she told me I should go home.
She never understood that part.
She was too nice.
It's done.
Not yet.
I don't know what to believe anymore.
I guess you know you're asking for trouble.
Just go.

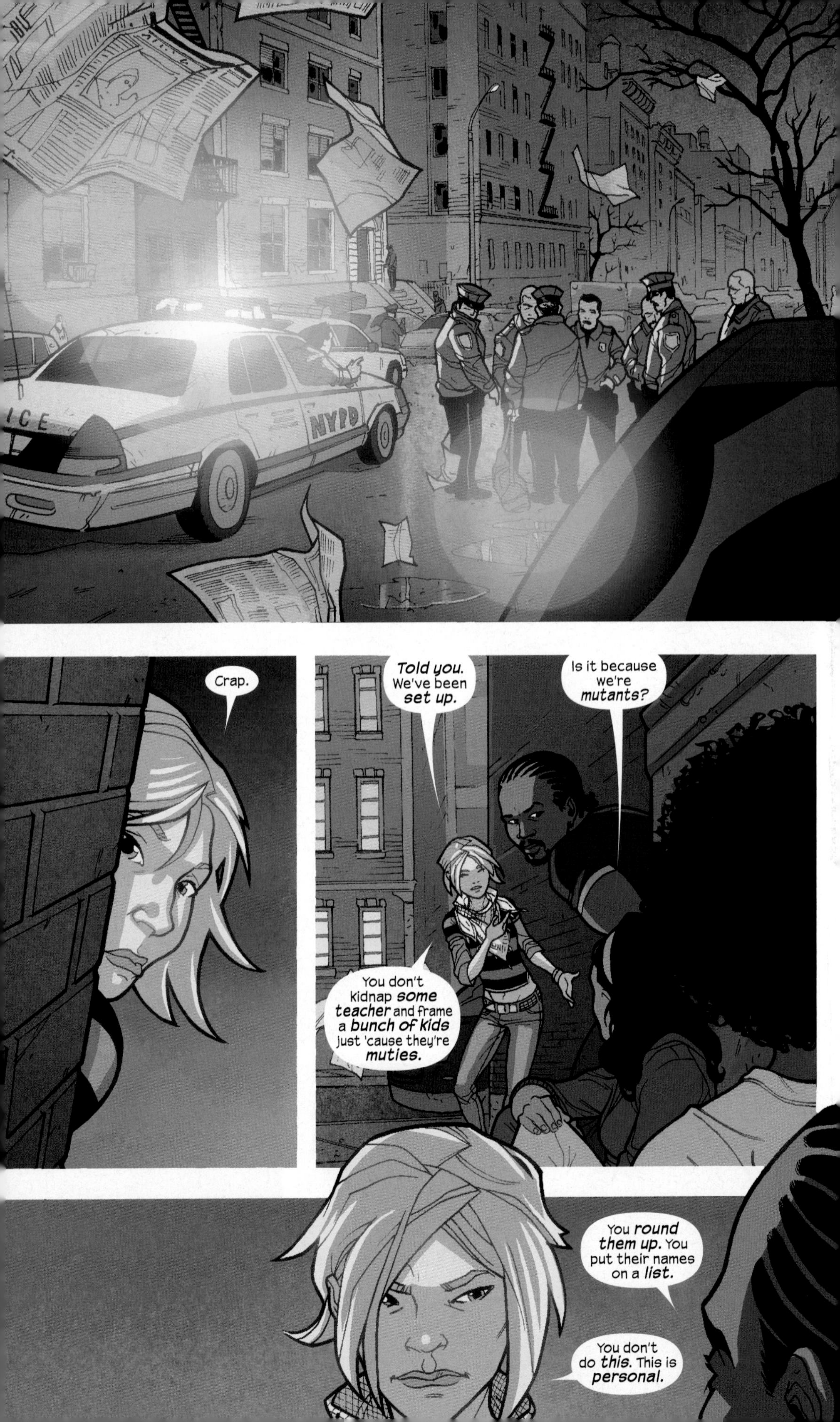
NYPD
Crap.
Told you. We've been set up.
Is it because we're mutants?
You don't kidnap some teacher and frame a bunch of kids just 'cause they're muties.
You round them up. You put their names on a list.
You don't do this. This is personal.

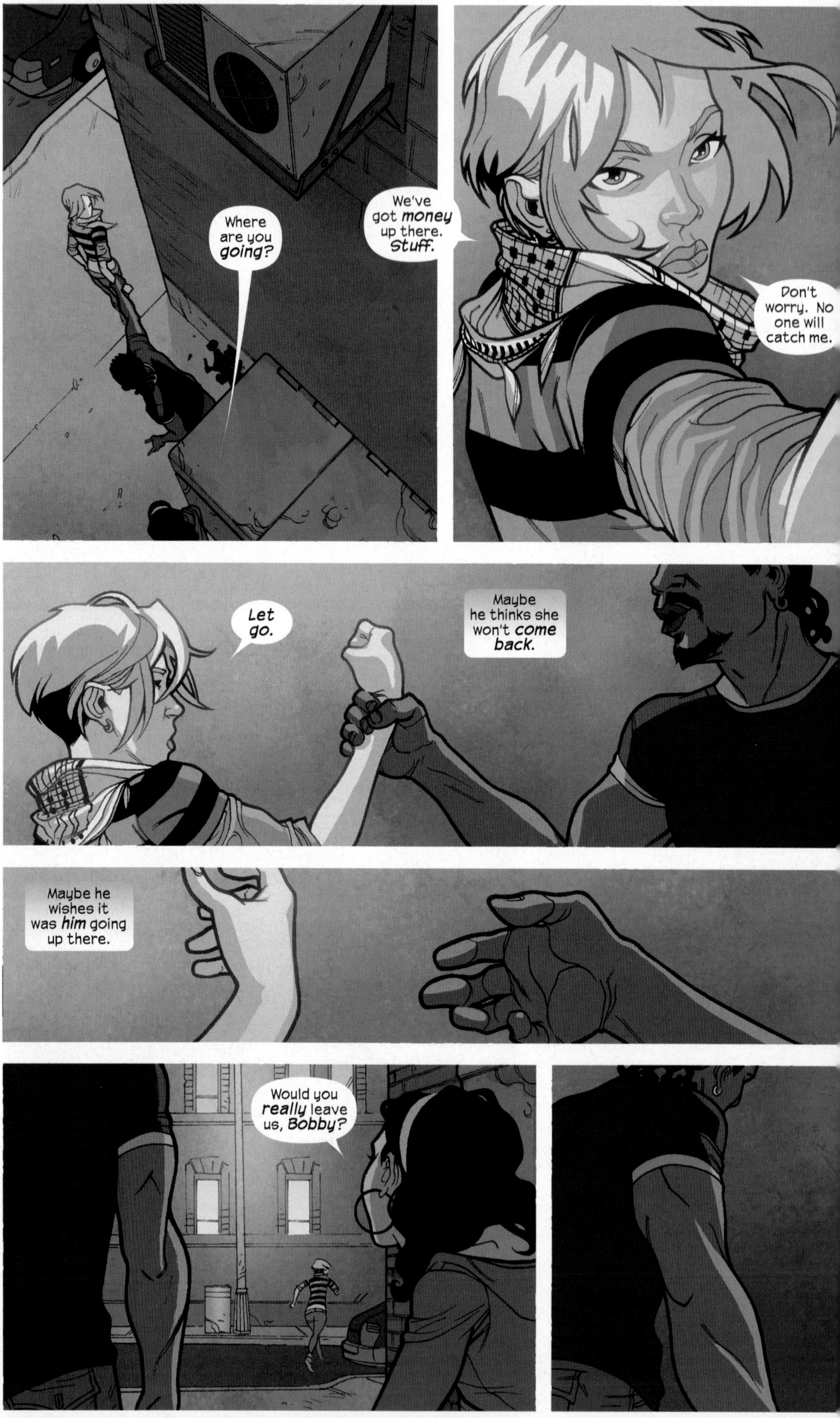
Where are you going?
We've got money up there. Stuff.
Don't worry. No one will catch me.
Let go.
Maybe he thinks she won't come back.
Maybe he wishes it was him going up there.
Would you really leave us, Bobby?

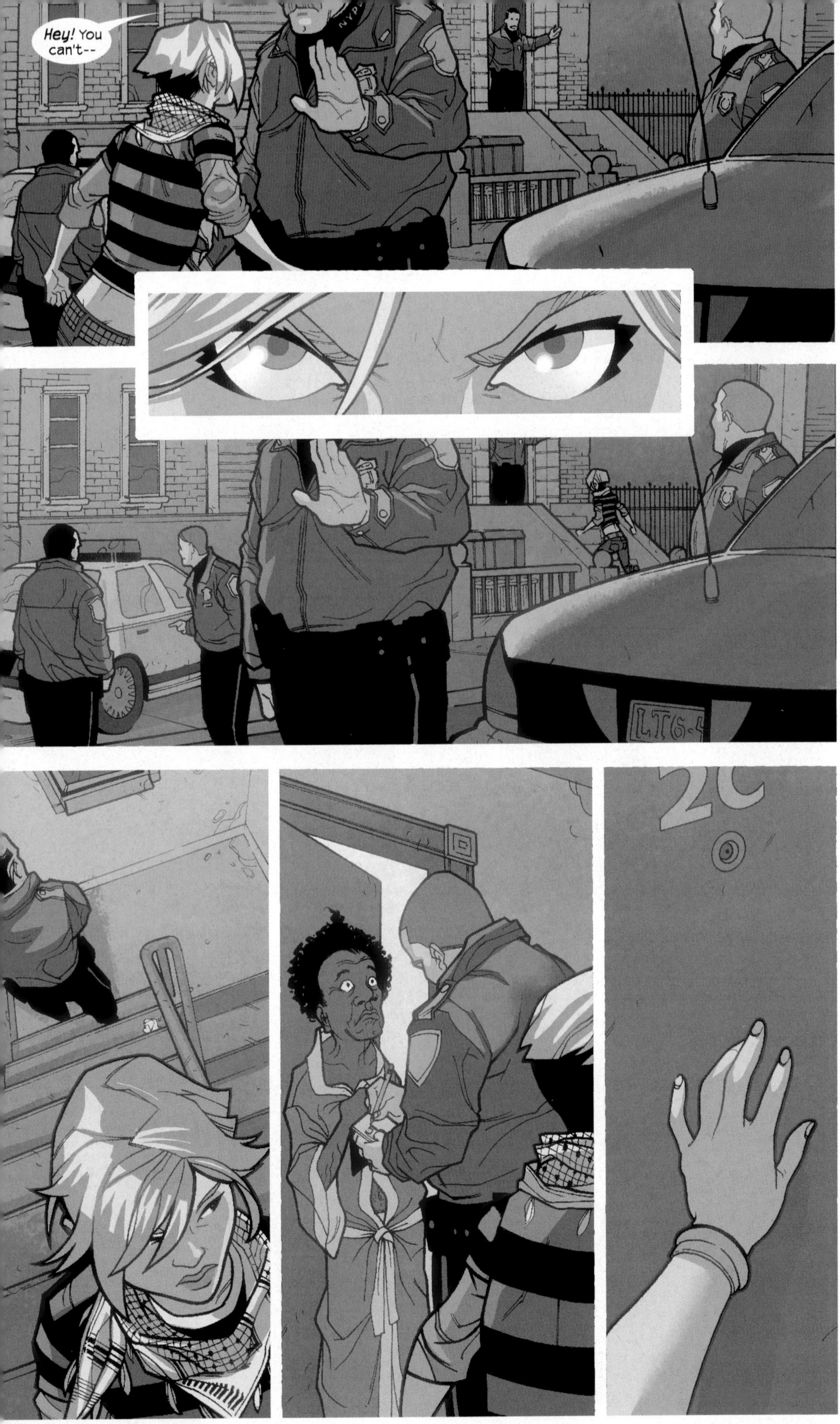
Hey! You can't--
2C

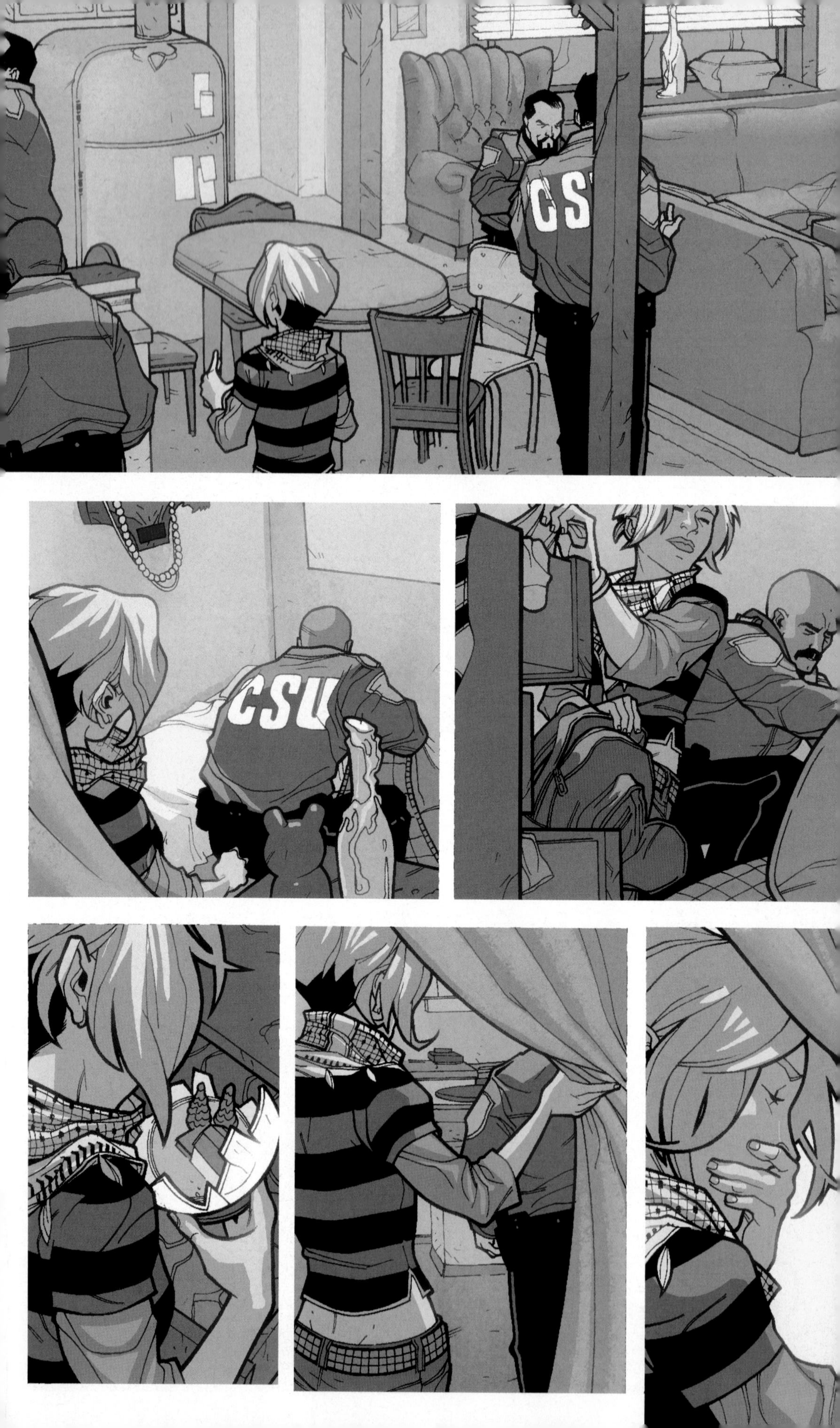
CSU
CSU

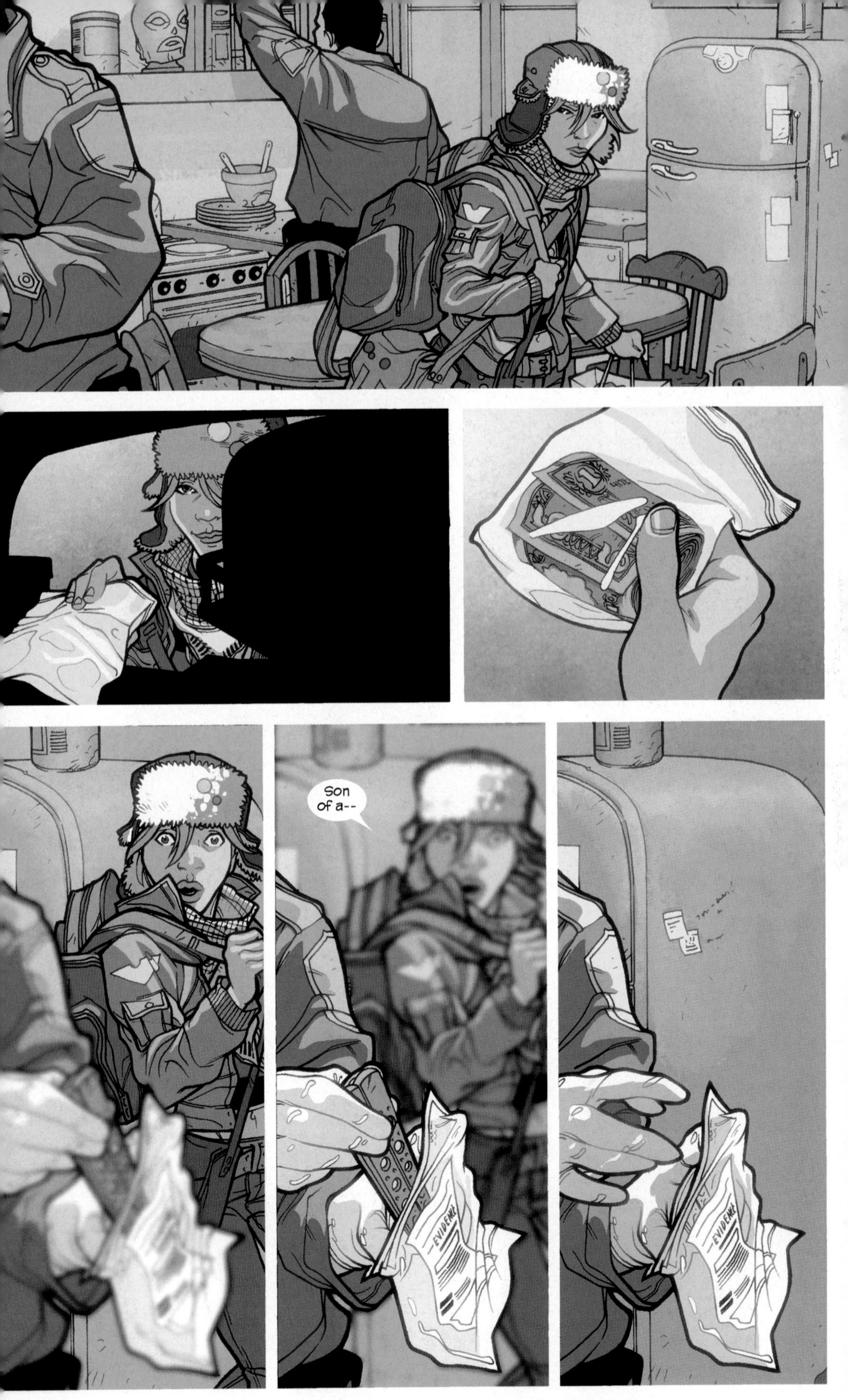
Son of a--
EVIDENCE

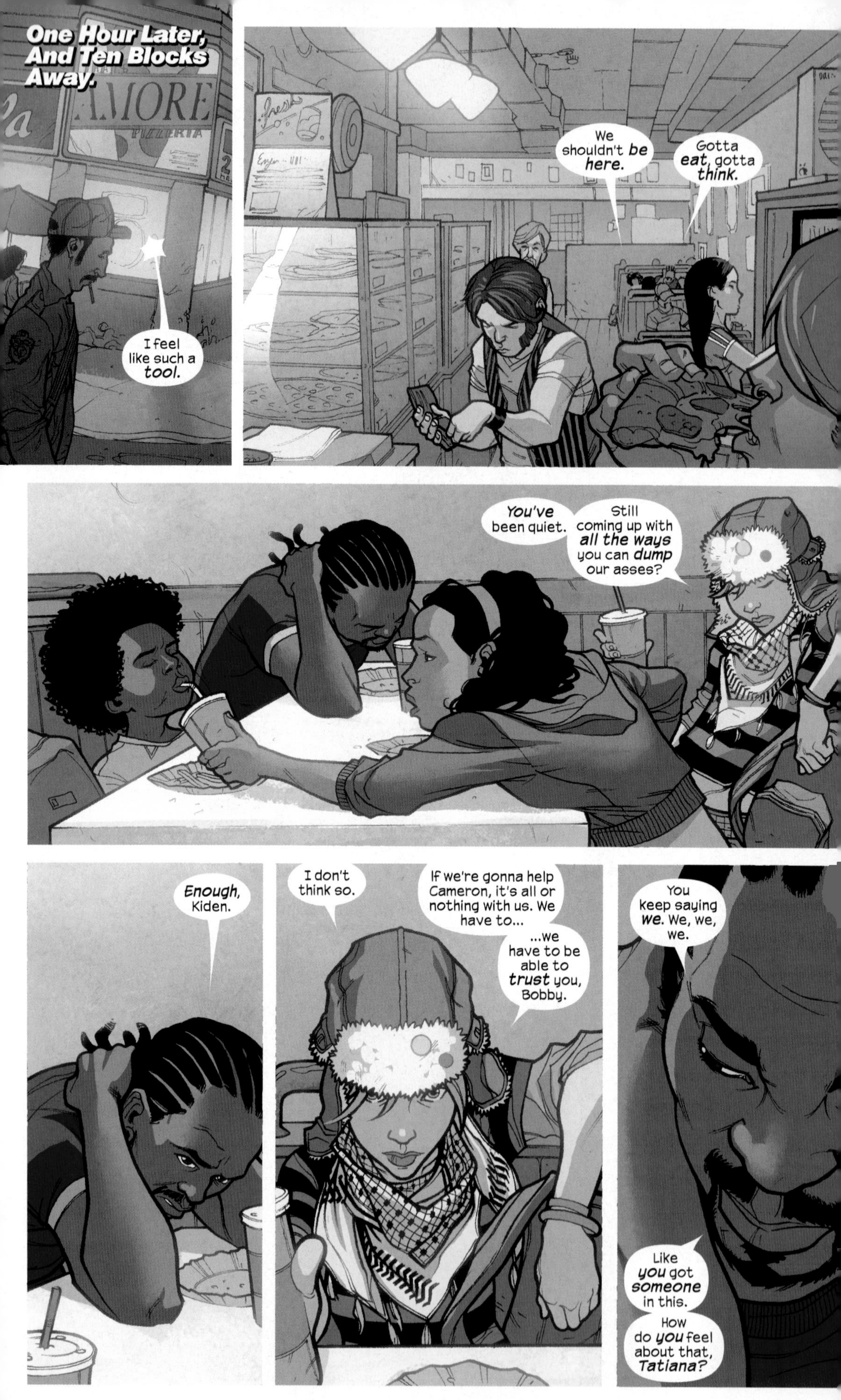
One Hour Later, And Ten Blocks Away.
AMORE
PIZZERIA
I feel like such a tool.
We shouldn't be here.
Gotta eat, gotta think.
You've been quiet.
Still coming up with all the ways you can dump our asses?
Enough, Kiden.
I don't think so.
If we're gonna help Cameron, it's all or nothing with us. We have to...
...we have to be able to trust you, Bobby.
You keep saying we. We, we, we.
Like you got someone in this.
How do you feel about that, Tatiana?

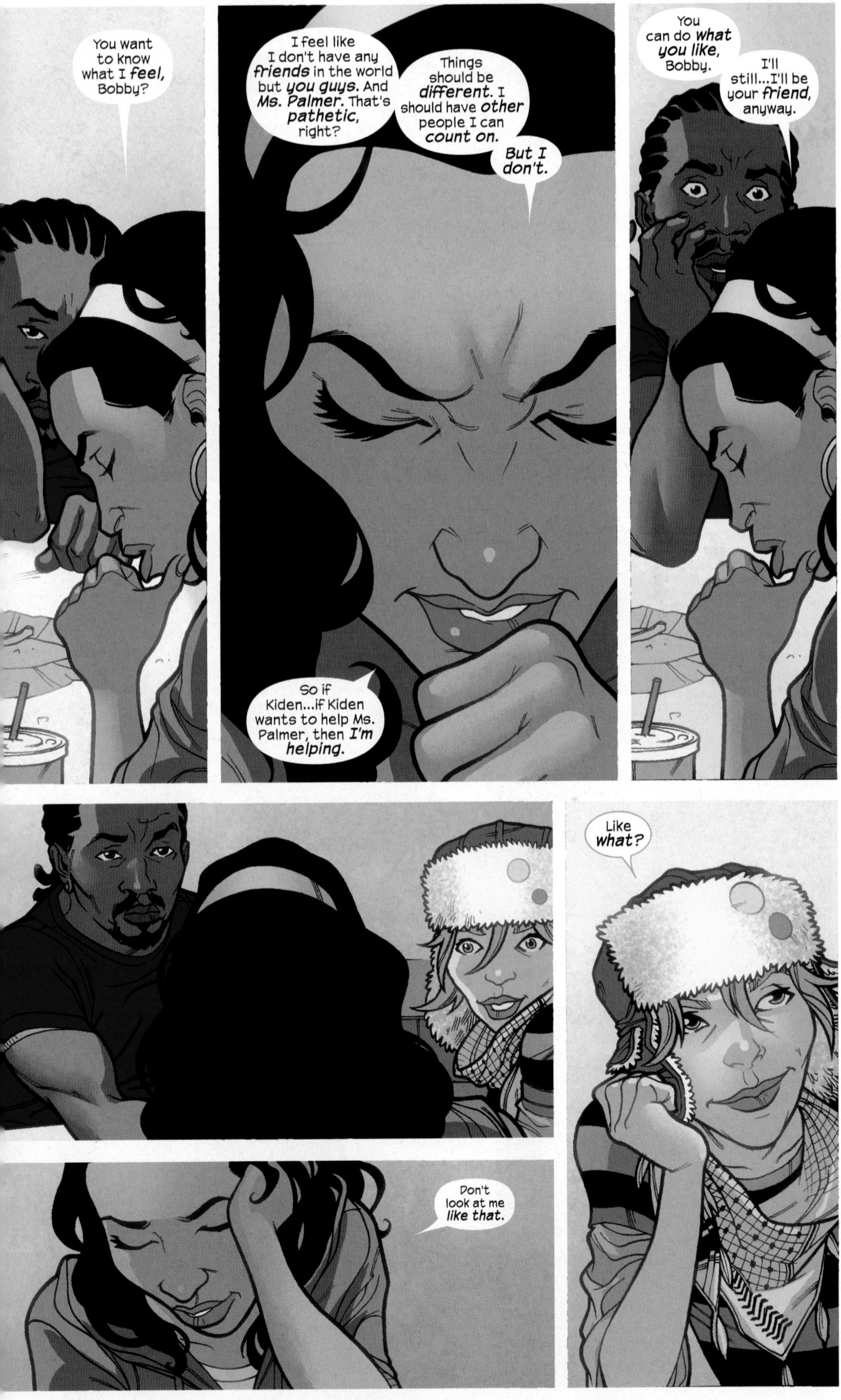
You want to know what I *feel,* Bobby?
I feel like I don't have any *friends* in the world but *you guys.* And *Ms. Palmer.* That's *pathetic,* right?
Things should be *different.* I should have *other* people I can *count on.*
But I don't.
So if Kiden...if Kiden wants to help Ms. Palmer, then *I'm helping.*
You can do *what you like,* Bobby.
I'll still...I'll be your *friend,* anyway.
Don't look at me *like that.*
Like *what?*

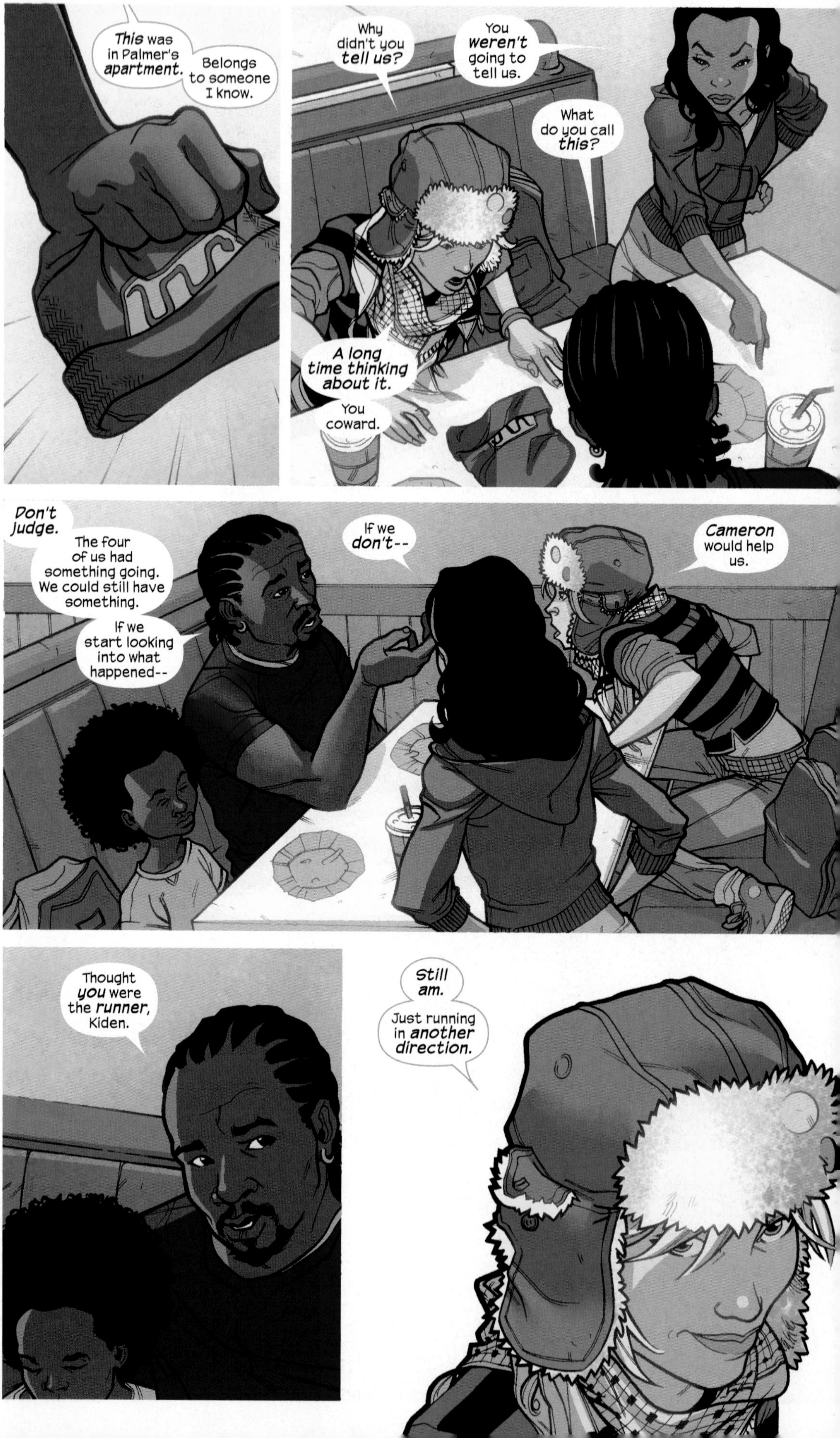
This was in Palmer's apartment.
Belongs to someone I know.
Why didn't you tell us?
You weren't going to tell us.
What do you call this?
A long time thinking about it.
You coward.
Don't judge.
The four of us had something going. We could still have something.
If we start looking into what happened--
If we don't--
Cameron would help us.
Thought you were the runner, Kiden.
Still am.
Just running in another direction.

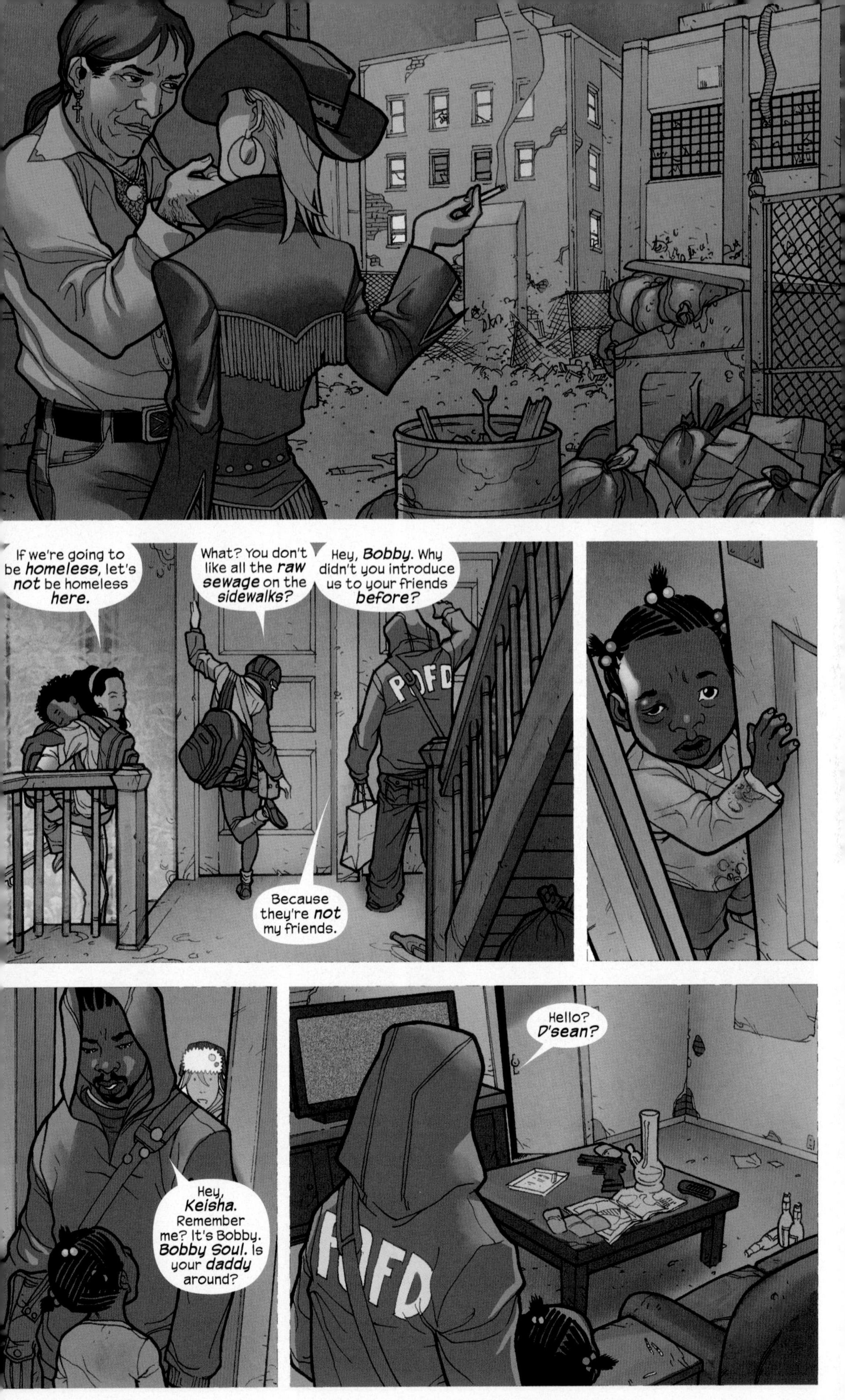
If we're going to be *homeless*, let's *not* be homeless *here.*
What? You don't like all the *raw sewage* on the *sidewalks?*
Hey, *Bobby.* Why didn't you introduce us to your friends *before?*
Because they're *not* my friends.
POFD
Hey, *Keisha.* Remember me? It's Bobby. *Bobby Soul.* Is your *daddy* around?
Hello? *D'sean?*
POFD

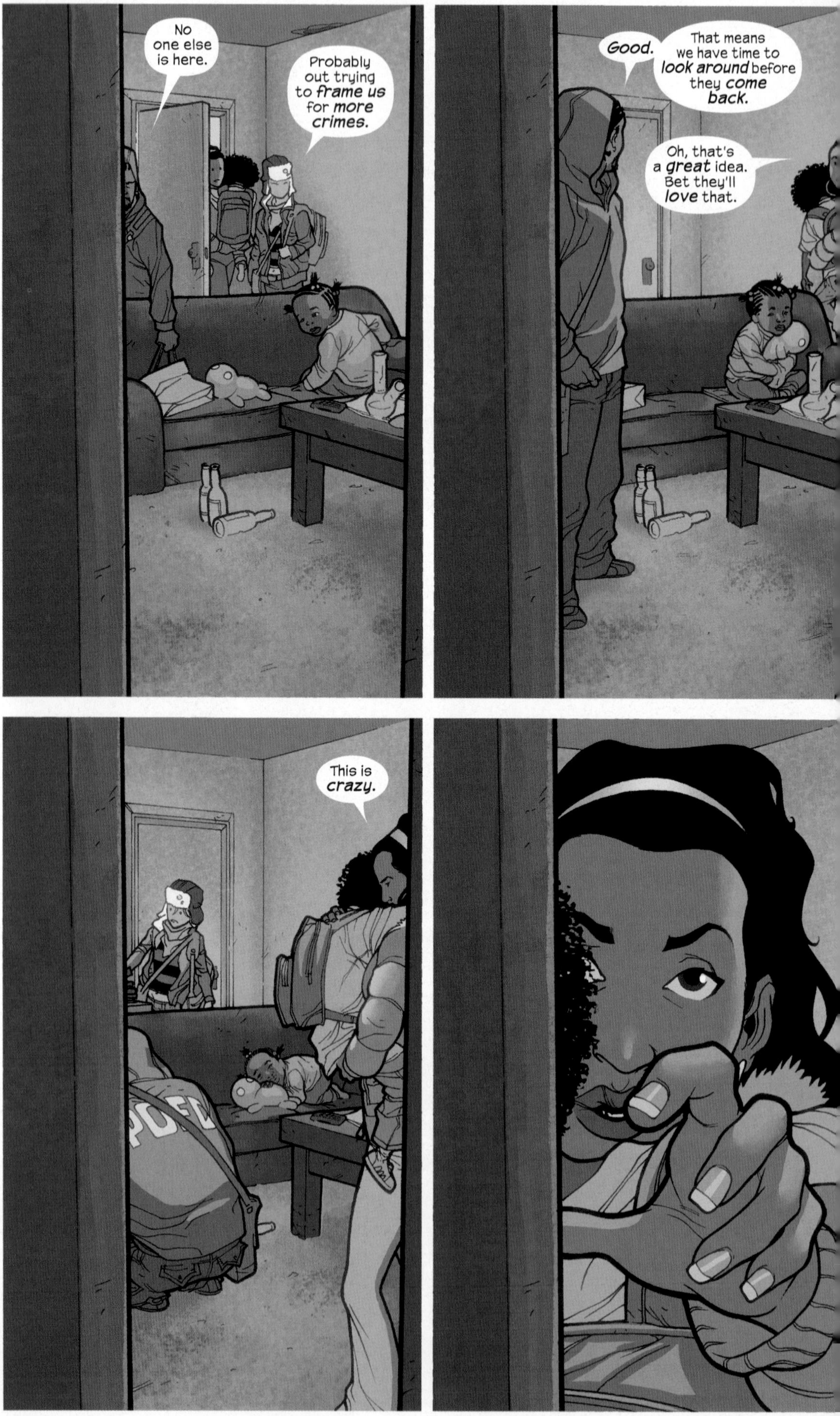
No one else is here.
Probably out trying to frame us for more crimes.
Good.
That means we have time to look around before they come back.
Oh, that's a great idea. Bet they'll love that.
This is crazy.

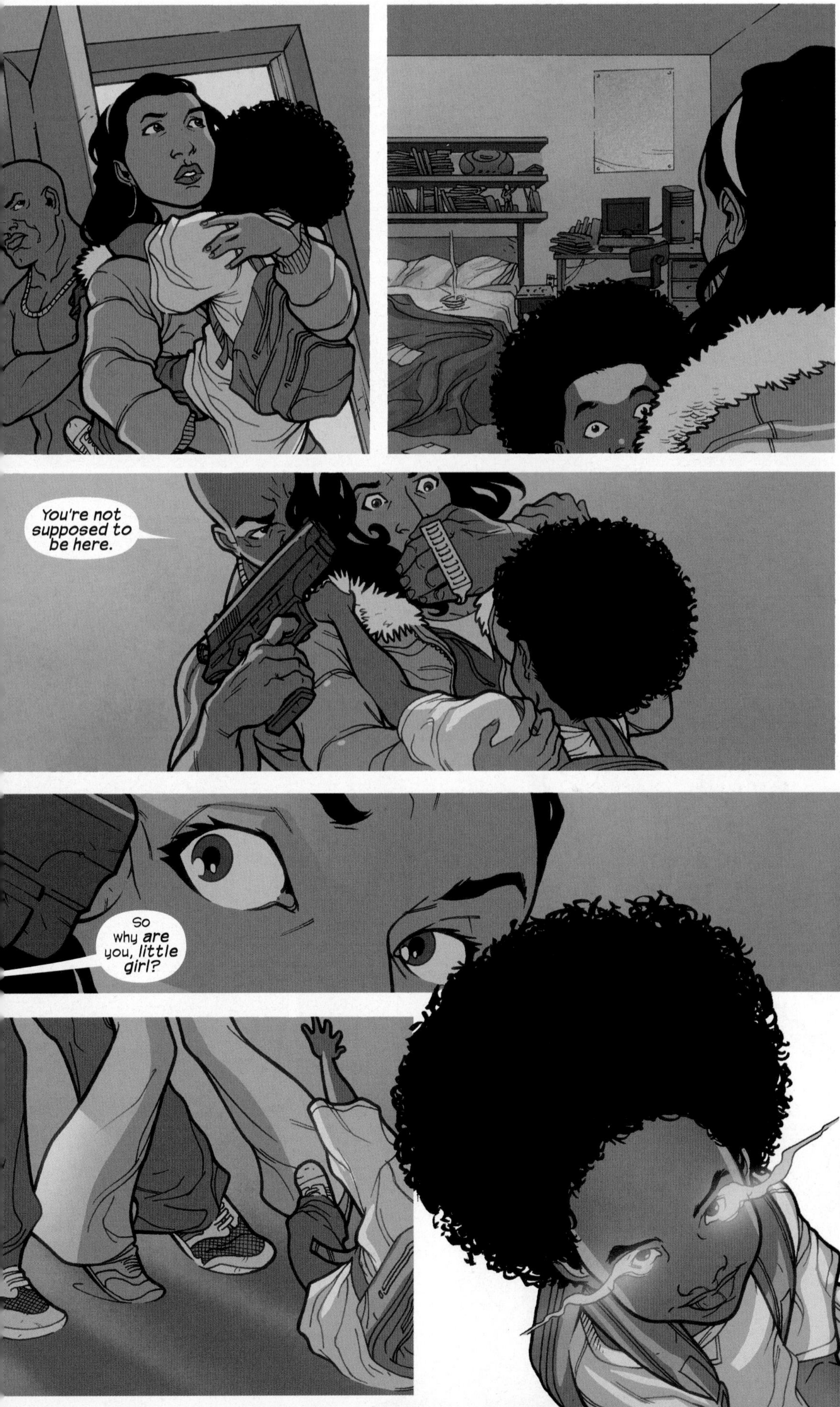
You're not supposed to be here.
So why are you, little girl?

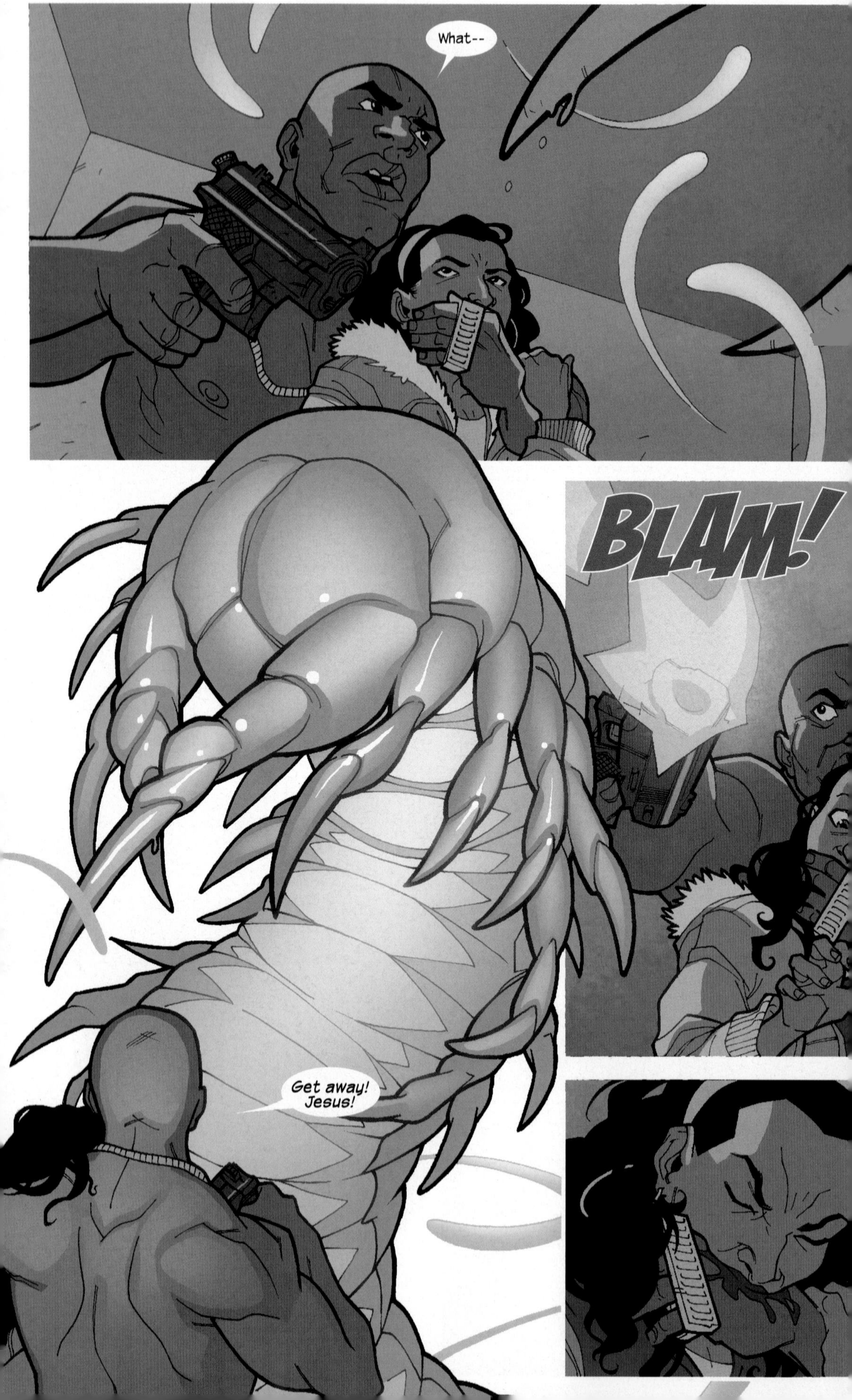
What--
BLAM!
Get away!
Jesus!

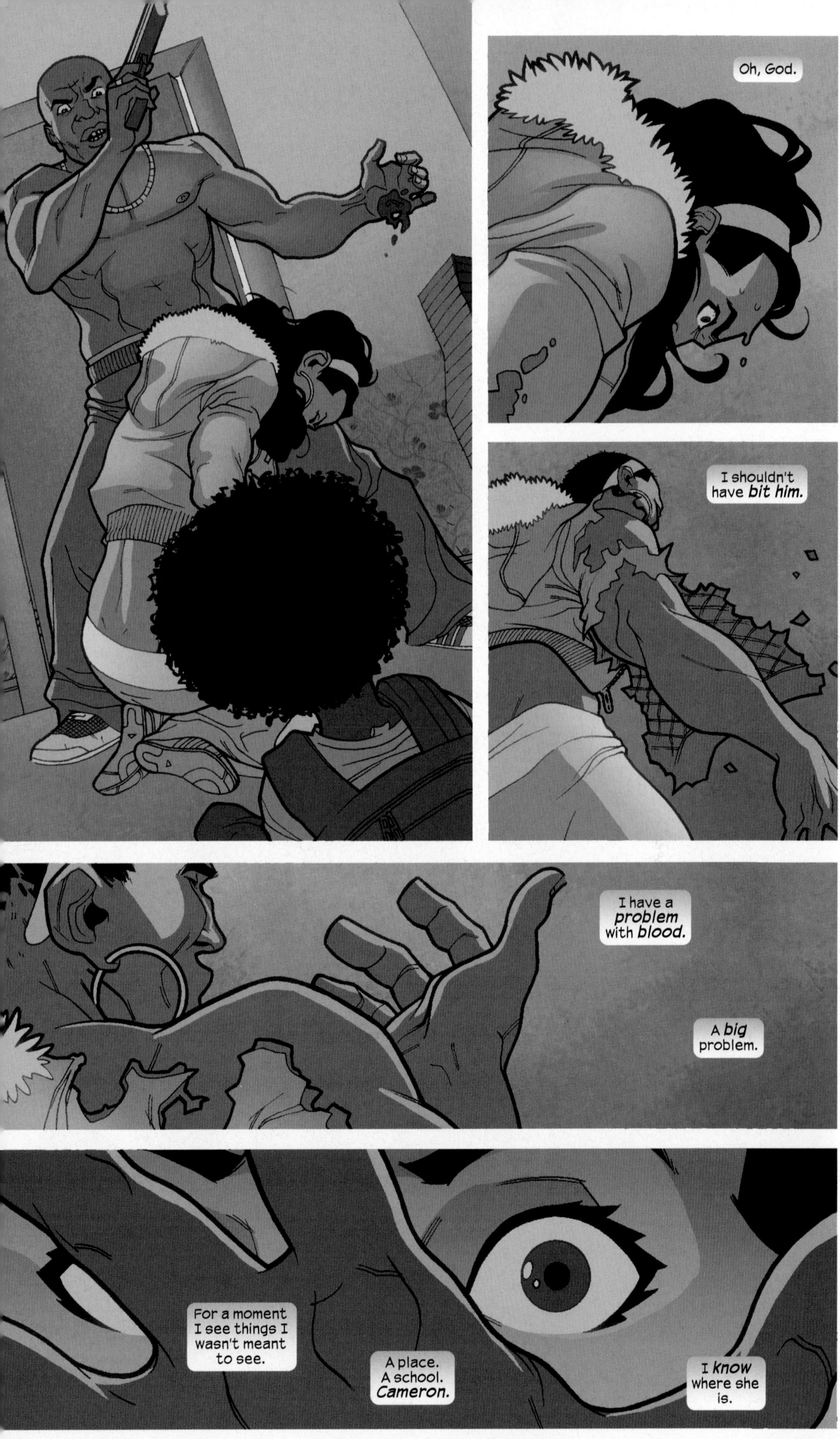

Oh, God.
I shouldn't have *bit him.*
I have a *problem* with *blood.*
A *big* problem.
For a moment I see things I wasn't meant to see.
A place. A school. *Cameron.*
I *know* where she is.

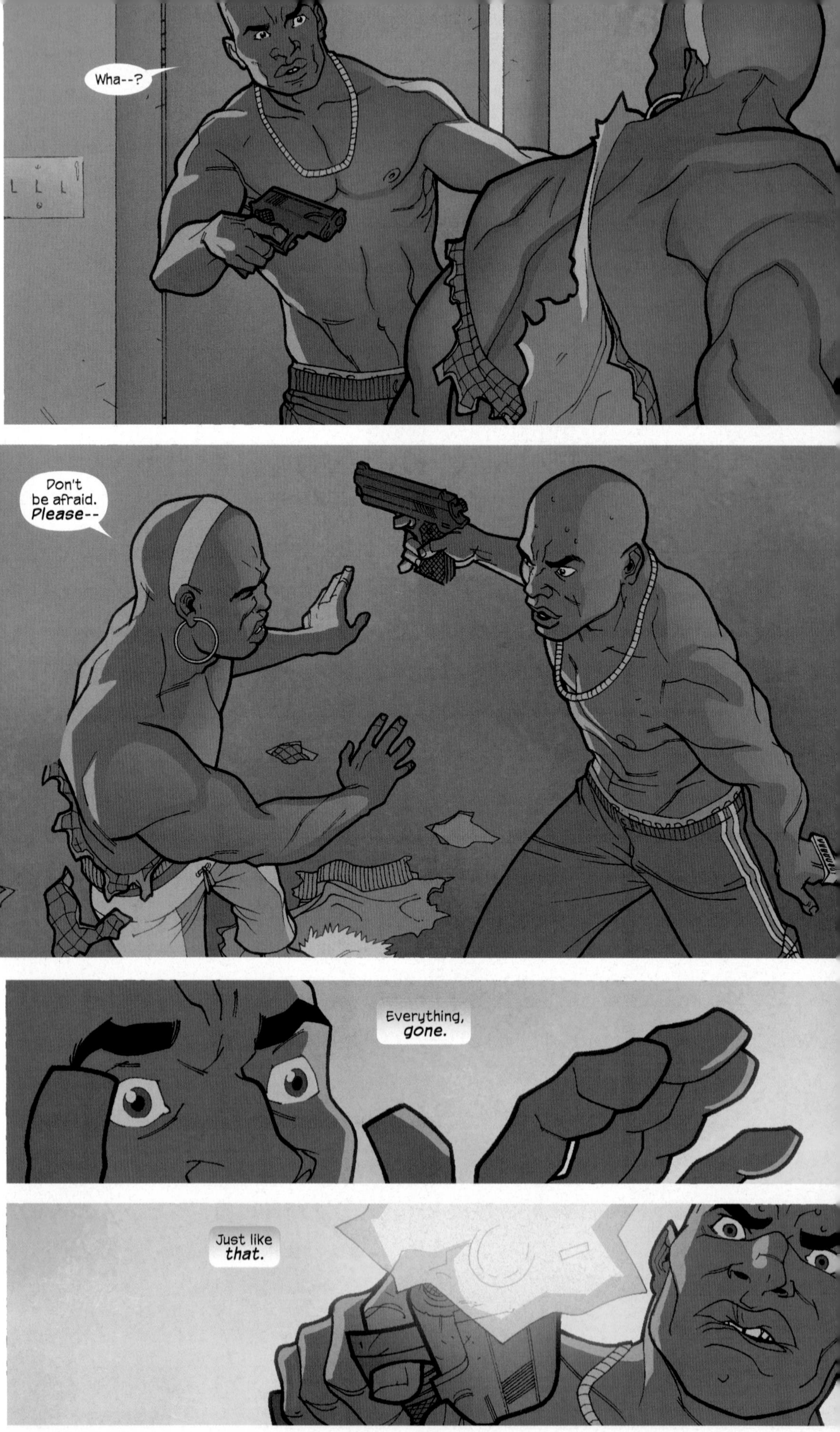

Wha--?
Don't be afraid. *Please--*
Everything, *gone.*
Just like *that.*

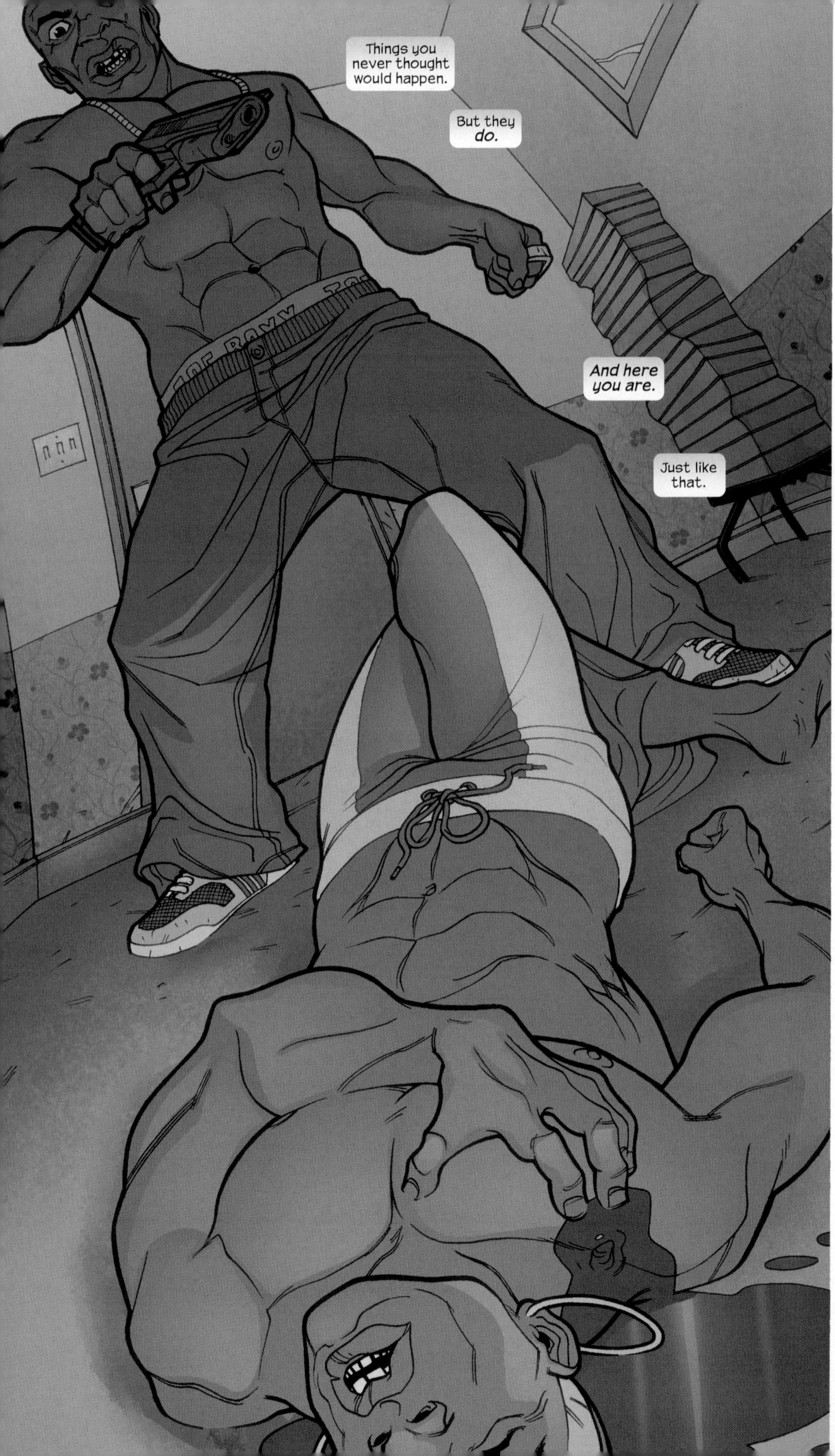
Things you never thought would happen.
But they *do.*
And here you are.
Just like that.

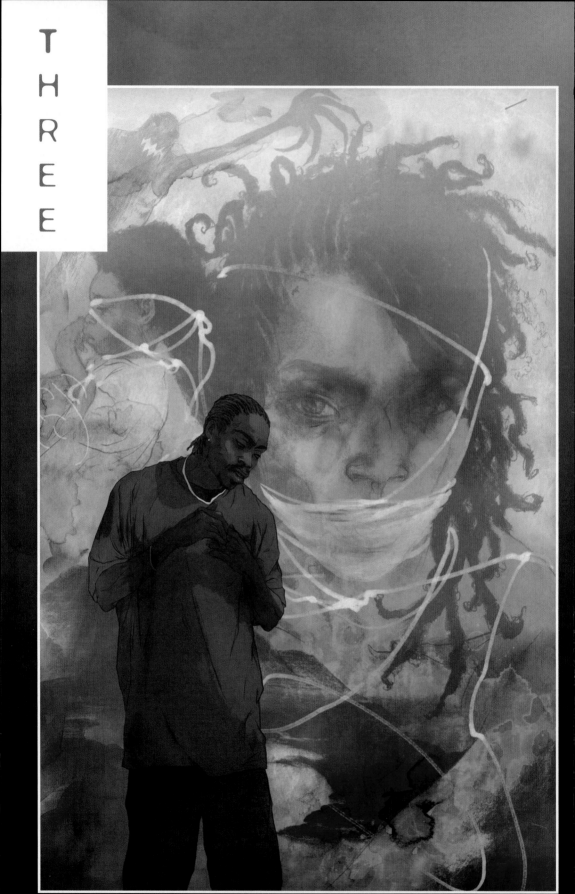

THREE

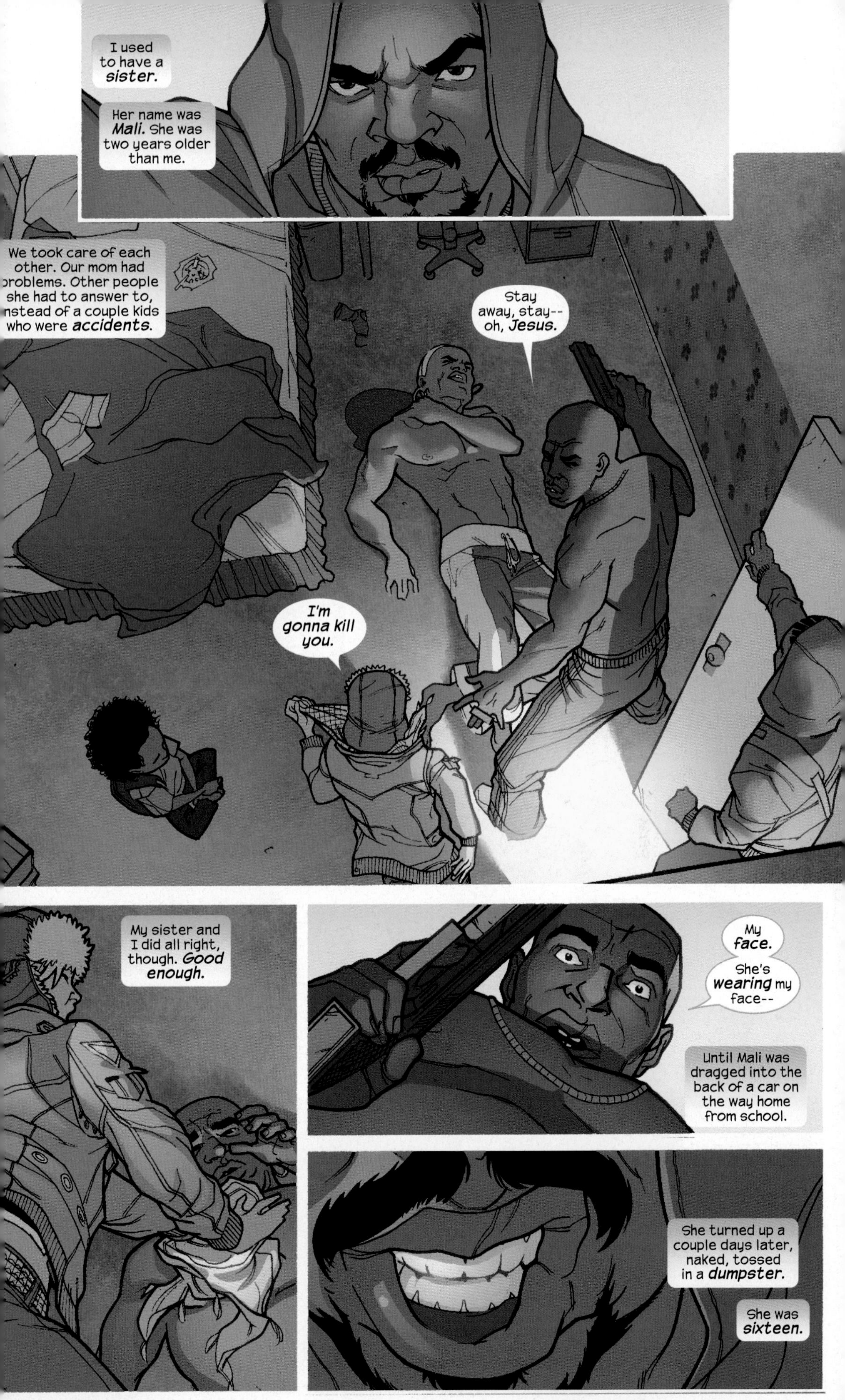

I used to have a sister.
Her name was Mali. She was two years older than me.
We took care of each other. Our mom had problems. Other people she had to answer to, instead of a couple kids who were accidents.
Stay away, stay-- oh, Jesus.
I'm gonna kill you.
My sister and I did all right, though. Good enough.
My face.
She's wearing my face--
Until Mali was dragged into the back of a car on the way home from school.
She turned up a couple days later, naked, tossed in a dumpster.
She was sixteen.

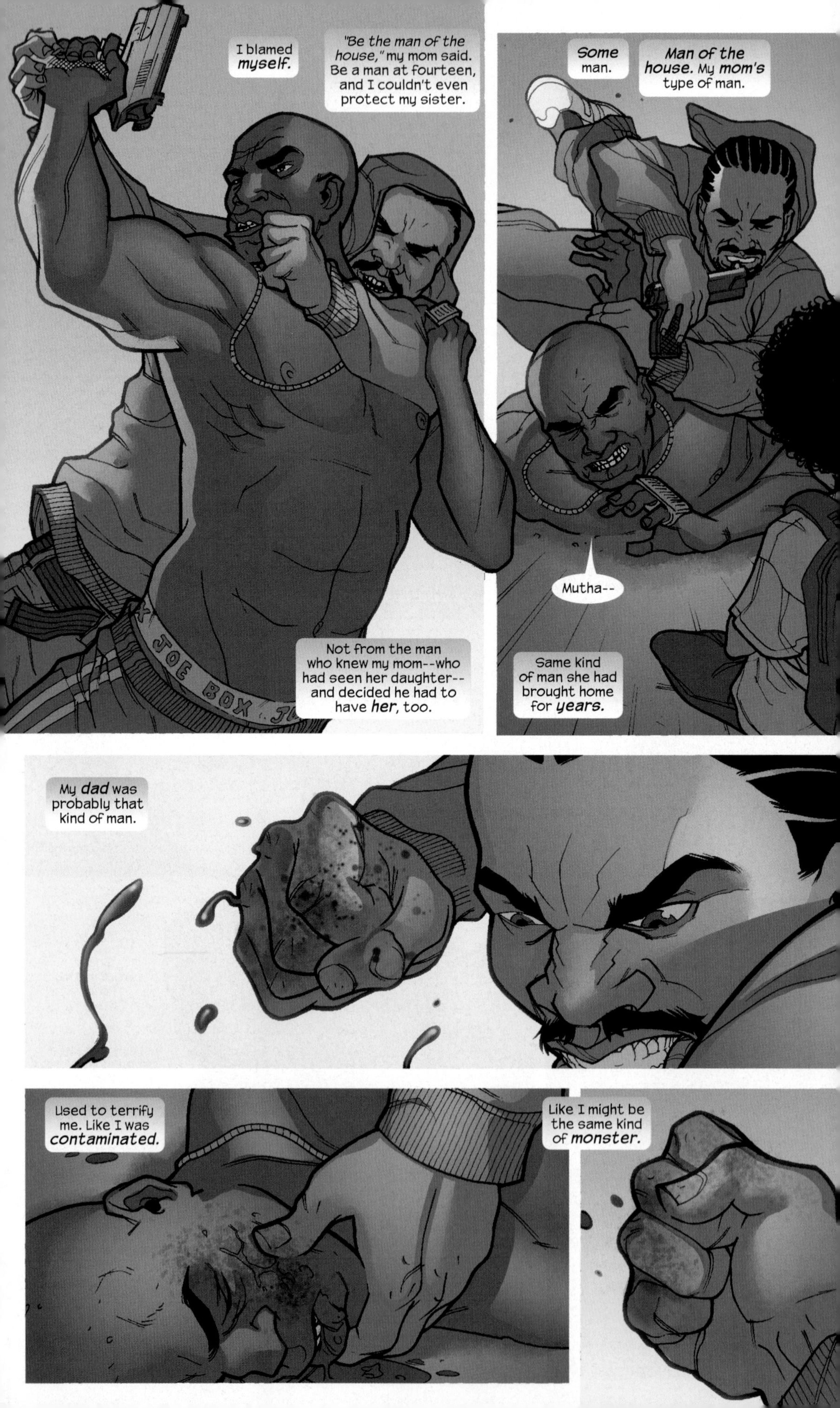

I blamed *myself.*
"Be the man of the house," my mom said. Be a man at fourteen, and I couldn't even protect my sister.
Not from the man who knew my mom--who had seen her daughter--and decided he had to have ***her***, too.
JOE BOX
Some man.
Man of the ***house.*** My ***mom's*** type of man.
Mutha--
Same kind of man she had brought home for ***years.***
My ***dad*** was probably that kind of man.
Used to terrify me. Like I was ***contaminated.***
Like I might be the same kind of ***monster.***

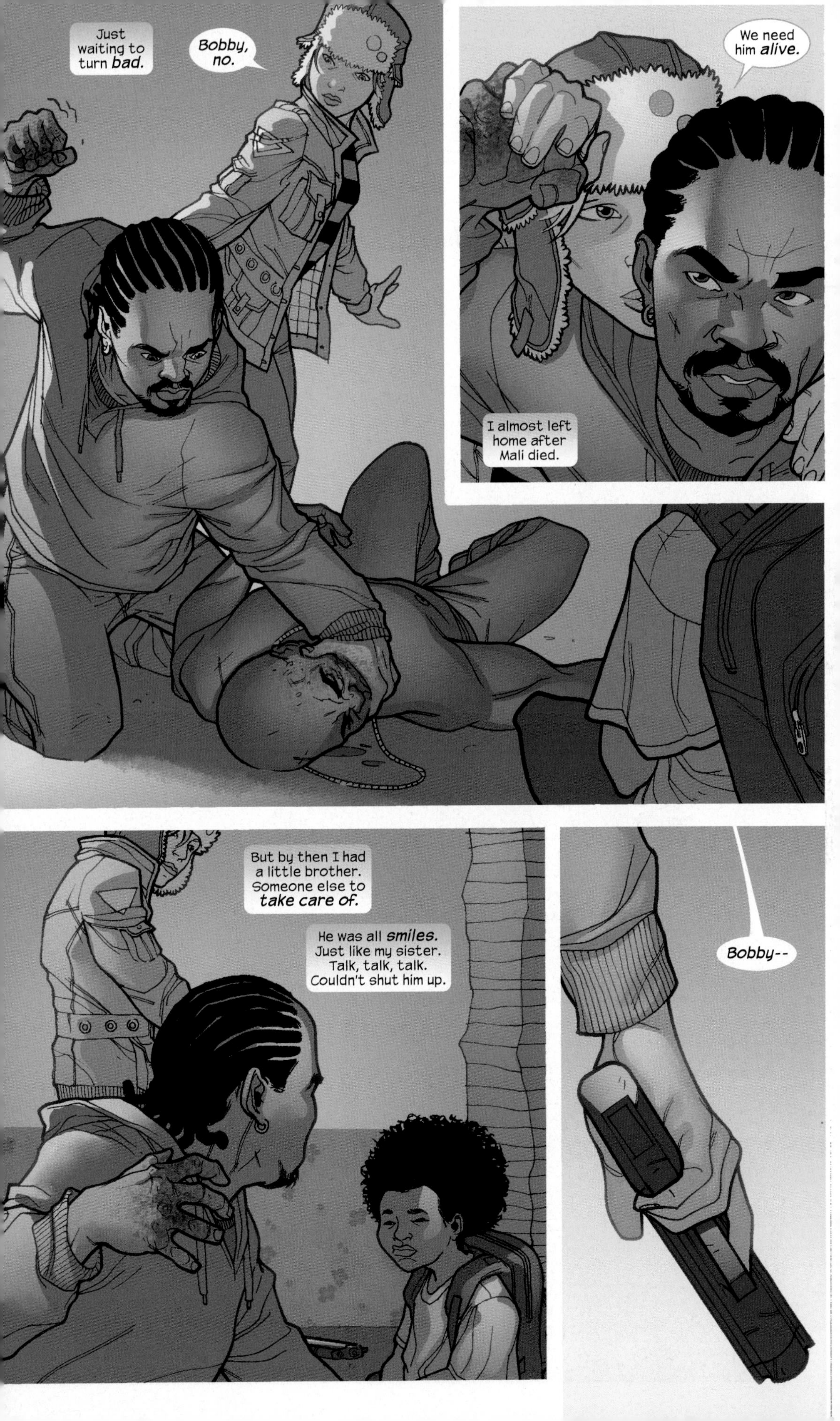

Just waiting to turn bad.
Bobby, no.
We need him alive.
I almost left home after Mali died.
But by then I had a little brother. Someone else to take care of.
He was all smiles. Just like my sister. Talk, talk, talk. Couldn't shut him up.
Bobby--

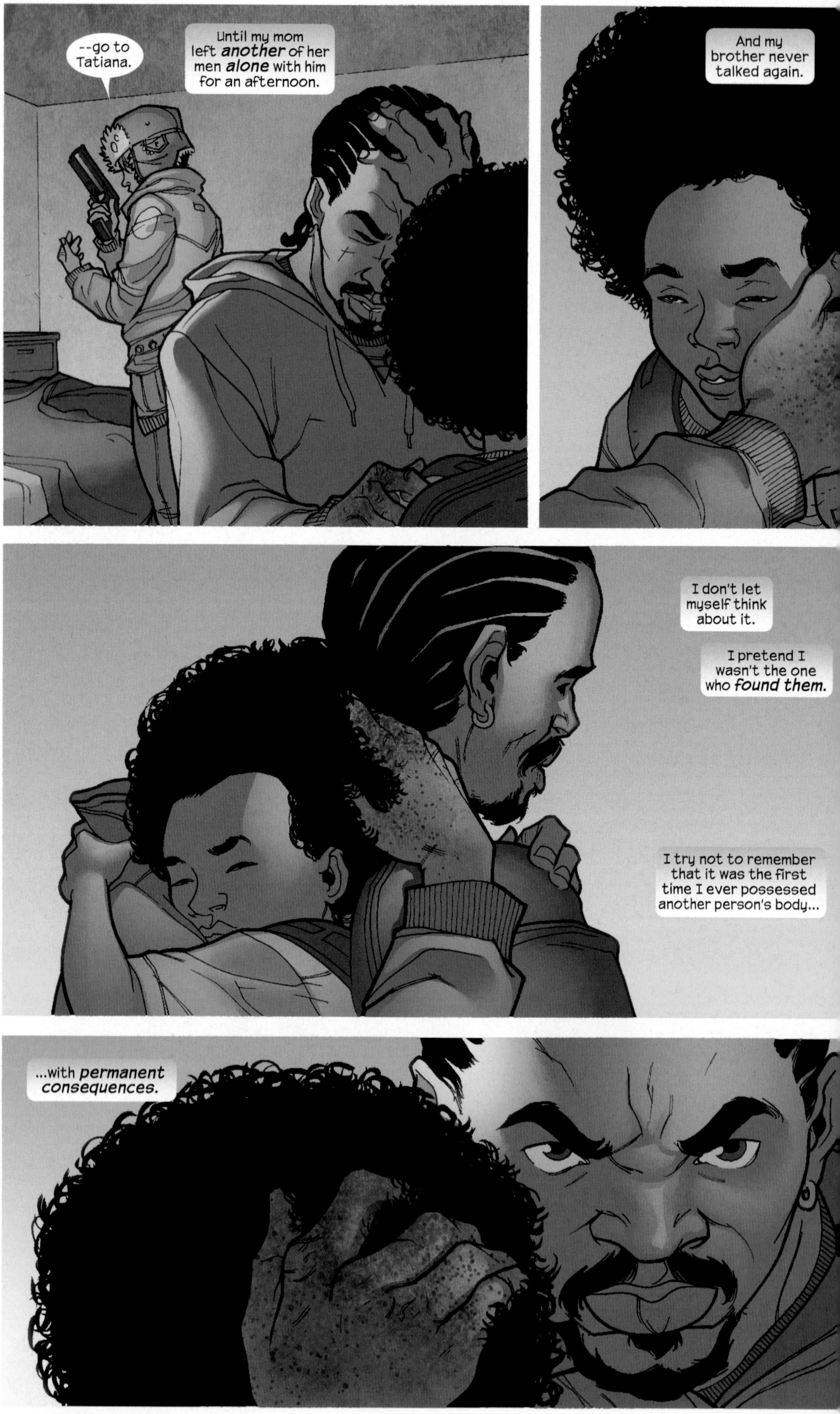
--go to Tatiana.
Until my mom left *another* of her men *alone* with him for an afternoon.
And my brother never talked again.
I don't let myself think about it.
I pretend I wasn't the one who *found them.*
I try not to remember that it was the first time I ever possessed another person's body...
...with *permanent consequences.*

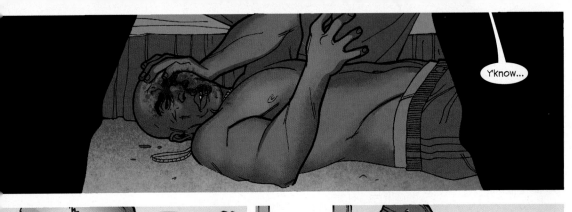

Y'know...

...I think I *like* this gun.

...get off... me.

Did I *hear* you right?

Did I hear you tell me to *do something?* I think my friend must have *damaged* your brain.

I really do.

'Cause, dude, you are *mine.* You are mine *all over.*

And if you think that girl stealing your face was *bad,* that ain't *nothing* compared to what *I'll* do.

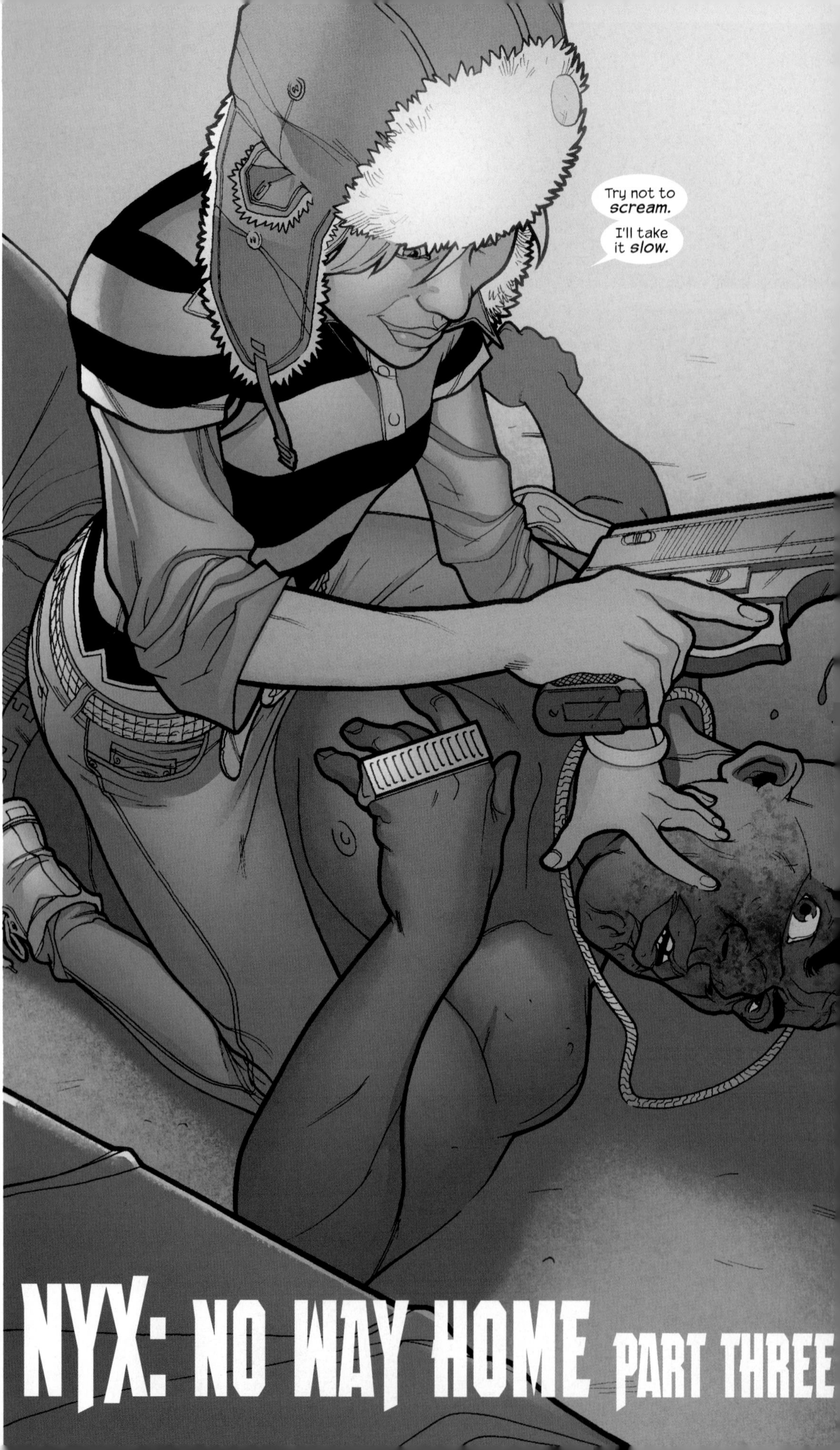
Try not to scream.
I'll take it slow.
NYX: NO WAY HOME PART THREE

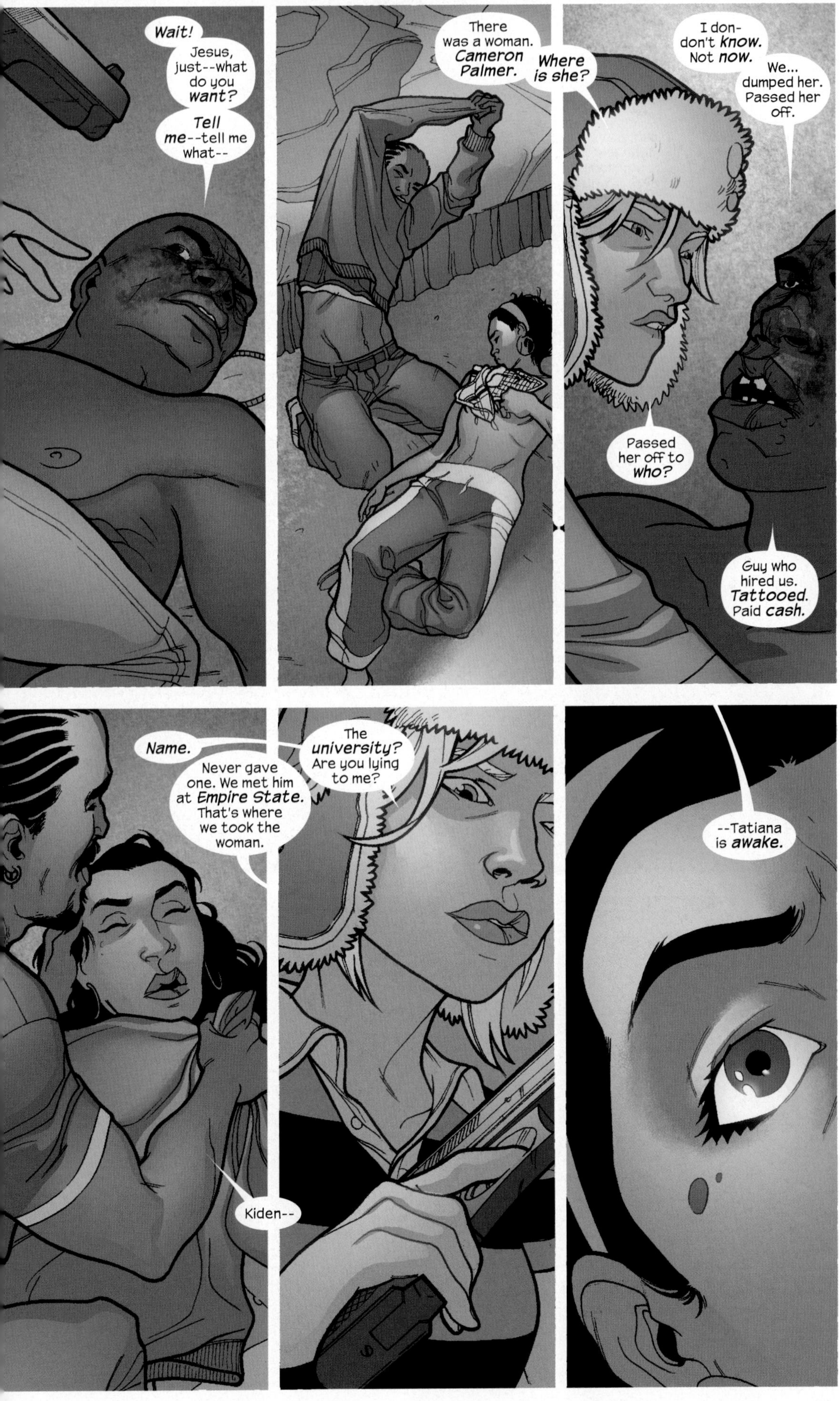
Wait!
Jesus, just--what do you want?
Tell me--tell me what--
There was a woman. Cameron Palmer.
Where is she?
I don-don't know. Not now.
We... dumped her. Passed her off.
Passed her off to who?
Guy who hired us. Tattooed. Paid cash.
Name.
Never gave one. We met him at Empire State. That's where we took the woman.
The university? Are you lying to me?
Kiden--
--Tatiana is awake.

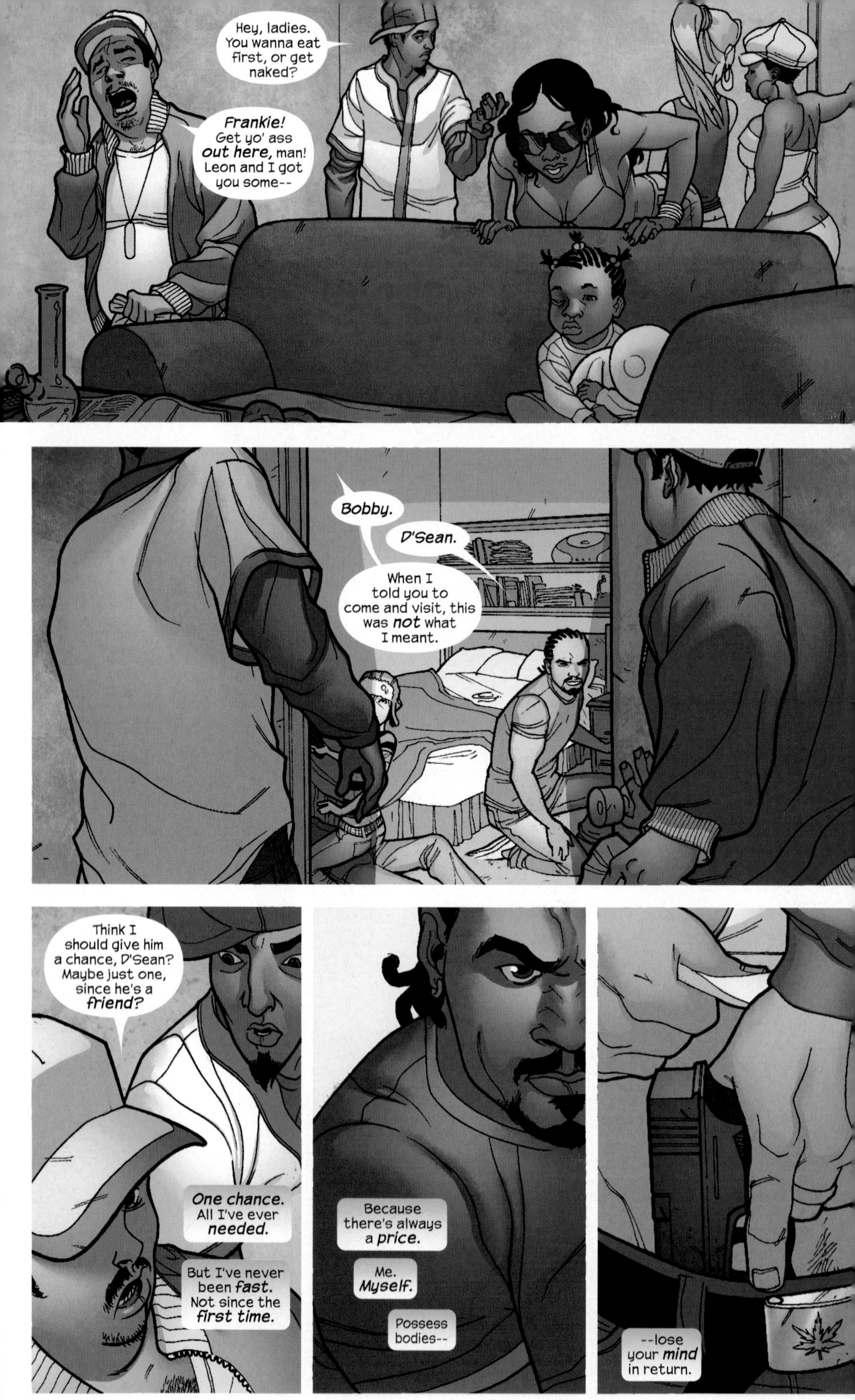

Hey, ladies. You wanna eat first, or get naked?
Frankie! Get yo' ass out here, man! Leon and I got you some--
Bobby.
D'Sean.
When I told you to come and visit, this was not what I meant.
Think I should give him a chance, D'Sean? Maybe just one, since he's a friend?
One chance. All I've ever needed.
But I've never been fast. Not since the first time.
Because there's always a price.
Me. Myself.
Possess bodies--
--lose your mind in return.

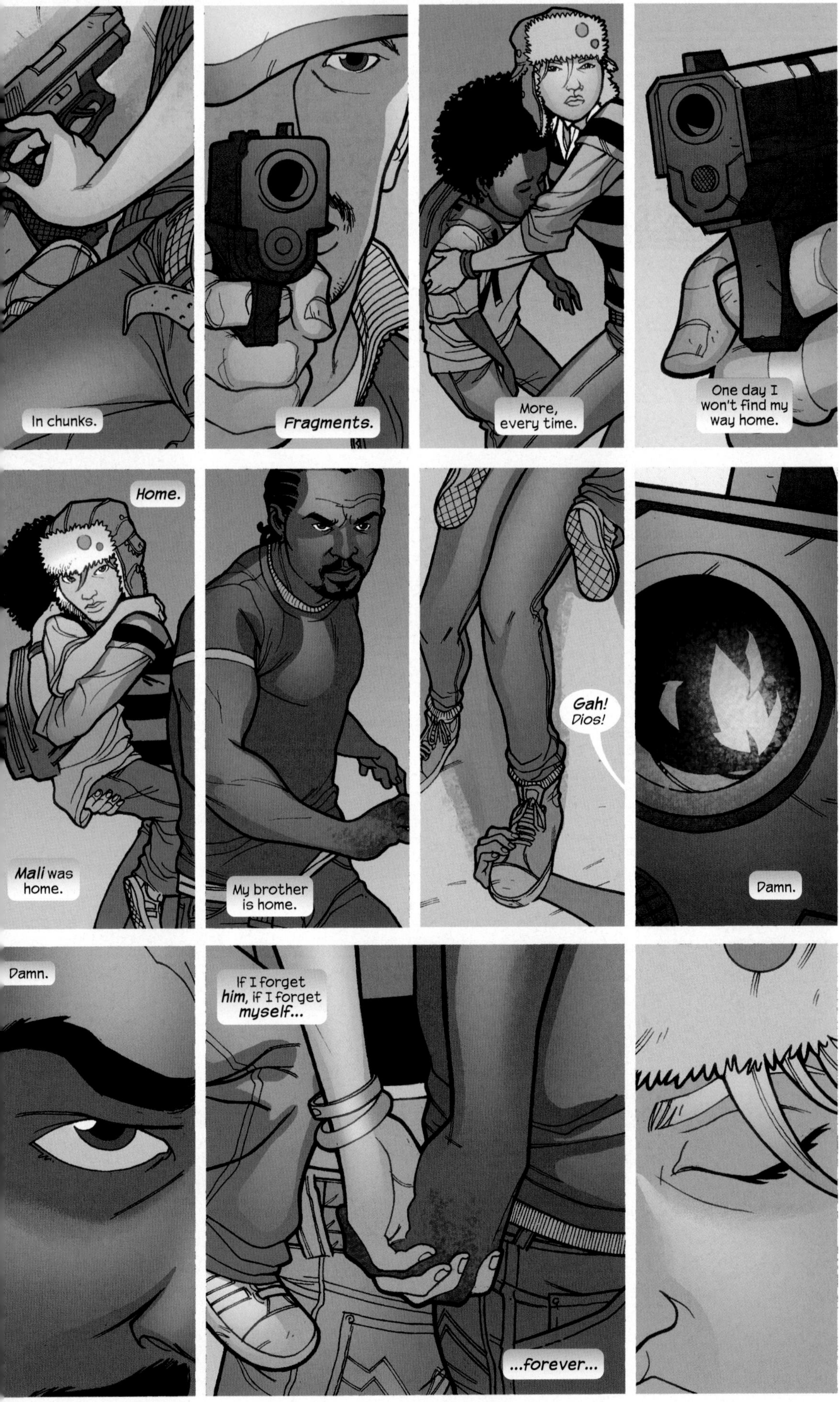

In chunks.
Fragments.
More, every time.
One day I won't find my way home.
Home.
Mali was home.
My brother is home.
Gah! *Dios!*
Damn.
Damn.
If I forget *him*, if I forget *myself*...
...forever...

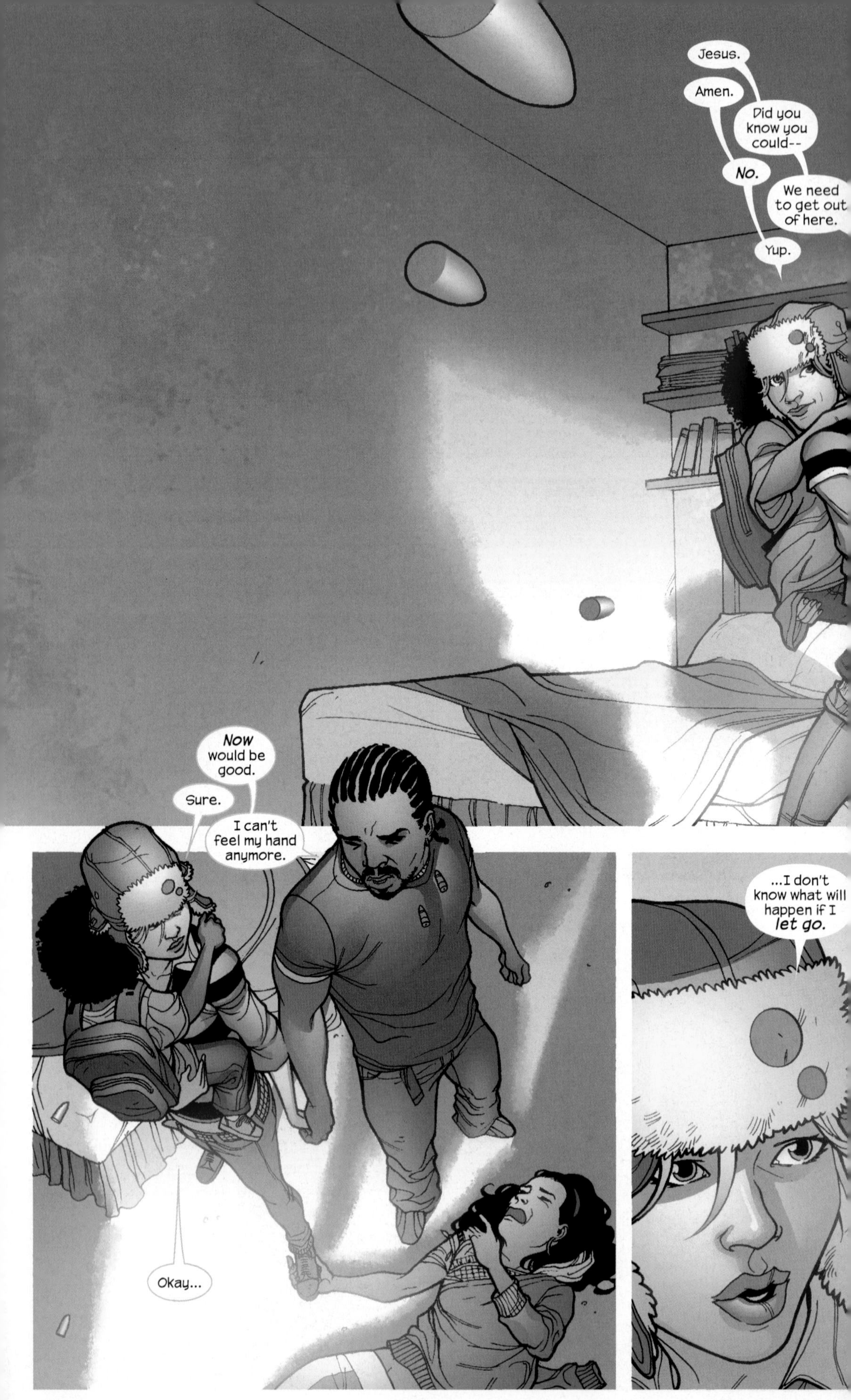
Jesus.
Amen.
Did you know you could--
No.
We need to get out of here.
Yup.
Now would be good.
Sure.
I can't feel my hand anymore.
Okay...
...I don't know what will happen if I let go.

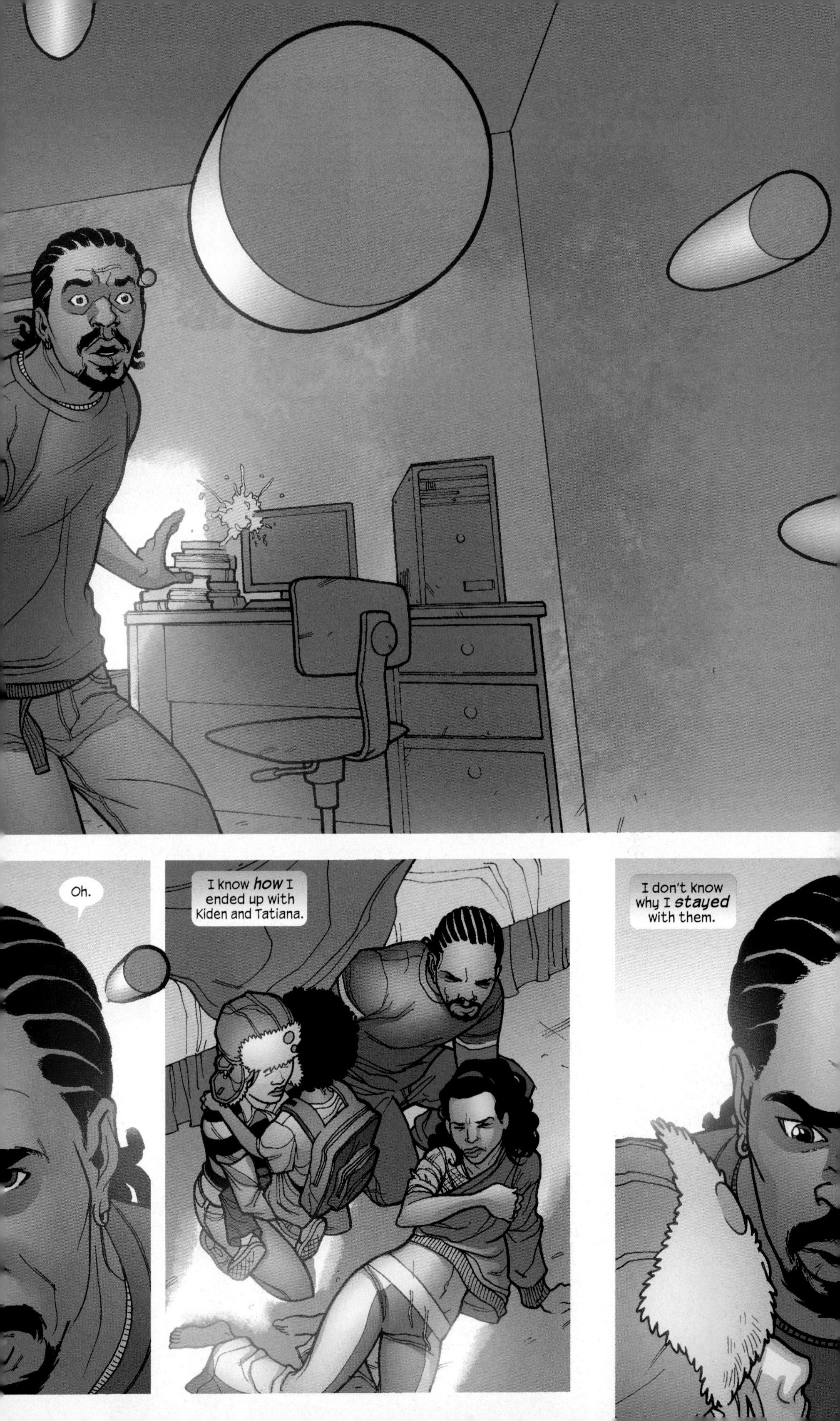
Oh.
I know how I ended up with Kiden and Tatiana.
I don't know why I stayed with them.

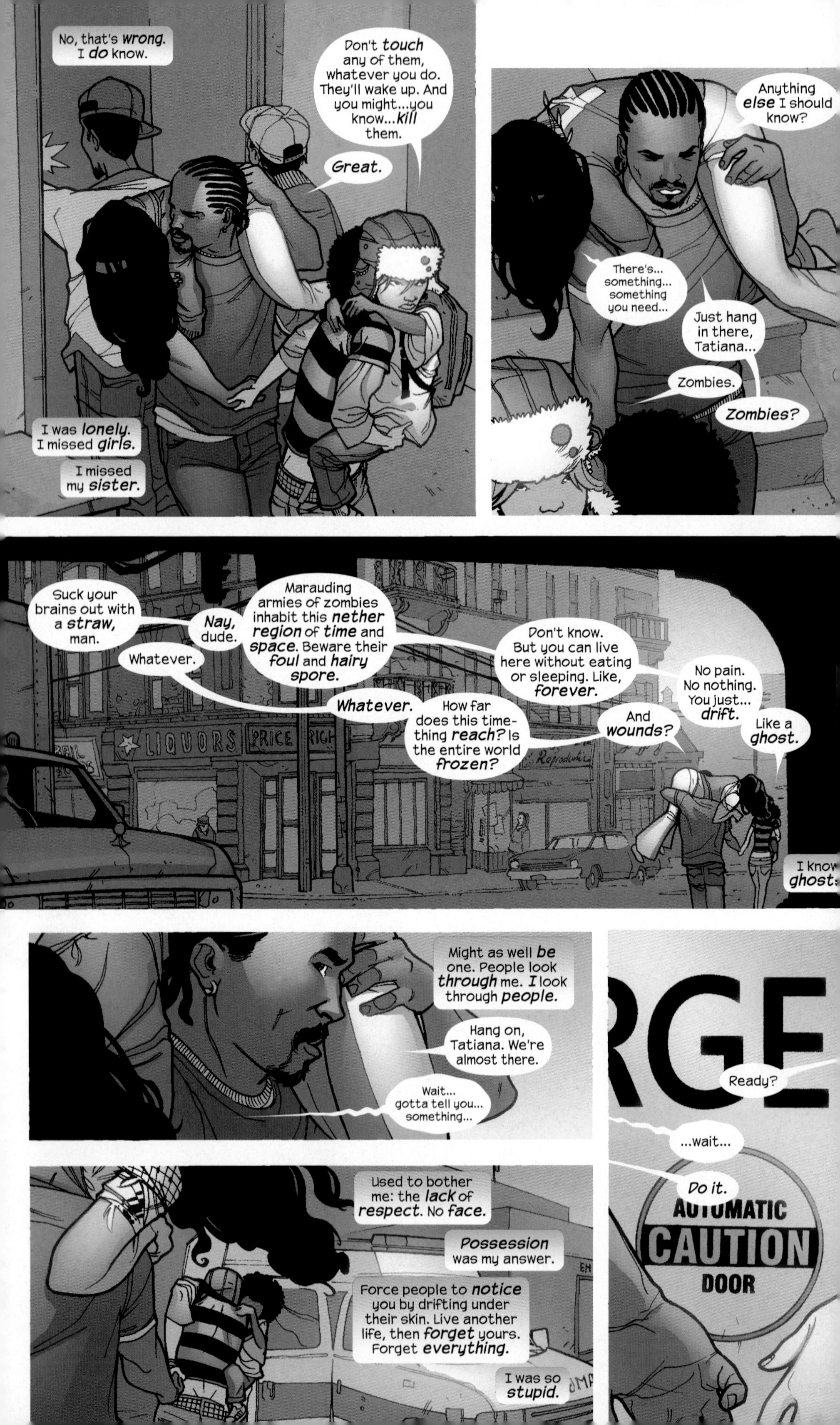
No, that's *wrong*. I *do* know.
Don't *touch* any of them, whatever you do. They'll wake up. And you might...you know...*kill* them.
Great.
I was *lonely*. I missed *girls*.
I missed my *sister*.
Anything *else* I should know?
There's... something... something you need...
Just hang in there, Tatiana...
Zombies.
Zombies?
Suck your brains out with a *straw*, man.
Nay, dude.
Marauding armies of zombies inhabit this *nether region* of *time* and *space*. Beware their *foul* and *hairy spore*.
Whatever.
Whatever.
How far does this time-thing *reach*? Is the entire world *frozen*?
Don't know. But you can live here without eating or sleeping. Like, *forever*.
And *wounds?*
No pain. No nothing. You just... *drift*.
Like a *ghost*.
LIQUORS
PRICE RIGH
Might as well *be* one. People look *through* me. *I* look through *people*.
Hang on, Tatiana. We're almost there.
Wait... gotta tell you... something...
Used to bother me: the *lack* of *respect*. No *face*.
Possession was my answer.
Force people to *notice* you by drifting under their skin. Live another life, then *forget* yours. Forget *everything*.
I was so *stupid*.
RGE
Ready?
...wait...
Do it.
AUTOMATIC
CAUTION
DOOR

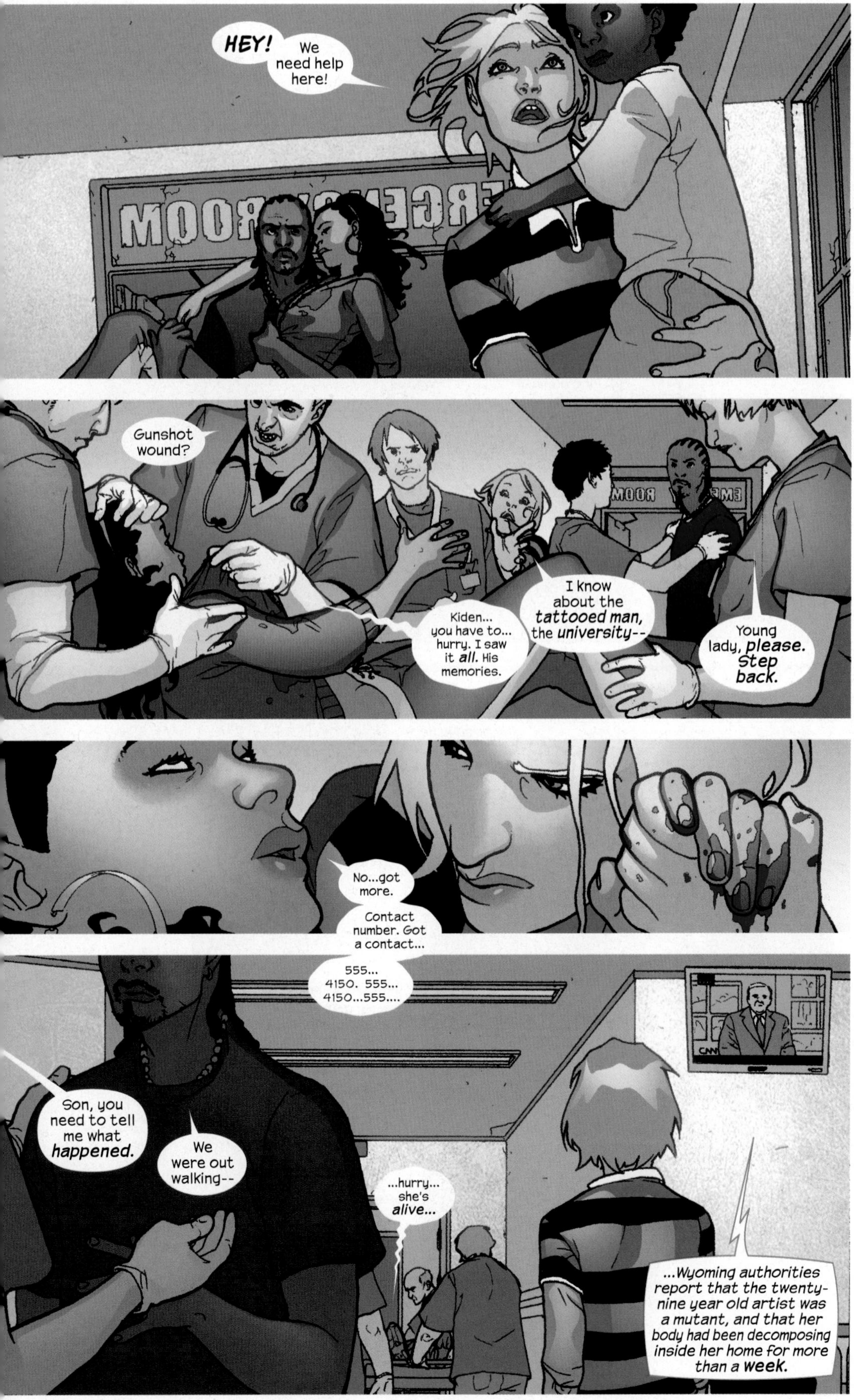
HEY! We need help here!
MOOR ROOM
Gunshot wound?
Kiden... you have to... hurry. I saw it all. His memories.
I know about the tattooed man, the university--
Young lady, please. Step back.
No...got more.
Contact number. Got a contact...
555... 4150. 555... 4150...555....
Son, you need to tell me what happened.
We were out walking--
...hurry... she's alive...
...Wyoming authorities report that the twenty-nine year old artist was a mutant, and that her body had been decomposing inside her home for more than a week.

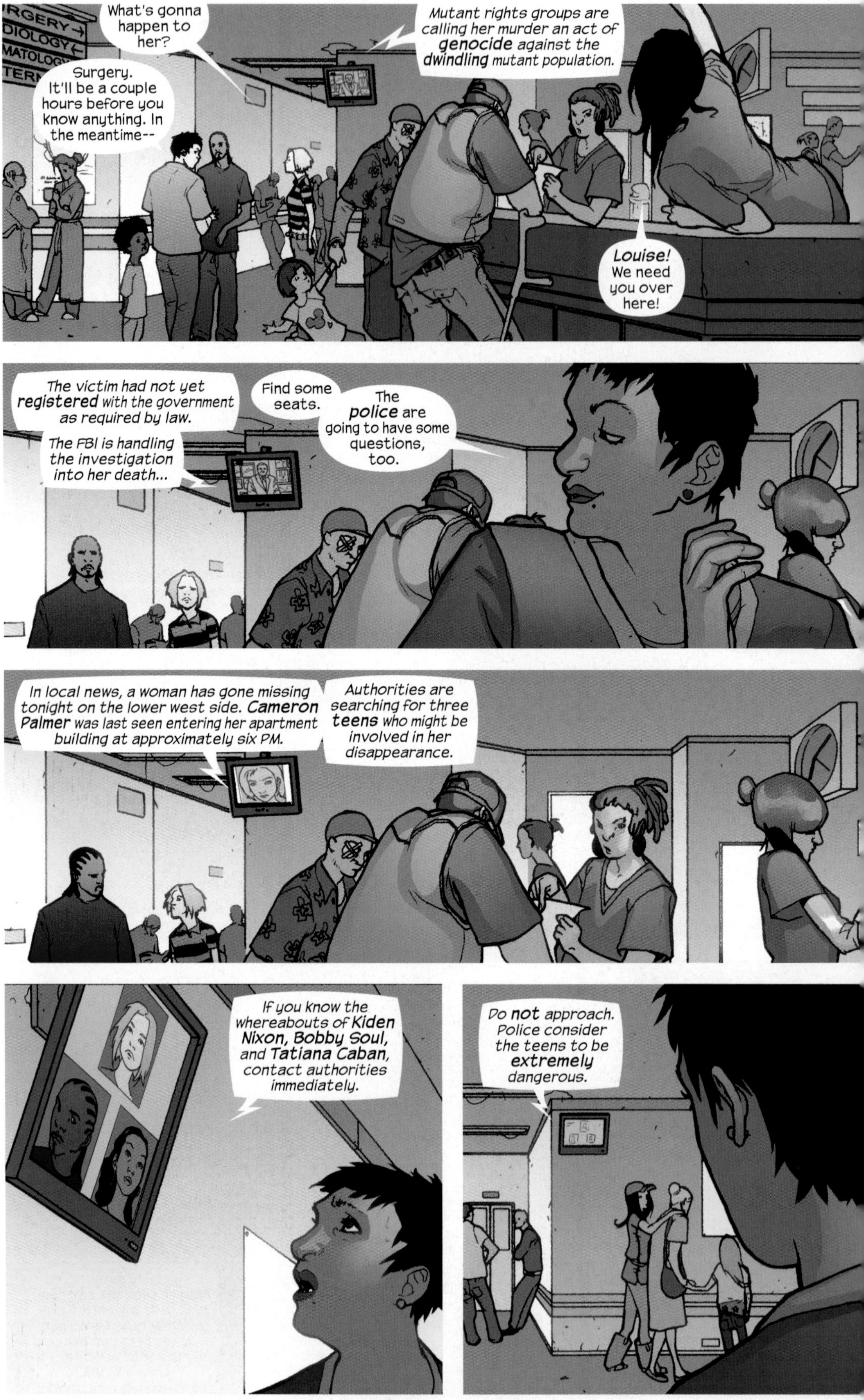
RGERY→
DIOLOGY←
MATOLOG
TERN
What's gonna happen to her?
Surgery. It'll be a couple hours before you know anything. In the meantime--
Mutant rights groups are calling her murder an act of genocide against the dwindling mutant population.
Louise! We need you over here!
The victim had not yet registered with the government as required by law.
The FBI is handling the investigation into her death...
Find some seats.
The police are going to have some questions, too.
In local news, a woman has gone missing tonight on the lower west side. Cameron Palmer was last seen entering her apartment building at approximately six PM.
Authorities are searching for three teens who might be involved in her disappearance.
If you know the whereabouts of Kiden Nixon, Bobby Soul, and Tatiana Caban, contact authorities immediately.
Do not approach. Police consider the teens to be extremely dangerous.

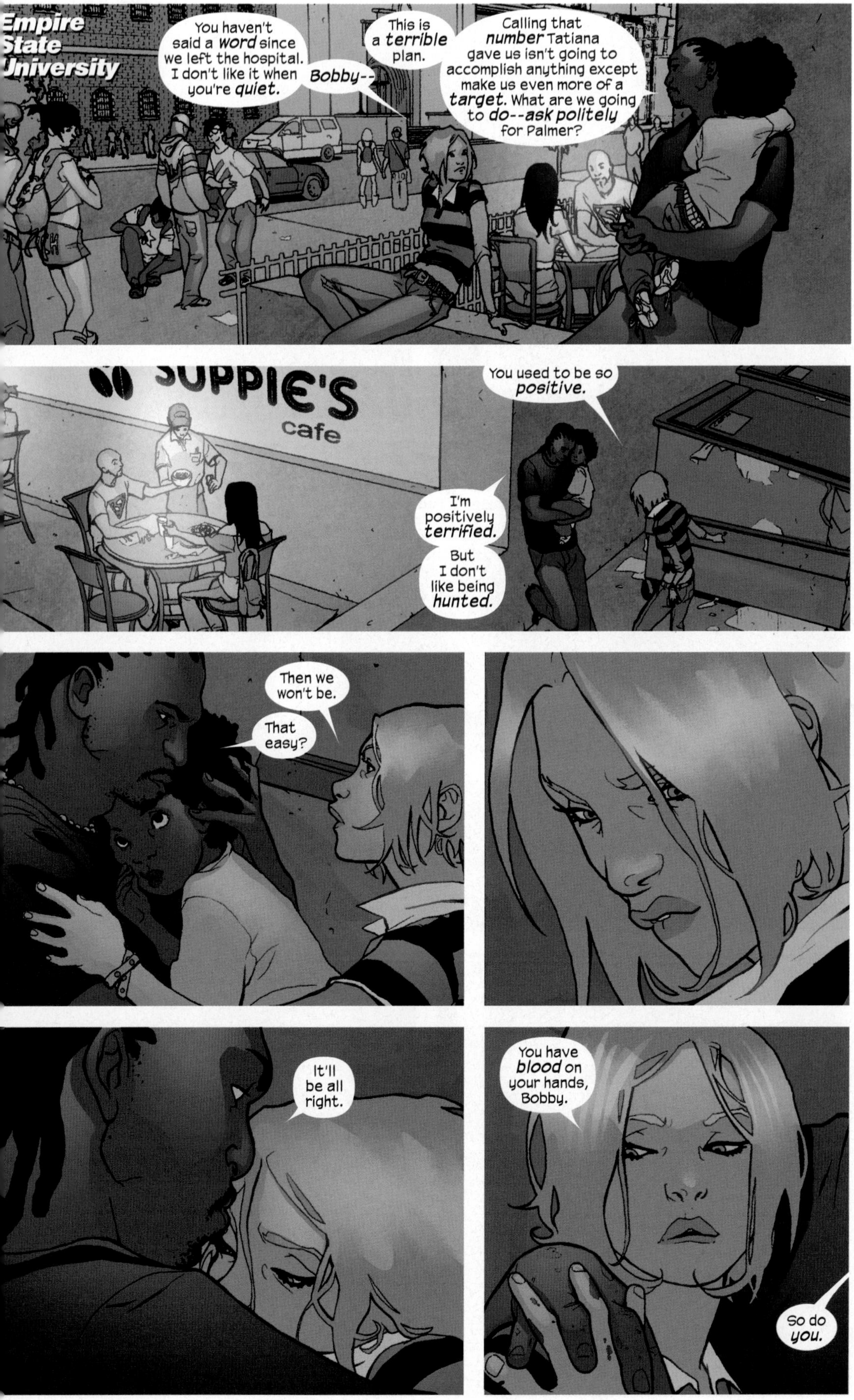
Empire State University
You haven't said a word since we left the hospital. I don't like it when you're quiet.
Bobby--
This is a terrible plan.
Calling that number Tatiana gave us isn't going to accomplish anything except make us even more of a target. What are we going to do--ask politely for Palmer?
SUPPIE'S cafe
You used to be so positive.
I'm positively terrified.
But I don't like being hunted.
Then we won't be.
That easy?
It'll be all right.
You have blood on your hands, Bobby.
So do you.

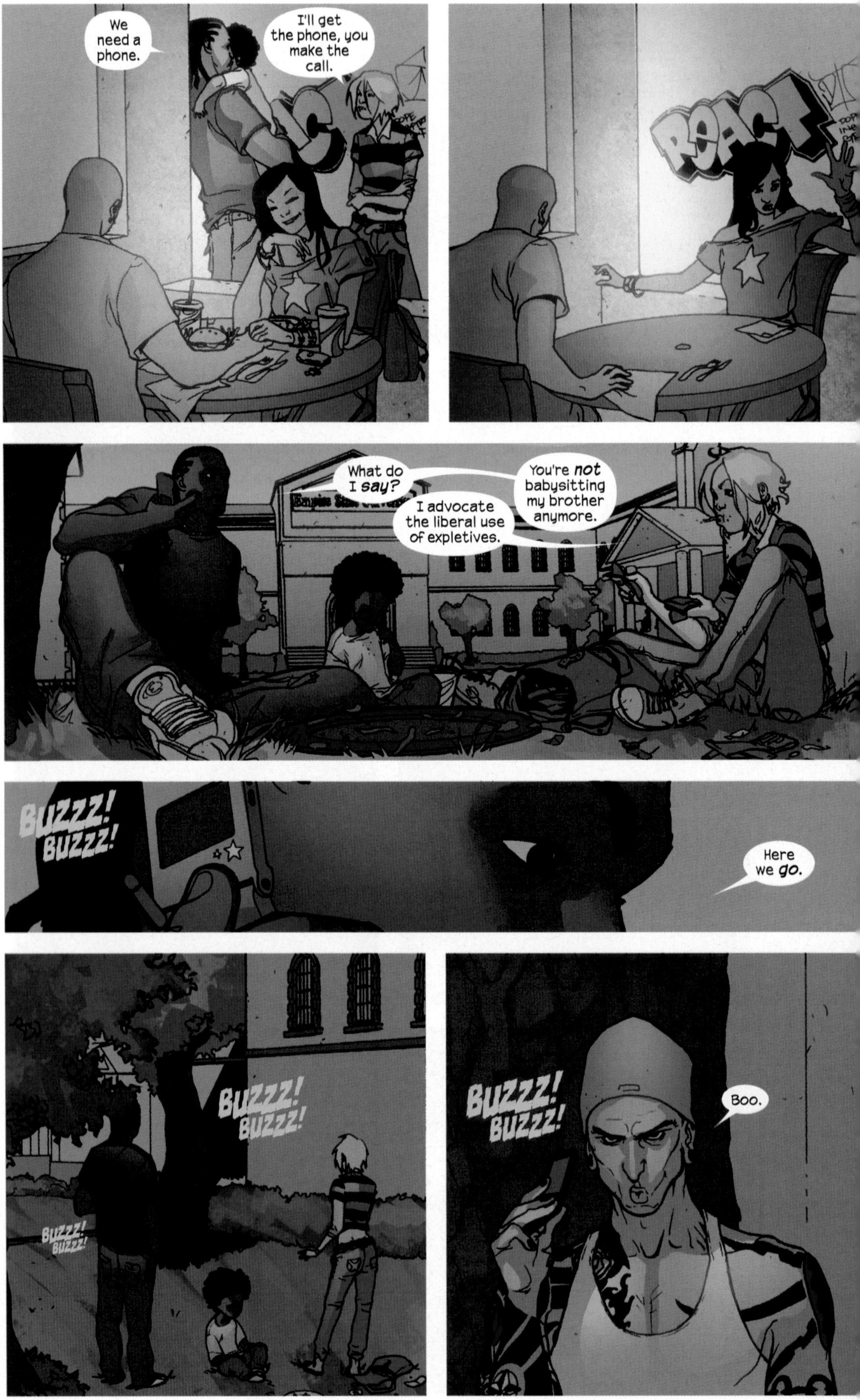
We need a phone.
I'll get the phone, you make the call.
ROACH
What do I *say*?
You're **not** babysitting my brother anymore.
I advocate the liberal use of expletives.
BUZZZ! BUZZZ!
Here we *go*.
BUZZZ! BUZZZ!
BUZZZ! BUZZZ!
BUZZZ! BUZZZ!
Boo.

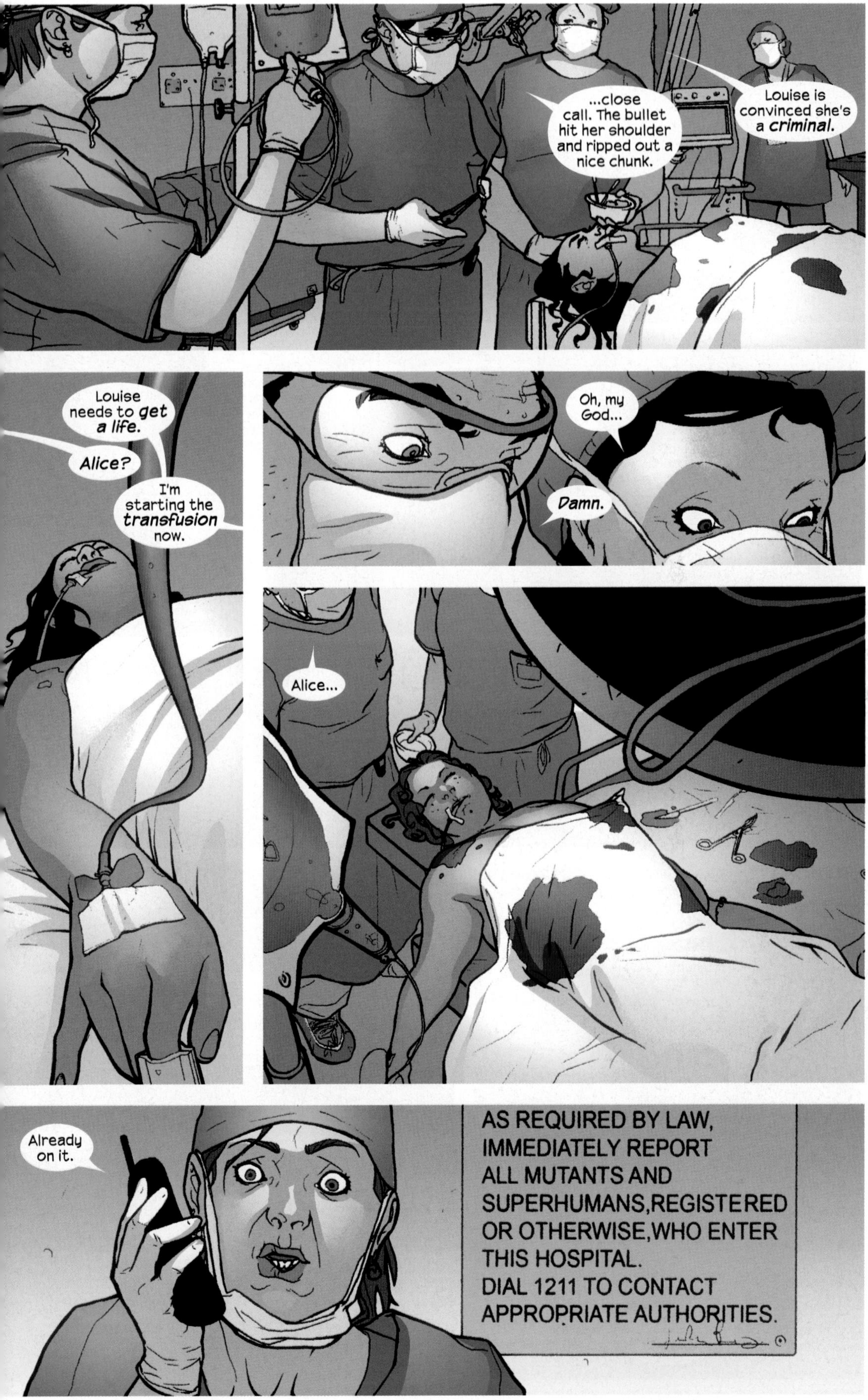
...close call. The bullet hit her shoulder and ripped out a nice chunk.
Louise is convinced she's a *criminal.*
Louise needs to *get a life.*
Alice?
I'm starting the *transfusion* now.
Oh, my God...
Damn.
Alice...
Already on it.
AS REQUIRED BY LAW, IMMEDIATELY REPORT ALL MUTANTS AND SUPERHUMANS, REGISTERED OR OTHERWISE, WHO ENTER THIS HOSPITAL.
DIAL 1211 TO CONTACT APPROPRIATE AUTHORITIES.

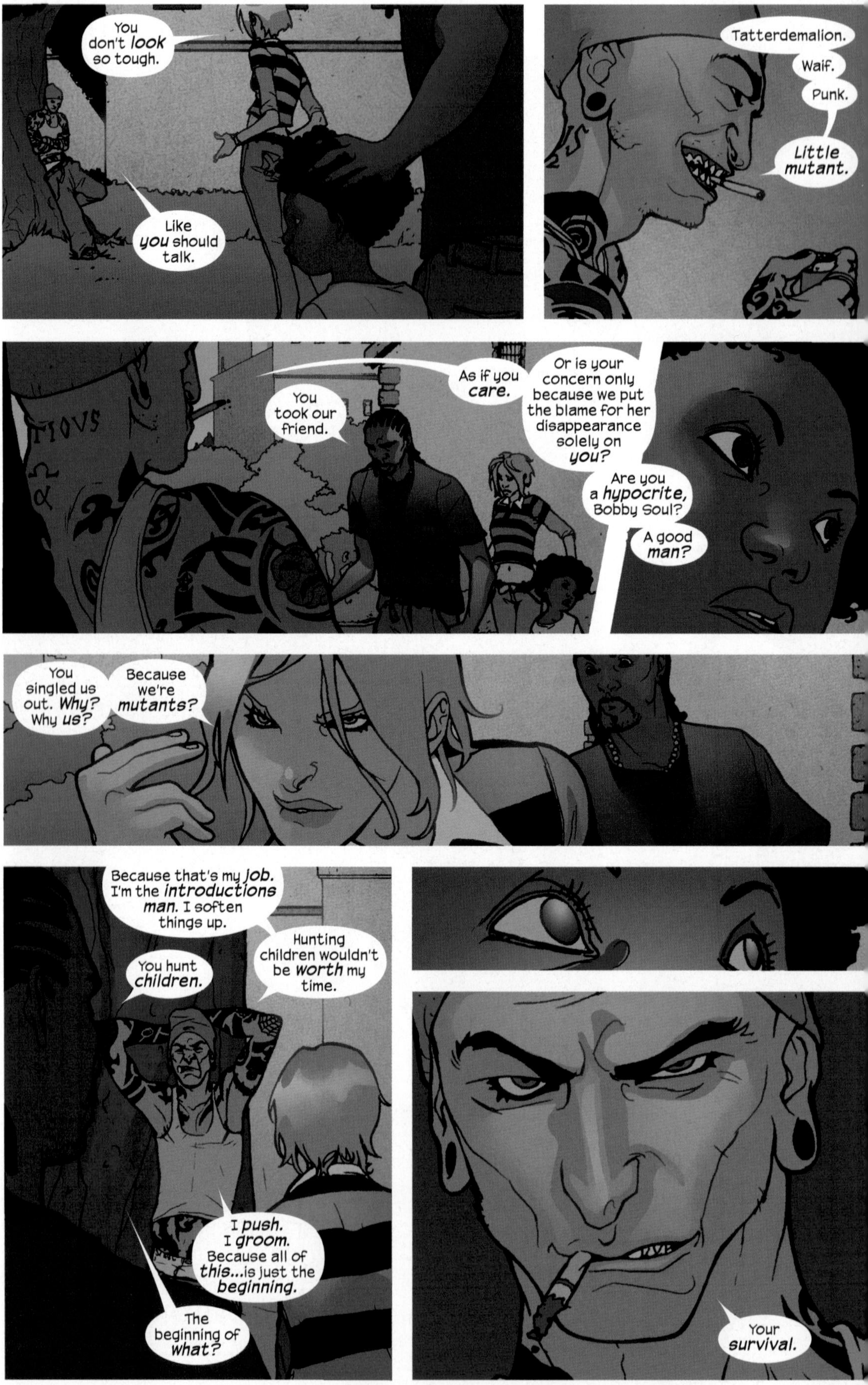
You don't *look* so tough.
Like *you* should talk.
Tatterdemalion.
Waif.
Punk.
Little mutant.
TIOVS
You took our friend.
As if you *care.*
Or is your concern only because we put the blame for her disappearance solely on *you?*
Are you a *hypocrite,* Bobby Soul?
A good *man?*
You singled us out. *Why?* Why *us?*
Because we're *mutants?*
Because that's my *job.* I'm the *introductions man.* I soften things up.
You hunt *children.*
Hunting children wouldn't be *worth* my time.
I *push.* I *groom.* Because all of *this*...is just the *beginning.*
The beginning of *what?*
Your *survival.*

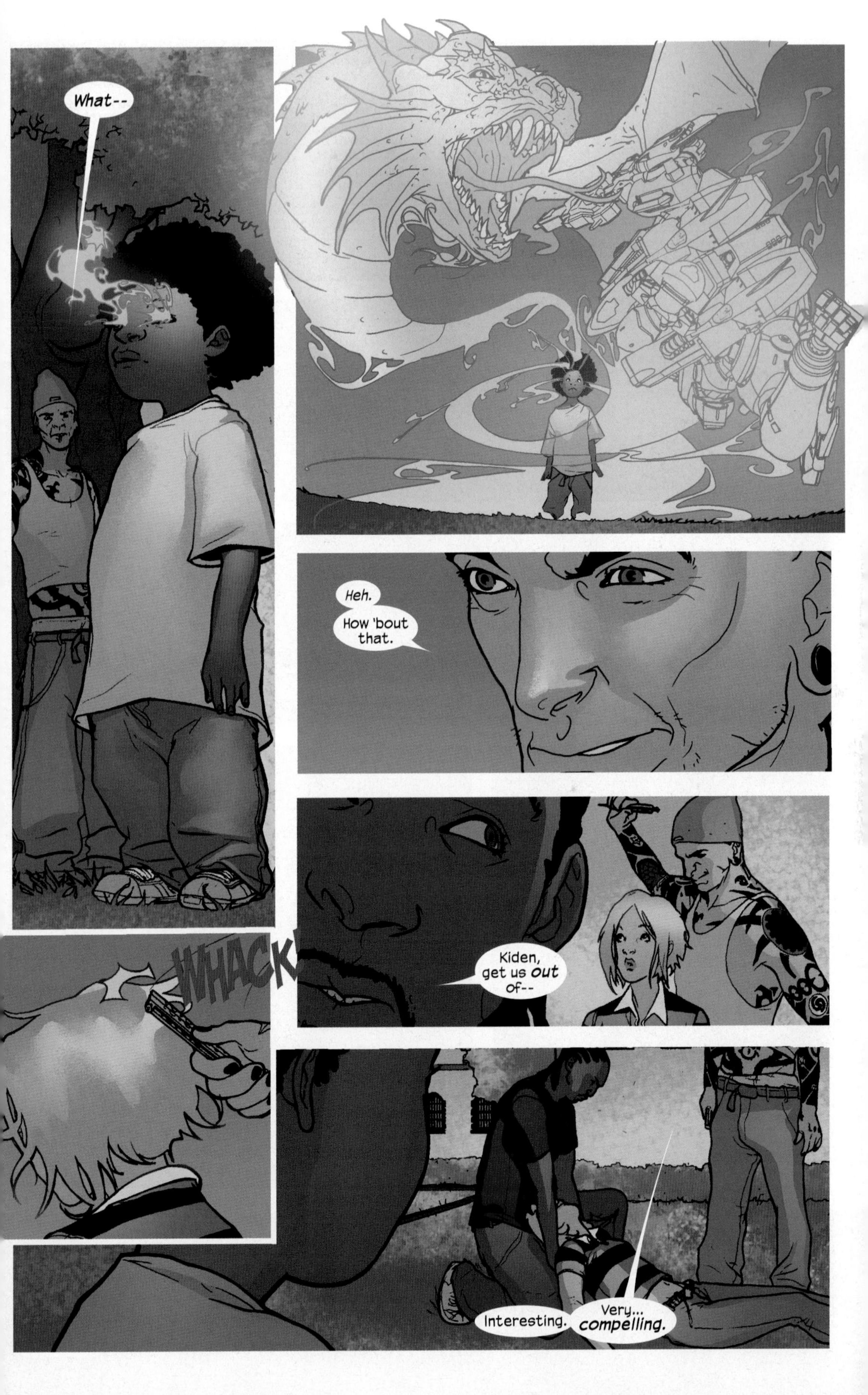
What--
Heh.
How 'bout that.
Kiden, get us *out* of--
WHACK!
Interesting.
Very... *compelling.*

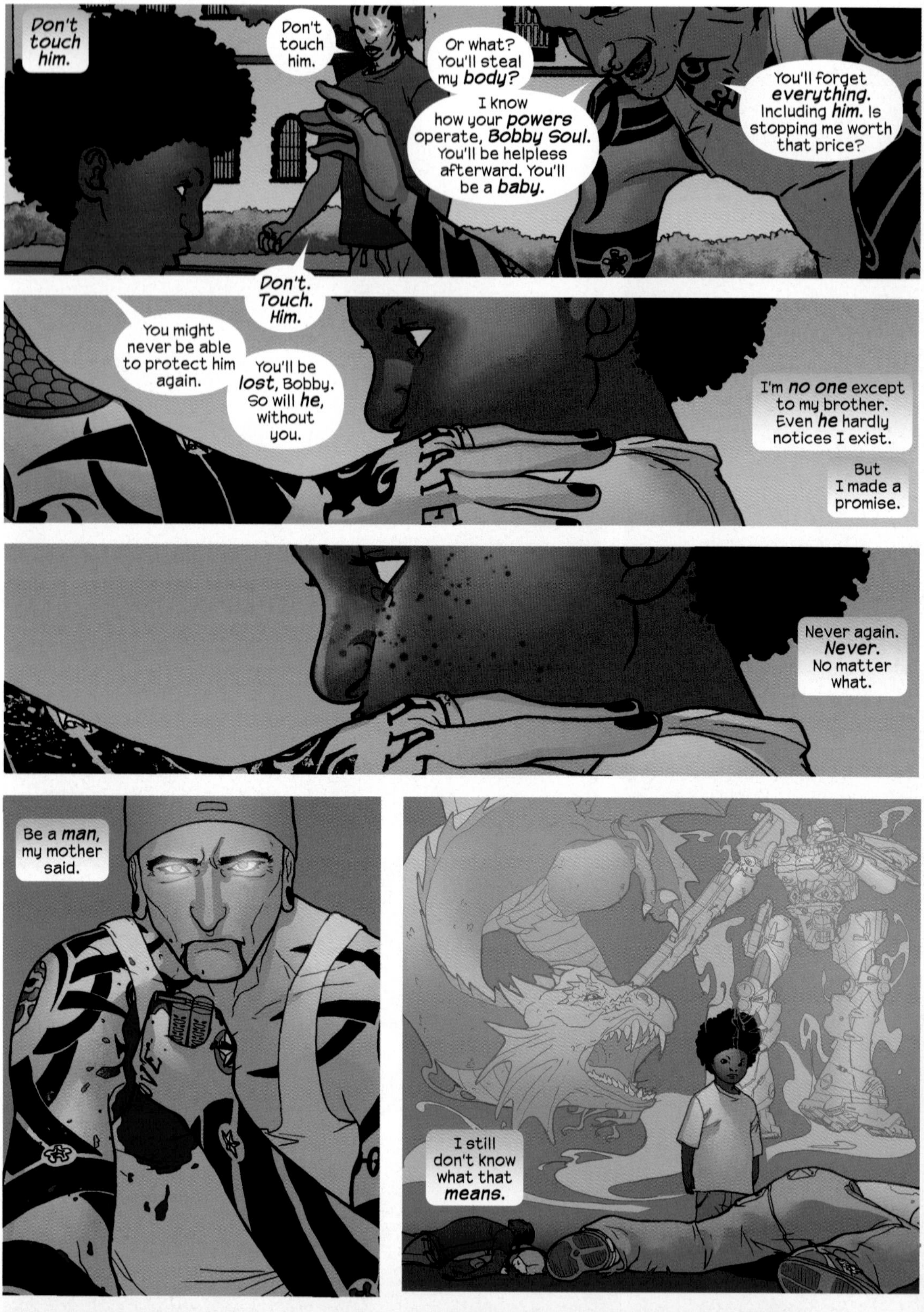
Don't touch him.
Don't touch him.
Or what? You'll steal my body?
I know how your powers operate, Bobby Soul. You'll be helpless afterward. You'll be a baby.
You'll forget everything. Including him. Is stopping me worth that price?
Don't. Touch. Him.
You might never be able to protect him again.
You'll be lost, Bobby. So will he, without you.
I'm no one except to my brother. Even he hardly notices I exist.
But I made a promise.
Never again. Never. No matter what.
Be a man, my mother said.
I still don't know what that means.

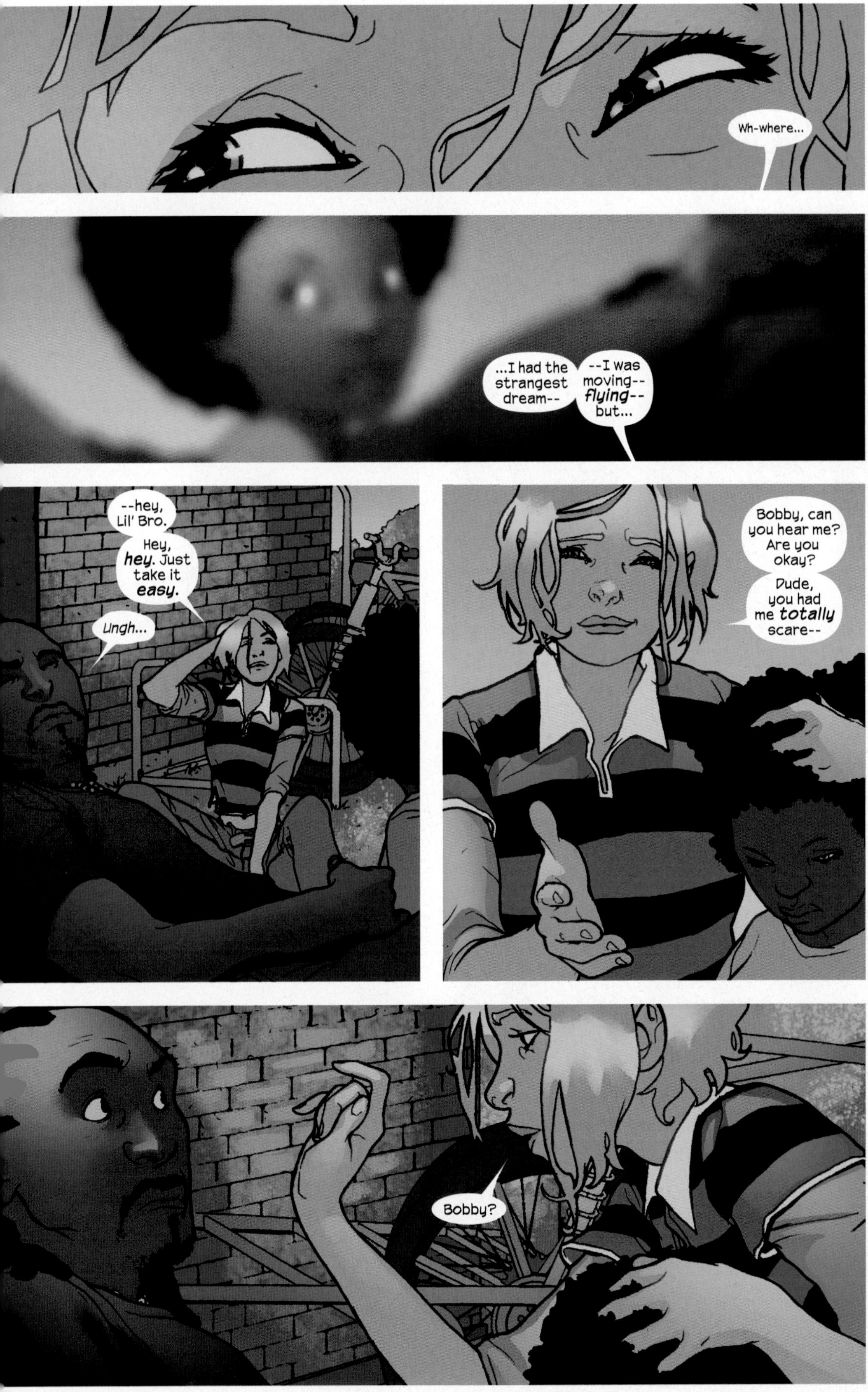
Wh-where...
...I had the strangest dream--
--I was moving--*flying*--but...
--hey, Lil' Bro.
Hey, *hey*. Just take it *easy*.
Ungh...
Bobby, can you hear me? Are you okay?
Dude, you had me *totally* scare--
Bobby?

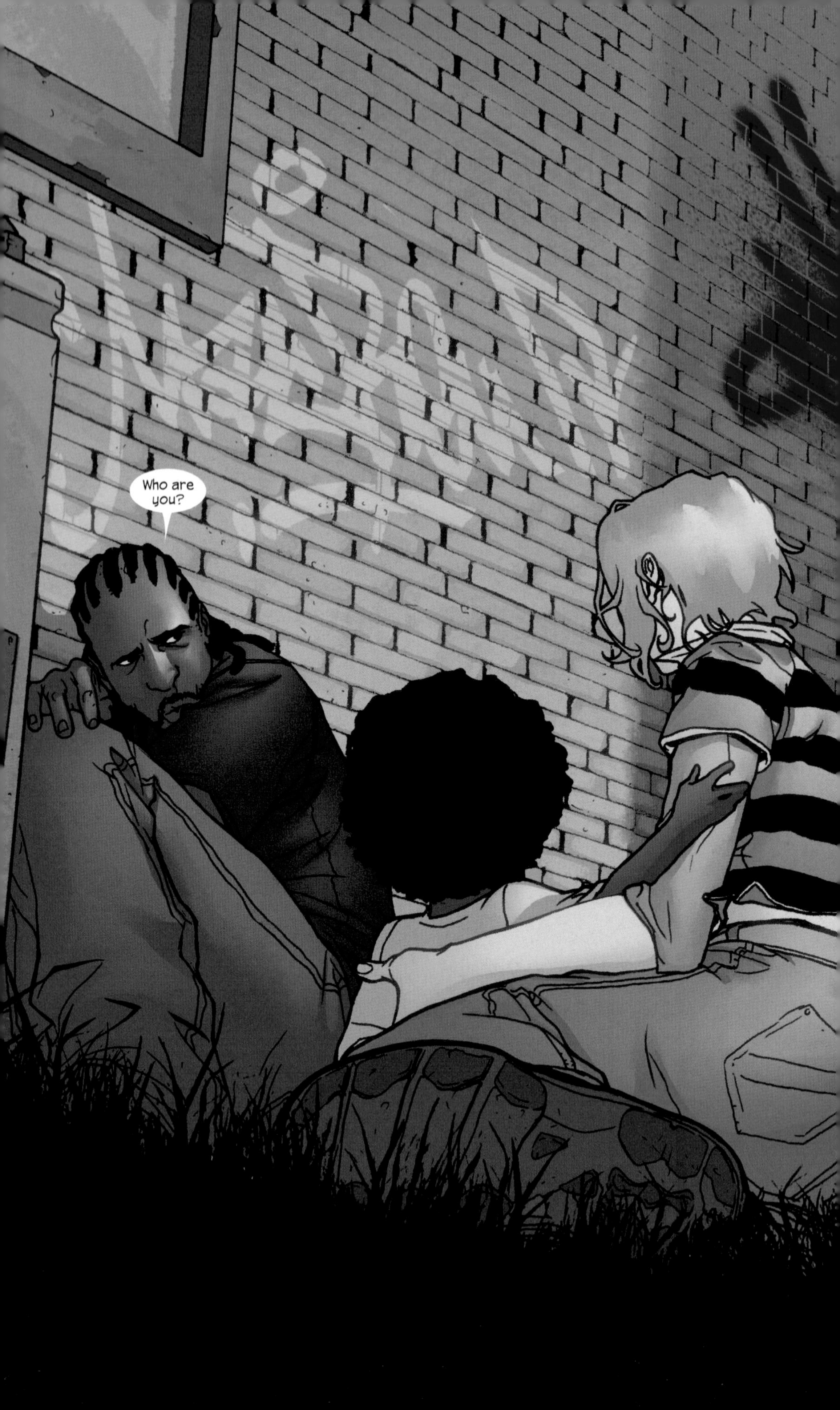
Who are you?

FOUR

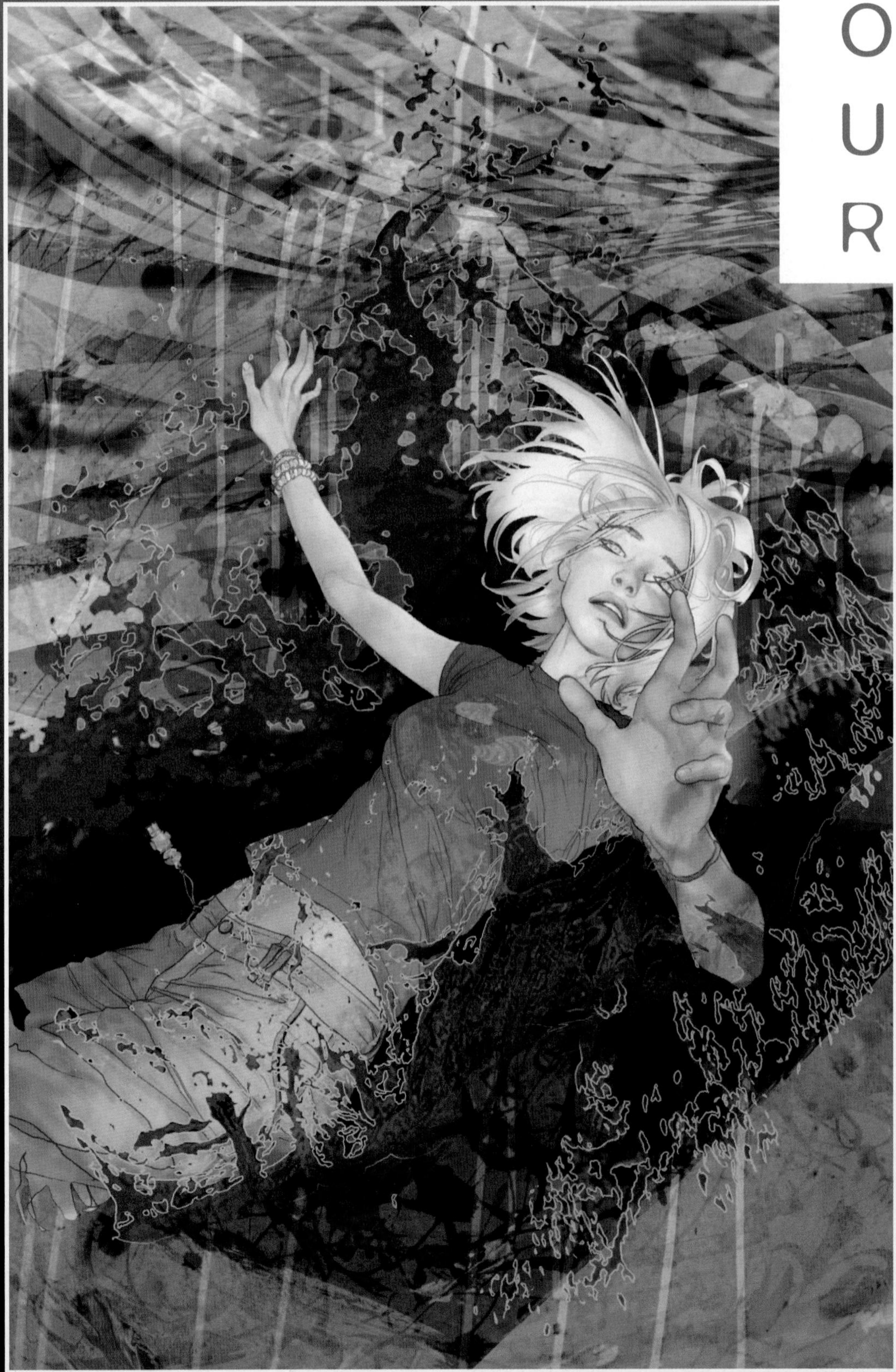

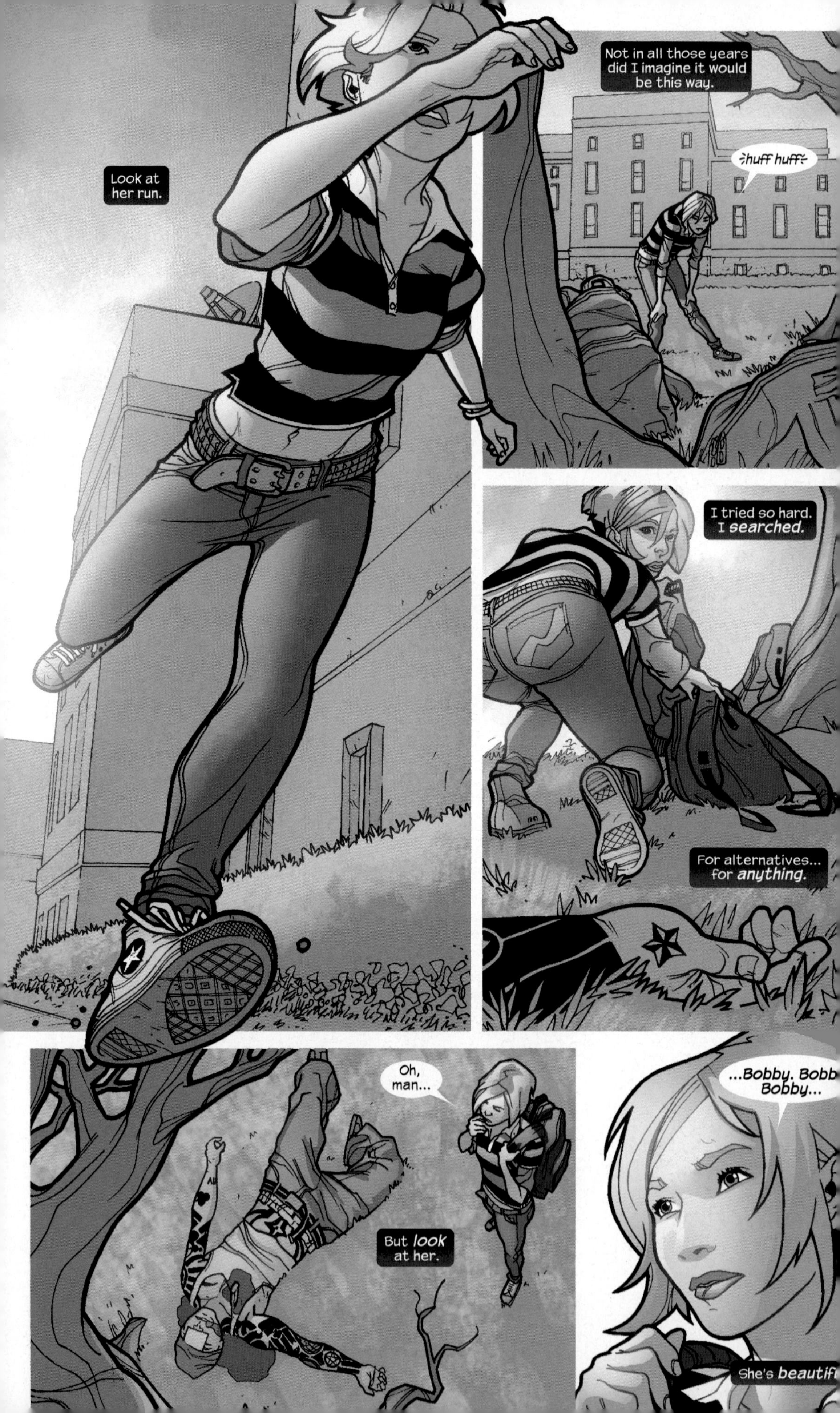
Look at her run.
Not in all those years did I imagine it would be this way.
huff huff
I tried so hard. I *searched.*
For alternatives... for *anything.*
Oh, man...
But *look* at her.
...Bobby. Bobb Bobby...
She's *beautif*

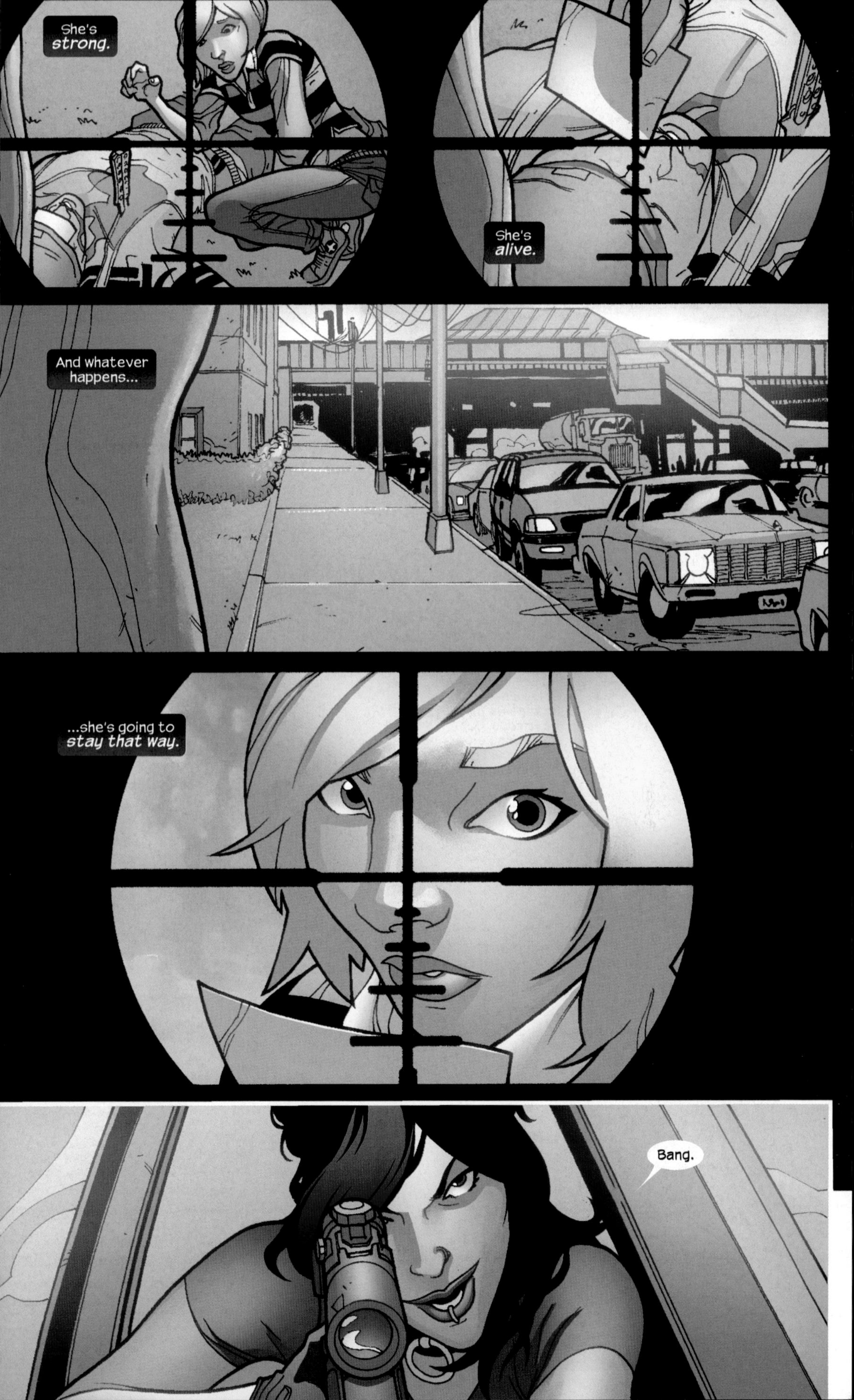
She's strong.
She's alive.
And whatever happens...
...she's going to stay that way.
Bang.

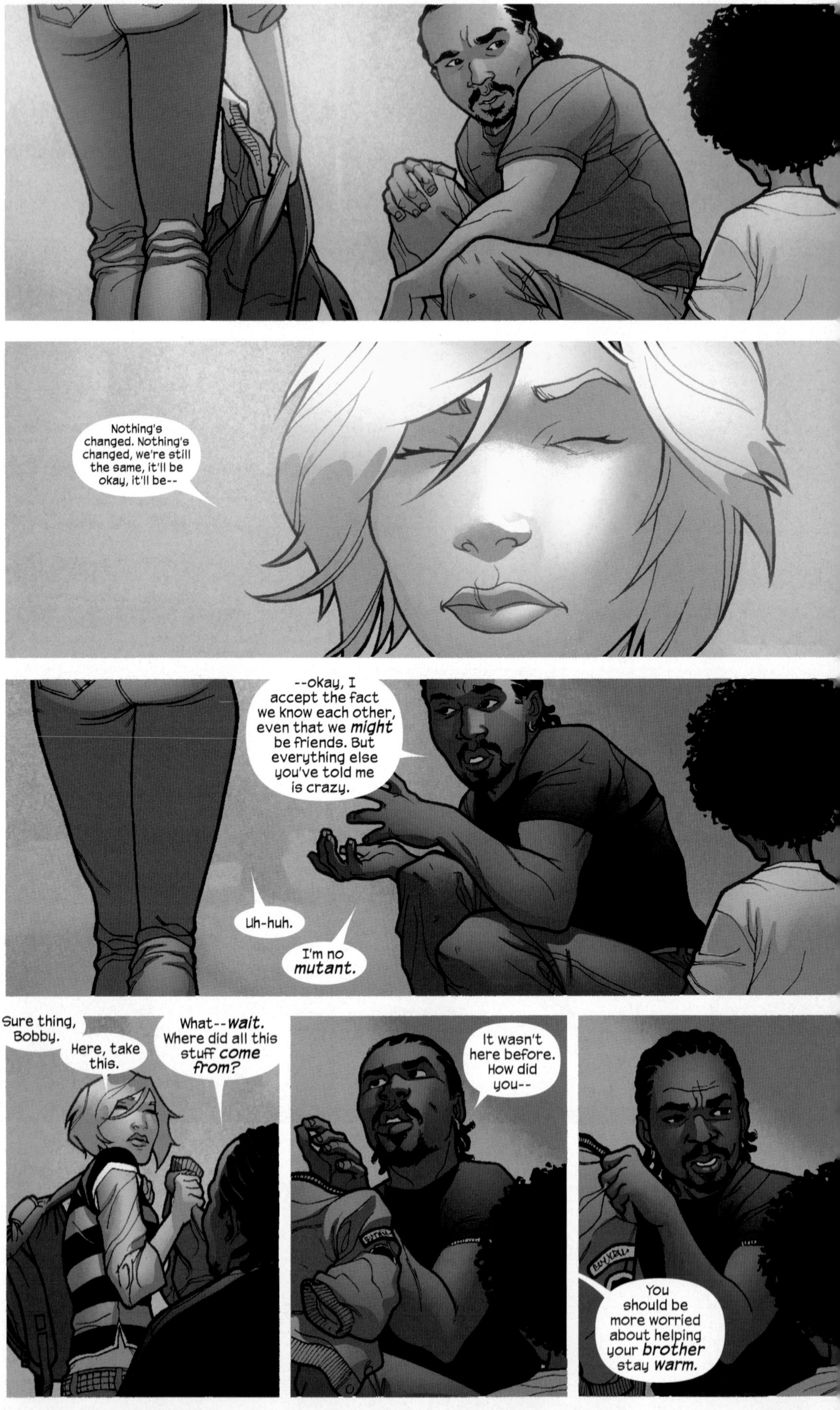

Nothing's changed. Nothing's changed, we're still the same, it'll be okay, it'll be--
--okay, I accept the fact we know each other, even that we *might* be friends. But everything else you've told me is crazy.
Uh-huh.
I'm no *mutant.*
Sure thing, Bobby.
Here, take this.
What--*wait.* Where did all this stuff *come from?*
It wasn't here before. How did you--
You should be more worried about helping your *brother* stay *warm.*

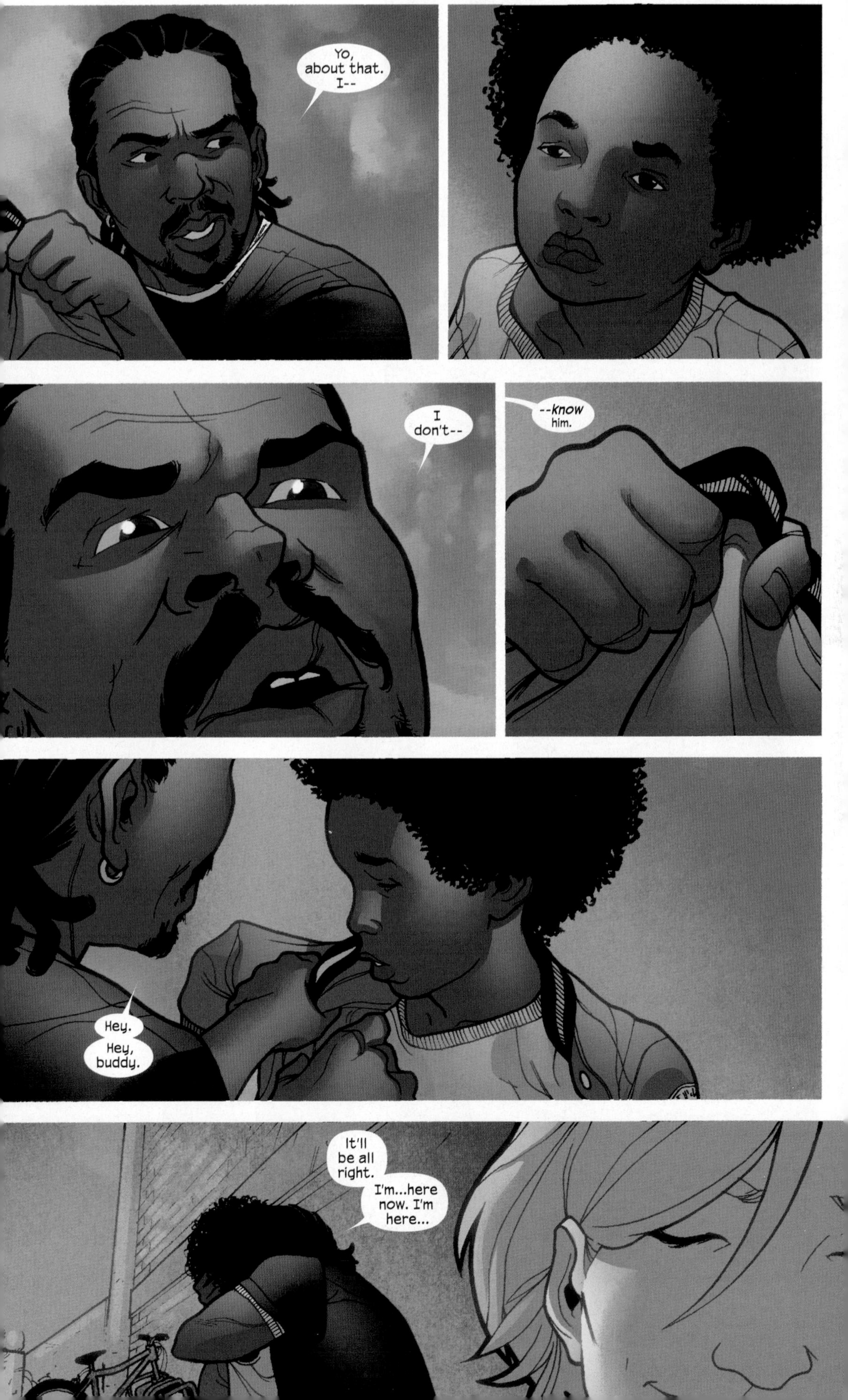
Yo, about that. I--
I don't--
--know him.
Hey.
Hey, buddy.
It'll be all right.
I'm...here now. I'm here...

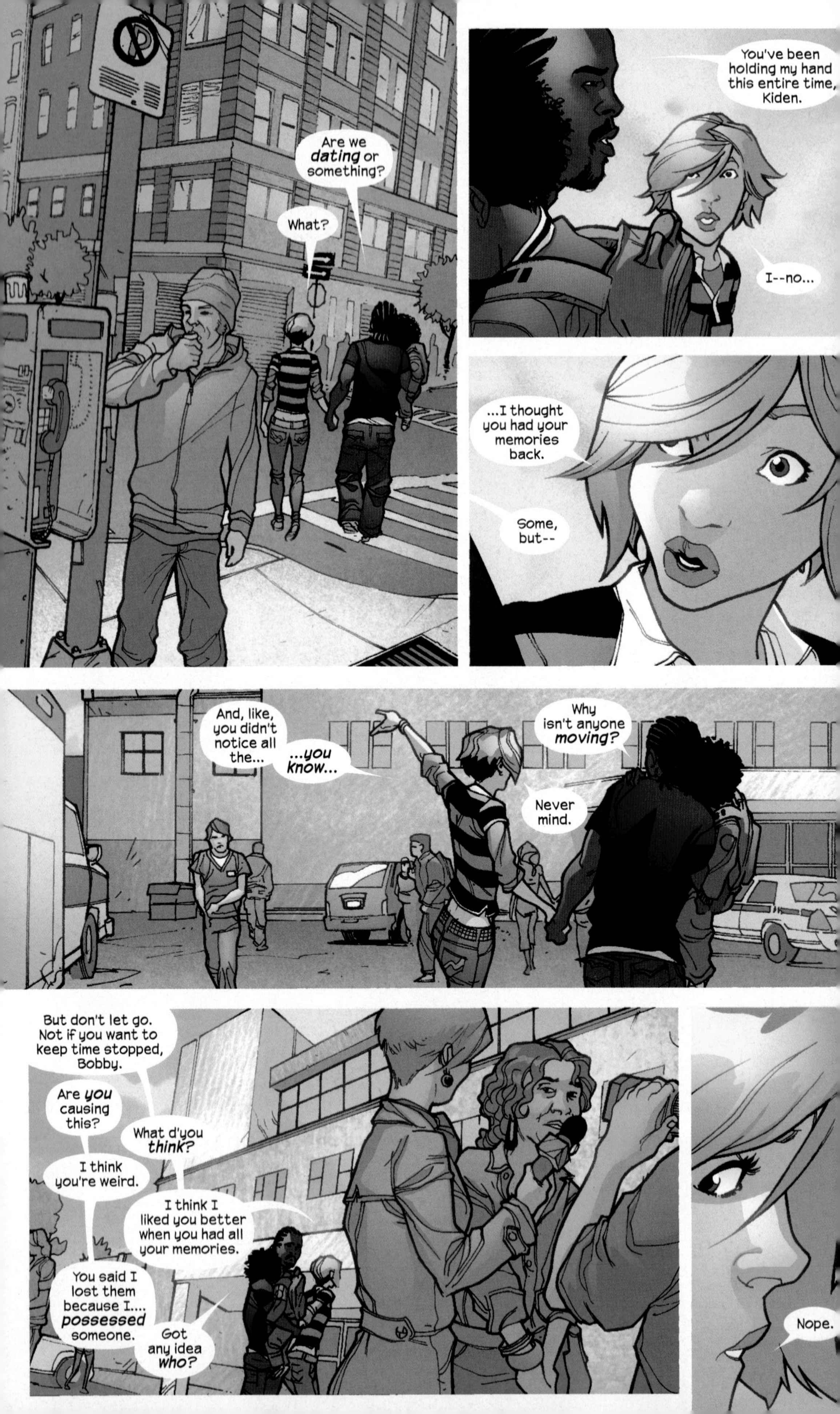
Are we *dating* or something?
What?
You've been holding my hand this entire time, Kiden.
I--no...
...I thought you had your memories back.
Some, but--
And, like, you didn't notice all the...
...you know...
Why isn't anyone *moving?*
Never mind.
But don't let go. Not if you want to keep time stopped, Bobby.
Are *you* causing this?
What d'you *think?*
I think you're weird.
I think I liked you better when you had all your memories.
You said I lost them because I.... *possessed* someone.
Got any idea *who?*
Nope.

I don't remember much, but this--

Something's happened.

I know that *symbol*...

...*military* dude. The kind that handles *mutants*.

You had a *sister*...

Do you think your friend is still here?

Tatiana.

Our friend.

Jeez, these guys are like *breadcrumbs*.

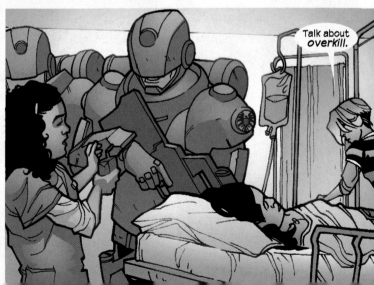

Talk about *overkill*.

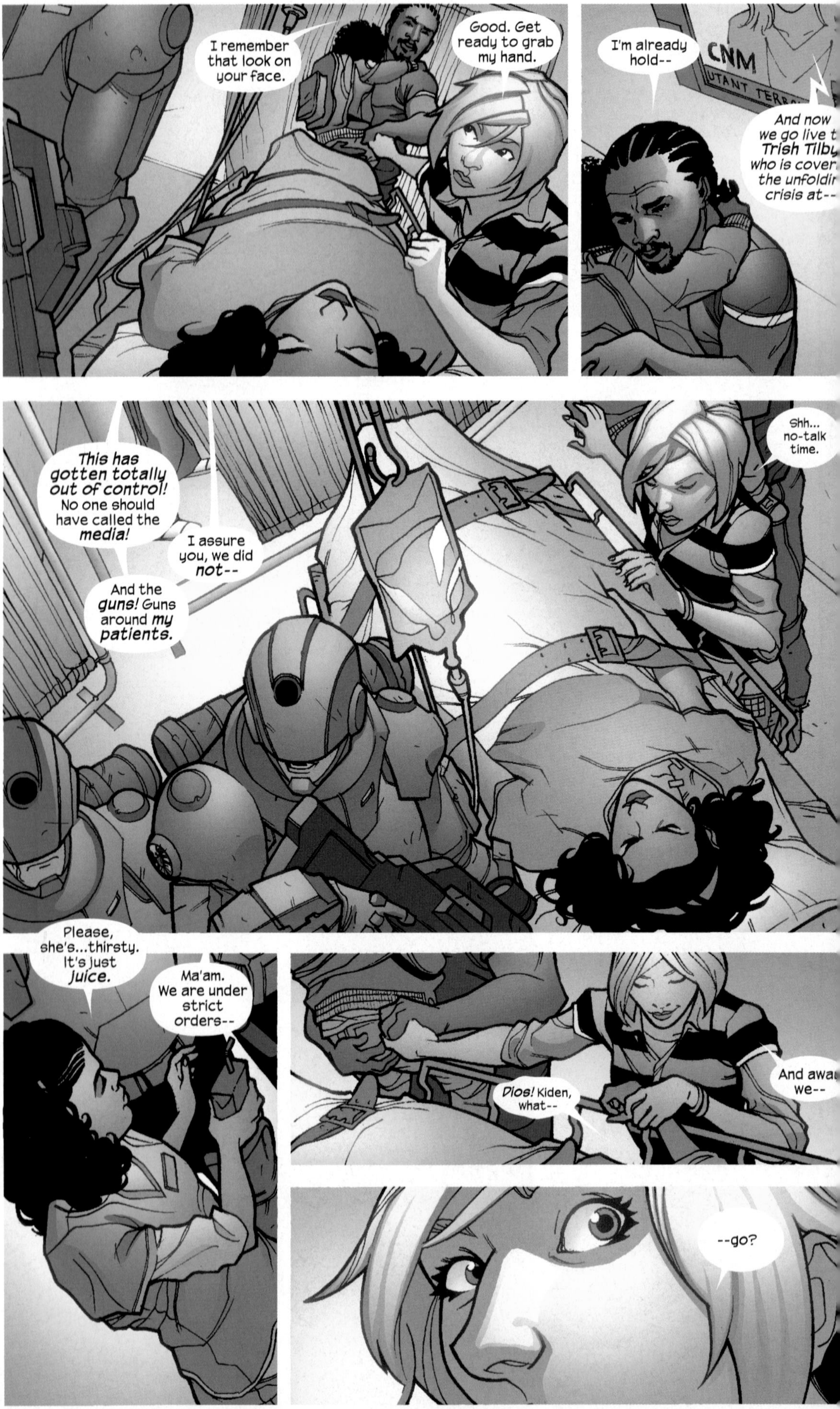

I remember that look on your face.
Good. Get ready to grab my hand.
I'm already hold--
CNM
And now we go live t
Trish Tilby
who is cover
the unfoldir
crisis at--
This has gotten totally out of control! No one should have called the media!
I assure you, we did not--
And the guns! Guns around my patients.
Shh... no-talk time.
Please, she's...thirsty. It's just juice.
Ma'am. We are under strict orders--
Dios! Kiden, what--
And awa
we--
--go?

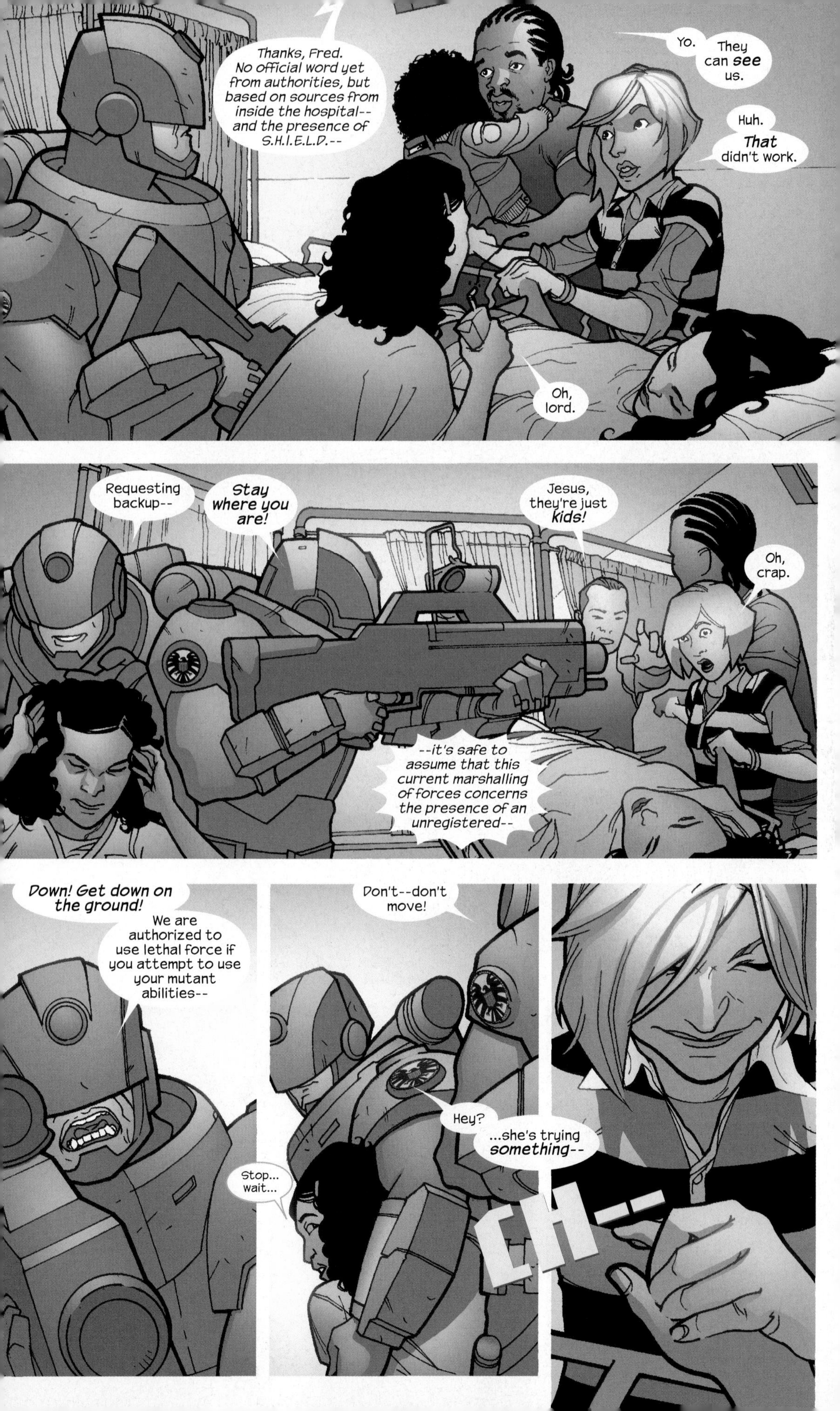
Thanks, Fred. No official word yet from authorities, but based on sources from inside the hospital-- and the presence of S.H.I.E.L.D.--
Yo.
They can see us.
Huh.
That didn't work.
Oh, lord.
Requesting backup--
Stay where you are!
Jesus, they're just kids!
Oh, crap.
--it's safe to assume that this current marshalling of forces concerns the presence of an unregistered--
Down! Get down on the ground!
We are authorized to use lethal force if you attempt to use your mutant abilities--
Don't--don't move!
Hey?
...she's trying something--
Stop... wait...
CH--

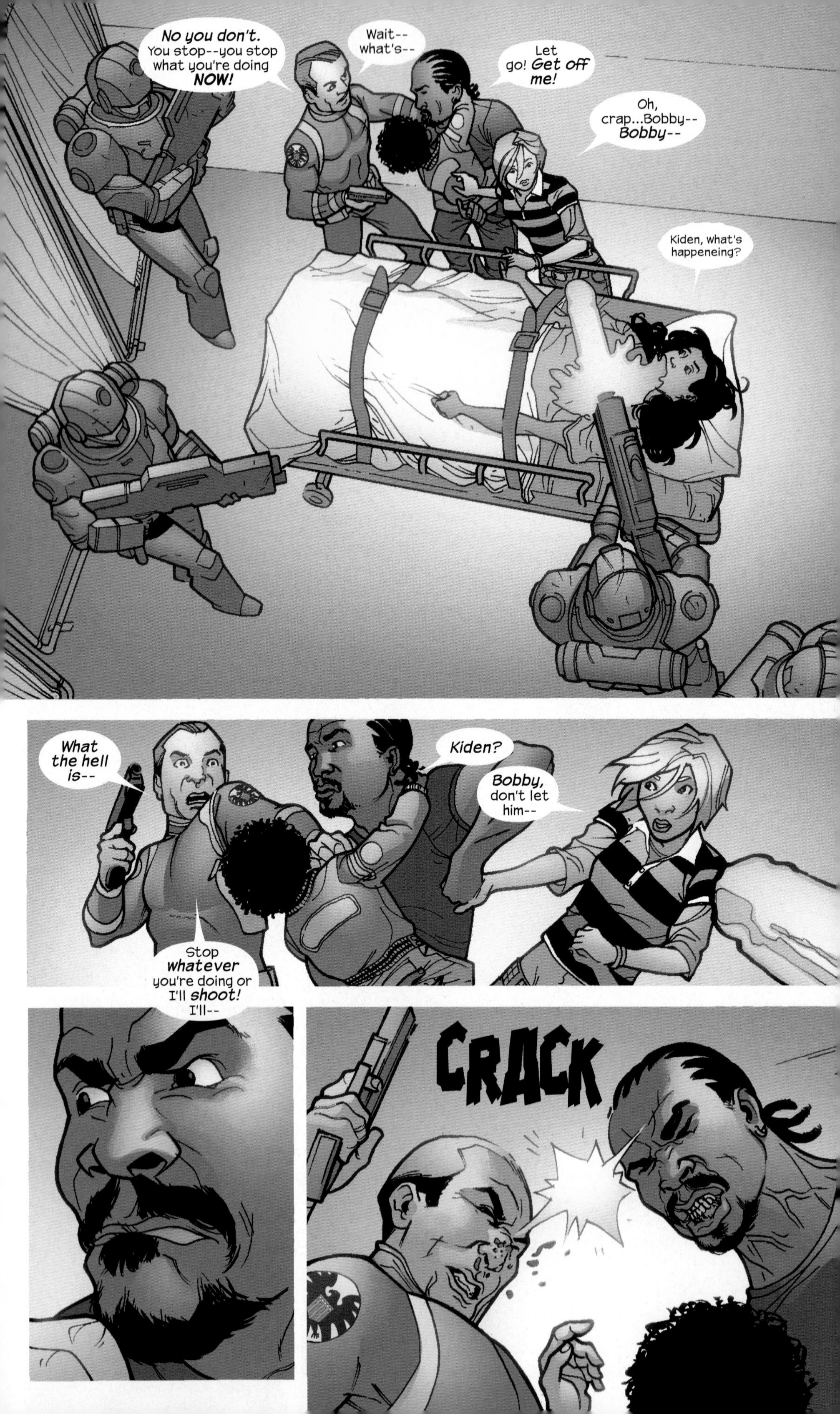

No you don't. You stop--you stop what you're doing NOW!
Wait-- what's--
Let go! Get off me!
Oh, crap...Bobby-- Bobby--
Kiden, what's happeneing?
What the hell is--
Kiden?
Bobby, don't let him--
Stop whatever you're doing or I'll shoot! I'll--
CRACK

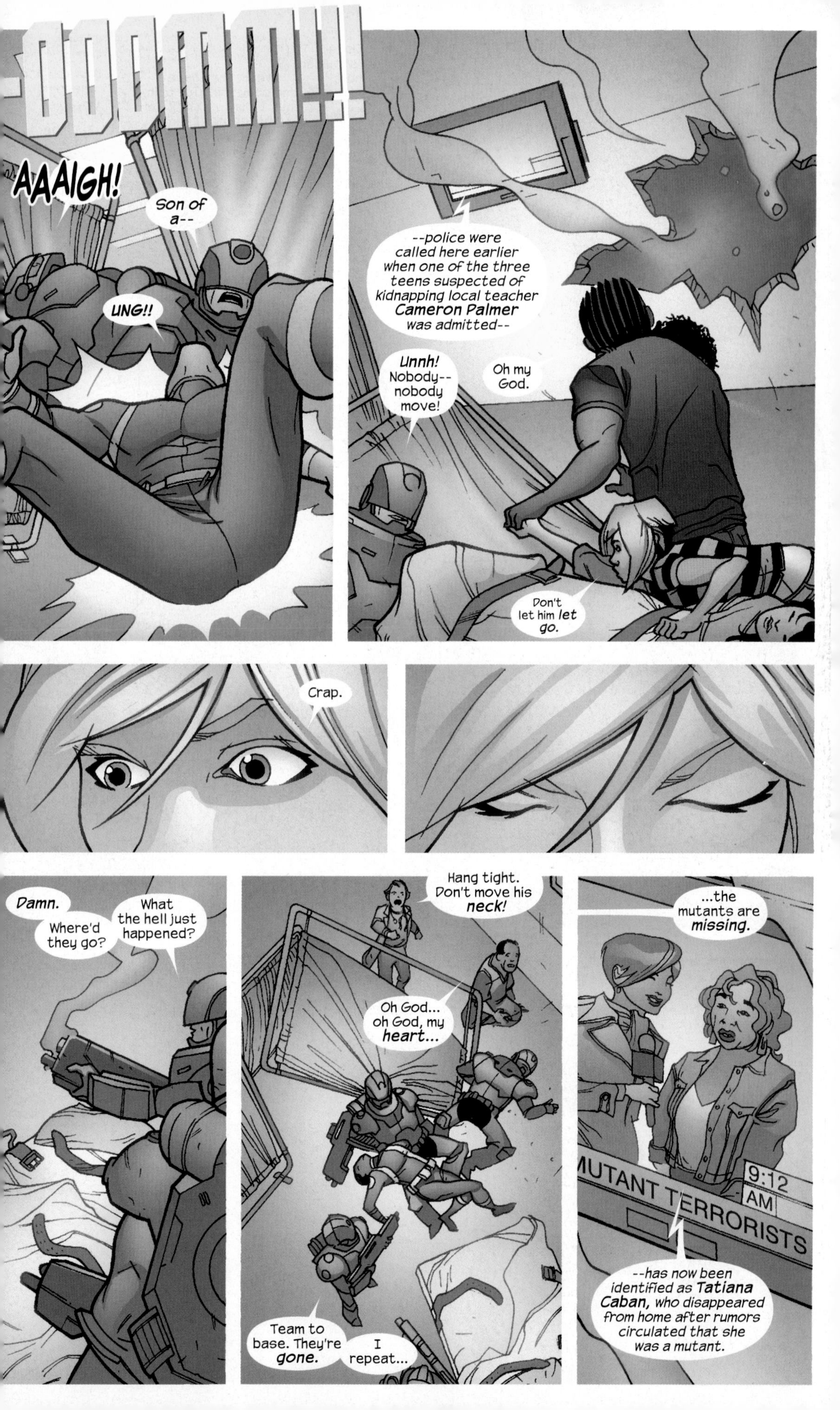
-OOOMM!!!
AAAIGH!
Son of a--
UNG!!
--police were called here earlier when one of the three teens suspected of kidnapping local teacher Cameron Palmer was admitted--
Unnh! Nobody-- nobody move!
Oh my God.
Don't let him let go.
Crap.
Damn.
Where'd they go?
What the hell just happened?
Hang tight. Don't move his neck!
Oh God... oh God, my heart...
Team to base. They're gone.
I repeat...
...the mutants are missing.
MUTANT TERRORISTS
9:12 AM
--has now been identified as Tatiana Caban, who disappeared from home after rumors circulated that she was a mutant.

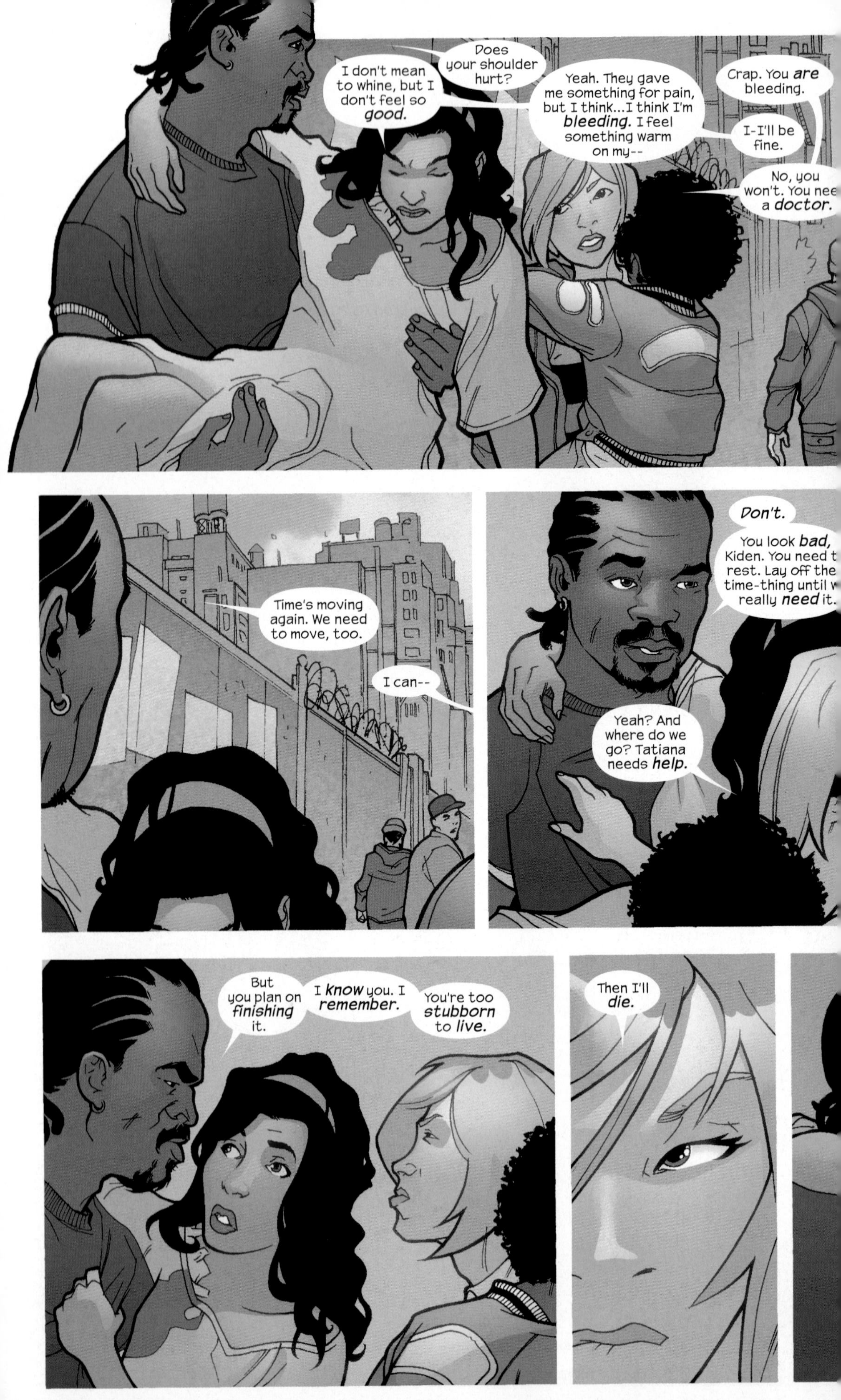
I don't mean to whine, but I don't feel so *good.*
Does your shoulder hurt?
Yeah. They gave me something for pain, but I think...I think I'm *bleeding.* I feel something warm on my--
Crap. You *are* bleeding.
I-I'll be fine.
No, you won't. You nee a *doctor.*
Time's moving again. We need to move, too.
I can--
Don't.
You look *bad,* Kiden. You need t rest. Lay off the time-thing until w really *need* it.
Yeah? And where do we go? Tatiana needs *help.*
But you plan on *finishing* it.
I *know* you. I *remember.*
You're too *stubborn* to *live.*
Then I'll *die.*

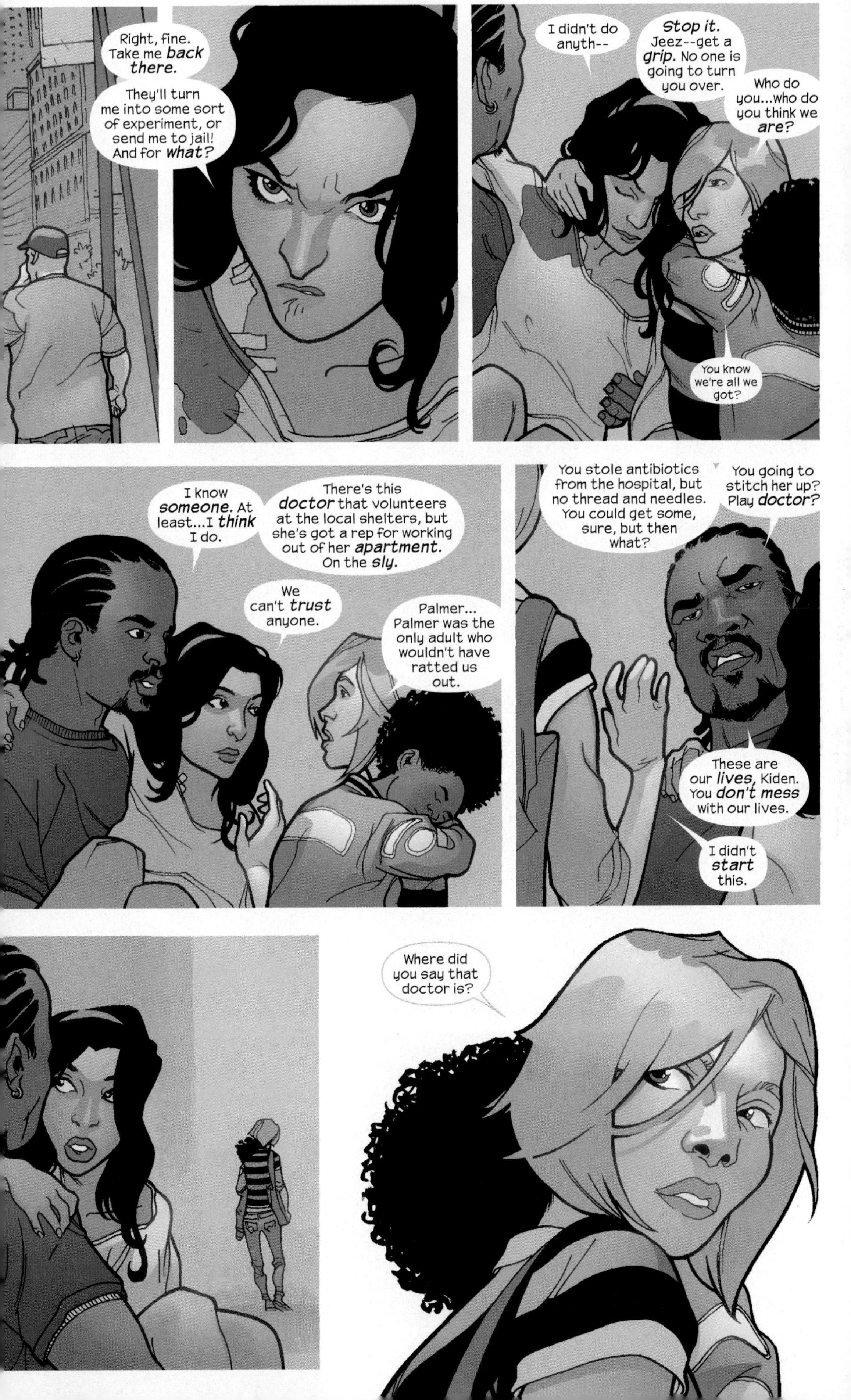

Right, fine. Take me back there.
They'll turn me into some sort of experiment, or send me to jail! And for what?
I didn't do anyth--
Stop it. Jeez--get a grip. No one is going to turn you over.
Who do you...who do you think we are?
You know we're all we got?
I know someone. At least...I think I do.
There's this doctor that volunteers at the local shelters, but she's got a rep for working out of her apartment. On the sly.
We can't trust anyone.
Palmer... Palmer was the only adult who wouldn't have ratted us out.
You stole antibiotics from the hospital, but no thread and needles. You could get some, sure, but then what?
You going to stitch her up? Play doctor?
These are our lives, Kiden. You don't mess with our lives.
I didn't start this.
Where did you say that doctor is?

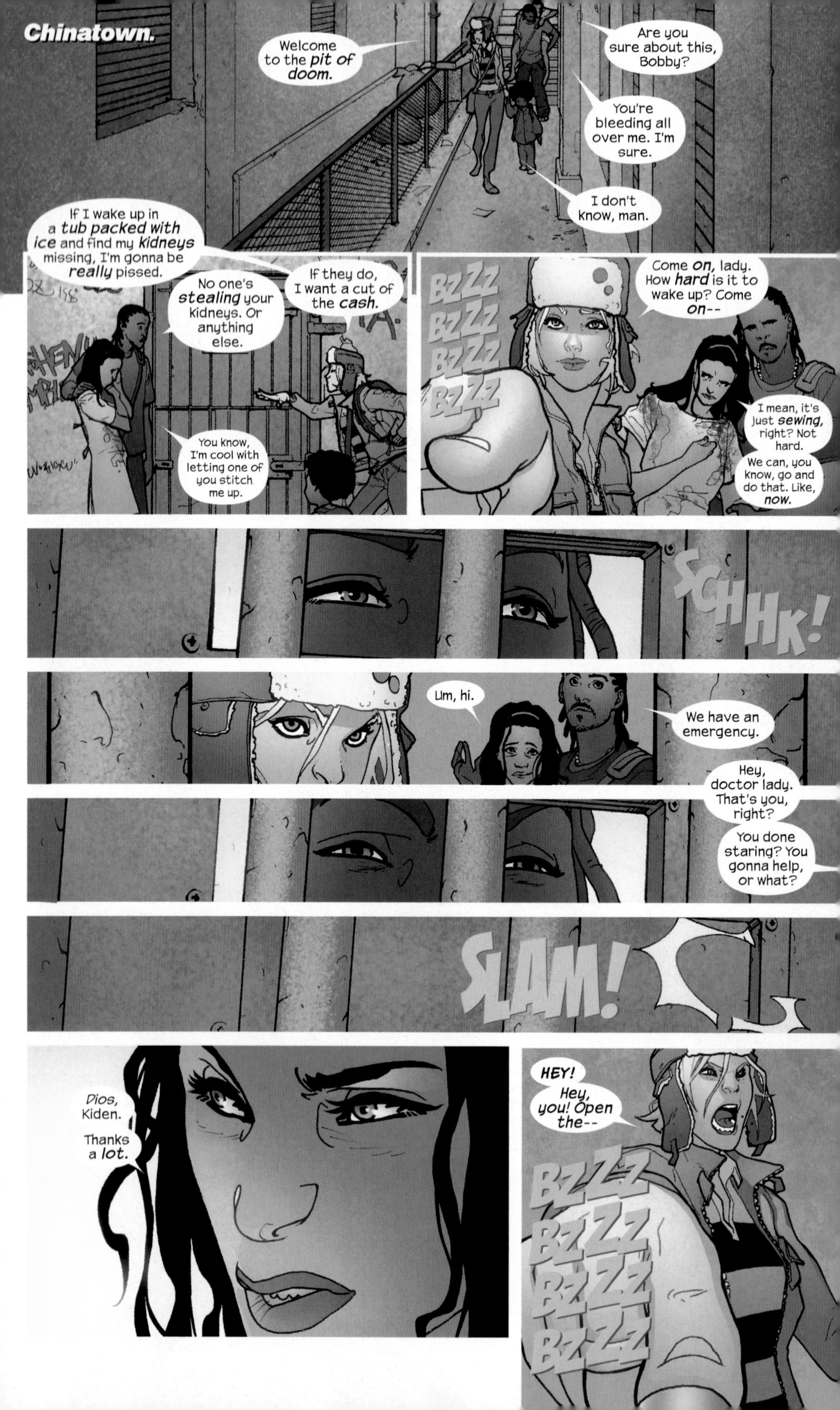
Chinatown.
Welcome to the pit of doom.
Are you sure about this, Bobby?
You're bleeding all over me. I'm sure.
I don't know, man.
If I wake up in a tub packed with ice and find my kidneys missing, I'm gonna be really pissed.
No one's stealing your kidneys. Or anything else.
If they do, I want a cut of the cash.
You know, I'm cool with letting one of you stitch me up.
BzZz BzZz BzZz BzZz
Come on, lady. How hard is it to wake up? Come on--
I mean, it's just sewing, right? Not hard.
We can, you know, go and do that. Like, now.
SCHHK!
Um, hi.
We have an emergency.
Hey, doctor lady. That's you, right?
You done staring? You gonna help, or what?
SLAM!
Dios, Kiden.
Thanks a lot.
HEY!
Hey, you! Open the--
BzZz BzZz BzZz BzZz

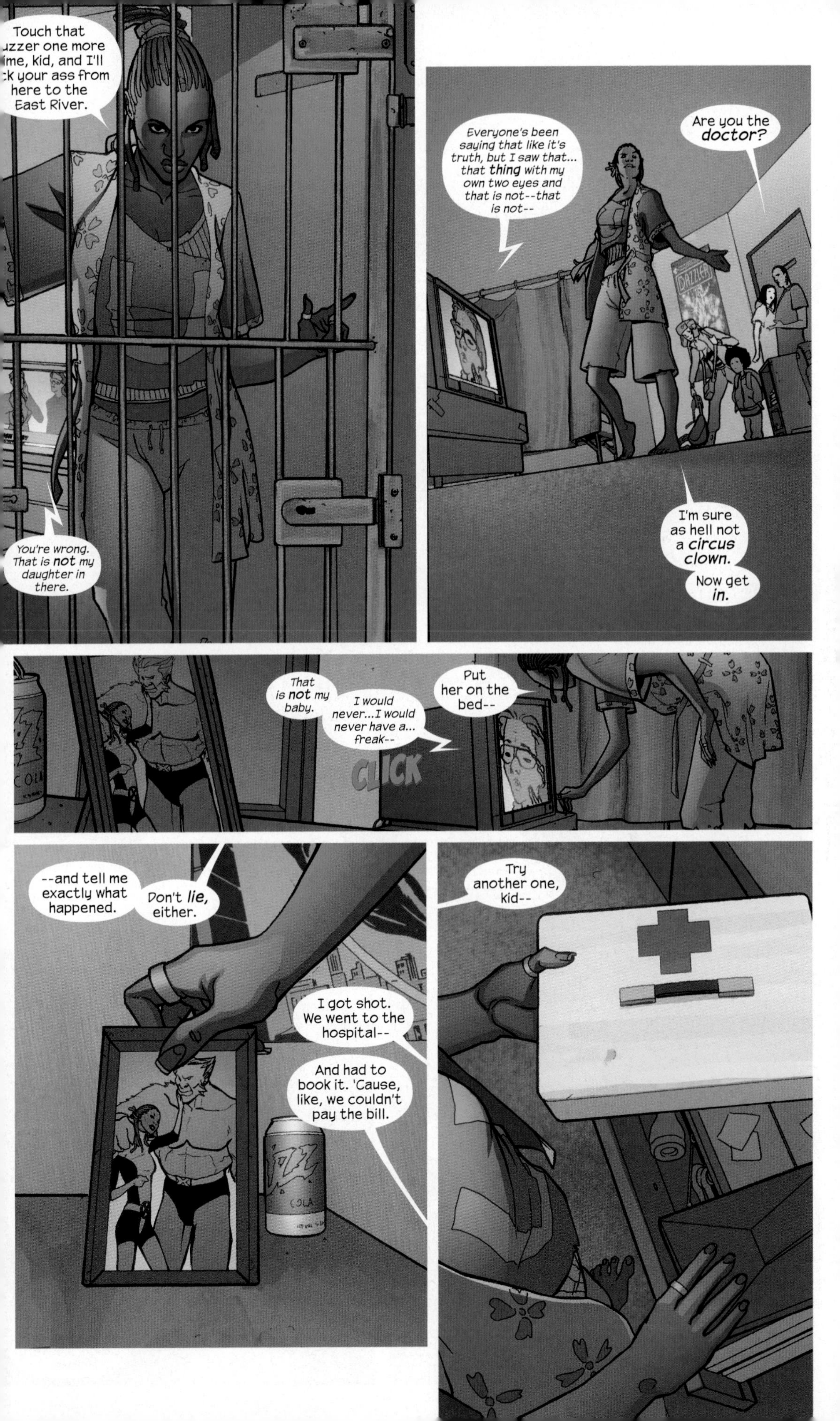

Touch that
-izzer one more
-ime, kid, and I'll
-:k your ass from
here to the
East River.
You're wrong. That is not my daughter in there.
Everyone's been saying that like it's truth, but I saw that... that thing with my own two eyes and that is not--that is not--
Are you the doctor?
DAZZLER
I'm sure as hell not a circus clown.
Now get in.
That is not my baby.
I would never...I would never have a... freak--
CLICK
Put her on the bed--
--and tell me exactly what happened.
Don't lie, either.
I got shot. We went to the hospital--
And had to book it. 'Cause, like, we couldn't pay the bill.
Try another one, kid--

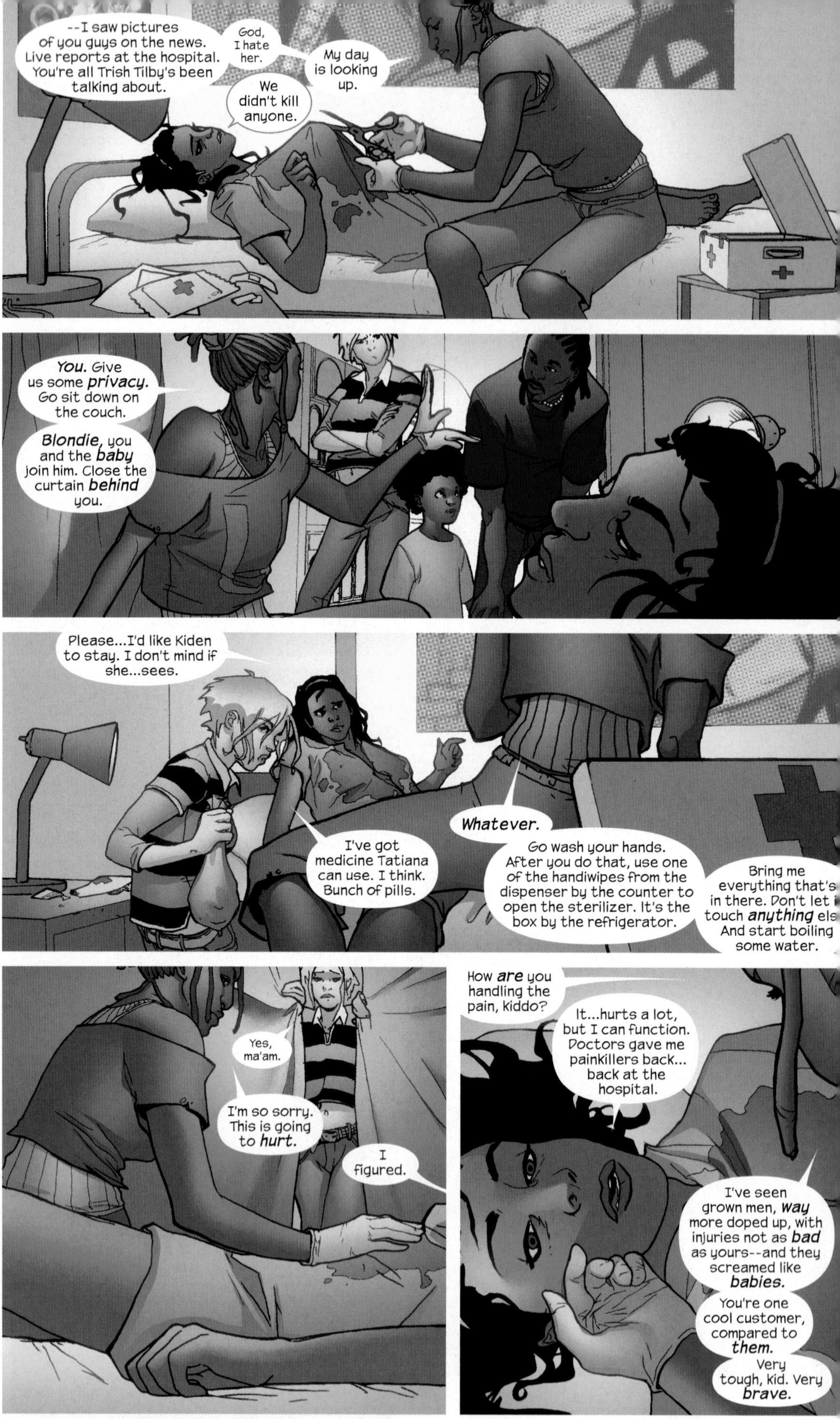
--I saw pictures of you guys on the news. Live reports at the hospital. You're all Trish Tilby's been talking about.
God, I hate her.
My day is looking up.
We didn't kill anyone.
You. Give us some privacy. Go sit down on the couch.
Blondie, you and the baby join him. Close the curtain behind you.
Please...I'd like Kiden to stay. I don't mind if she...sees.
I've got medicine Tatiana can use. I think. Bunch of pills.
Whatever.
Go wash your hands. After you do that, use one of the handiwipes from the dispenser by the counter to open the sterilizer. It's the box by the refrigerator.
Bring me everything that's in there. Don't let i touch anything els And start boiling some water.
Yes, ma'am.
I'm so sorry. This is going to hurt.
I figured.
How are you handling the pain, kiddo?
It...hurts a lot, but I can function. Doctors gave me painkillers back... back at the hospital.
I've seen grown men, way more doped up, with injuries not as bad as yours--and they screamed like babies.
You're one cool customer, compared to them.
Very tough, kid. Very brave.

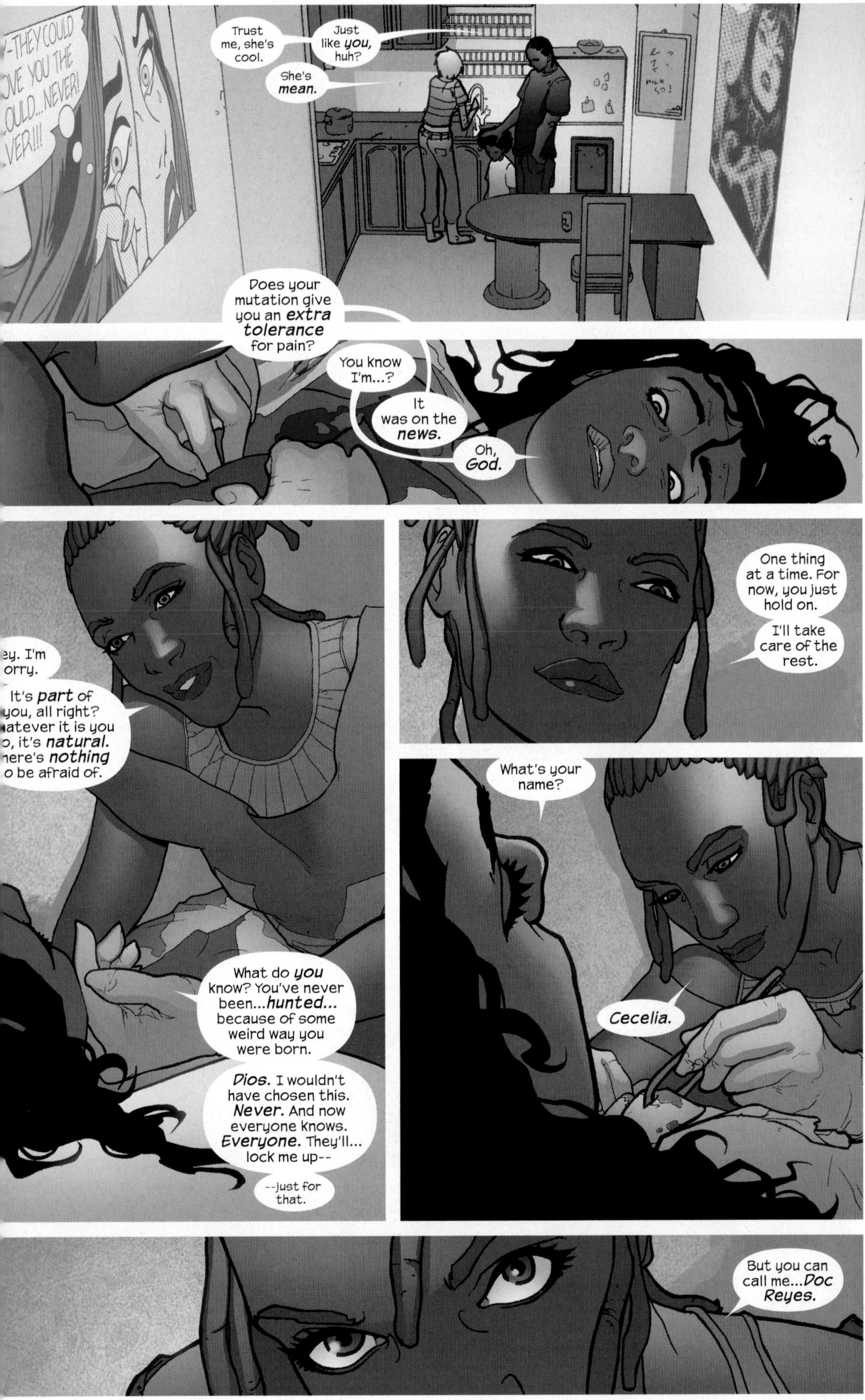

-THEY COULD
OVE YOU THE
OULD...NEVER!
VER!!!
Trust me, she's cool.
Just like *you*, huh?
She's *mean*.
Does your mutation give you an *extra tolerance* for pain?
You know I'm...?
It was on the *news*.
Oh, *God*.
ey. I'm orry.
It's *part* of you, all right? atever it is you o, it's *natural*. here's *nothing* o be afraid of.
One thing at a time. For now, you just hold on.
I'll take care of the rest.
What do *you* know? You've never been...*hunted*... because of some weird way you were born.
Dios. I wouldn't have chosen this. *Never*. And now everyone knows. *Everyone*. They'll... lock me up--
--just for that.
What's your name?
Cecelia.
But you can call me...*Doc Reyes*.

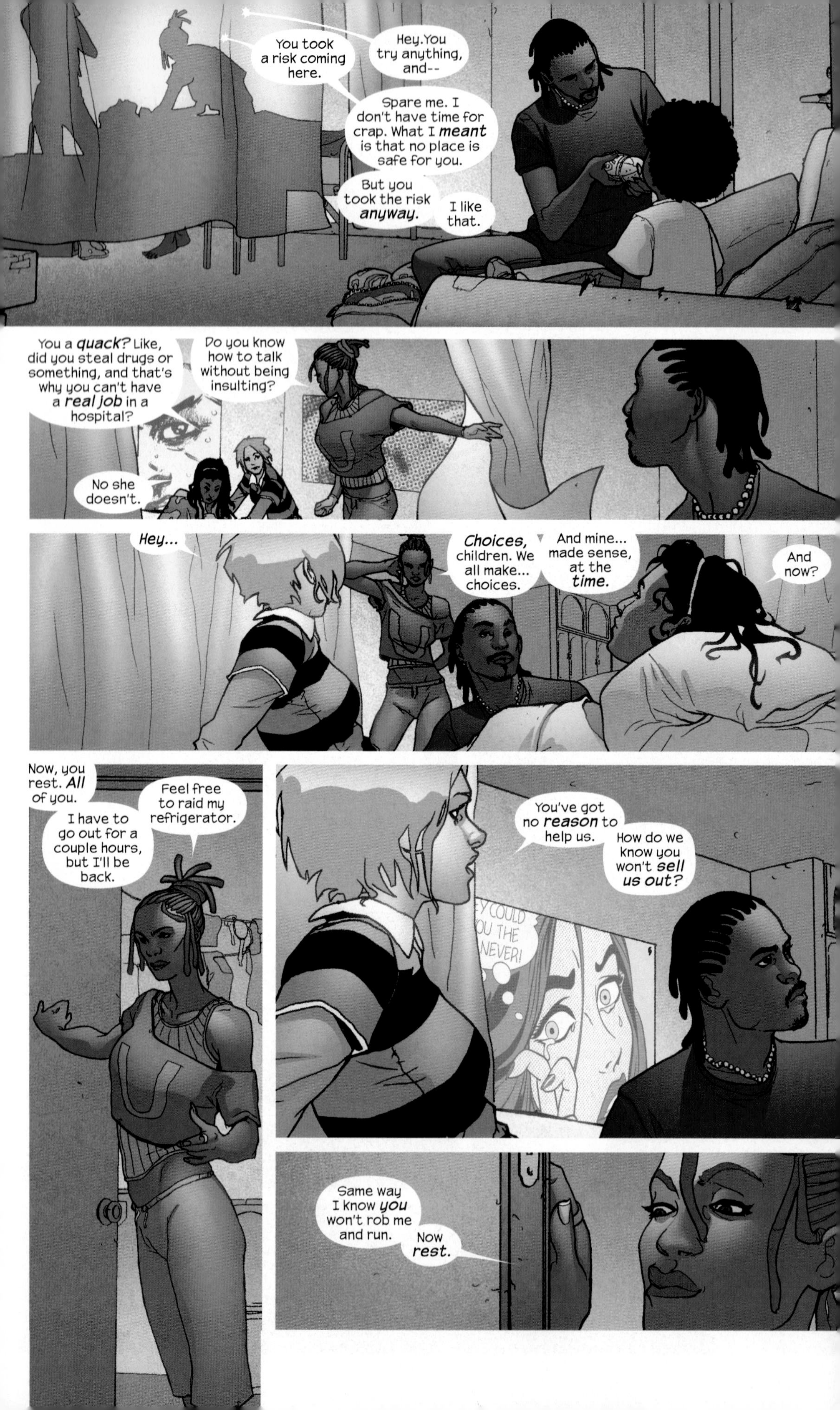

Hey.You try anything, and--
You took a risk coming here.
Spare me. I don't have time for crap. What I *meant* is that no place is safe for you.
But you took the risk *anyway.*
I like that.
You a *quack?* Like, did you steal drugs or something, and that's why you can't have a *real job* in a hospital?
Do you know how to talk without being insulting?
No she doesn't.
Hey...
Choices, children. We all make... choices.
And mine... made sense, at the *time.*
And now?
Now, you rest. *All* of you.
I have to go out for a couple hours, but I'll be back.
Feel free to raid my refrigerator.
You've got no *reason* to help us.
How do we know you won't *sell us out?*
Same way I know *you* won't rob me and run.
Now *rest.*

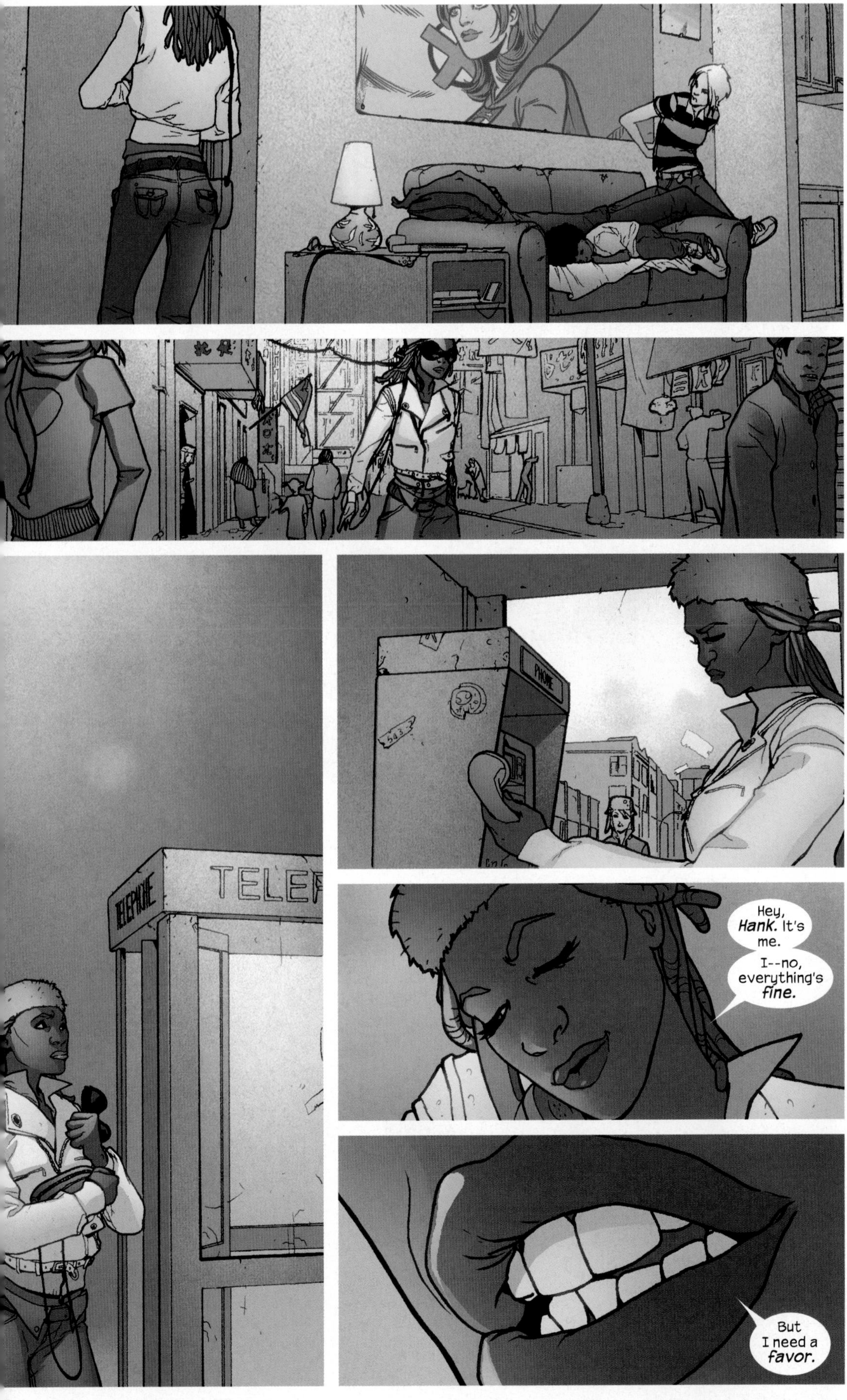
TELEPHONE
TELEP
PHONE
Hey, Hank. It's me.
I--no, everything's fine.
But I need a favor.

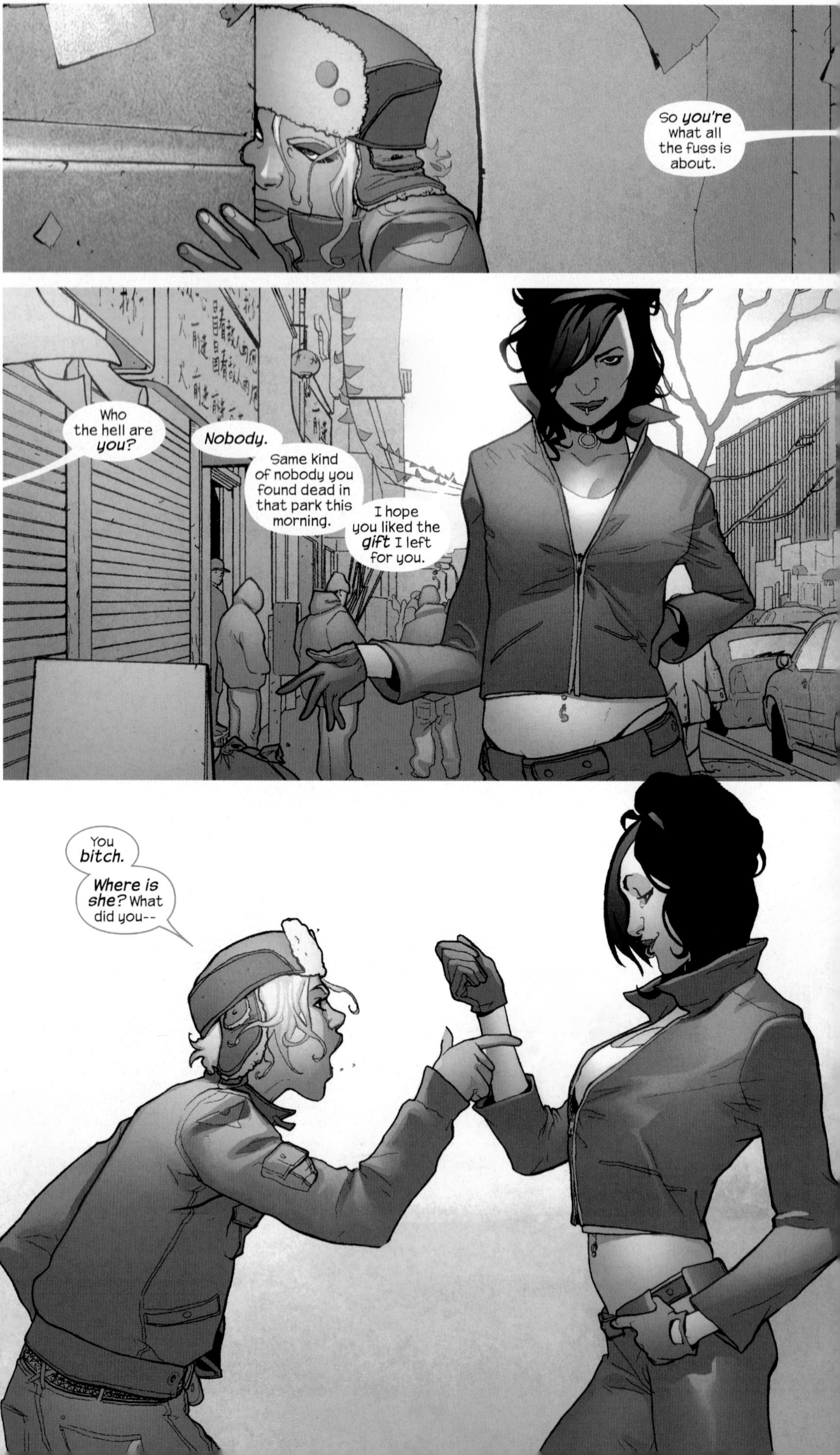
So you're what all the fuss is about.
Who the hell are you?
Nobody.
Same kind of nobody you found dead in that park this morning.
I hope you liked the gift I left for you.
You bitch.
Where is she? What did you--

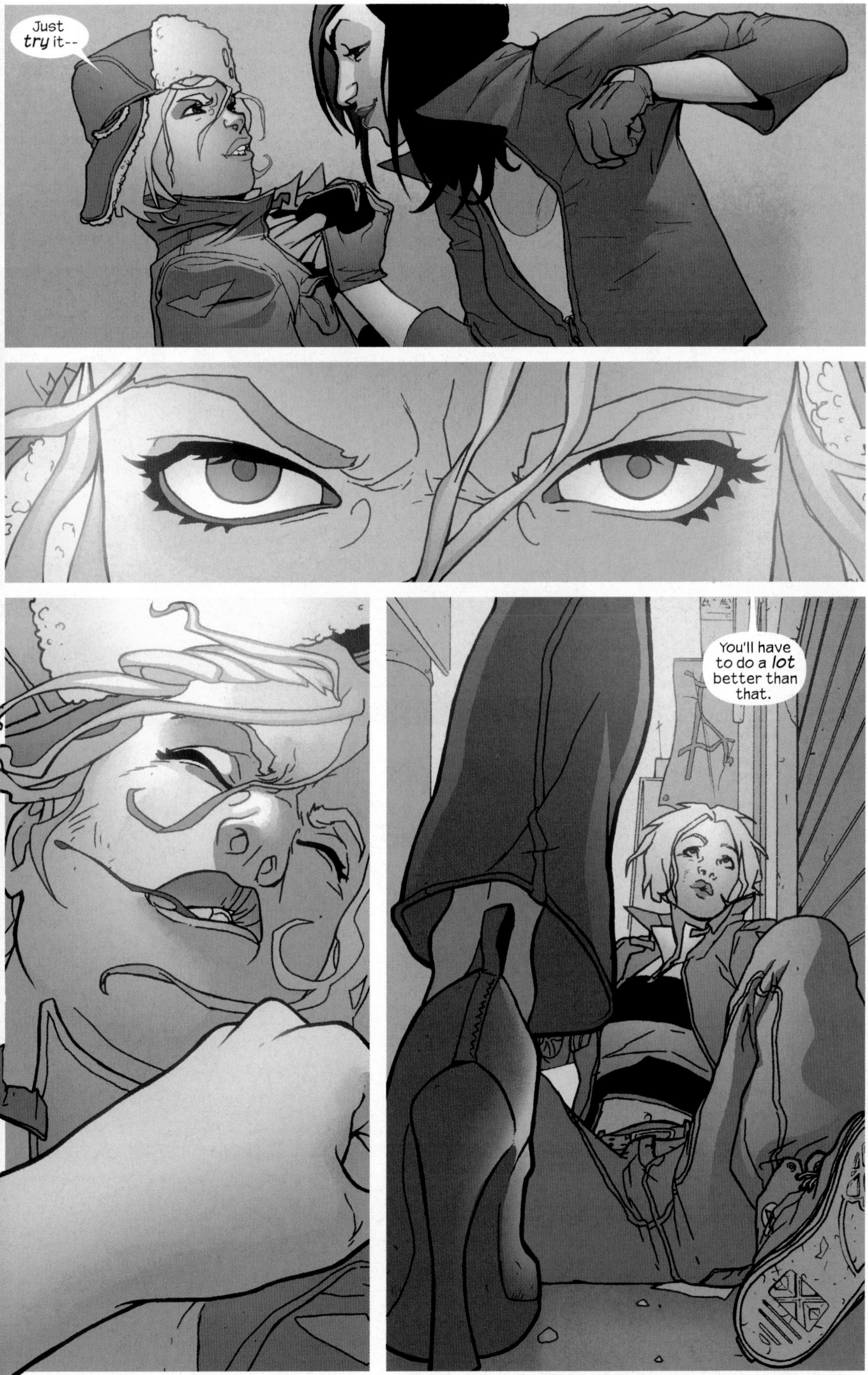

Just *try* it--
You'll have to do a *lot* better than that.

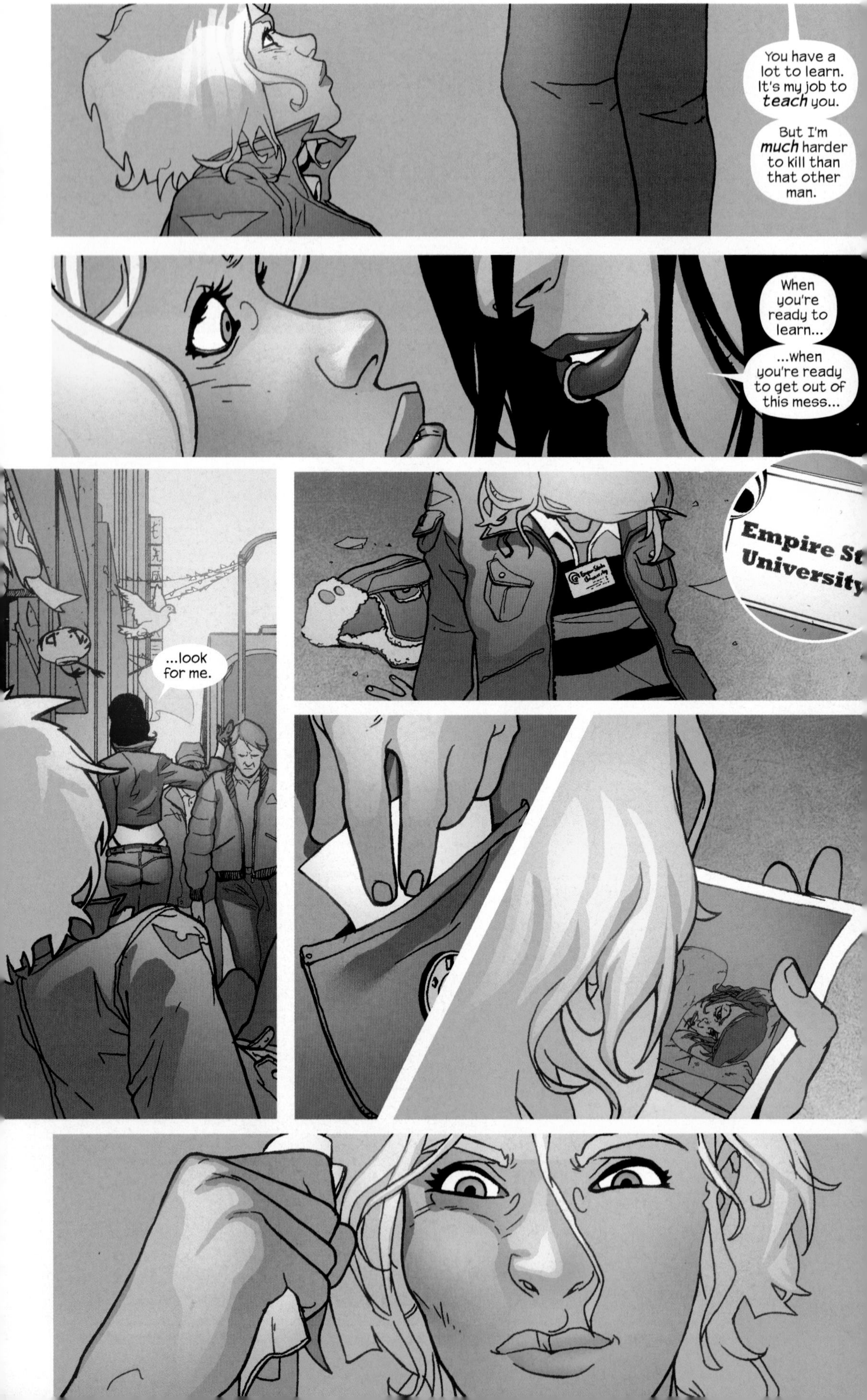
You have a lot to learn. It's my job to *teach* you.
But I'm *much* harder to kill than that other man.
When you're ready to learn...
...when you're ready to get out of this mess...
...look for me.
Empire St University

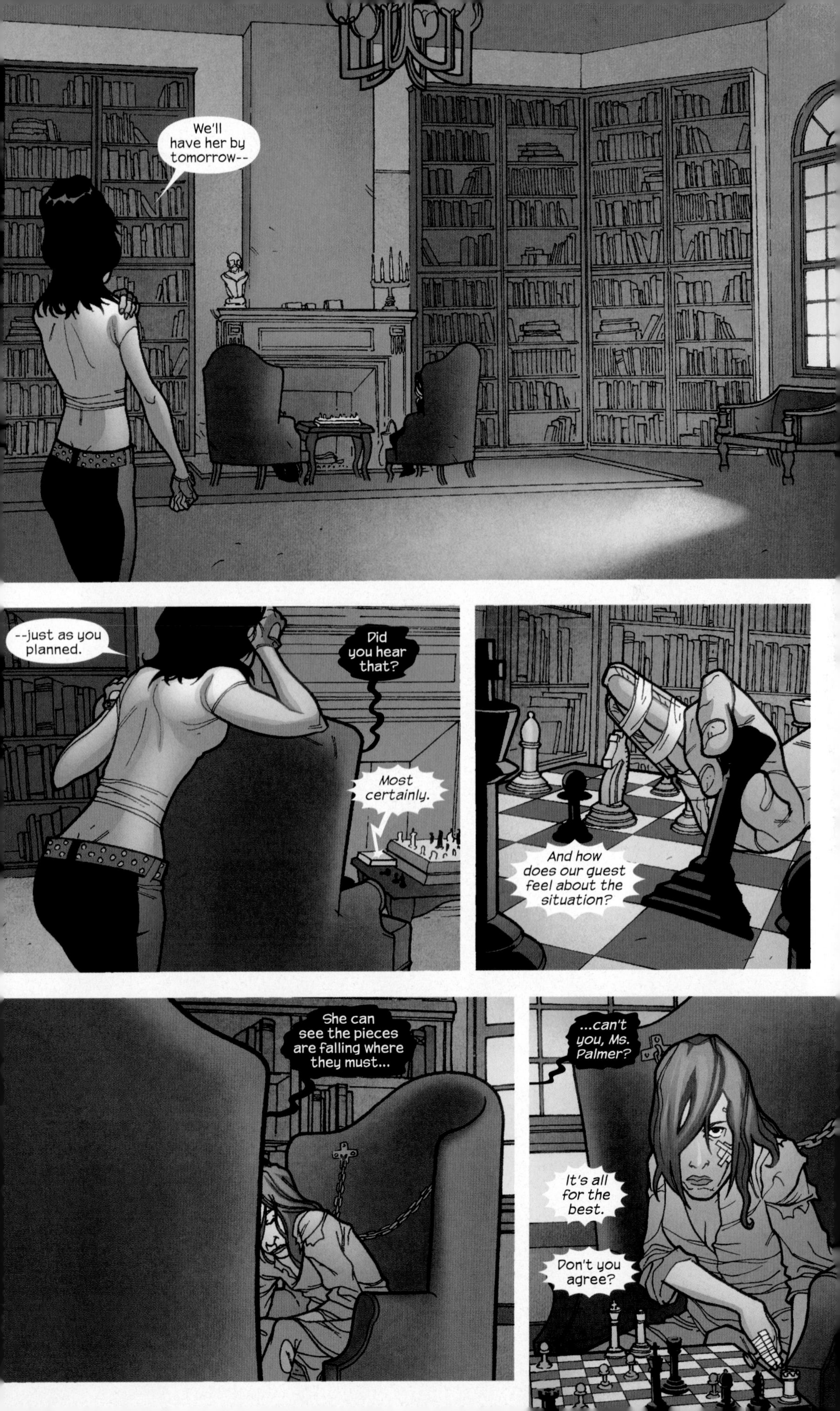
We'll have her by tomorrow--
--just as you planned.
Did you hear that?
Most certainly.
And how does our guest feel about the situation?
She can see the pieces are falling where they must...
...can't you, Ms. Palmer?
It's all for the best.
Don't you agree?

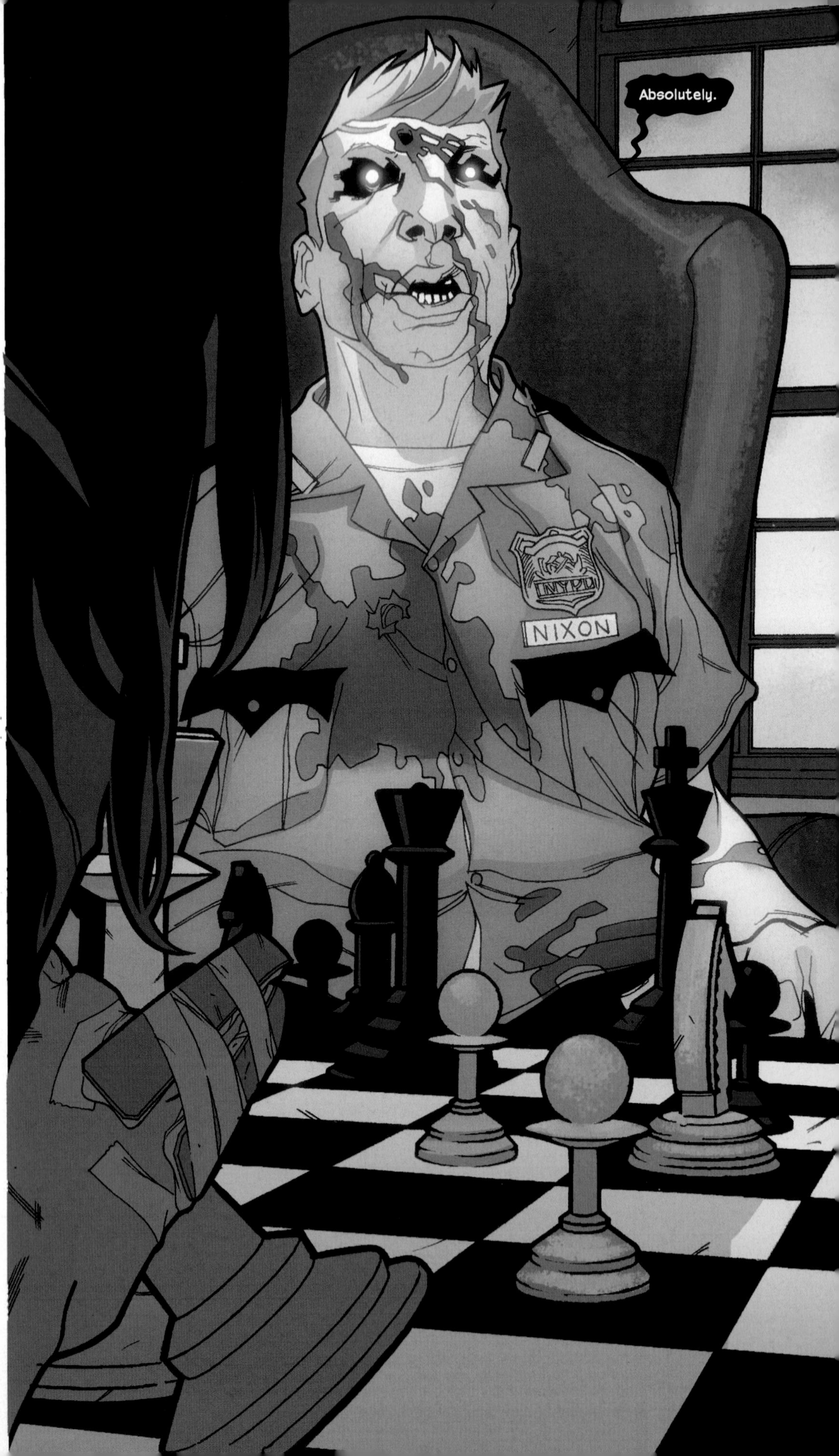
Absolutely.
NYPD
NIXON

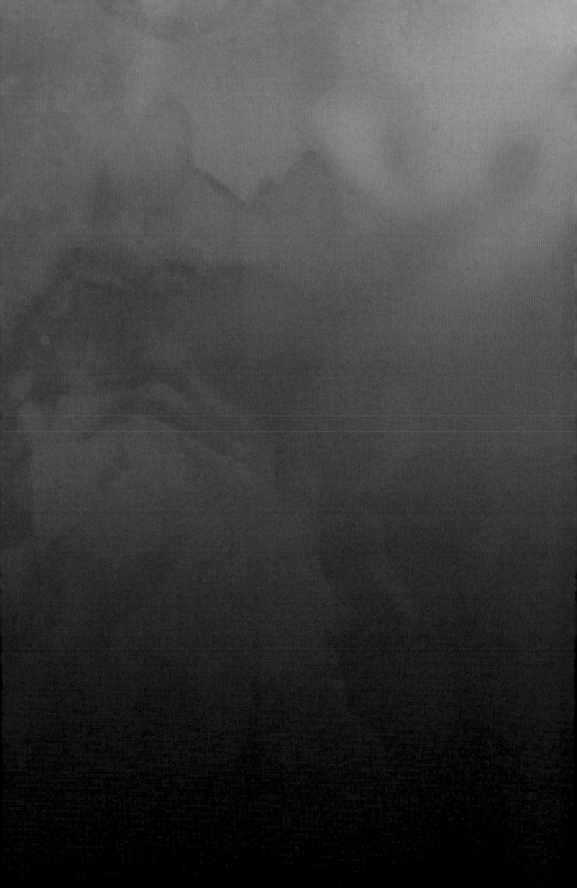

FIVE

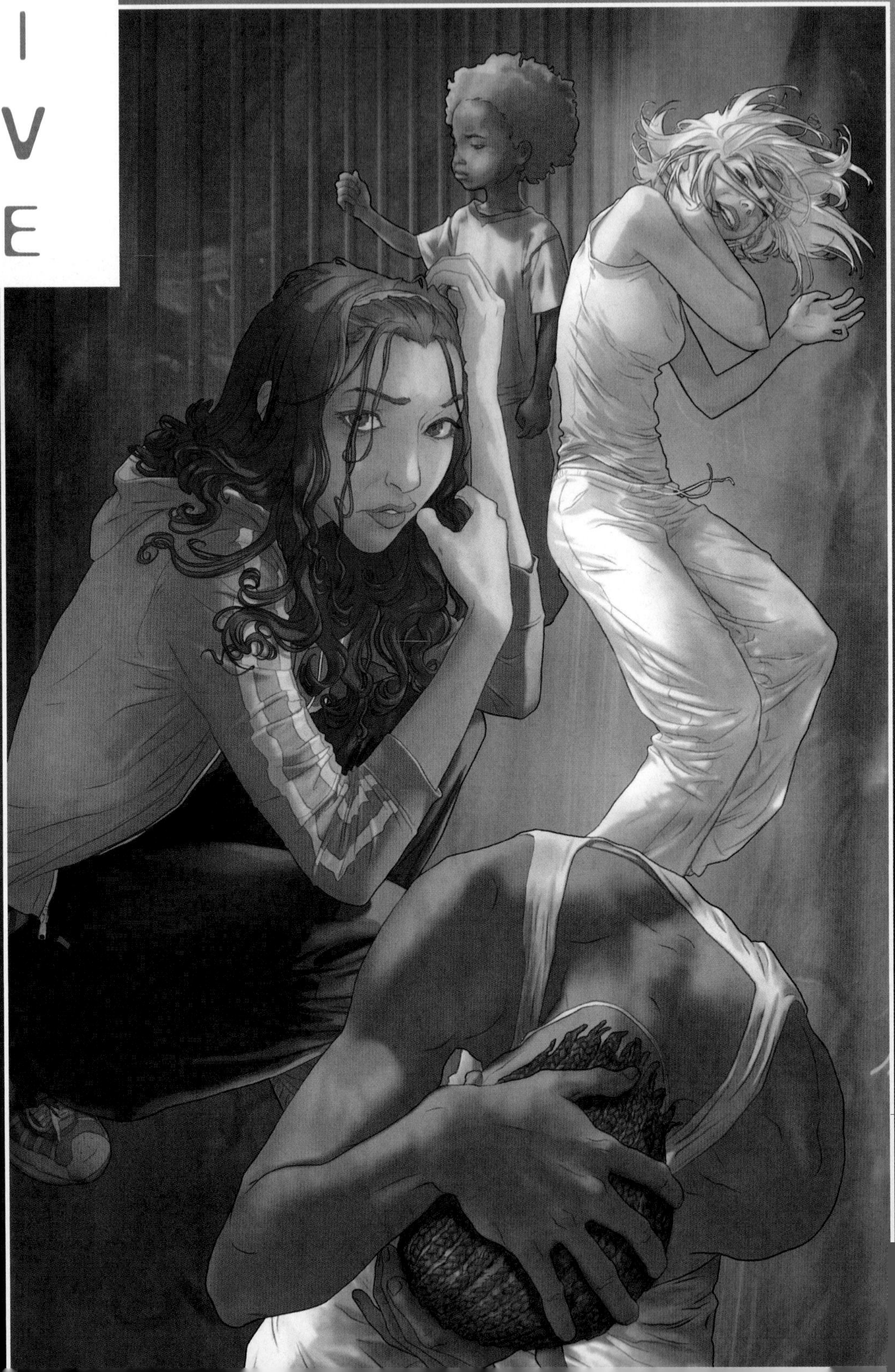

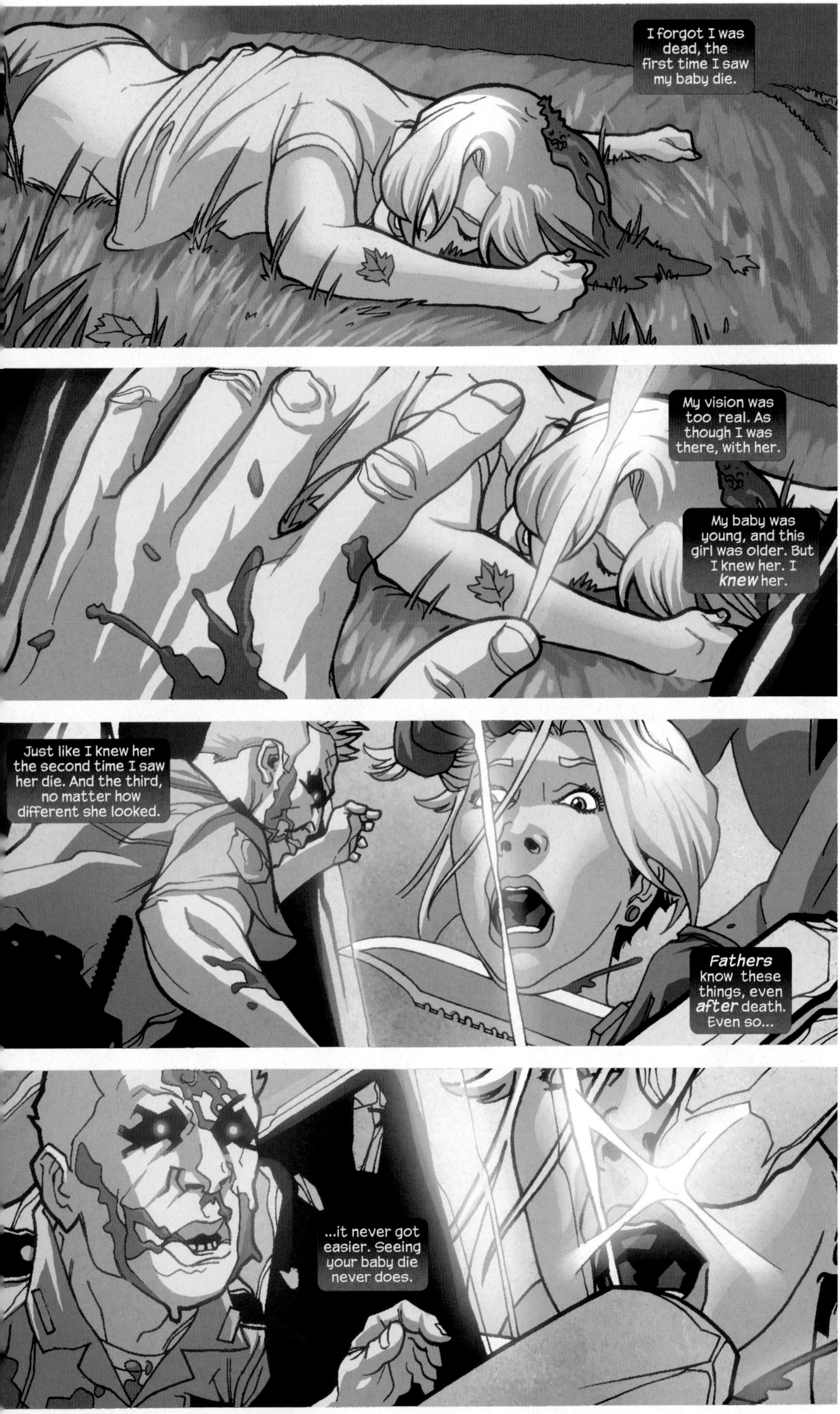
I forgot I was dead, the first time I saw my baby die.
My vision was too real. As though I was there, with her.
My baby was young, and this girl was older. But I knew her. I *knew* her.
Just like I knew her the second time I saw her die. And the third, no matter how different she looked.
Fathers know these things, even *after* death. Even so...
...it never got easier. Seeing your baby die never does.

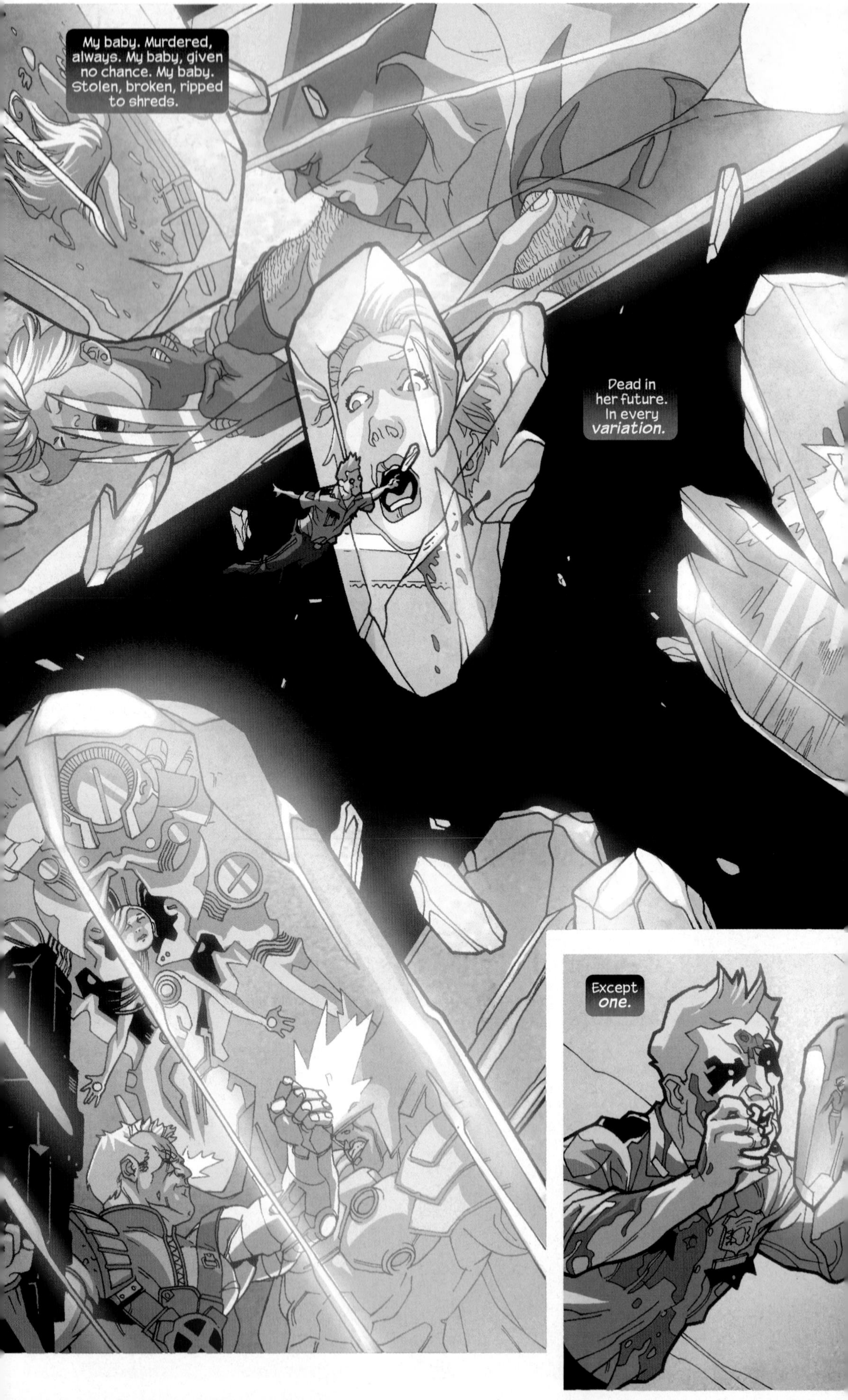
My baby. Murdered, always. My baby, given no chance. My baby. Stolen, broken, ripped to shreds.
Dead in her future. In every *variation.*
Except *one.*

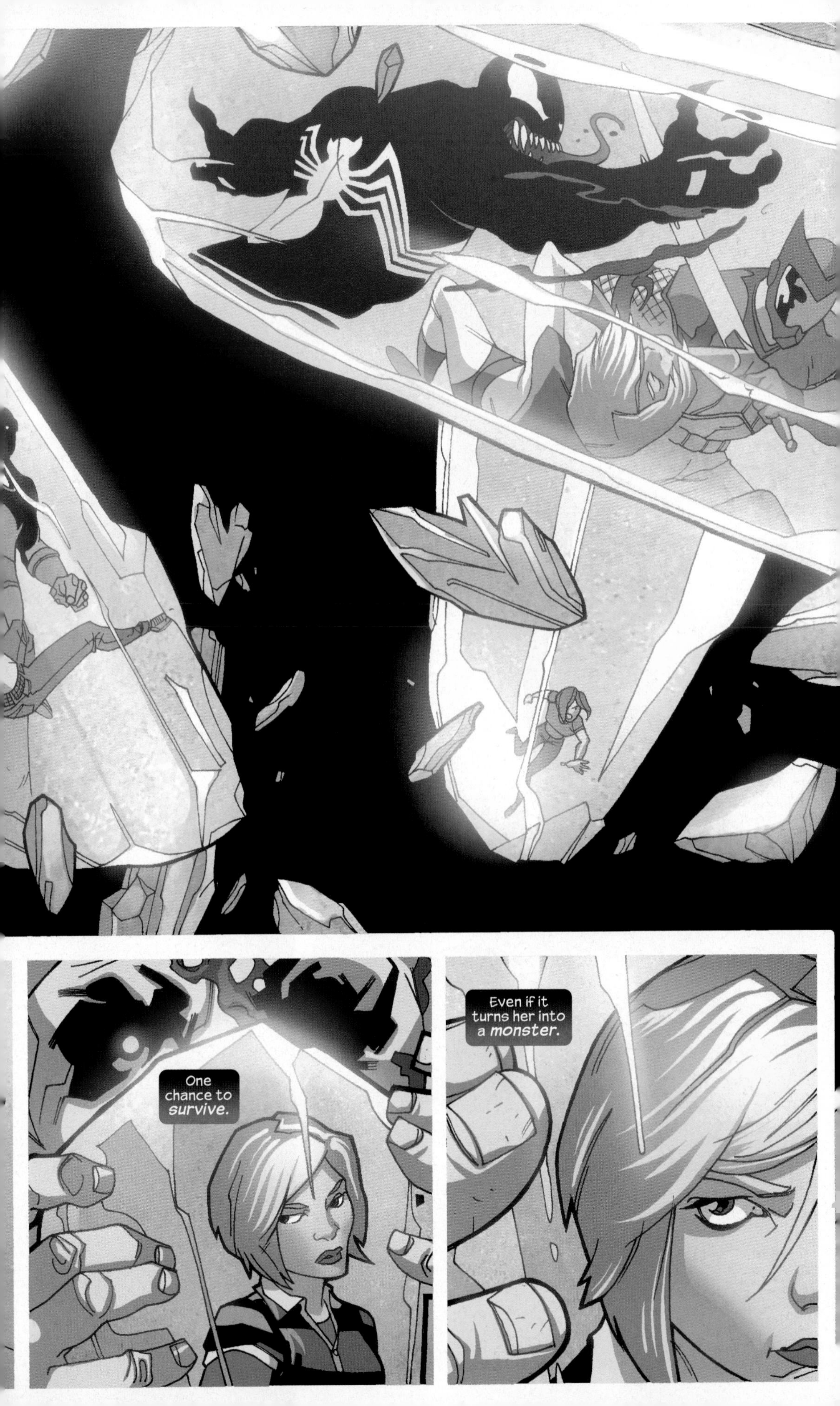
One chance to *survive*.
Even if it turns her into a *monster*.

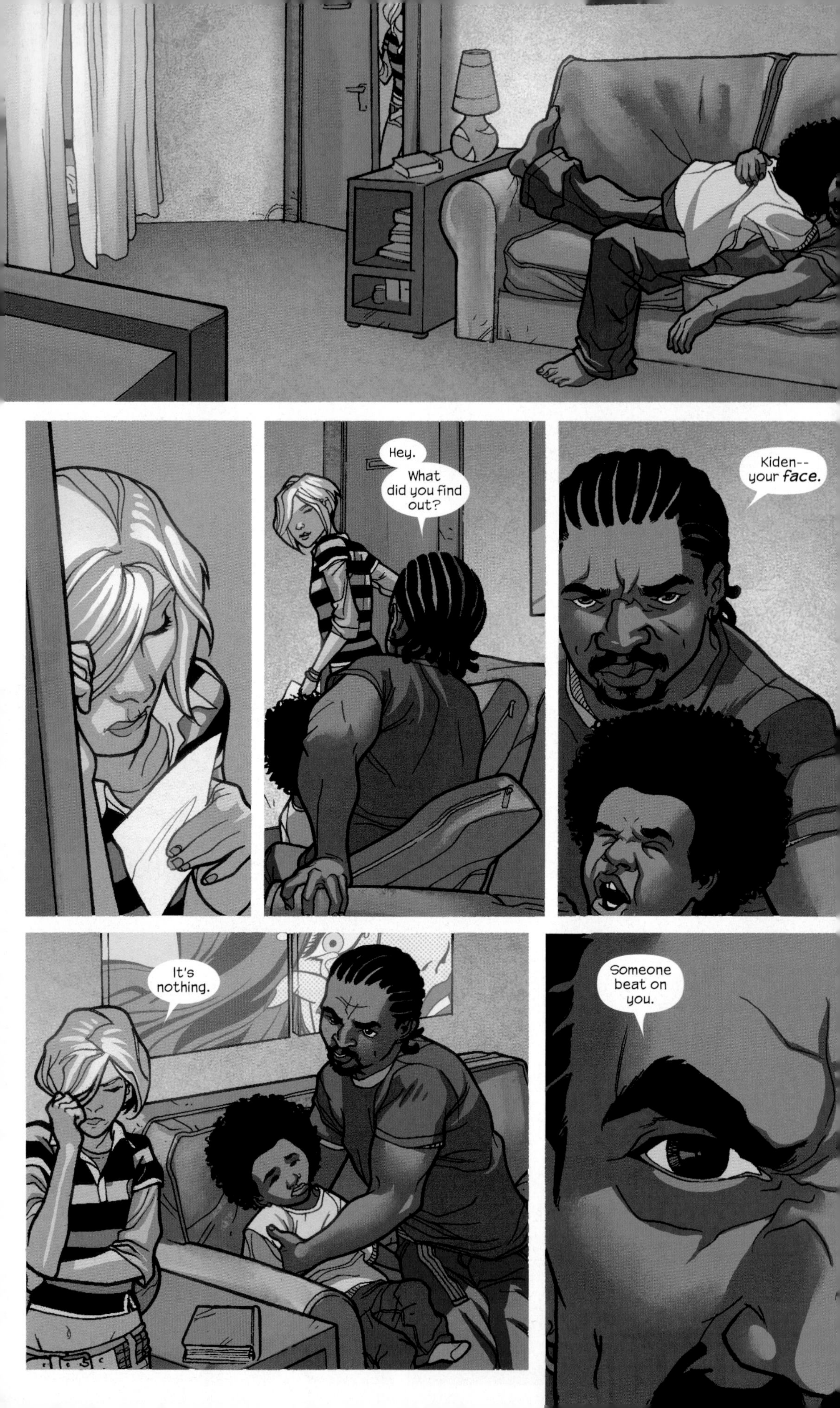
Hey.
What did you find out?
Kiden-- your *face*.
It's nothing.
Someone beat on you.

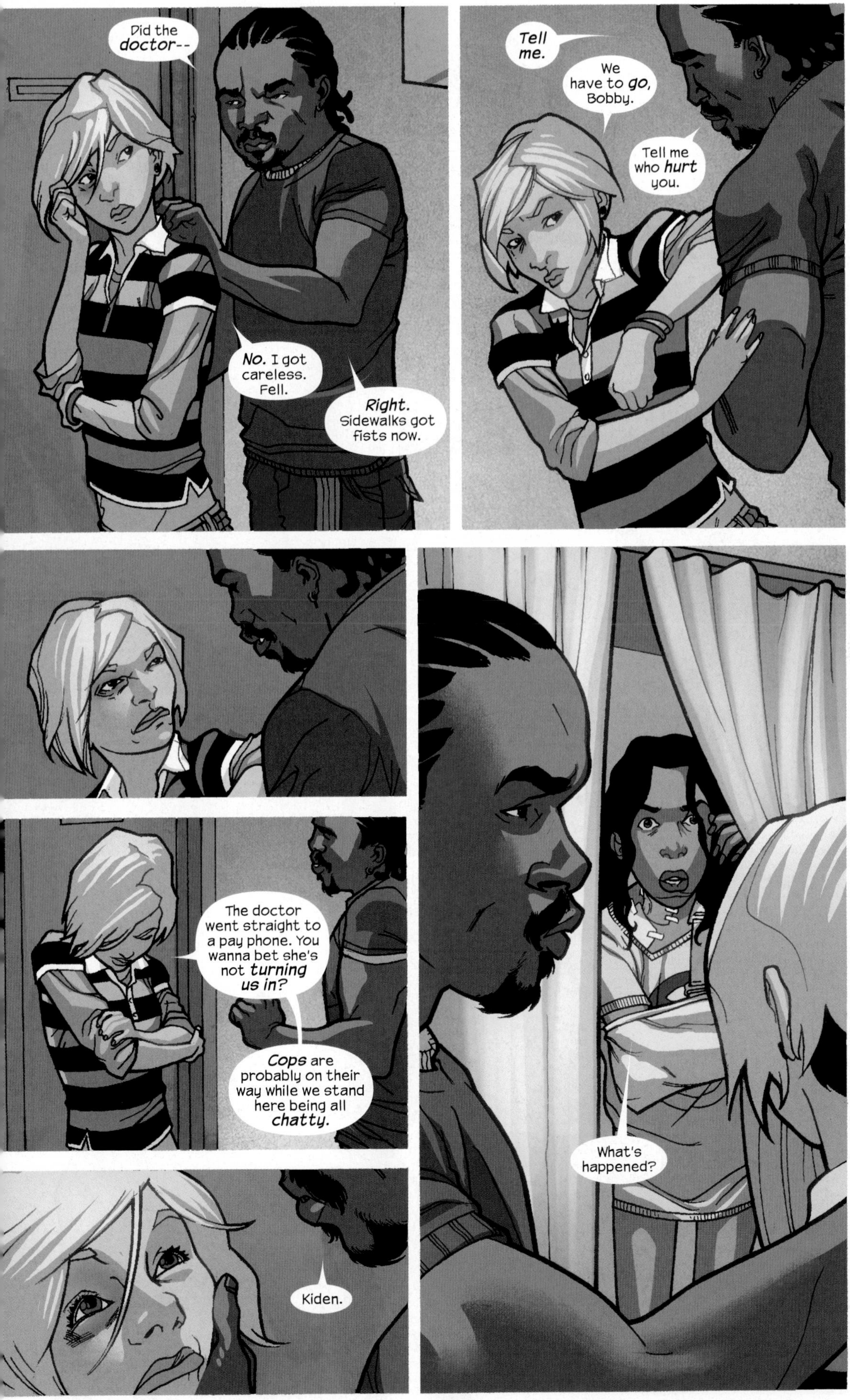
Did the doctor--
No. I got careless. Fell.
Right. Sidewalks got fists now.
Tell me.
We have to go, Bobby.
Tell me who hurt you.
The doctor went straight to a pay phone. You wanna bet she's not turning us in?
Cops are probably on their way while we stand here being all chatty.
Kiden.
What's happened?

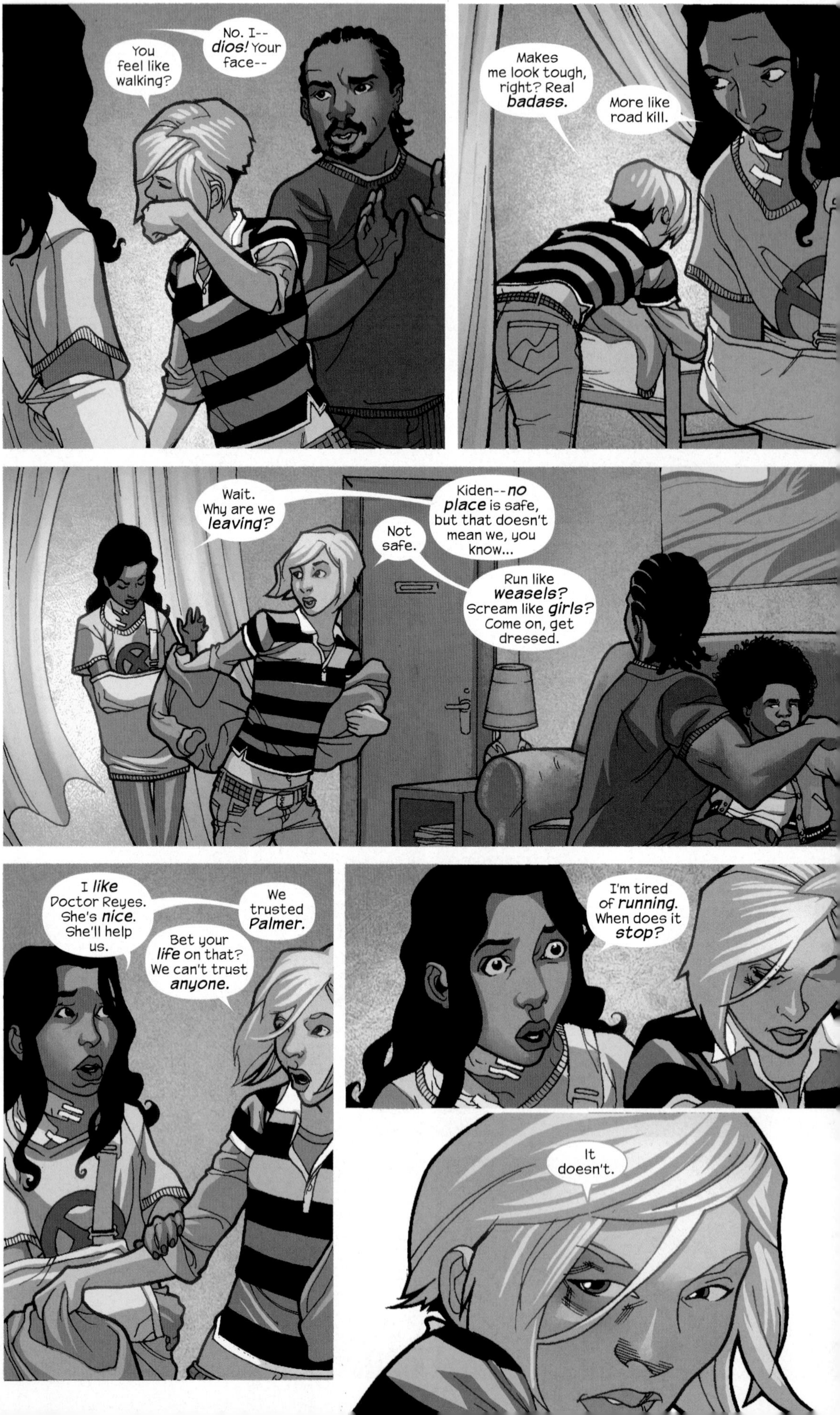
No. I--
dios! Your face--
You feel like walking?
Makes me look tough, right? Real **badass.**
More like road kill.
Wait. Why are we *leaving?*
Kiden--***no place*** is safe, but that doesn't mean we, you know...
Not safe.
Run like *weasels?* Scream like *girls?* Come on, get dressed.
I *like* Doctor Reyes. She's *nice.* She'll help us.
We trusted *Palmer.*
Bet your *life* on that? We can't trust *anyone.*
I'm tired of *running.* When does it *stop?*
It doesn't.

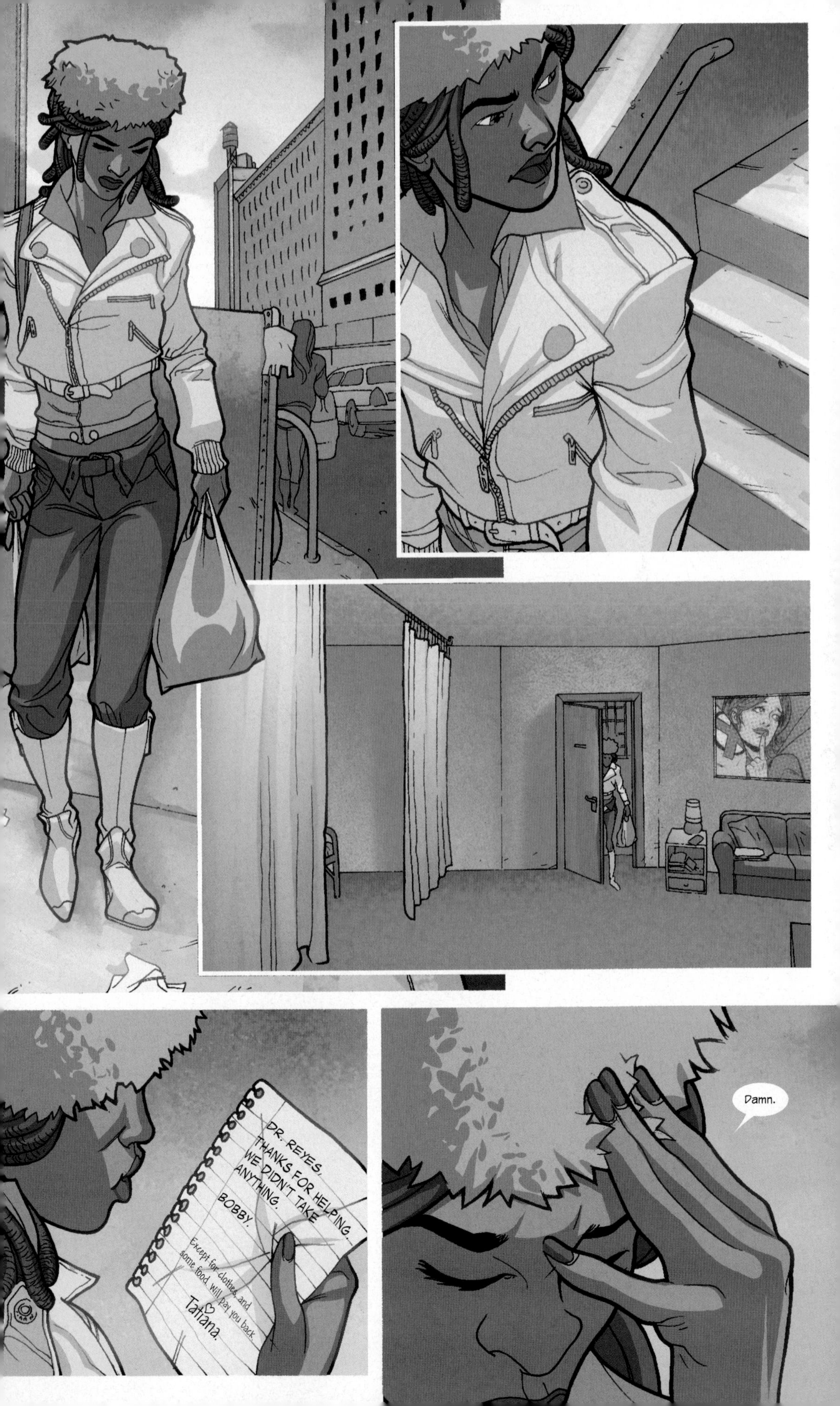
DR. REYES,
THANKS FOR HELPING.
WE DIDN'T TAKE ANYTHING.
BOBBY.
Except for clothes, and some food. Will pay you back.
Tatiana.
Damn.

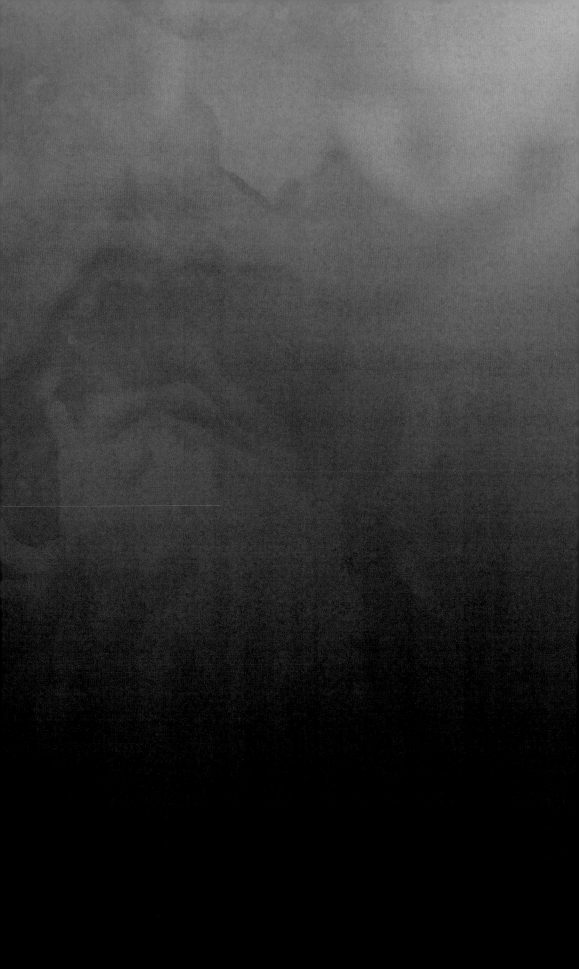

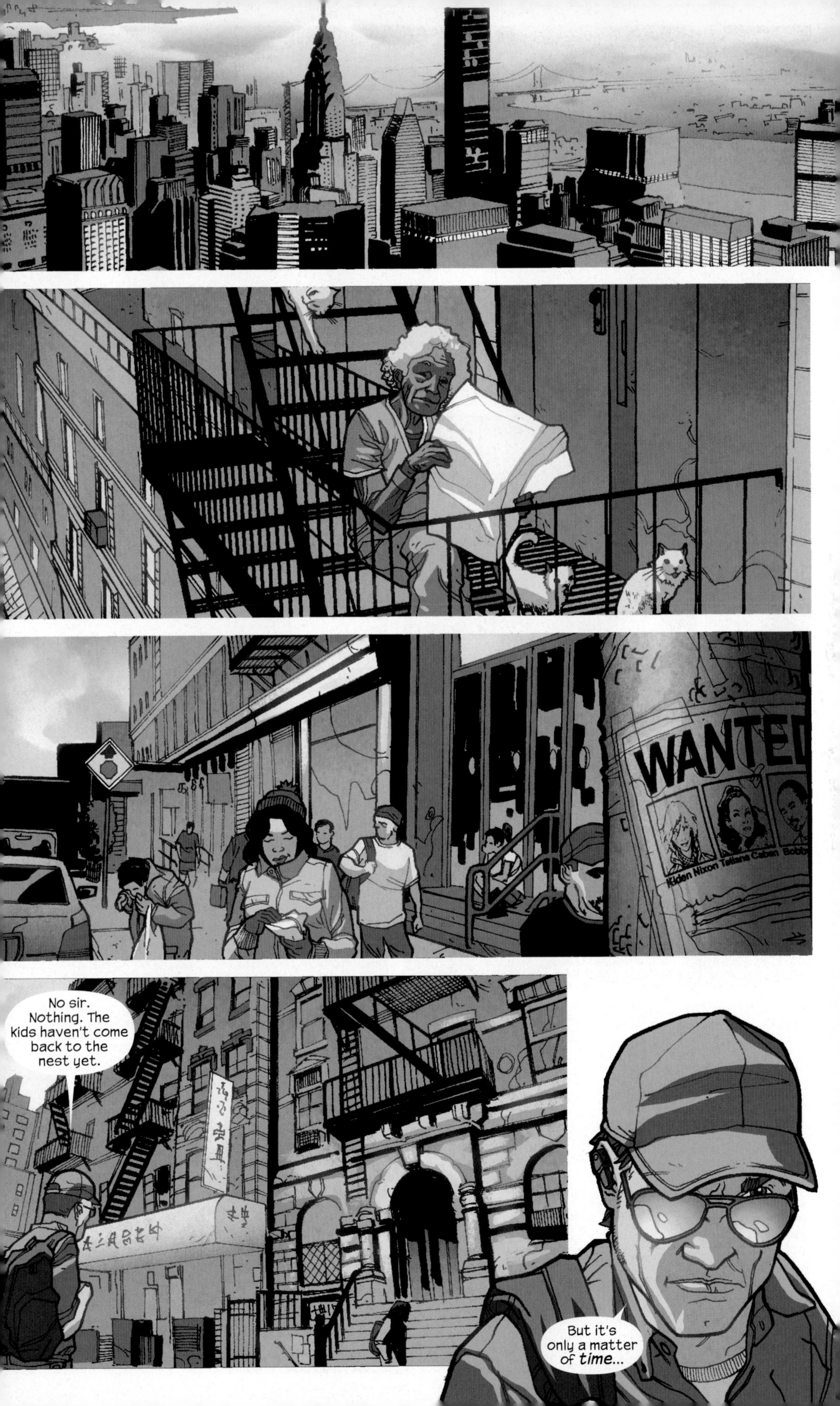

WANTED
Kiden Nixon
Tatiana Caban
Bobb
No sir. Nothing. The kids haven't come back to the nest yet.
But it's only a matter of *time*...

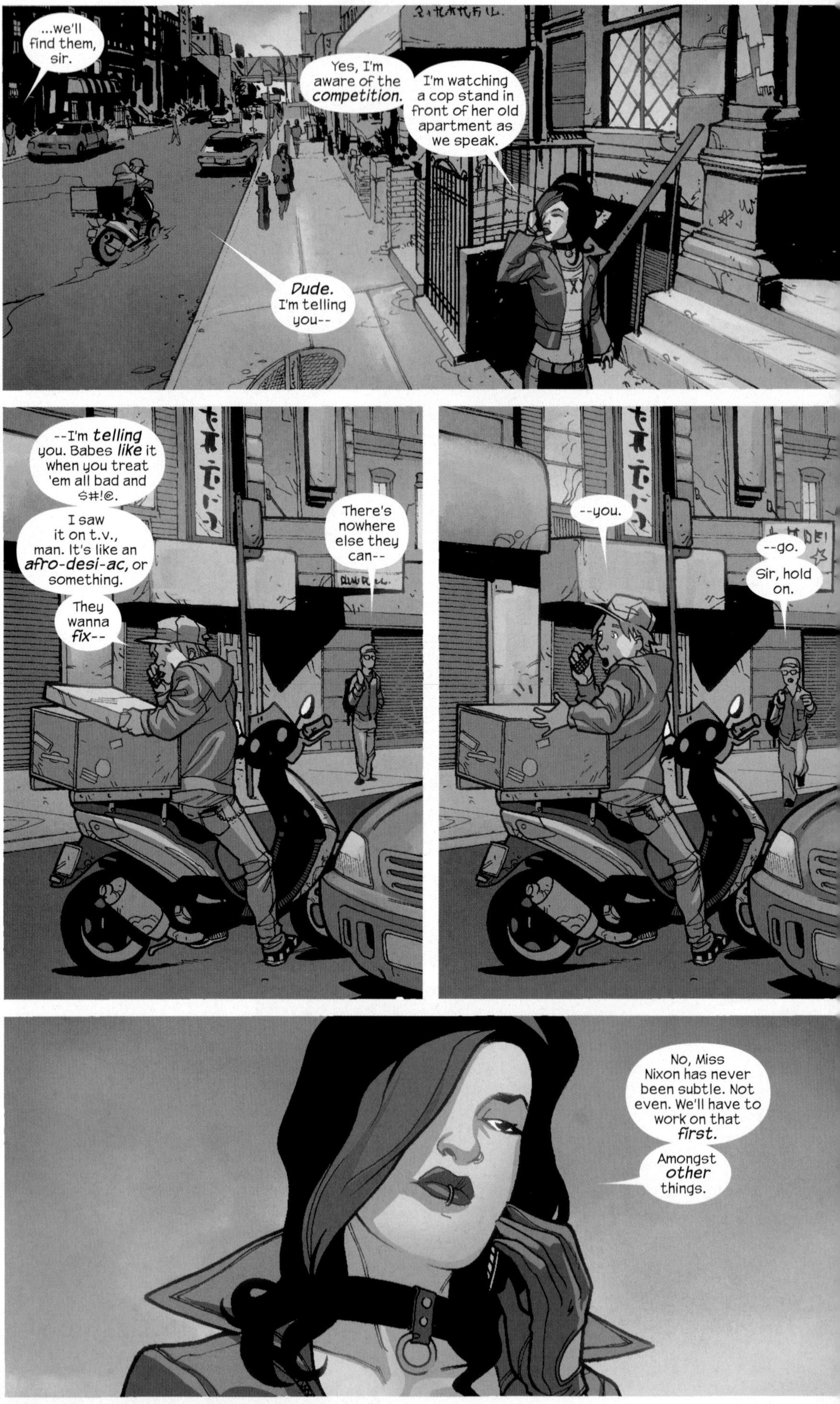
...we'll find them, sir.
Yes, I'm aware of the competition.
I'm watching a cop stand in front of her old apartment as we speak.
Dude. I'm telling you--
--I'm telling you. Babes like it when you treat 'em all bad and $#!@.
I saw it on t.v., man. It's like an afro-desi-ac, or something.
They wanna fix--
There's nowhere else they can--
--you.
--go.
Sir, hold on.
No, Miss Nixon has never been subtle. Not even. We'll have to work on that first.
Amongst other things.

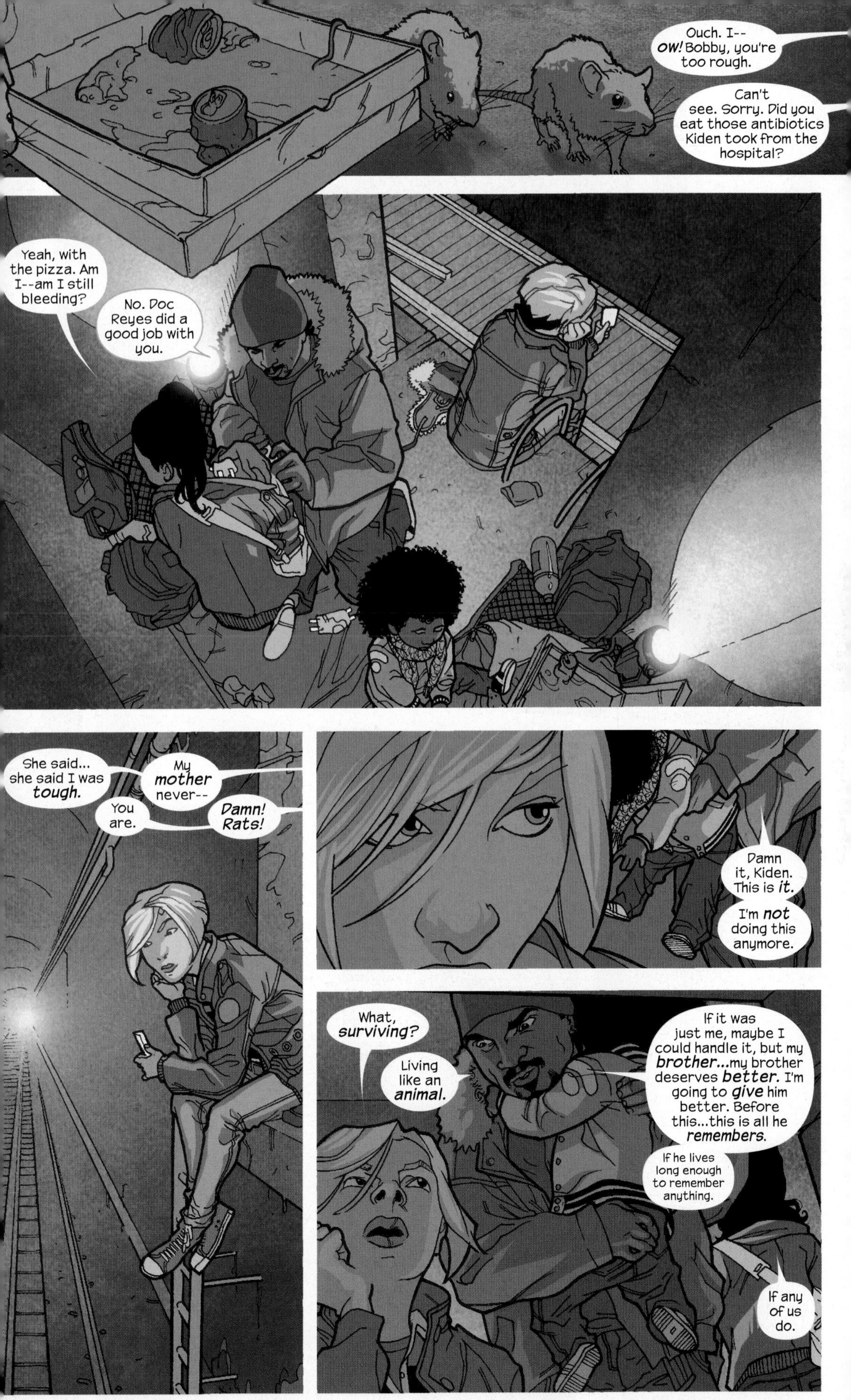
Ouch. I-- *OW!* Bobby, you're too rough.
Can't see. Sorry. Did you eat those antibiotics Kiden took from the hospital?
Yeah, with the pizza. Am I--am I still bleeding?
No. Doc Reyes did a good job with you.
She said... she said I was **tough.**
My **mother** never--
You are.
Damn! Rats!
Damn it, Kiden. This is *it.*
I'm **not** doing this anymore.
What, *surviving?*
Living like an *animal.*
If it was just me, maybe I could handle it, but my **brother...**my brother deserves **better**. I'm going to **give** him better. Before this...this is all he *remembers.*
If he lives long enough to remember anything.
If any of us do.

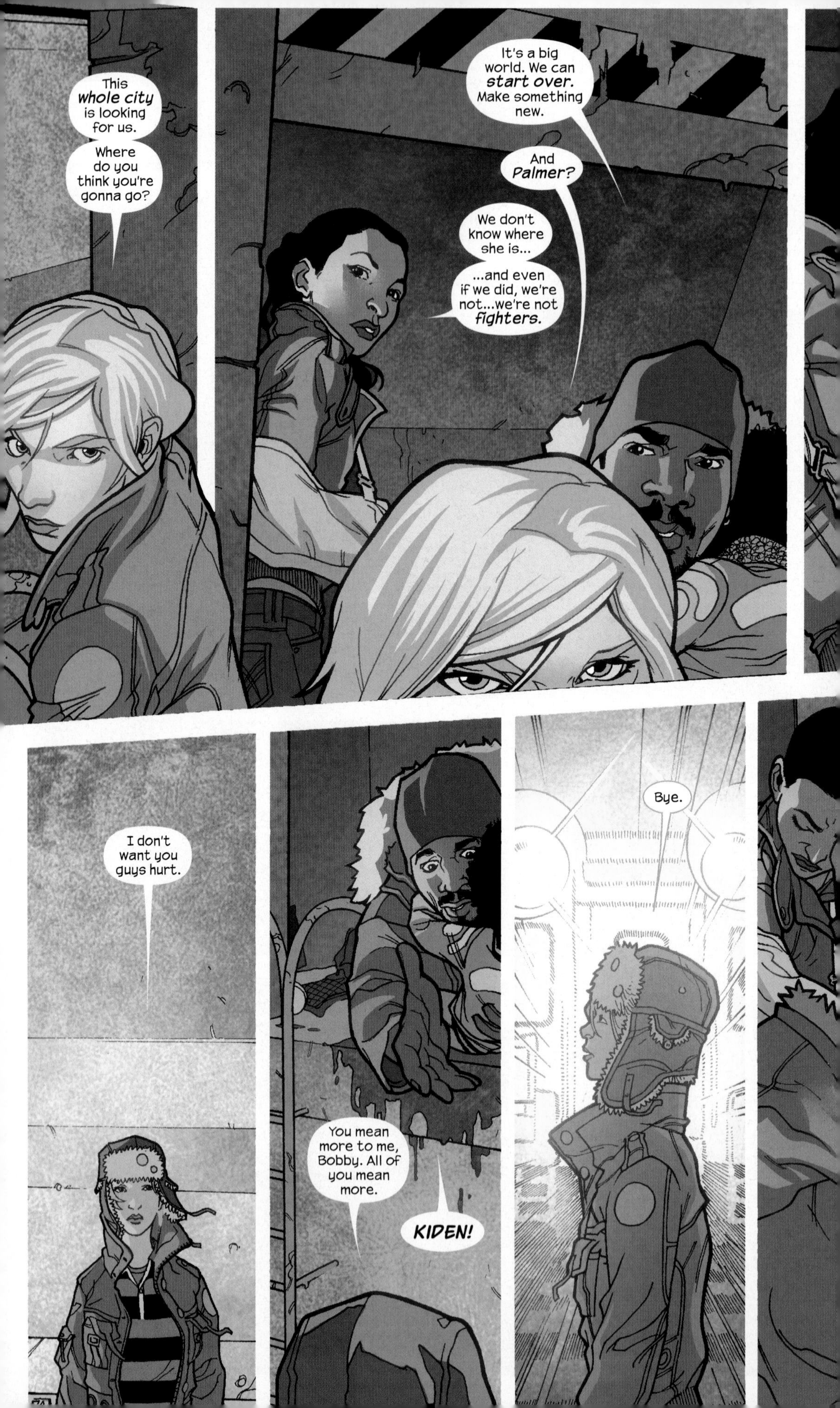
This whole city is looking for us.
Where do you think you're gonna go?
It's a big world. We can start over. Make something new.
And Palmer?
We don't know where she is...
...and even if we did, we're not...we're not fighters.
I don't want you guys hurt.
You mean more to me, Bobby. All of you mean more.
KIDEN!
Bye.

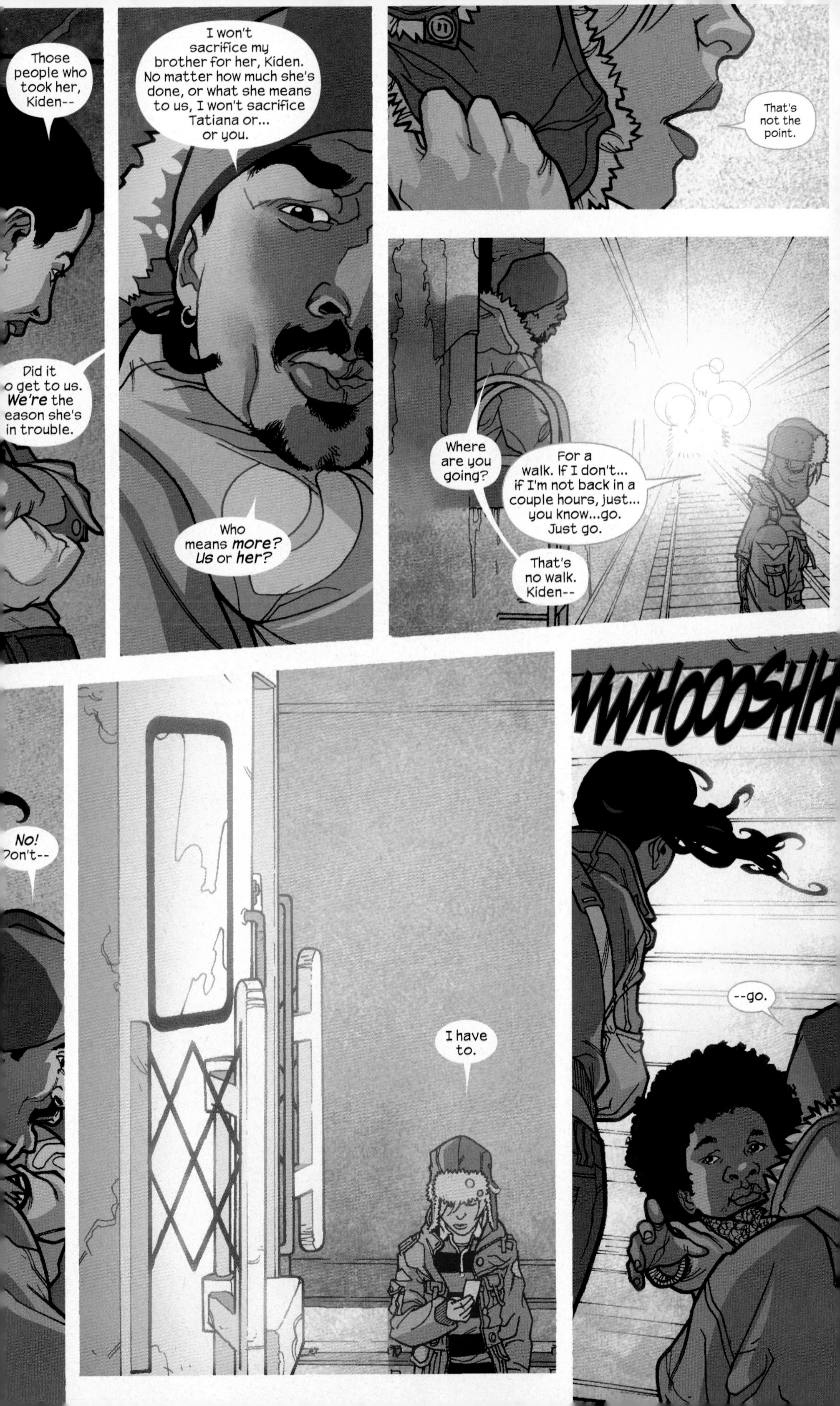

Those people who took her, Kiden--
I won't sacrifice my brother for her, Kiden. No matter how much she's done, or what she means to us, I won't sacrifice Tatiana or... or you.
That's not the point.
Did it o get to us. *We're* the eason she's in trouble.
Who means *more*? *Us* or *her*?
Where are you going?
For a walk. If I don't... if I'm not back in a couple hours, just... you know...go. Just go.
That's no walk. Kiden--
No! Don't--
I have to.
WHOOOSHH
--go.

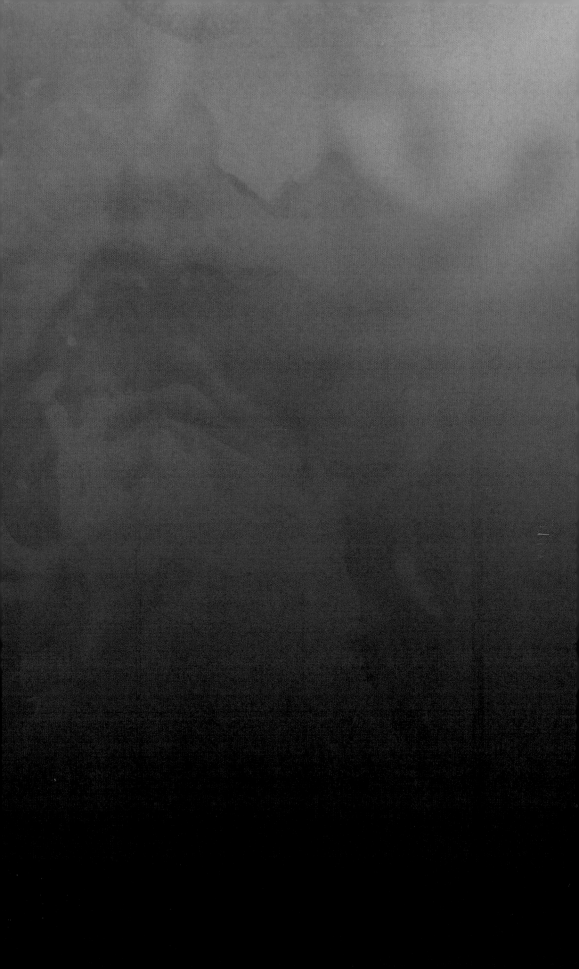

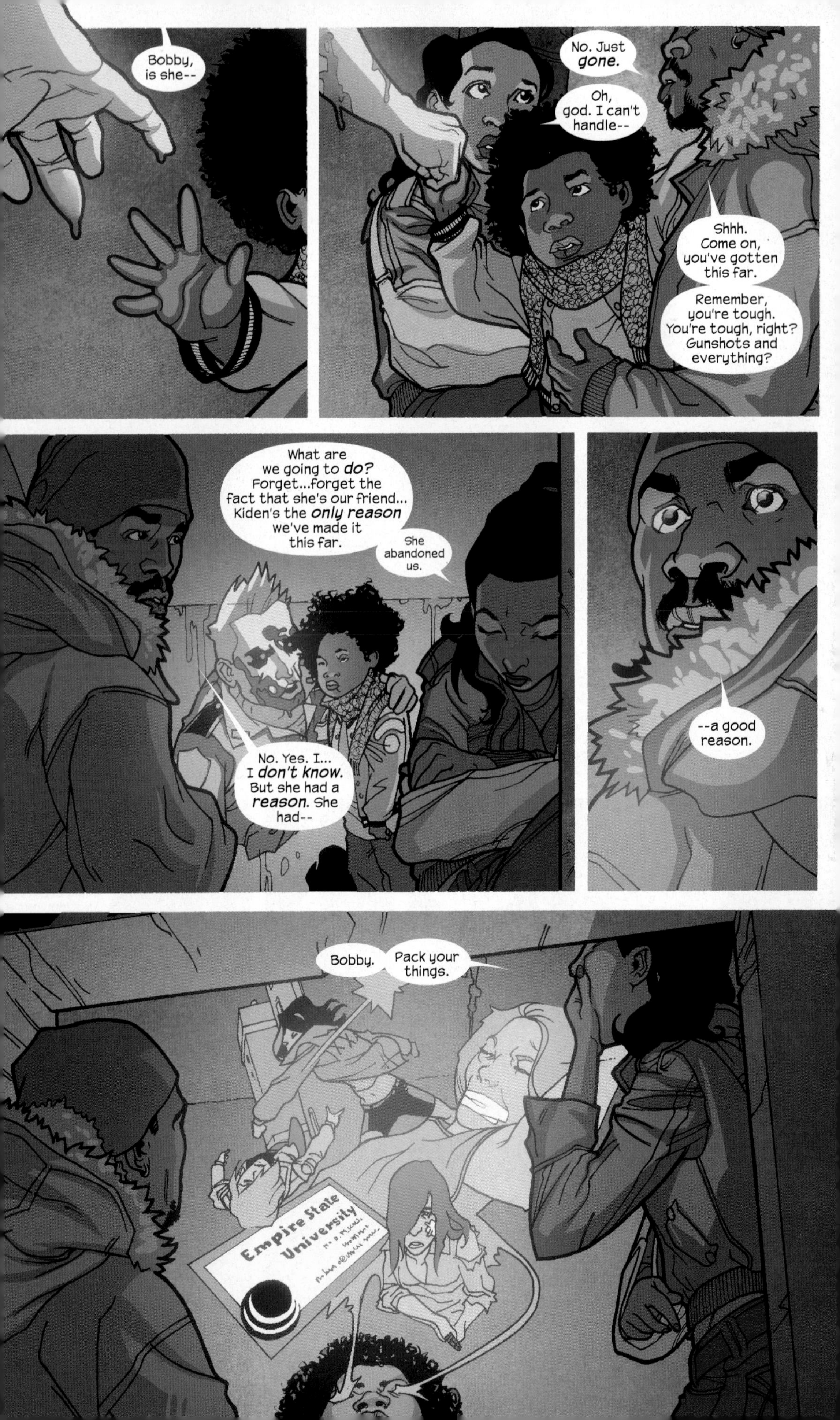

Bobby, is she--
No. Just gone.
Oh, god. I can't handle--
Shhh. Come on, you've gotten this far.
Remember, you're tough. You're tough, right? Gunshots and everything?
What are we going to do? Forget...forget the fact that she's our friend... Kiden's the only reason we've made it this far.
She abandoned us.
No. Yes. I... I don't know. But she had a reason. She had--
--a good reason.
Bobby.
Pack your things.
Empire State University

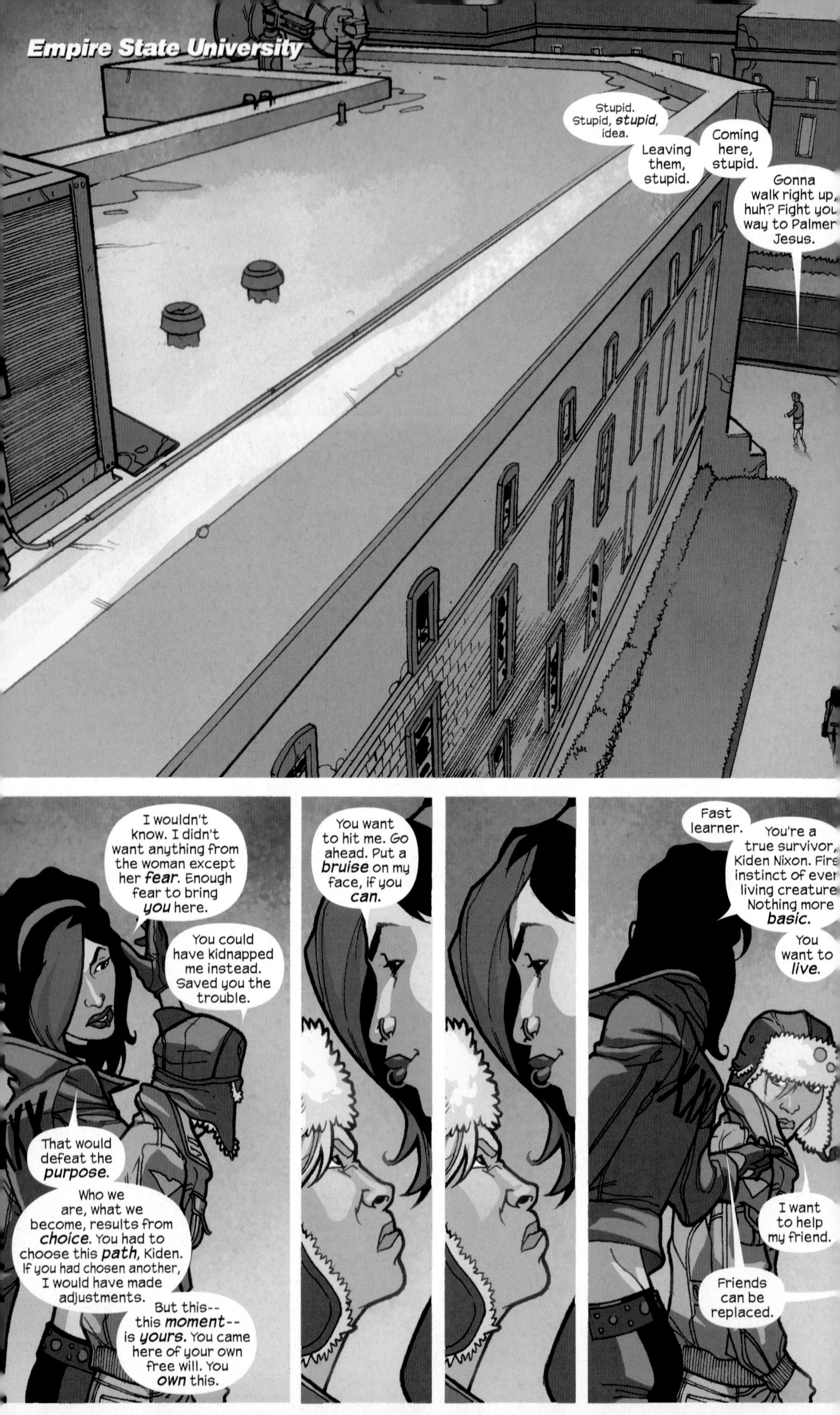
Empire State University
Stupid. Stupid, *stupid*, idea.
Leaving them, stupid.
Coming here, stupid.
Gonna walk right up, huh? Fight you way to Palmer Jesus.
I wouldn't know. I didn't want anything from the woman except her *fear*. Enough fear to bring *you* here.
You could have kidnapped me instead. Saved you the trouble.
That would defeat the *purpose*.
Who we are, what we become, results from *choice*. You had to choose this *path*, Kiden. If you had chosen another, I would have made adjustments.
But this-- this *moment*-- is *yours*. You came here of your own free will. You *own* this.
You want to hit me. Go ahead. Put a *bruise* on my face, if you *can*.
Fast learner.
You're a true survivor, Kiden Nixon. Fire instinct of ever living creature Nothing more *basic*.
You want to *live*.
I want to help my friend.
Friends can be replaced.

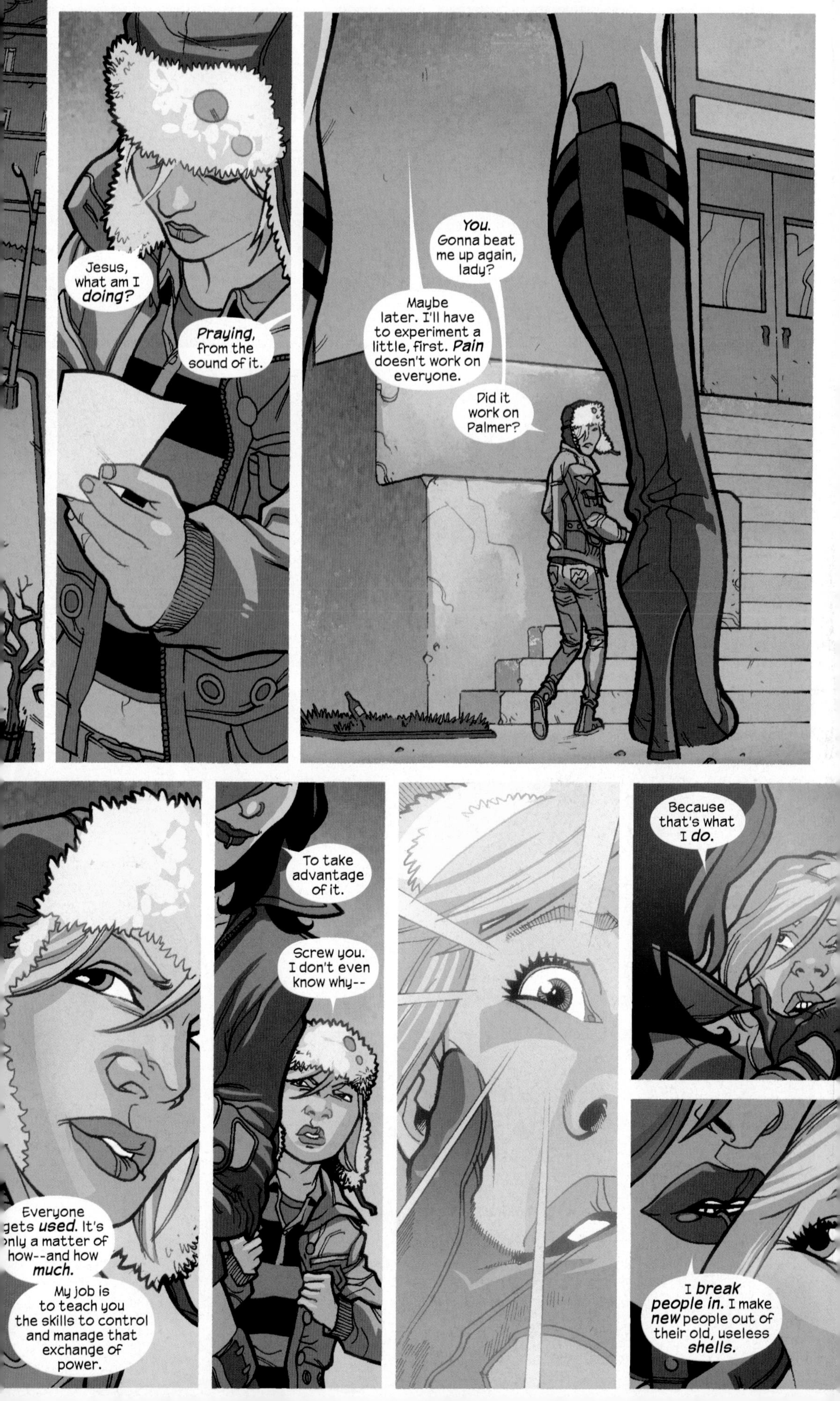

Jesus, what am I *doing?*
Praying, from the sound of it.
You. Gonna beat me up again, lady?
Maybe later. I'll have to experiment a little, first. *Pain* doesn't work on everyone.
Did it work on Palmer?
Everyone gets *used.* It's only a matter of how--and how *much.*
My job is to teach you the skills to control and manage that exchange of power.
To take advantage of it.
Screw you. I don't even know why--
Because that's what I *do.*
I *break people in.* I make *new* people out of their old, useless *shells.*

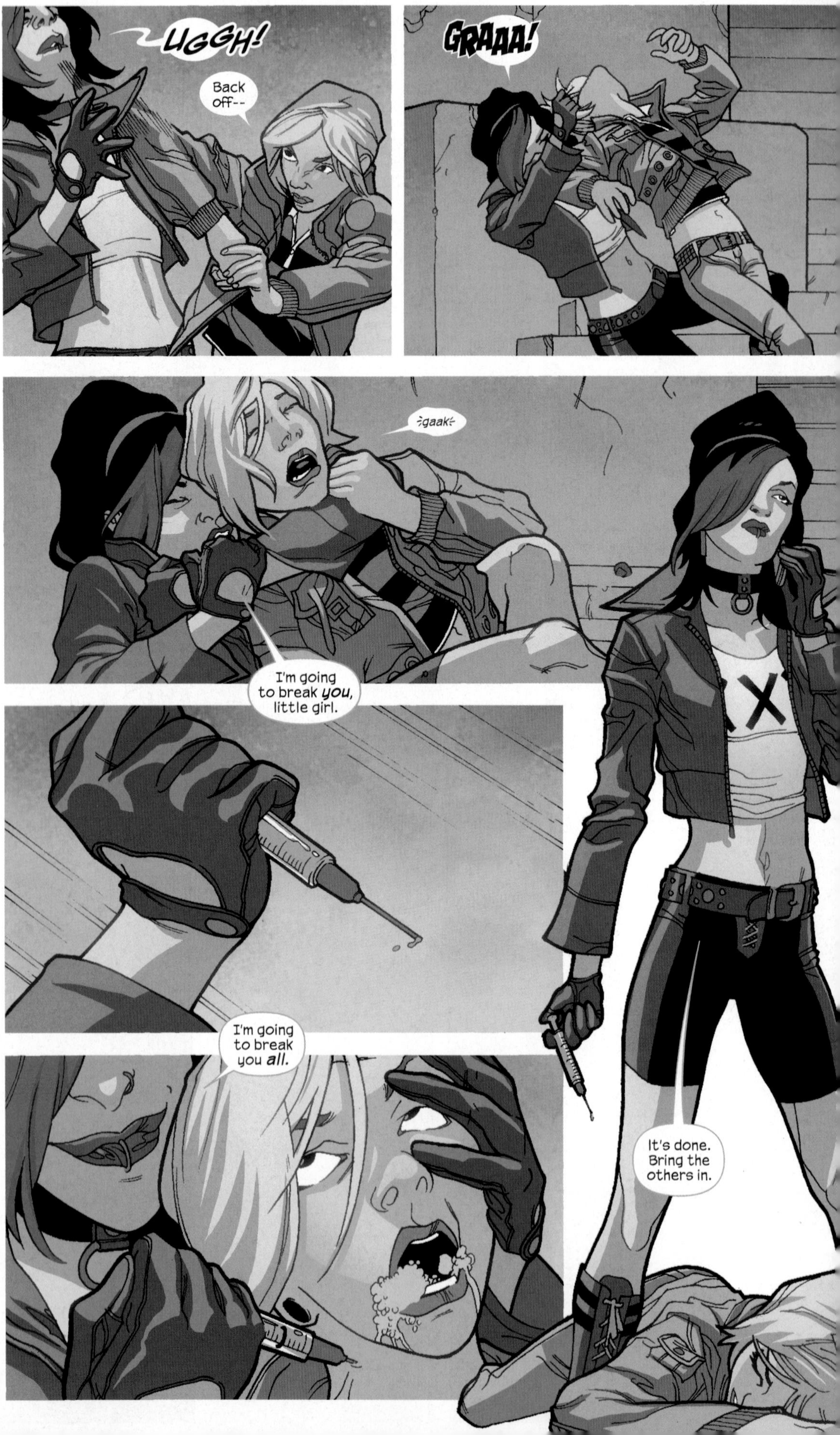
UGGH!
Back off--
GRAAA!
gaak
I'm going to break you, little girl.
I'm going to break you all.
It's done. Bring the others in.

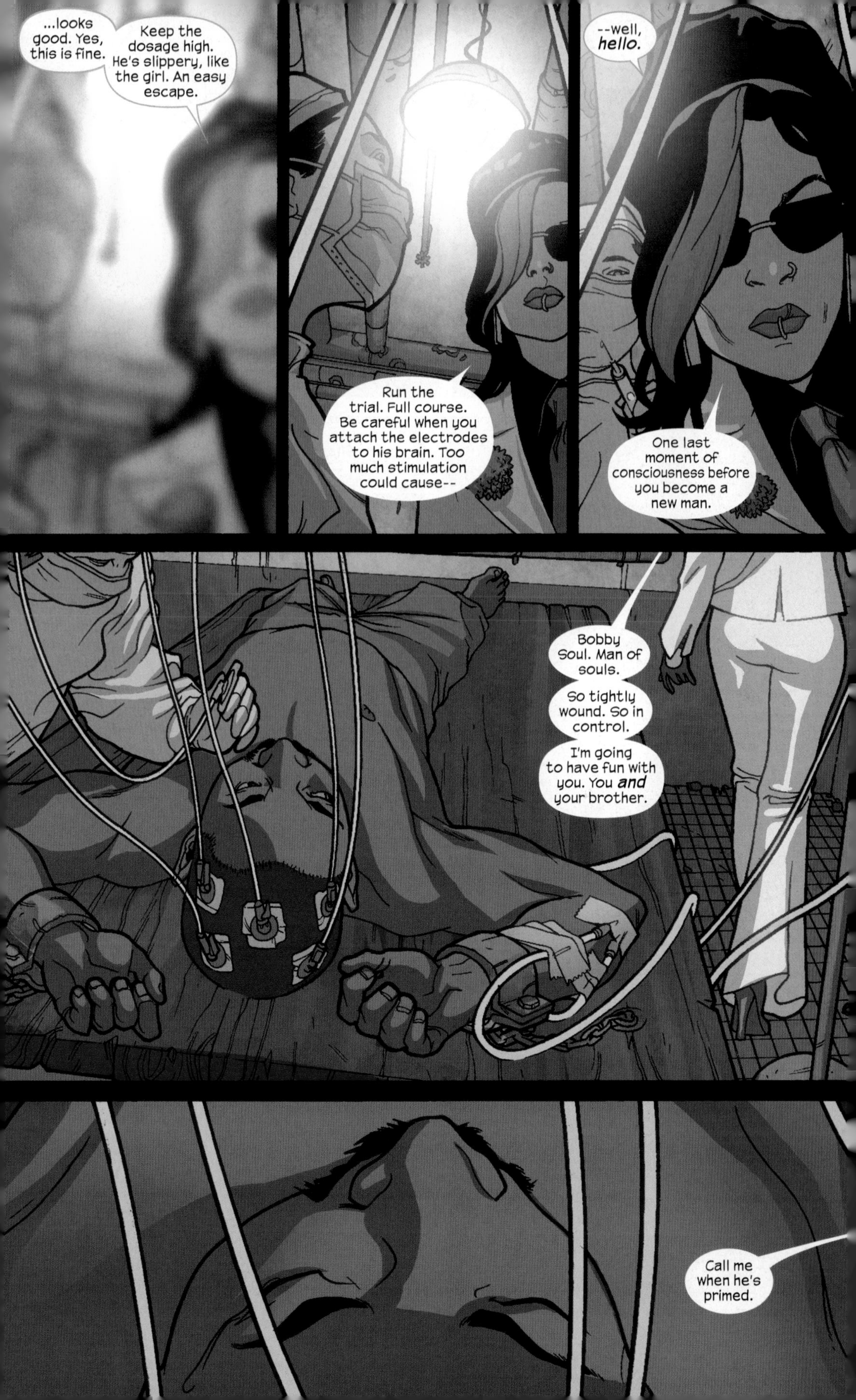
...looks good. Yes, this is fine.
Keep the dosage high. He's slippery, like the girl. An easy escape.
Run the trial. Full course. Be careful when you attach the electrodes to his brain. Too much stimulation could cause--
--well, *hello.*
One last moment of consciousness before you become a new man.
Bobby Soul. Man of souls.
So tightly wound. So in control.
I'm going to have fun with you. You *and* your brother.
Call me when he's primed.

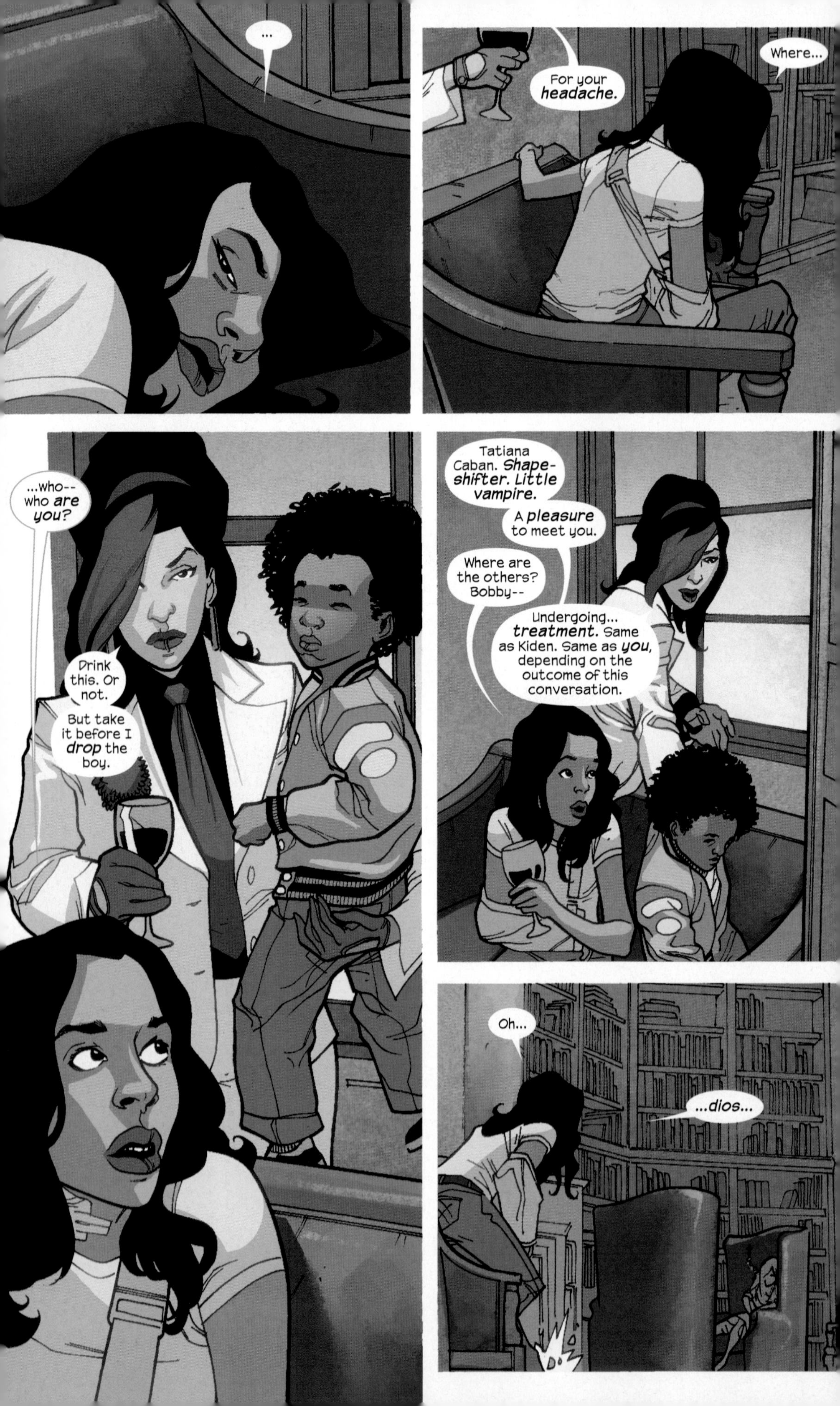

...
For your headache.
Where...
...who-- who are you?
Drink this. Or not.
But take it before I drop the boy.
Tatiana Caban. Shape-shifter. Little vampire.
A pleasure to meet you.
Where are the others? Bobby--
Undergoing... treatment. Same as Kiden. Same as you, depending on the outcome of this conversation.
Oh...
...dios...

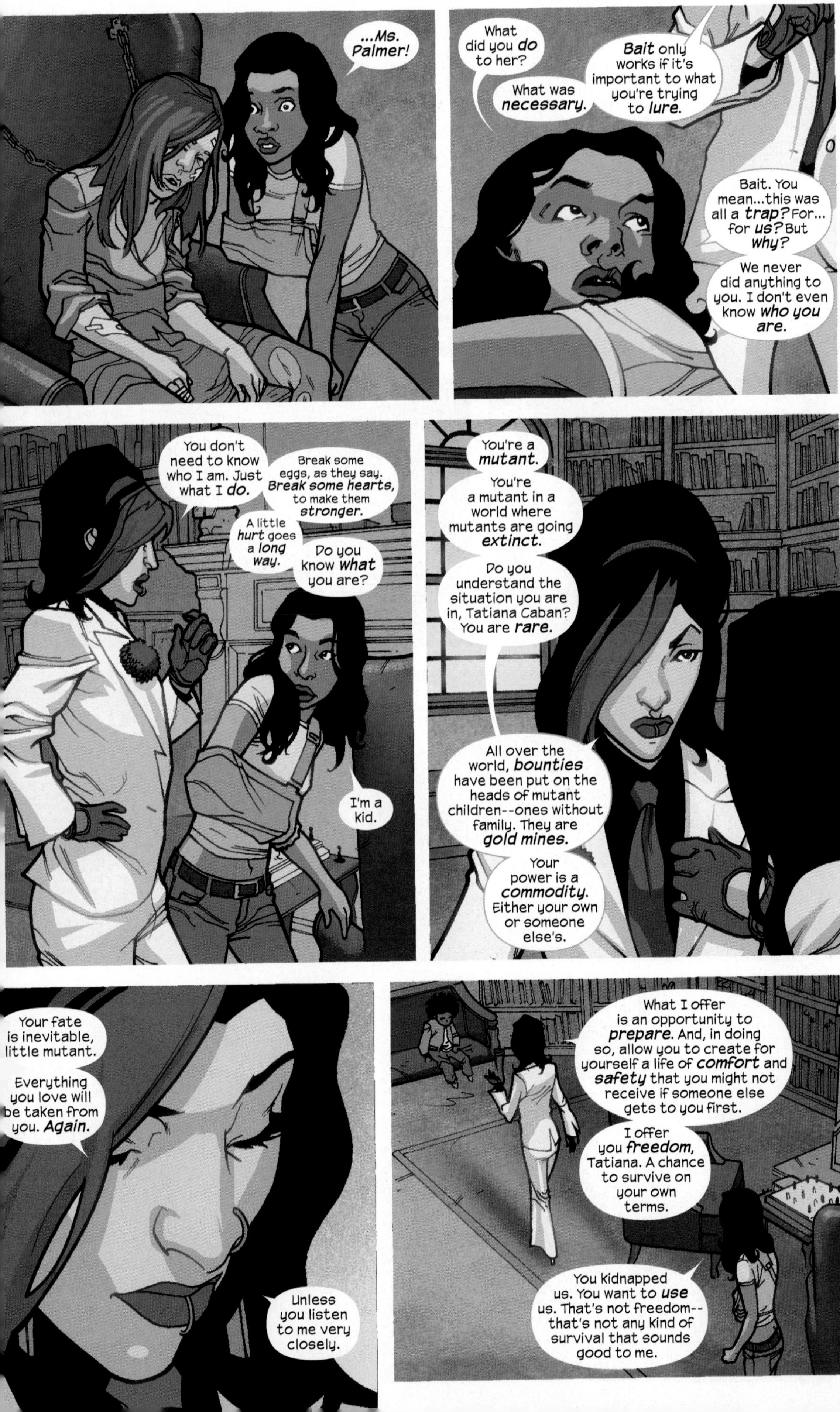
...Ms. Palmer!
What did you do to her?
What was necessary.
Bait only works if it's important to what you're trying to lure.
Bait. You mean...this was all a trap? For... for us? But why?
We never did anything to you. I don't even know who you are.
You don't need to know who I am. Just what I do.
Break some eggs, as they say. Break some hearts, to make them stronger.
A little hurt goes a long way.
Do you know what you are?
I'm a kid.
You're a mutant.
You're a mutant in a world where mutants are going extinct.
Do you understand the situation you are in, Tatiana Caban? You are rare.
All over the world, bounties have been put on the heads of mutant children--ones without family. They are gold mines.
Your power is a commodity. Either your own or someone else's.
Your fate is inevitable, little mutant.
Everything you love will be taken from you. Again.
Unless you listen to me very closely.
What I offer is an opportunity to prepare. And, in doing so, allow you to create for yourself a life of comfort and safety that you might not receive if someone else gets to you first.
I offer you freedom, Tatiana. A chance to survive on your own terms.
You kidnapped us. You want to use us. That's not freedom--that's not any kind of survival that sounds good to me.

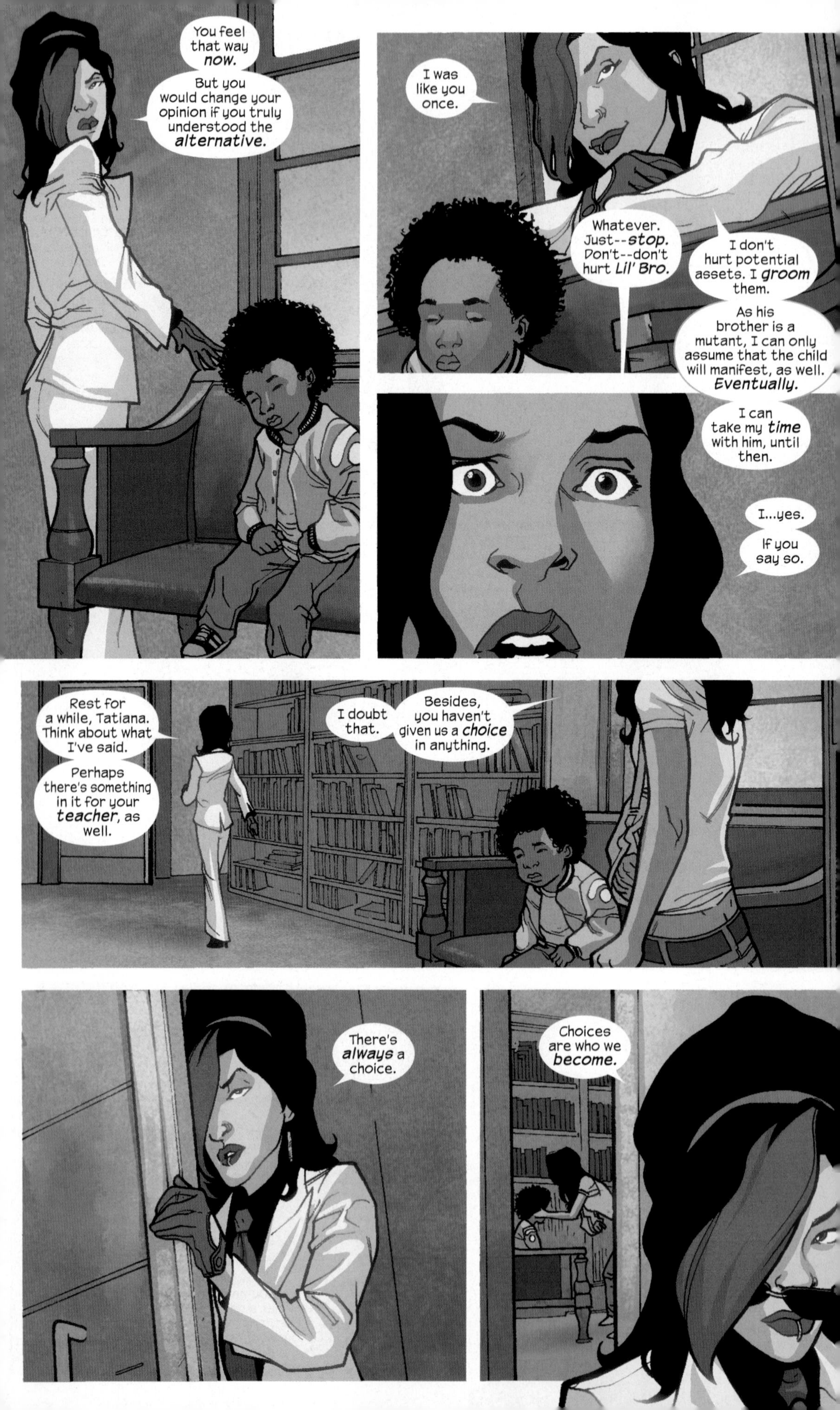
You feel that way *now.*
But you would change your opinion if you truly understood the *alternative.*
I was like you once.
Whatever. Just--*stop.* Don't--don't hurt *Lil' Bro.*
I don't hurt potential assets. I *groom* them.
As his brother is a mutant, I can only assume that the child will manifest, as well. *Eventually.*
I can take my *time* with him, until then.
I...yes.
If you say so.
Rest for a while, Tatiana. Think about what I've said.
Perhaps there's something in it for your *teacher*, as well.
I doubt that.
Besides, you haven't given us a *choice* in anything.
There's *always* a choice.
Choices are who we *become.*

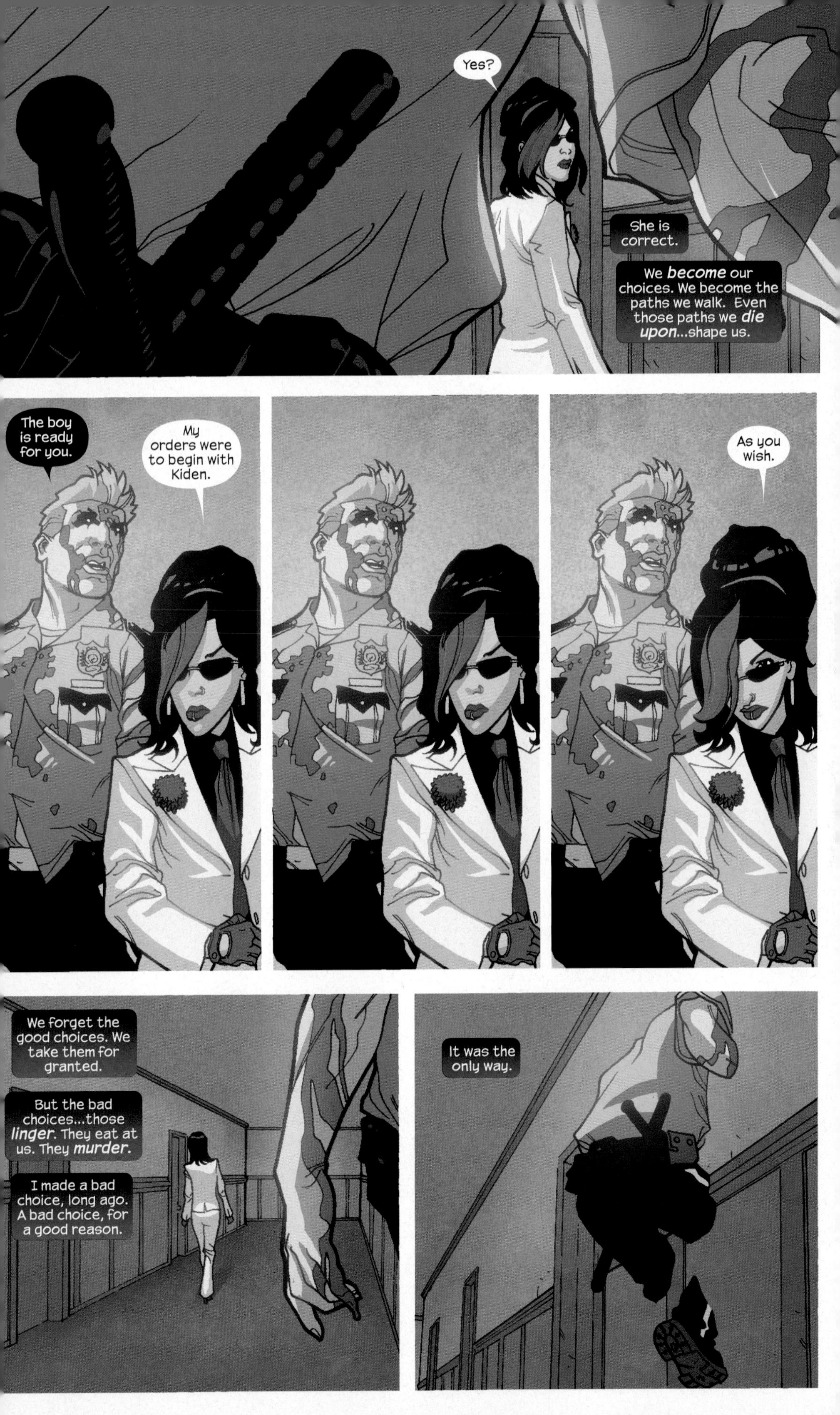

Yes?
She is correct.
We **become** our choices. We become the paths we walk. Even those paths we **die upon**...shape us.
The boy is ready for you.
My orders were to begin with Kiden.
As you wish.
We forget the good choices. We take them for granted.
But the bad choices...those **linger**. They eat at us. They **murder**.
I made a bad choice, long ago. A bad choice, for a good reason.
It was the only way.

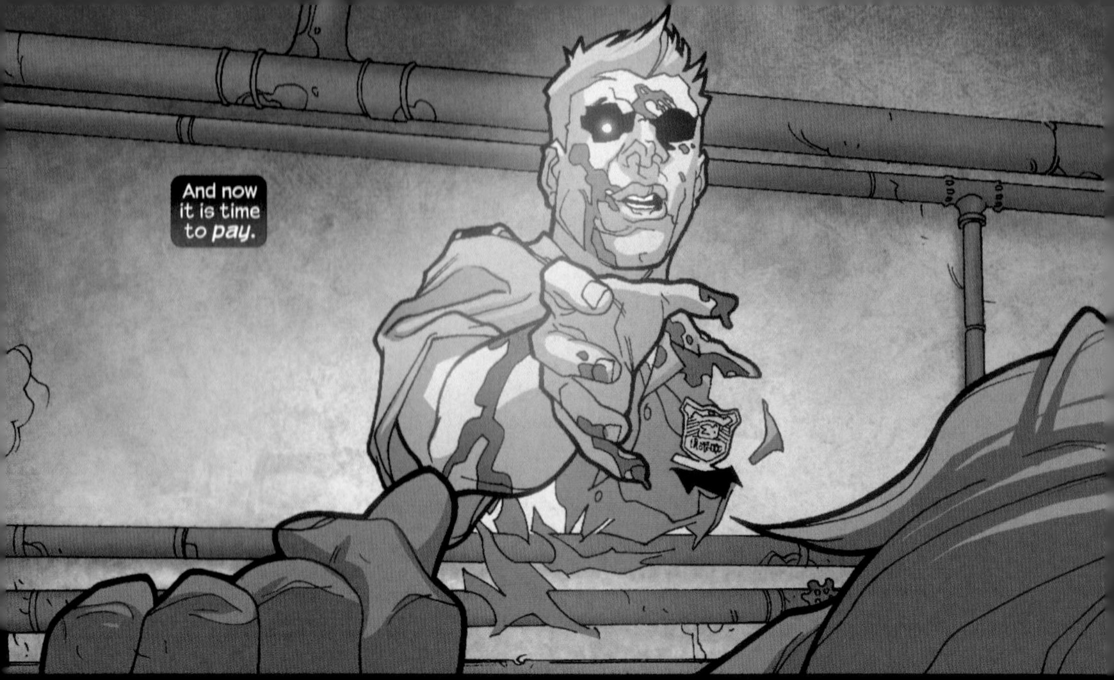
And now it is time to *pay*.

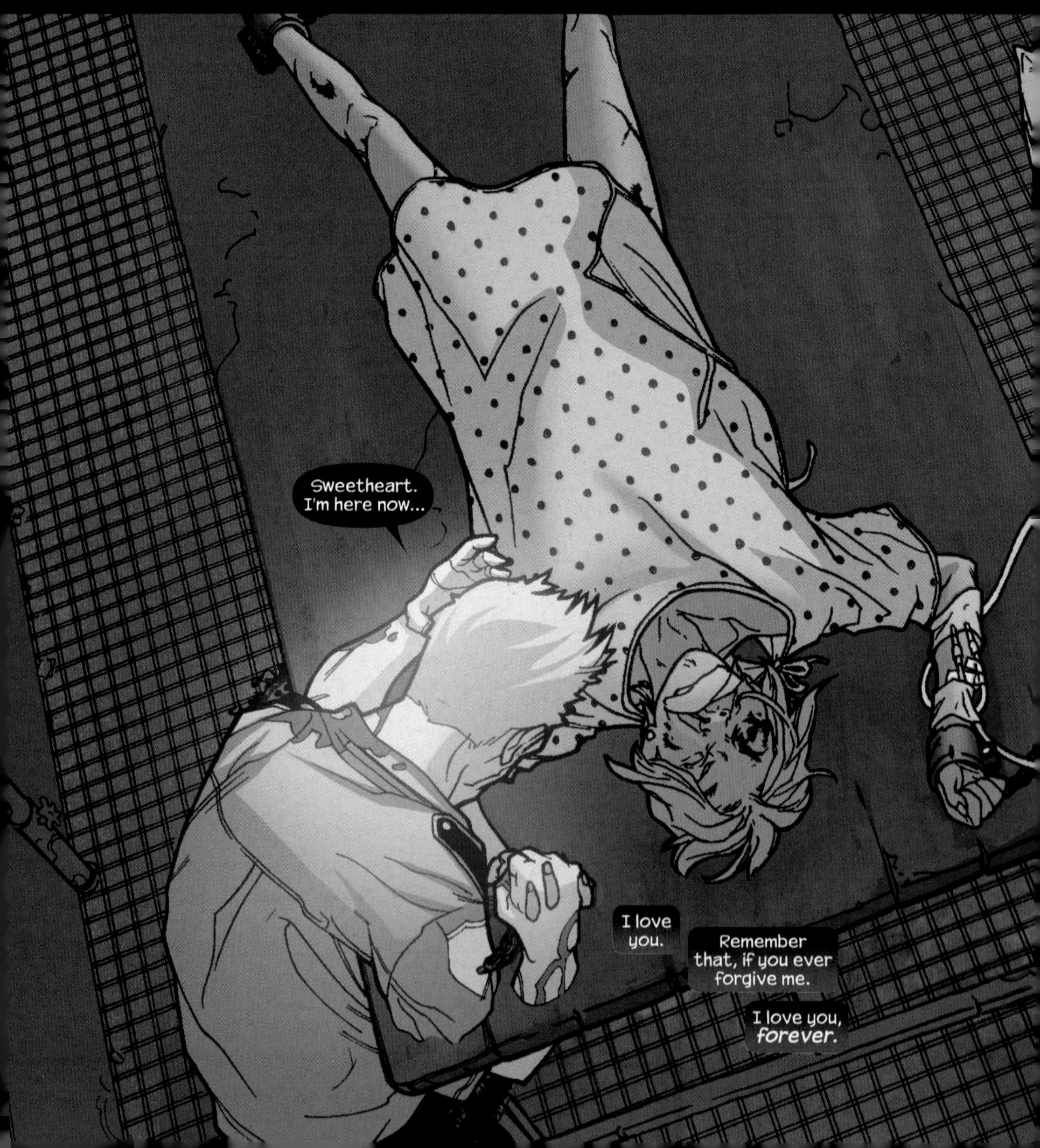
Sweetheart. I'm here now...
I love you.
Remember that, if you ever forgive me.
I love you, *forever*.

SIX

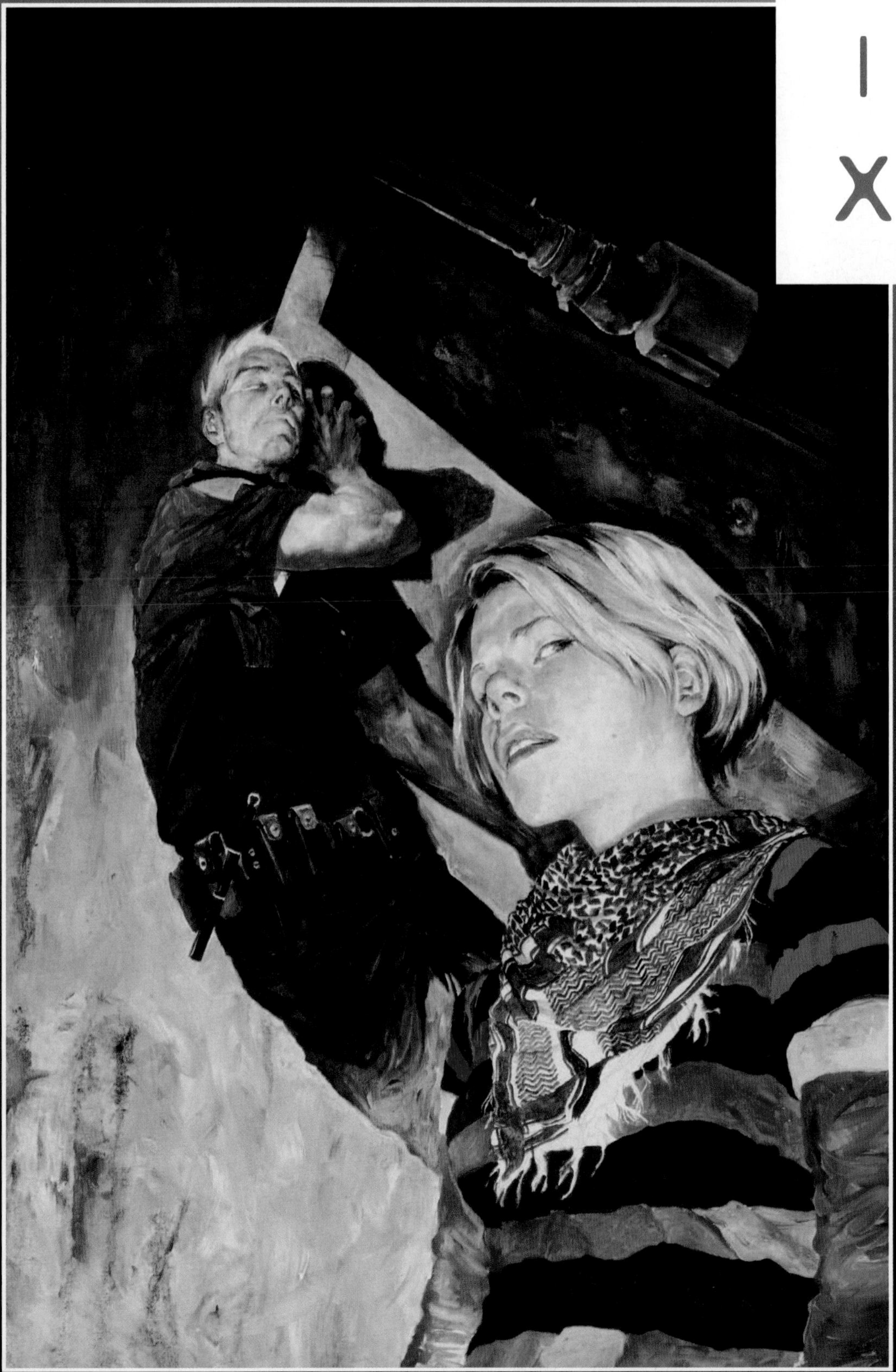

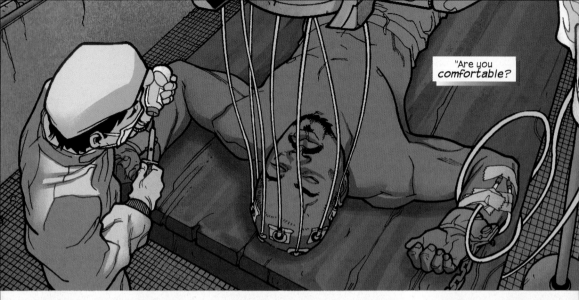

"Are you *comfortable?*

"Perhaps some refreshments, before we start...

"Tea? Soda? Some *cocaine?*

"Yes, I was teasing. *Such* a tease.

"So...don't be *shy*.

"Really, do sit down.

"Sit. *Down.*

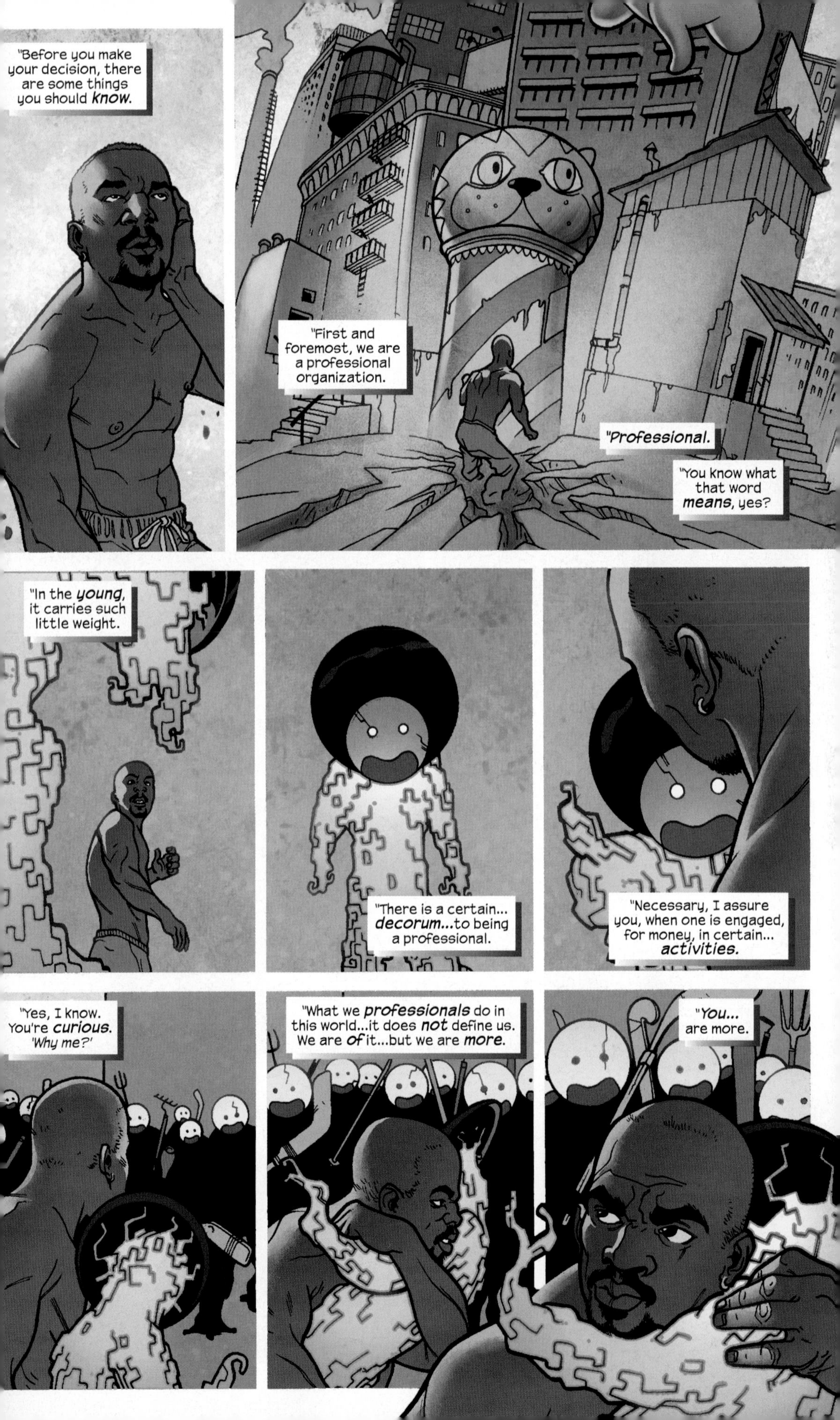
"Before you make your decision, there are some things you should *know*.
"First and foremost, we are a professional organization.
"*Professional.*
"You know what that word *means*, yes?
"In the *young*, it carries such little weight.
"There is a certain... *decorum*...to being a professional.
"Necessary, I assure you, when one is engaged, for money, in certain... *activities.*
"Yes, I know. You're *curious*. *'Why me?'*
"What we *professionals* do in this world...it does *not* define us. We are *of* it...but we are *more*.
"*You*... are more.

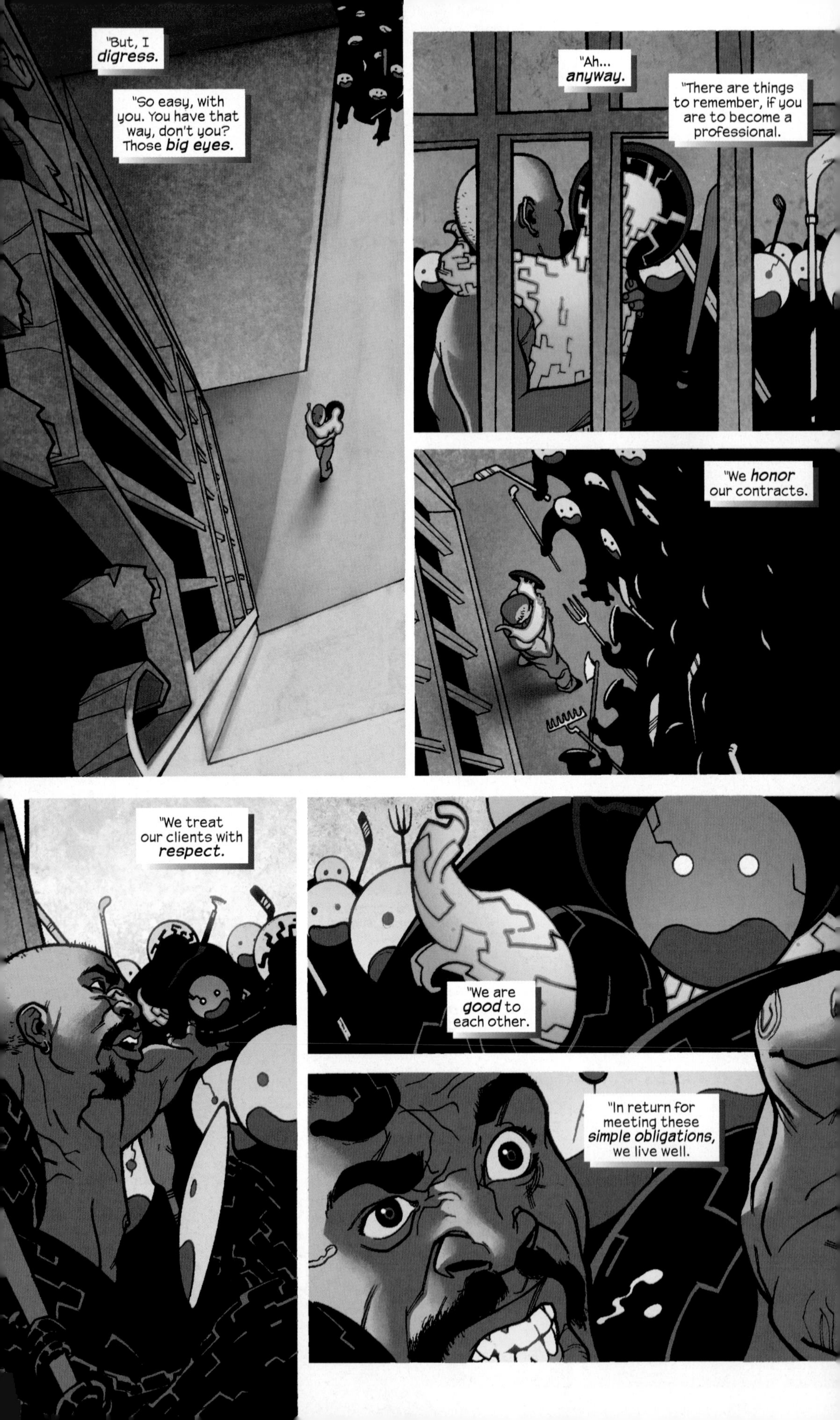
"But, I *digress*.
"So easy, with you. You have that way, don't you? Those *big eyes*.
"Ah... *anyway*.
"There are things to remember, if you are to become a professional.
"We *honor* our contracts.
"We treat our clients with *respect*.
"We are *good* to each other.
"In return for meeting these *simple obligations*, we live well.

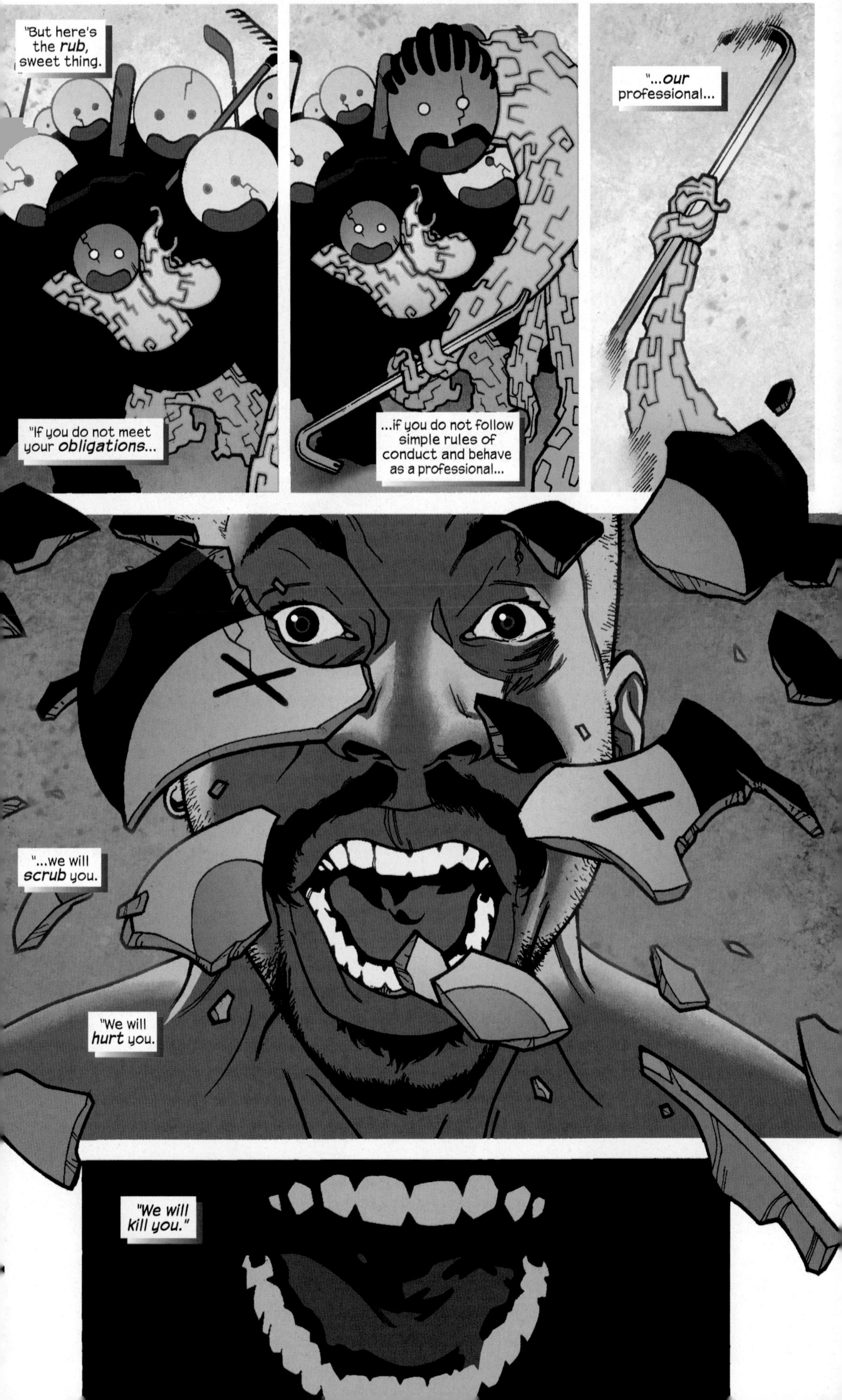
"But here's the *rub*, sweet thing.
"If you do not meet your *obligations*...
...if you do not follow simple rules of conduct and behave as a professional...
"...*our* professional...
"...we will *scrub* you.
"We will *hurt* you.
"We will kill you."

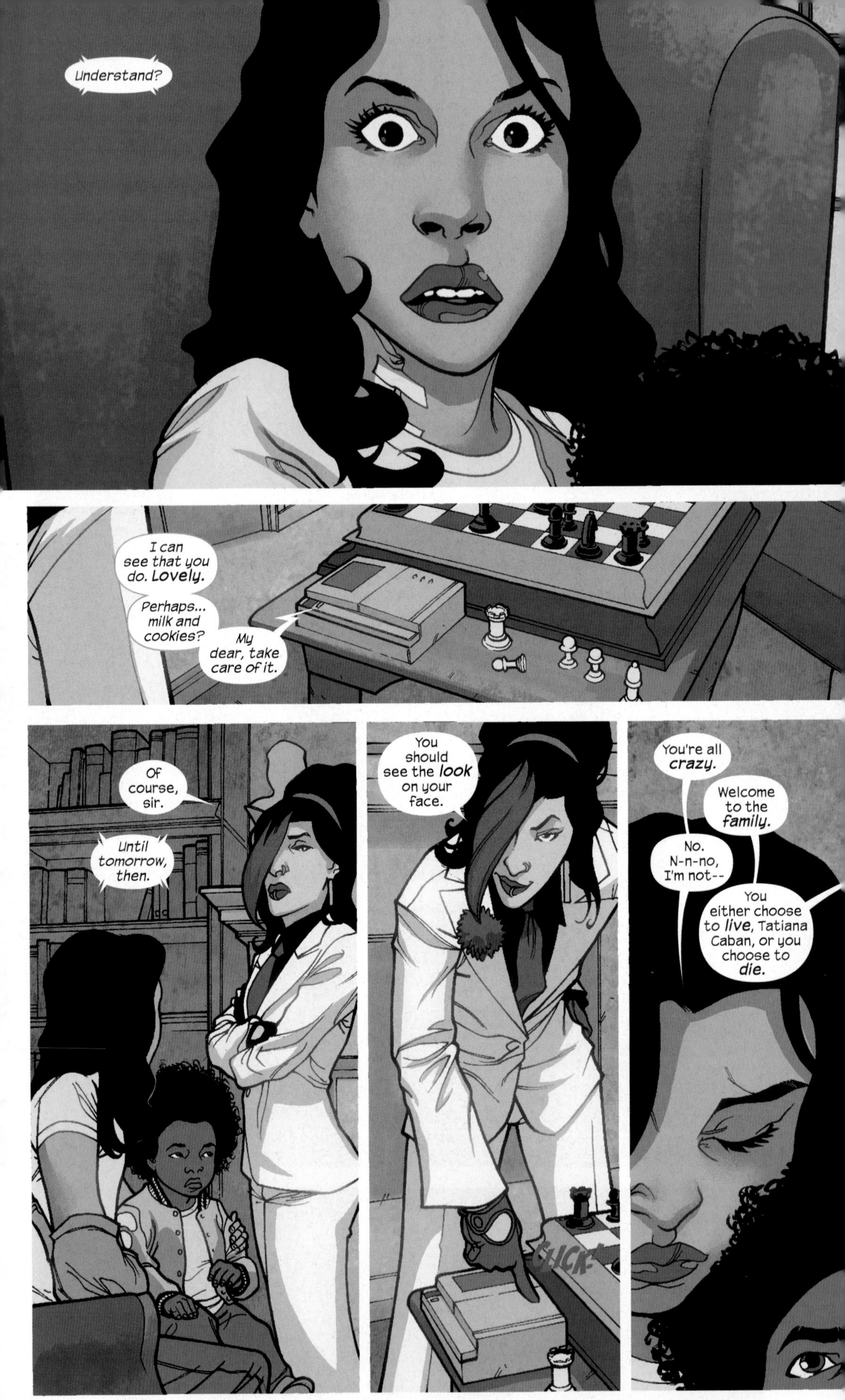

Understand?
I can see that you do. Lovely.
Perhaps... milk and cookies?
My dear, take care of it.
Of course, sir.
Until tomorrow, then.
You should see the look on your face.
CLICK
You're all crazy.
Welcome to the family.
No. N-n-no, I'm not--
You either choose to live, Tatiana Caban, or you choose to die.

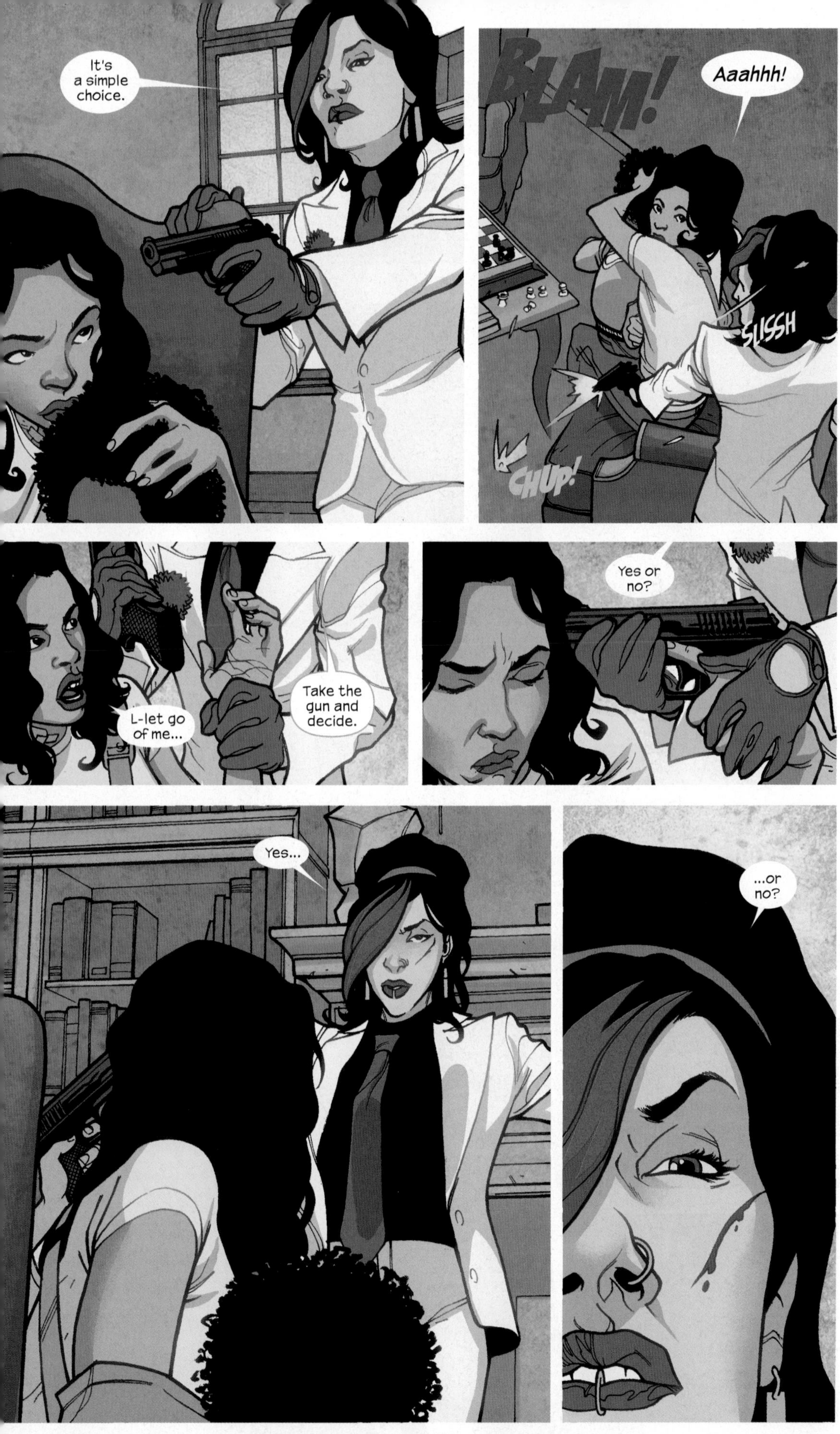
It's a simple choice.
BLAM!
Aaahhh!
SLISSH
CHUP!
L-let go of me...
Take the gun and decide.
Yes or no?
Yes...
...or no?

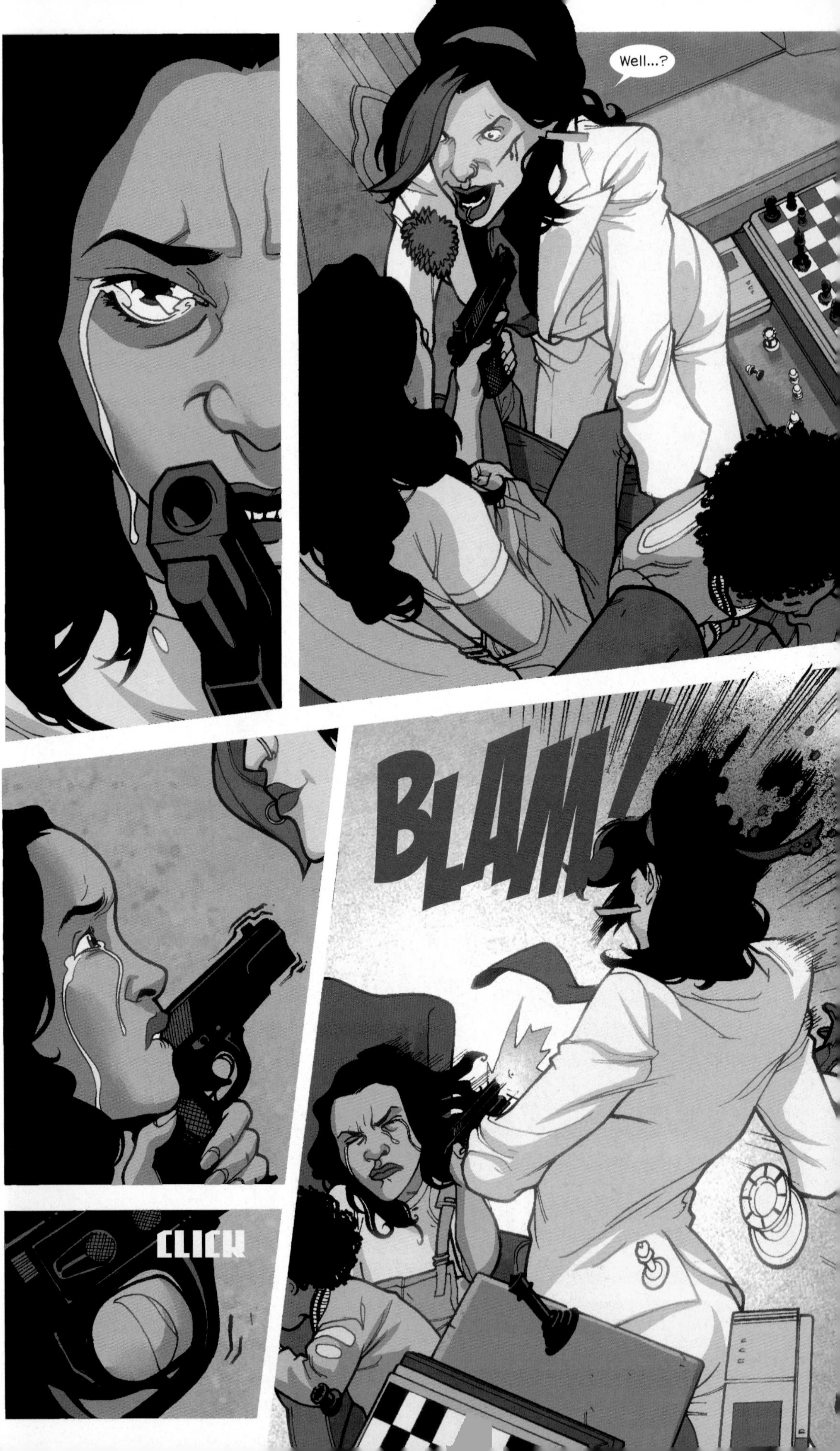
Well...?
CLICK
BLAM!

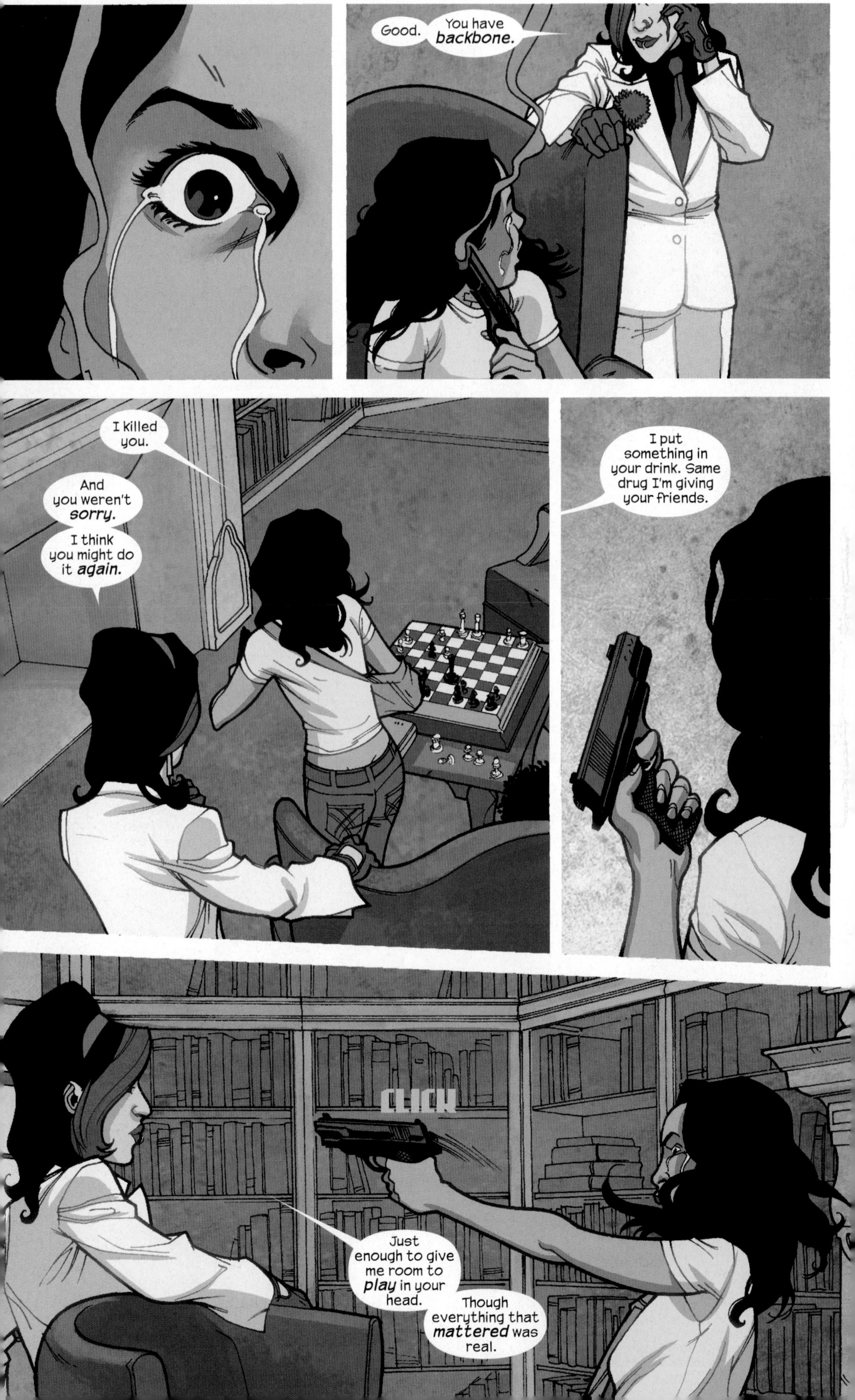
Good.
You have *backbone.*
I killed you.
And you weren't *sorry.*
I think you might do it *again.*
I put something in your drink. Same drug I'm giving your friends.
CLICK
Just enough to give me room to *play* in your head.
Though everything that *mattered* was real.

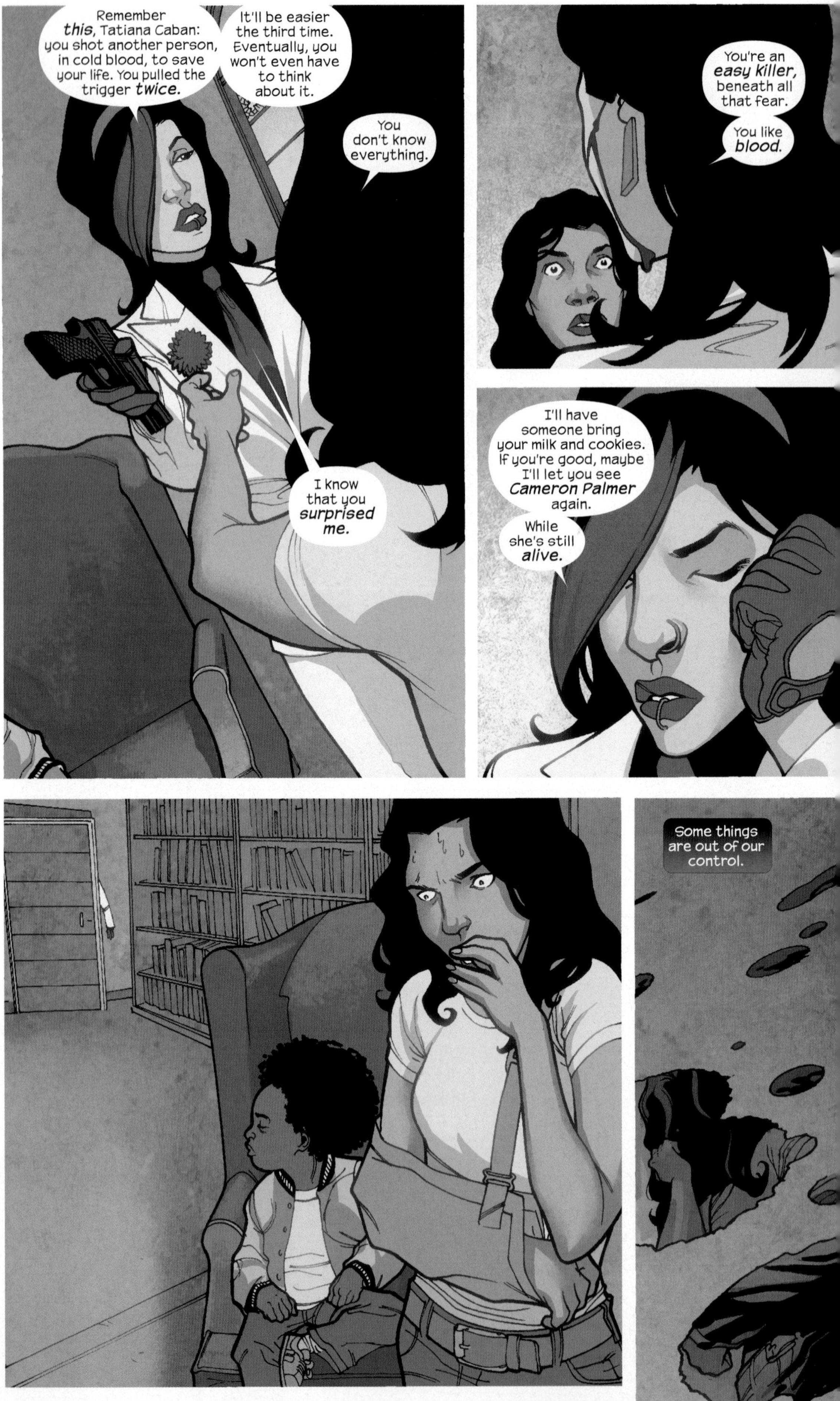

Remember *this*, Tatiana Caban: you shot another person, in cold blood, to save your life. You pulled the trigger *twice.*
It'll be easier the third time. Eventually, you won't even have to think about it.
You don't know everything.
I know that you *surprised me.*
You're an *easy killer,* beneath all that fear.
You like *blood.*
I'll have someone bring your milk and cookies. If you're good, maybe I'll let you see *Cameron Palmer* again.
While she's still *alive.*
Some things are out of our control.

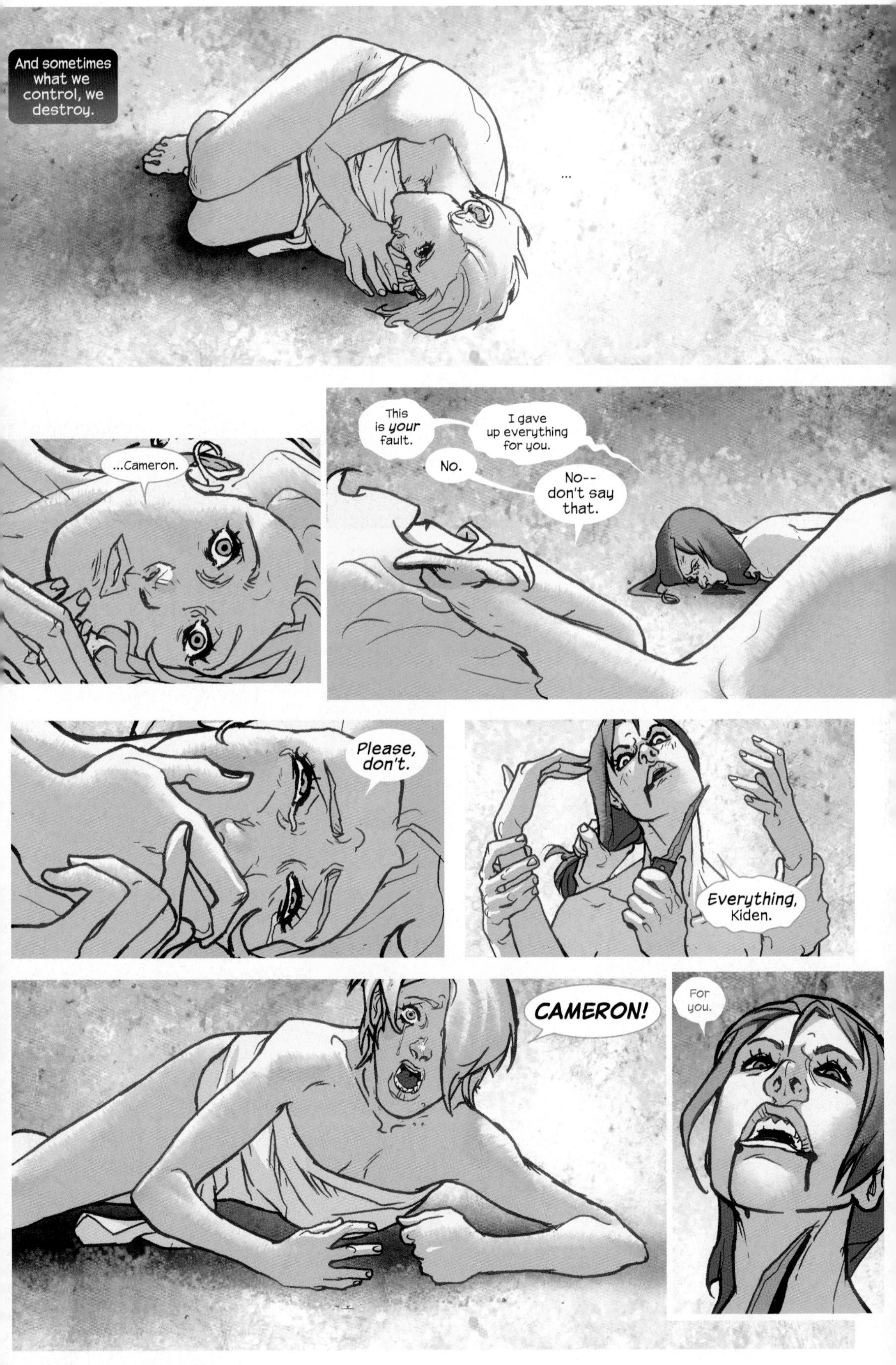

And sometimes what we control, we destroy.
...
...Cameron.
This is *your* fault.
I gave up everything for you.
No.
No-- don't say that.
Please, don't.
Everything, Kiden.
CAMERON!
For you.

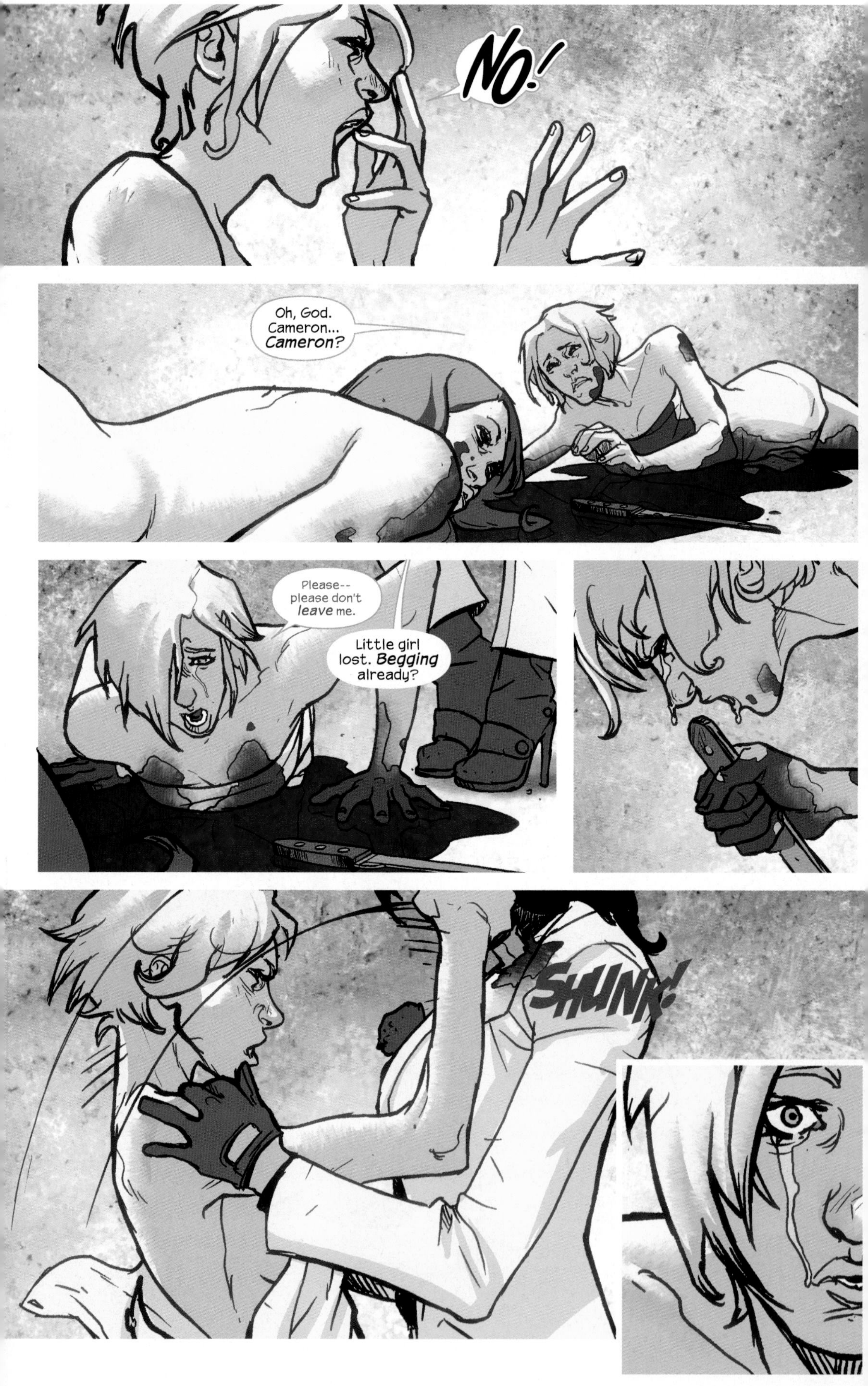
NO!
Oh, God. Cameron... *Cameron*?
Please-- please don't *leave* me.
Little girl lost. *Begging* already?
SHUNK!

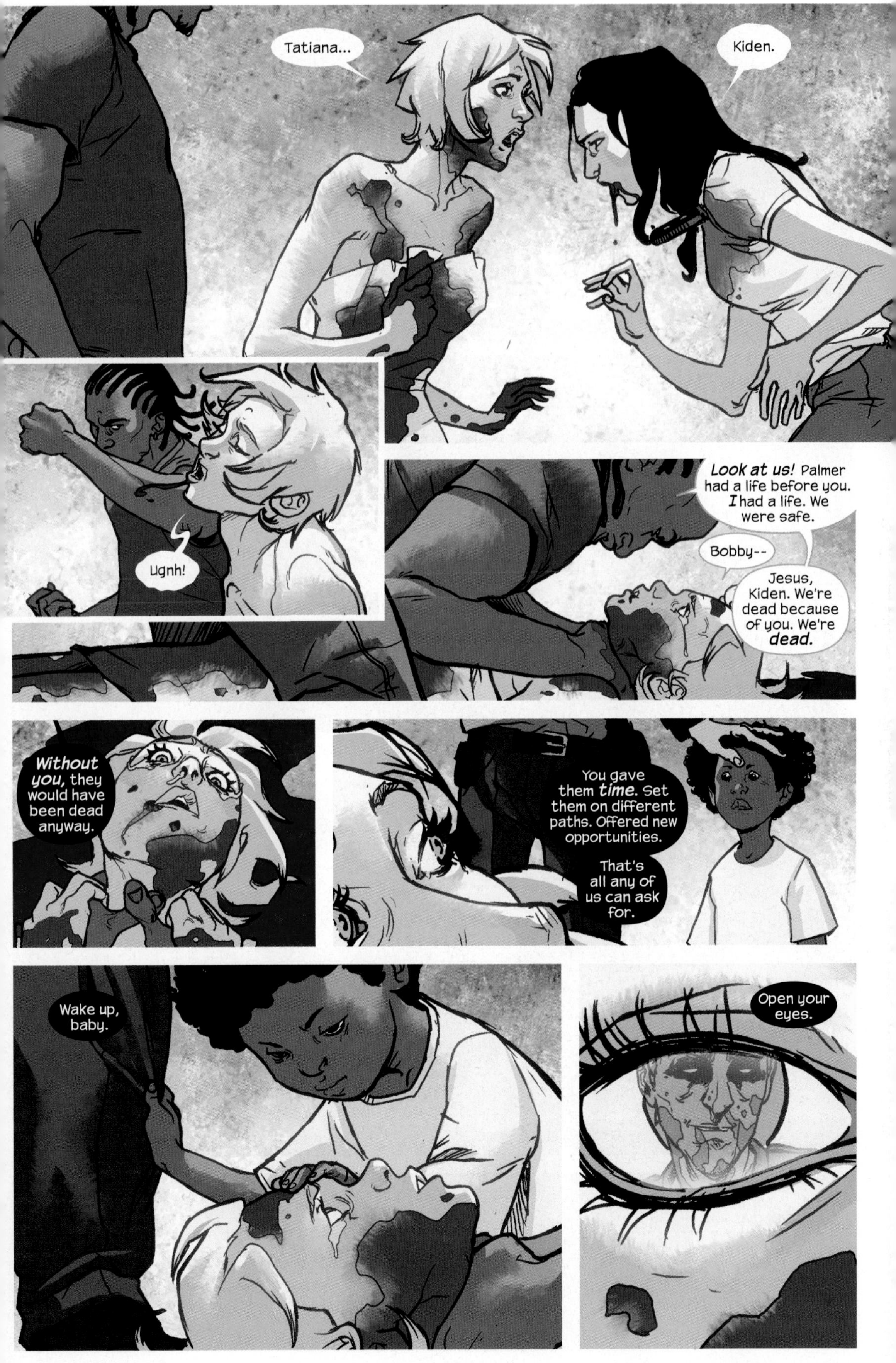

Tatiana...
Kiden.
Ugnh!
Look at us! Palmer had a life before you. I had a life. We were safe.
Bobby--
Jesus, Kiden. We're dead because of you. We're dead.
Without you, they would have been dead anyway.
You gave them time. Set them on different paths. Offered new opportunities.
That's all any of us can ask for.
Wake up, baby.
Open your eyes.

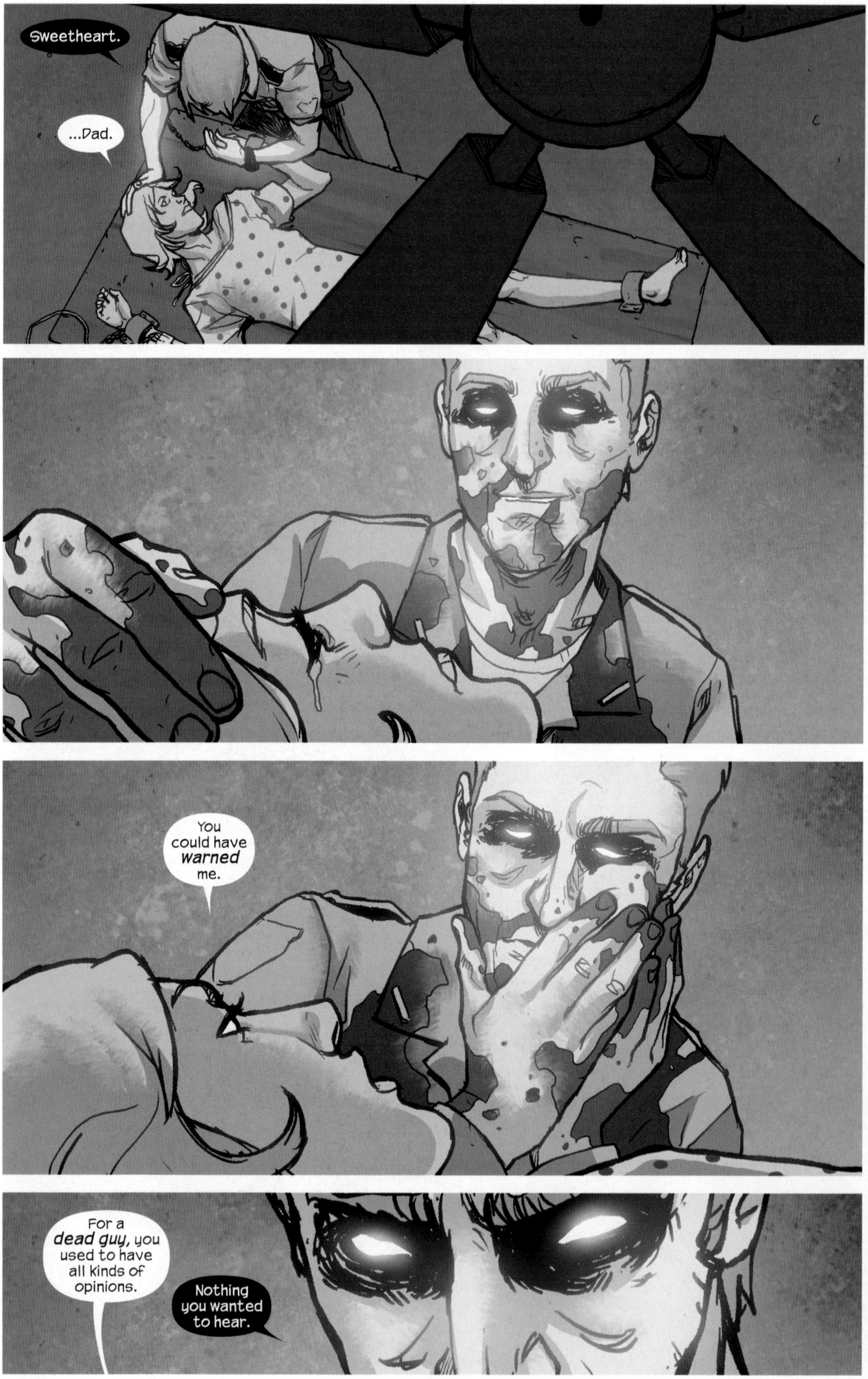
Sweetheart.
...Dad.
You could have *warned* me.
For a *dead guy,* you used to have all kinds of opinions.
Nothing you wanted to hear.

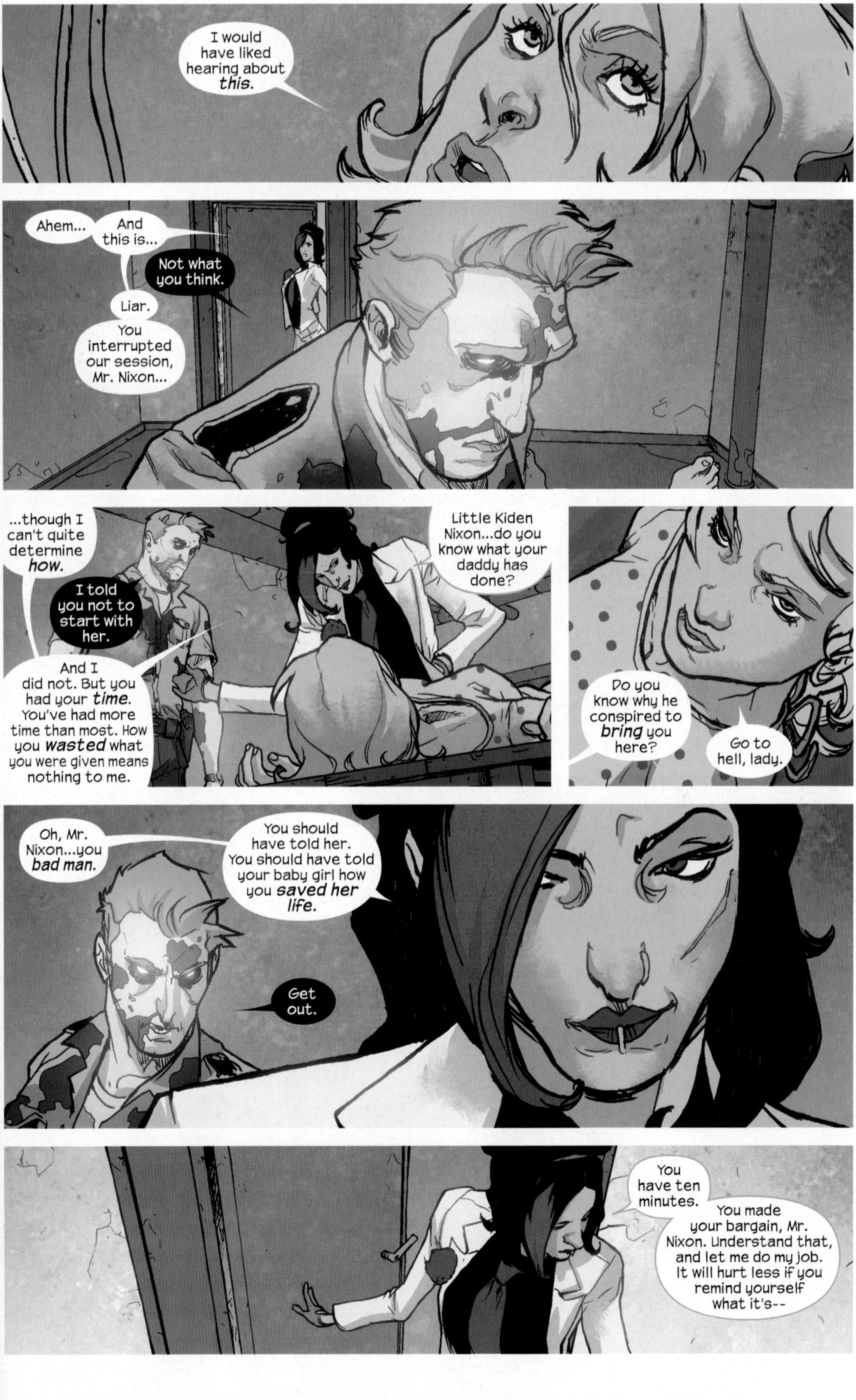

I would have liked hearing about *this.*
Ahem...
And this is...
Not what you think.
Liar.
You interrupted our session, Mr. Nixon...
...though I can't quite determine *how.*
I told you not to start with her.
And I did not. But you had your *time.* You've had more time than most. How you *wasted* what you were given means nothing to me.
Little Kiden Nixon...do you know what your daddy has done?
Do you know why he conspired to *bring* you here?
Go to hell, lady.
Oh, Mr. Nixon...you *bad man.*
You should have told her. You should have told your baby girl how you *saved her life.*
Get out.
You have ten minutes.
You made your bargain, Mr. Nixon. Understand that, and let me do my job. It will hurt less if you remind yourself what it's--

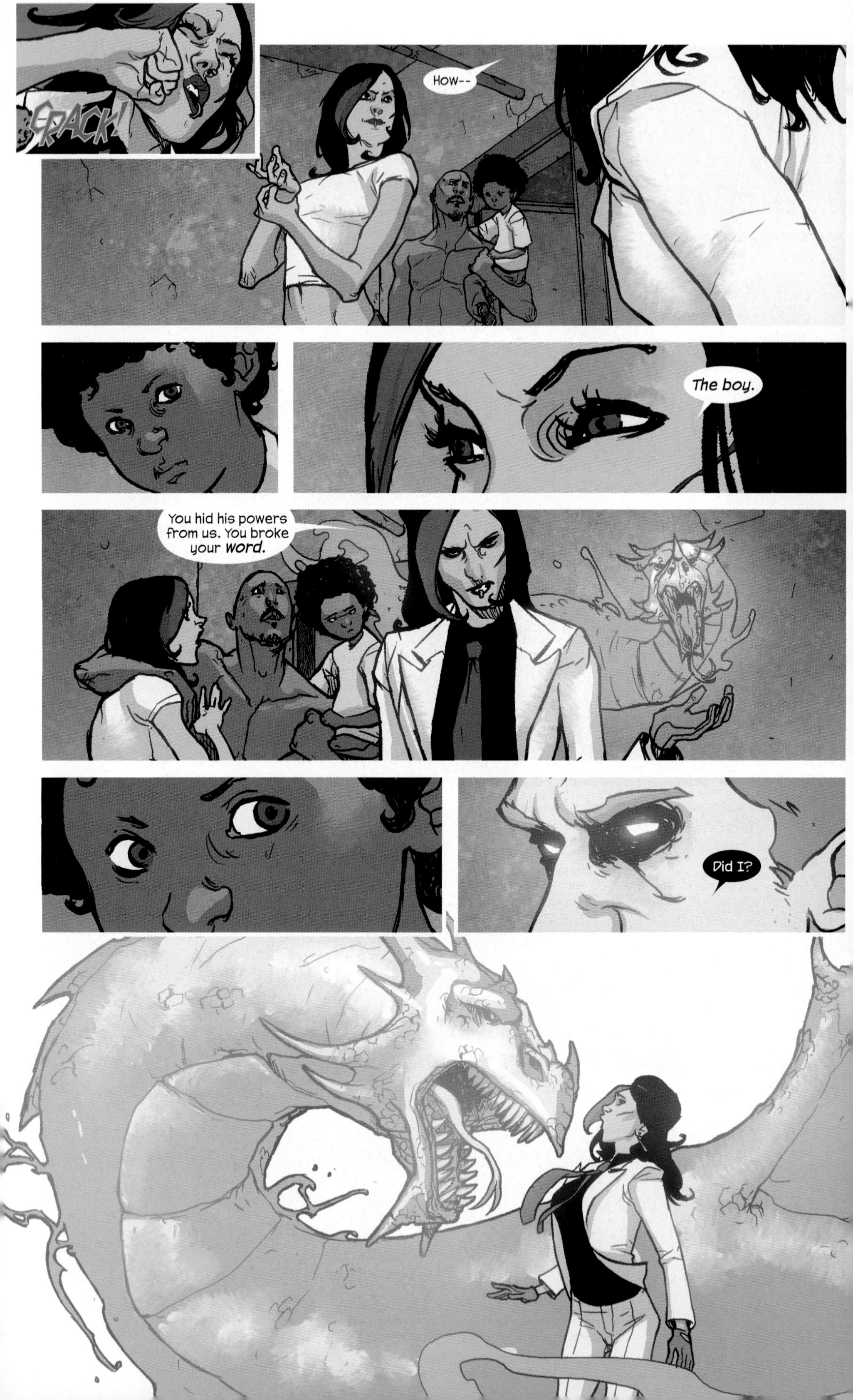
CRACK!
How--
The boy.
You hid his powers from us. You broke your word.
Did I?

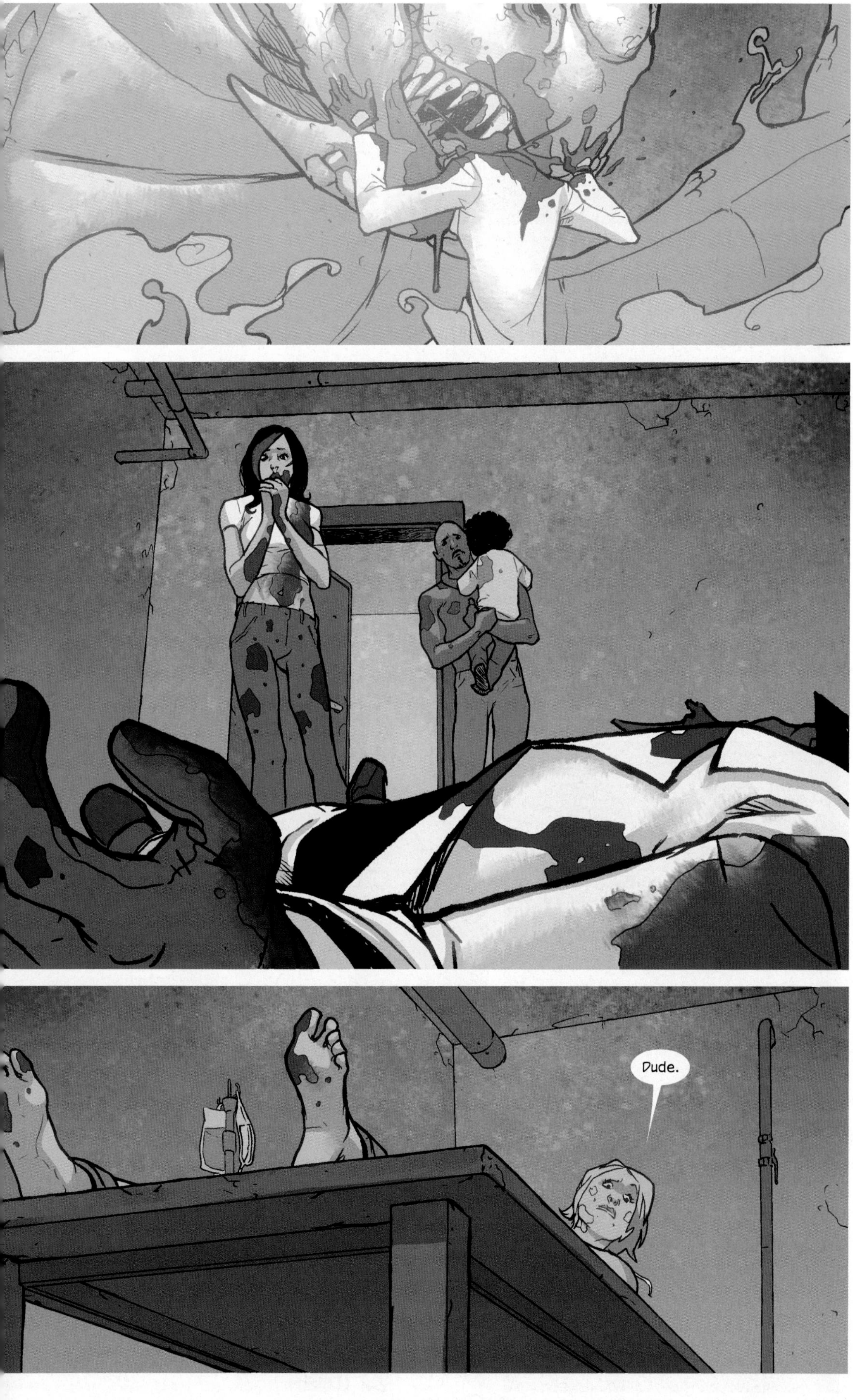
Dude.

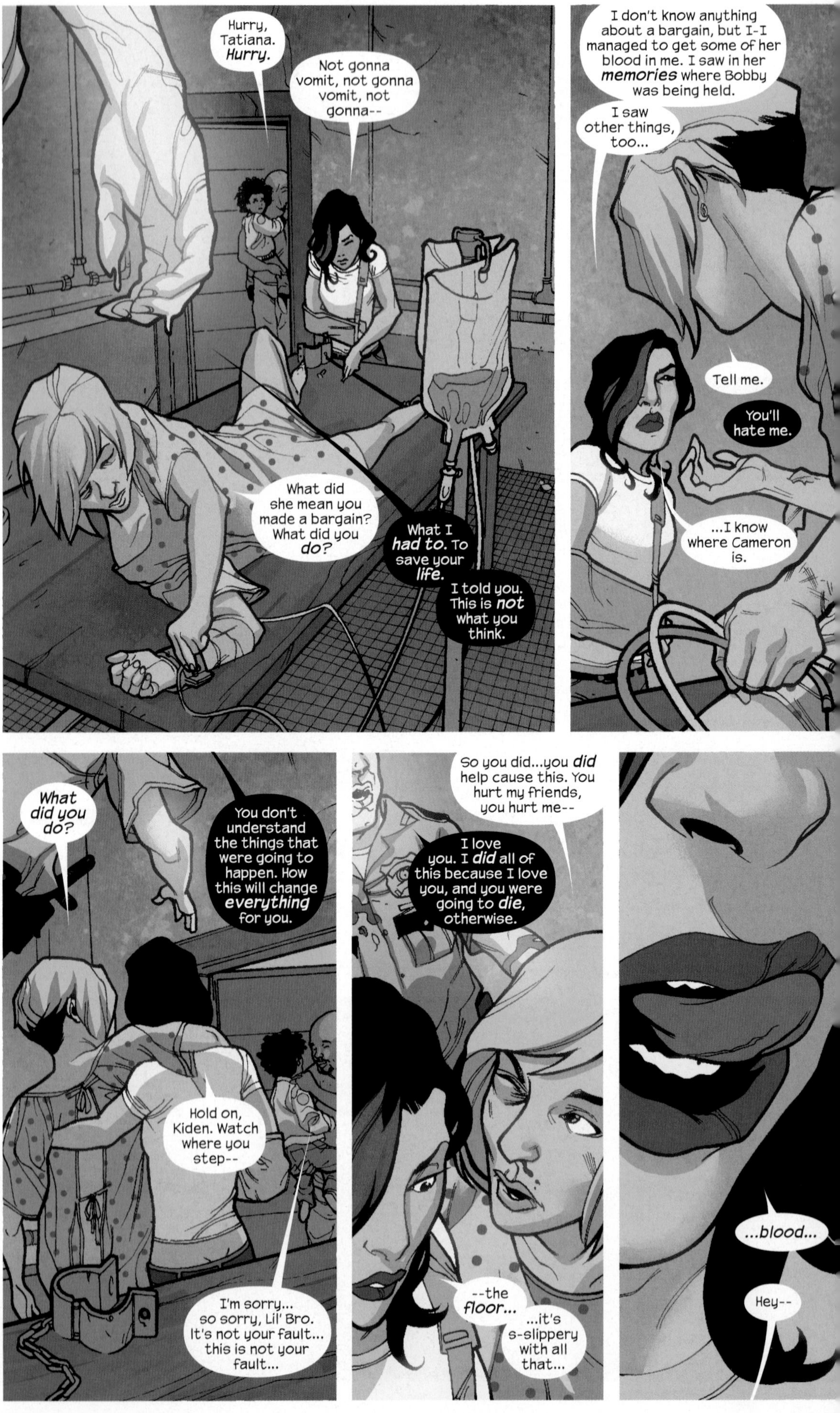

Hurry, Tatiana. *Hurry.*
Not gonna vomit, not gonna vomit, not gonna--
What did she mean you made a bargain? What did you *do?*
What I *had to.* To save your *life.*
I told you. This is *not* what you think.
I don't know anything about a bargain, but I-I managed to get some of her blood in me. I saw in her *memories* where Bobby was being held.
I saw other things, too...
Tell me.
You'll hate me.
...I know where Cameron is.
What did you do?
You don't understand the things that were going to happen. How this will change *everything* for you.
Hold on, Kiden. Watch where you step--
I'm sorry... so sorry, Lil' Bro. It's not your fault... this is not your fault...
So you did...you *did* help cause this. You hurt my friends, you hurt me--
I love you. I *did* all of this because I love you, and you were going to *die,* otherwise.
--the *floor...*
...it's s-slippery with all that...
...blood...
Hey--

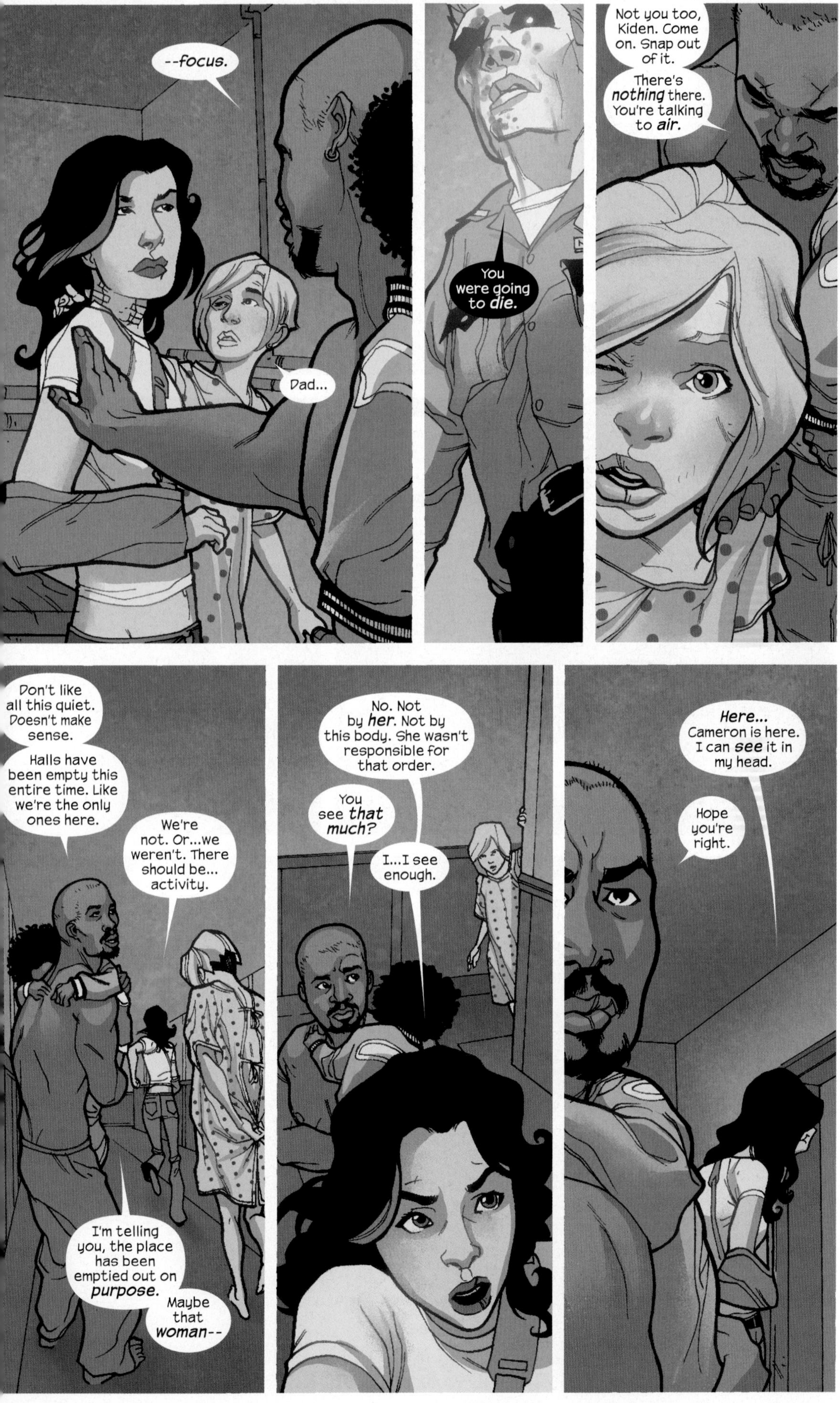
--focus.
Dad...
You were going to die.
Not you too, Kiden. Come on. Snap out of it.
There's nothing there. You're talking to air.
Don't like all this quiet. Doesn't make sense.
Halls have been empty this entire time. Like we're the only ones here.
We're not. Or...we weren't. There should be... activity.
I'm telling you, the place has been emptied out on purpose.
Maybe that woman--
No. Not by her. Not by this body. She wasn't responsible for that order.
You see that much?
I...I see enough.
Here... Cameron is here. I can see it in my head.
Hope you're right.

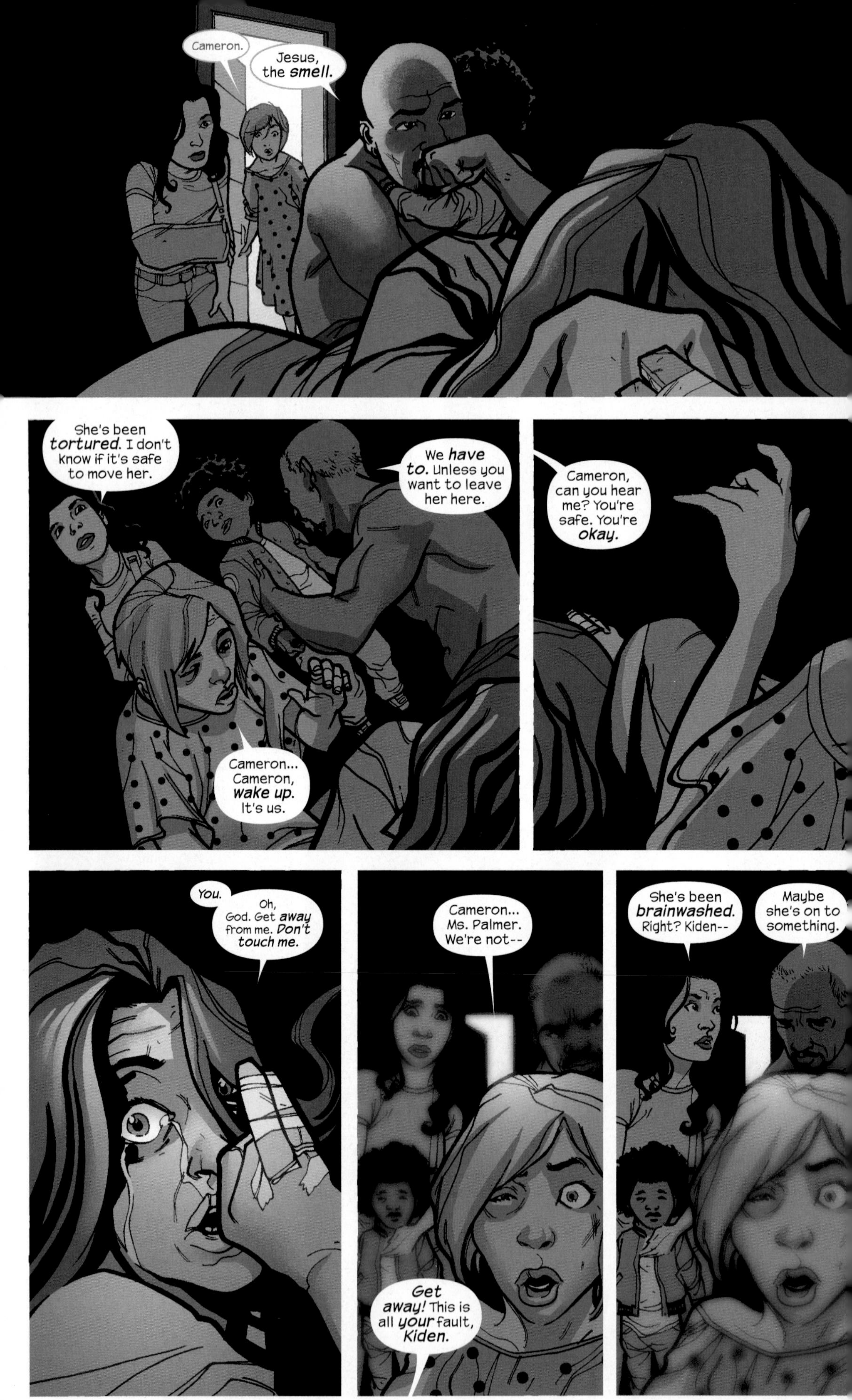

Cameron.
Jesus, the smell.
She's been tortured. I don't know if it's safe to move her.
We have to. Unless you want to leave her here.
Cameron... Cameron, wake up. It's us.
Cameron, can you hear me? You're safe. You're okay.
You.
Oh, God. Get away from me. Don't touch me.
Cameron... Ms. Palmer. We're not--
Get away! This is all your fault, Kiden.
She's been brainwashed. Right? Kiden--
Maybe she's on to something.

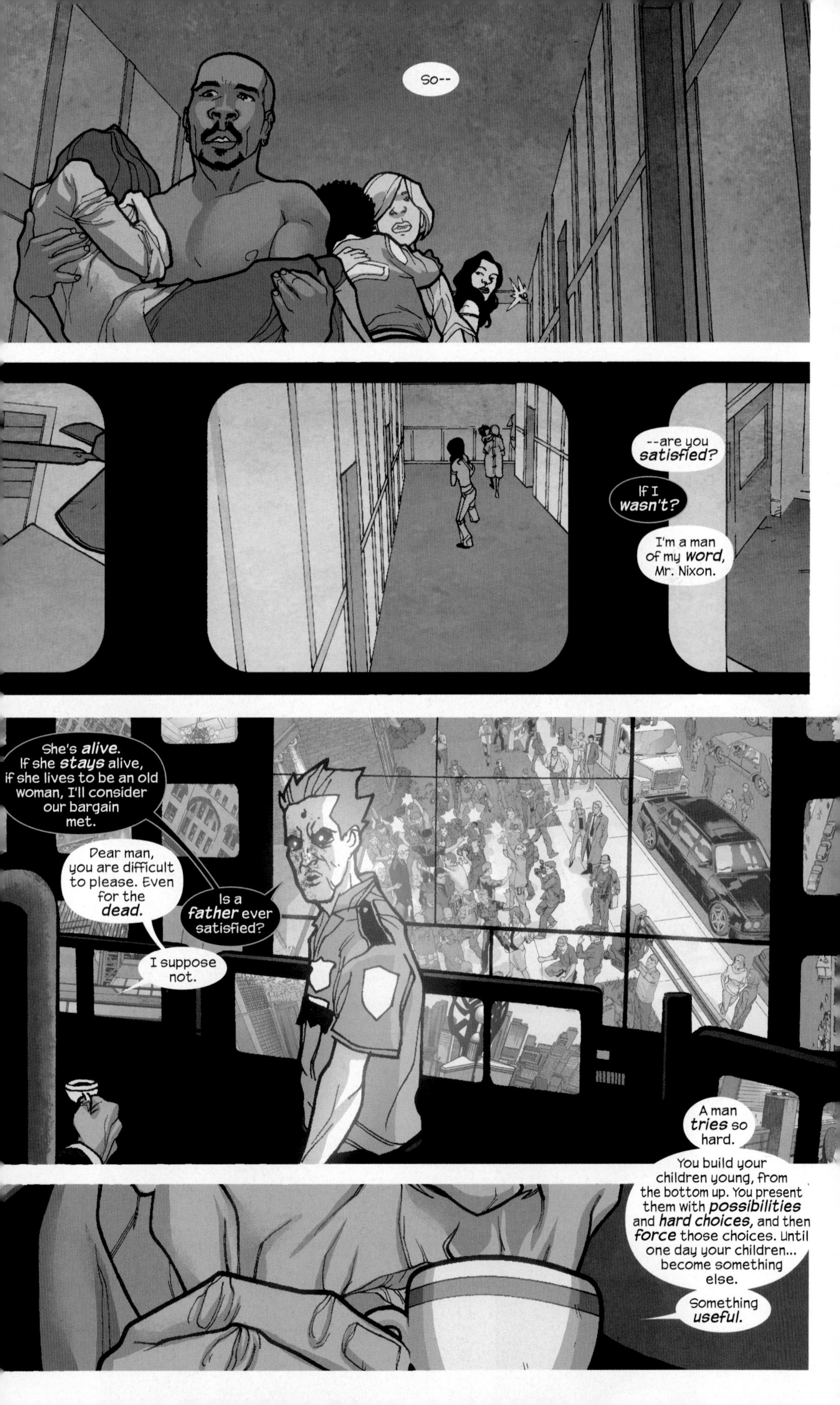
So--
--are you satisfied?
If I wasn't?
I'm a man of my word, Mr. Nixon.
She's alive. If she stays alive, if she lives to be an old woman, I'll consider our bargain met.
Dear man, you are difficult to please. Even for the dead.
Is a father ever satisfied?
I suppose not.
A man tries so hard.
You build your children young, from the bottom up. You present them with possibilities and hard choices, and then force those choices. Until one day your children... become something else.
Something useful.

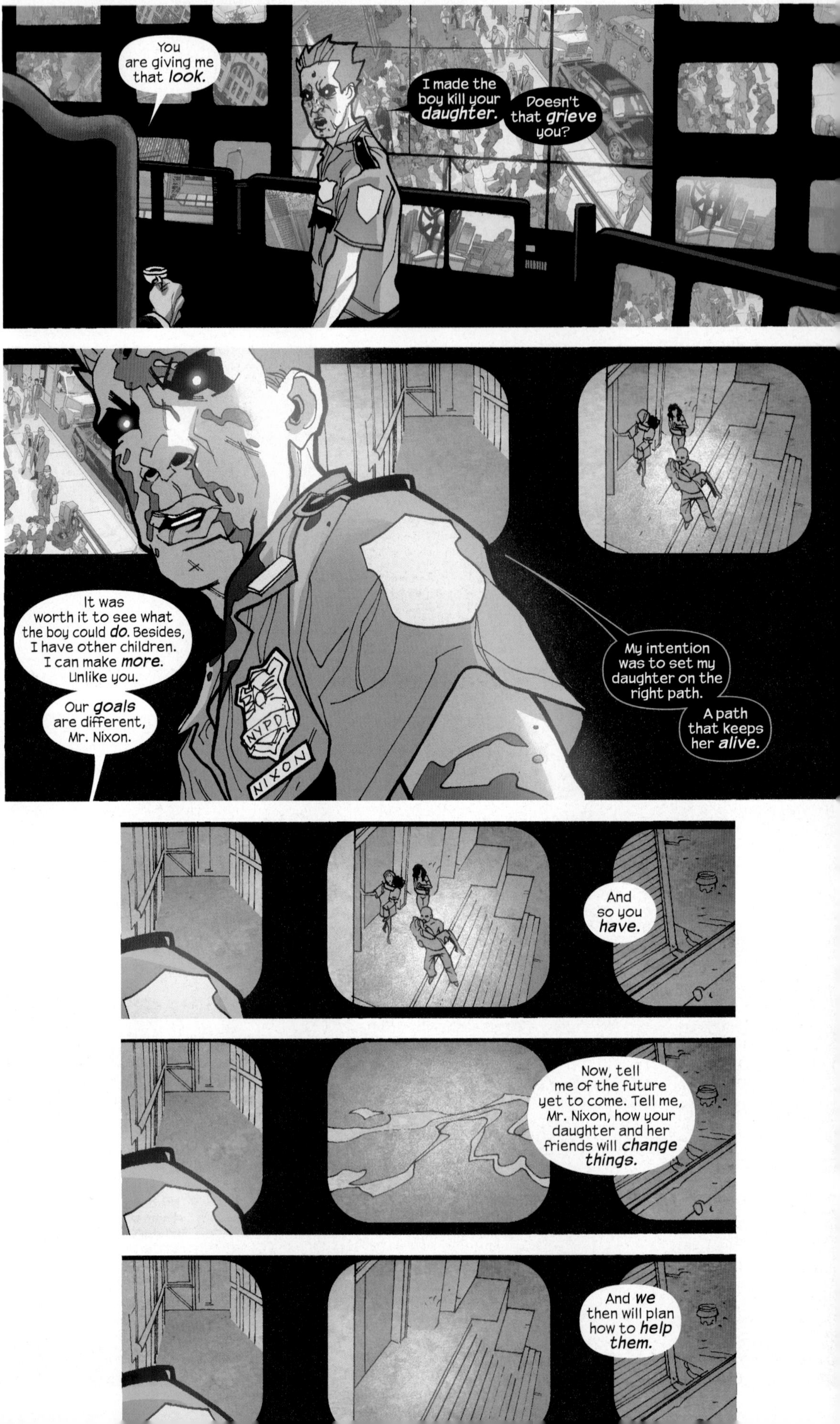

You are giving me that look.
I made the boy kill your daughter.
Doesn't that grieve you?
It was worth it to see what the boy could do. Besides, I have other children. I can make more. Unlike you.
Our goals are different, Mr. Nixon.
My intention was to set my daughter on the right path.
A path that keeps her alive.
NYPD
NIXON
And so you have.
Now, tell me of the future yet to come. Tell me, Mr. Nixon, how your daughter and her friends will change things.
And we then will plan how to help them.

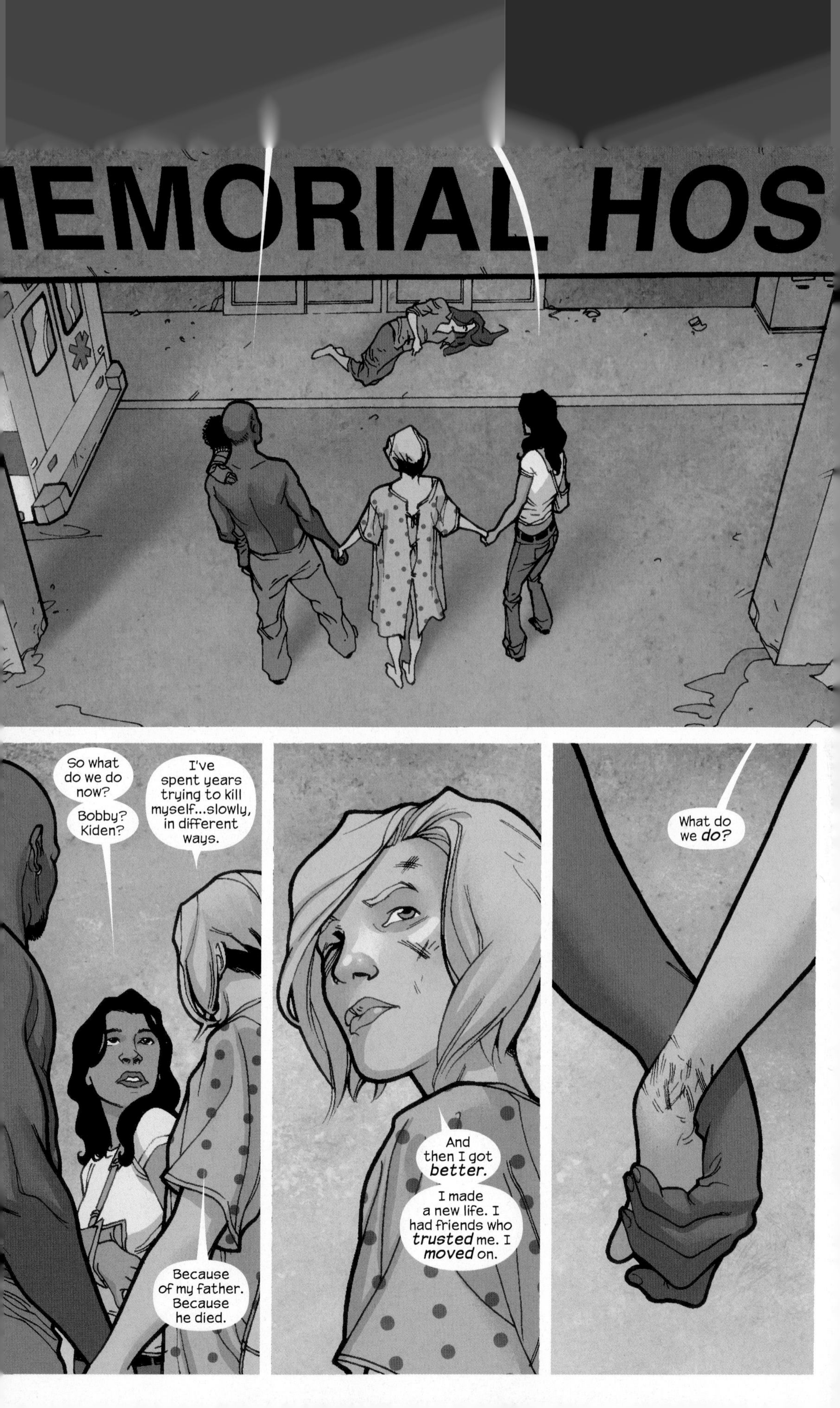
MEMORIAL HOS
So what do we do now?
Bobby? Kiden?
I've spent years trying to kill myself...slowly, in different ways.
Because of my father. Because he died.
And then I got better.
I made a new life. I had friends who trusted me. I moved on.
What do we do?

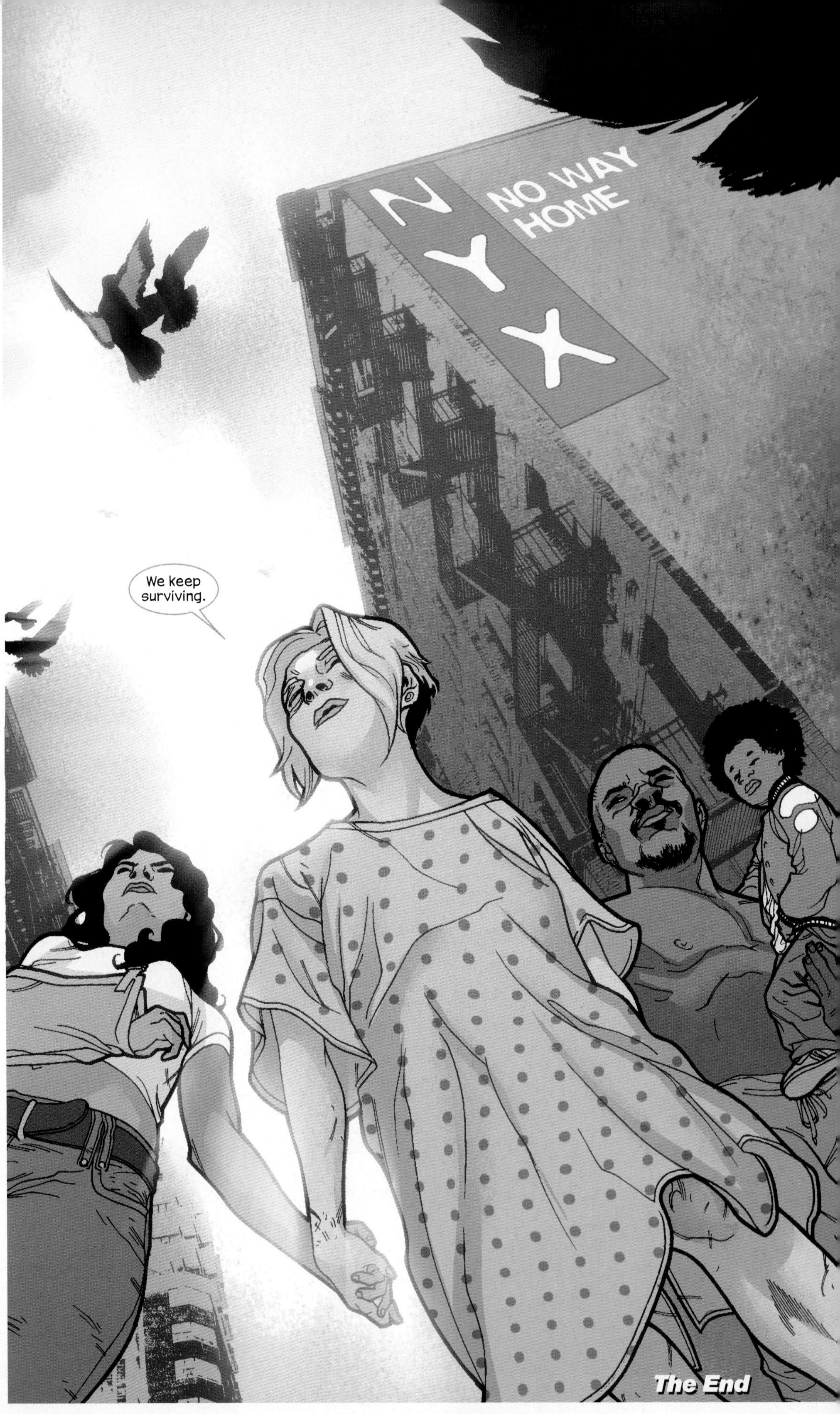
NYX
NO WAY HOME
We keep surviving.
The End

O N E

variant by
Jo Chen

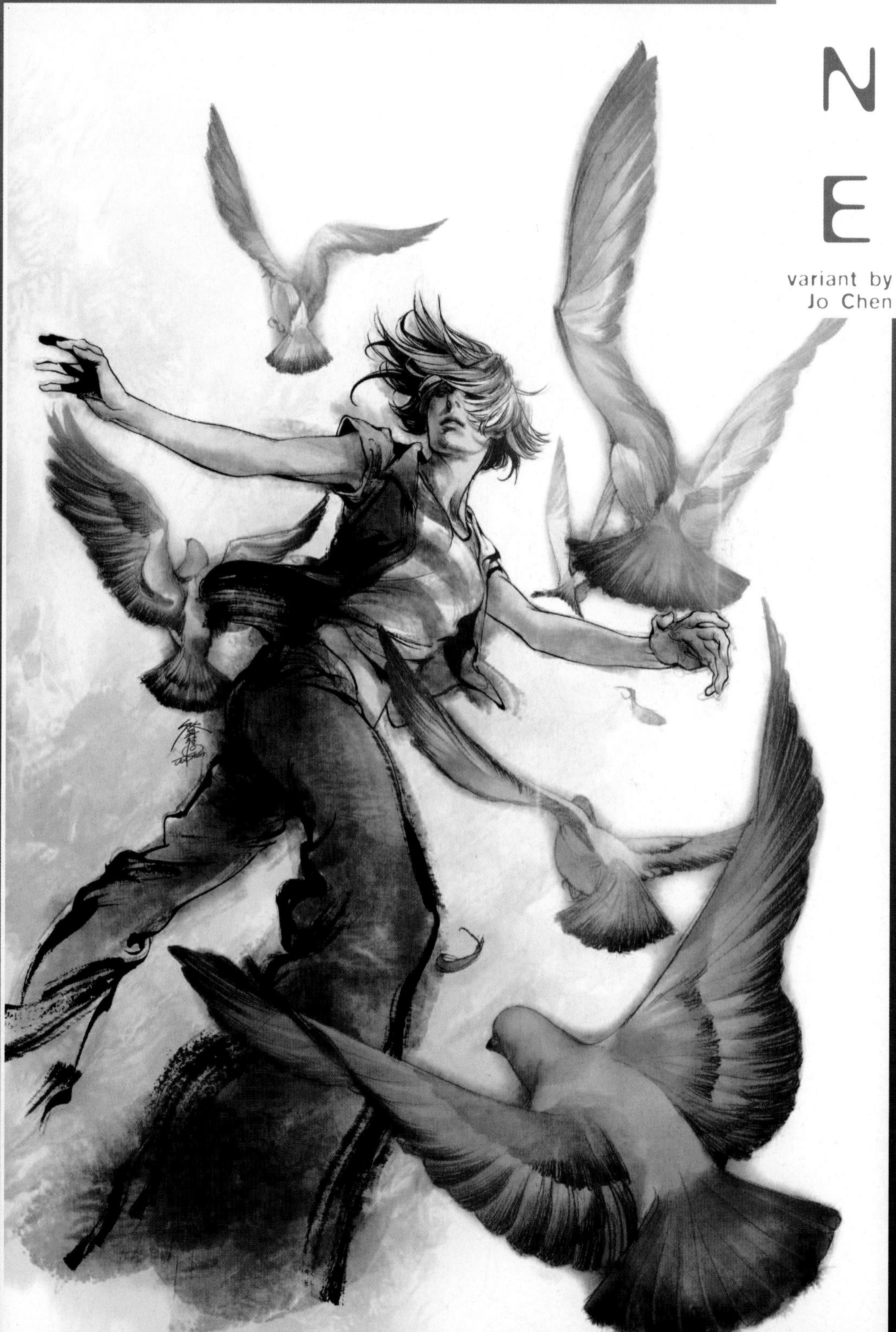

N Y X

TATIANA

CHARACTER DESIGN BY
KALMAN ANDRASOFSZKY

CHARACTER DESIGN BY
KALMAN ANDRASOFSZKY

NYX

KIDEN

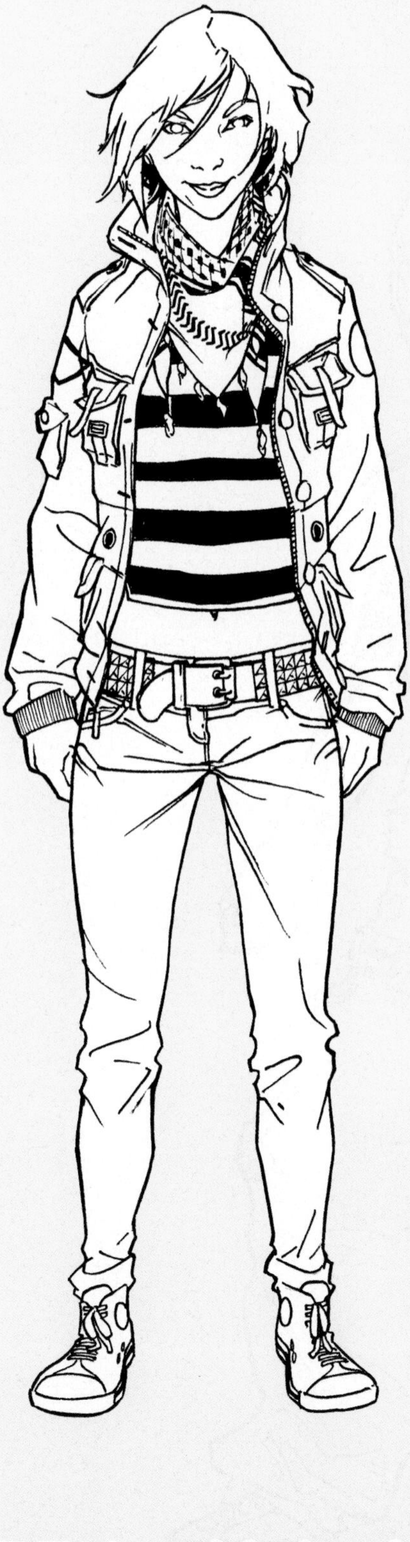

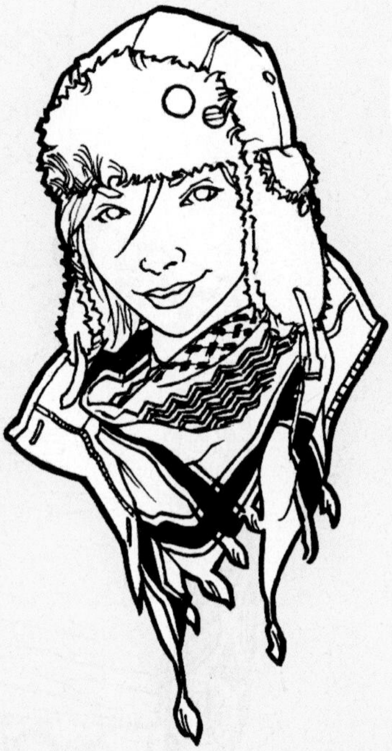

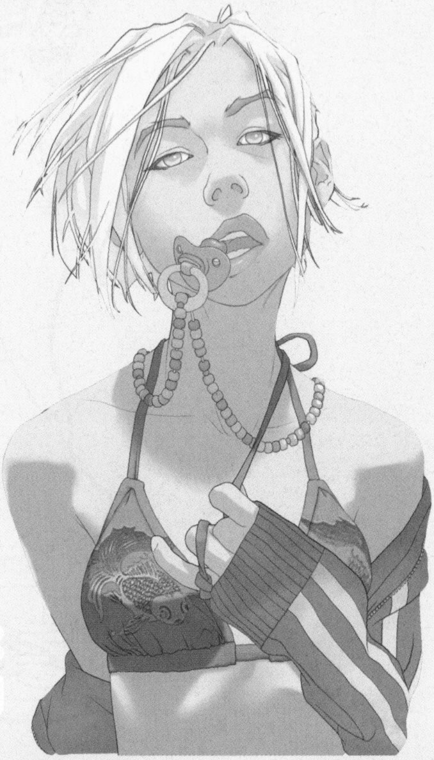

KIDEN by original series artist
JOSH MIDDLETON

NYX

TATTOO MAN

CHARACTER DESIGN BY
KALMAN ANDRASOFSZKY

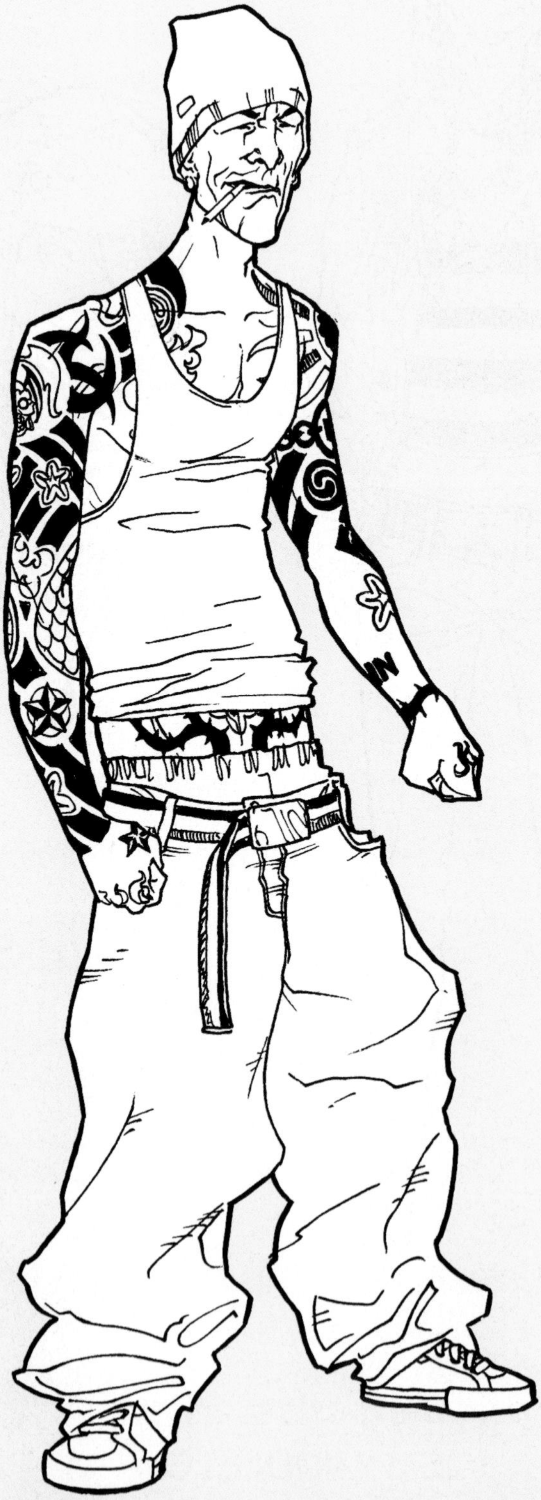

CHARACTER DESIGN BY
KALMAN ANDRASOFSZKY

NYX

BOBBY & LIL' BRO

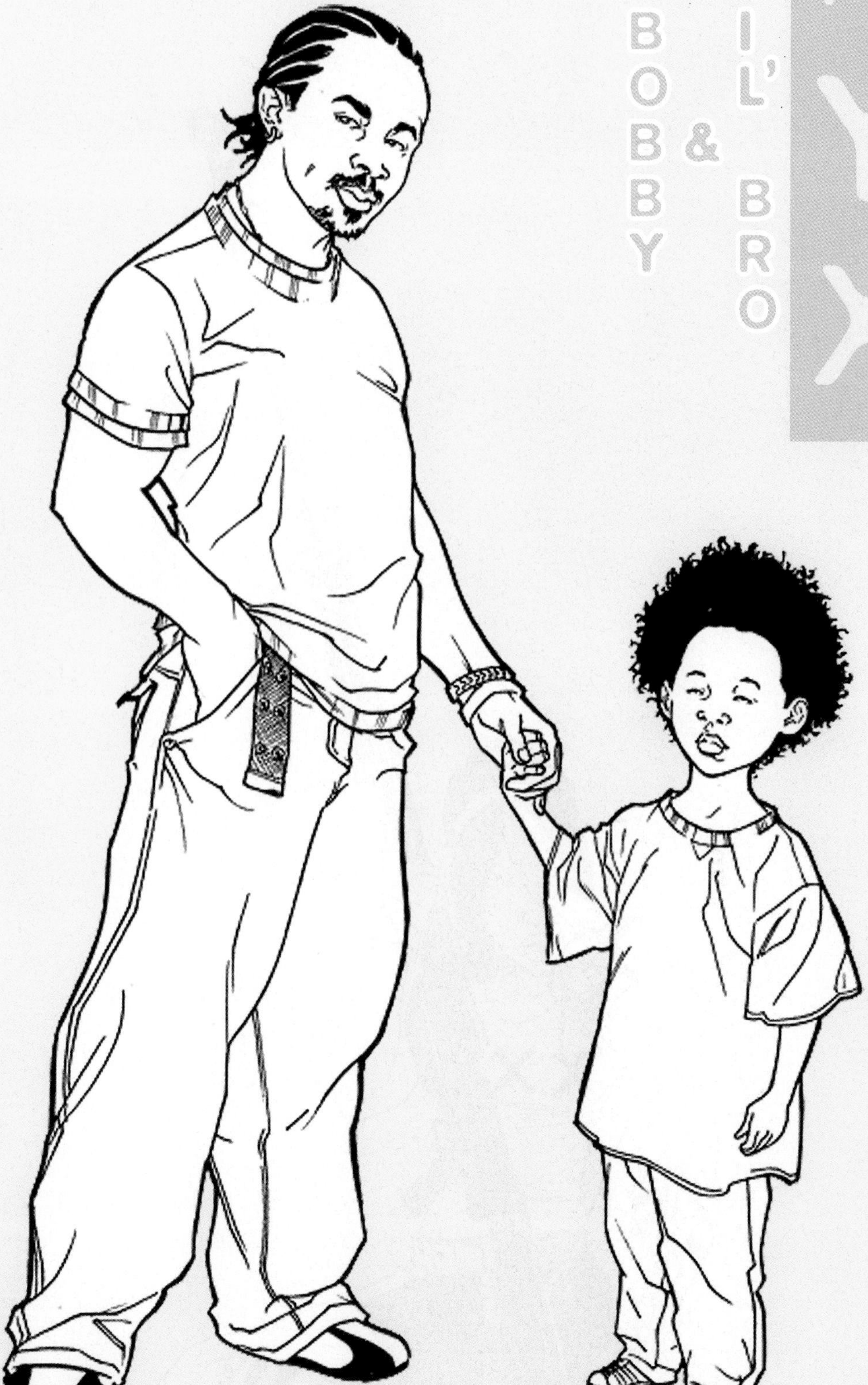

NYX

SNIPER CHICK

CHARACTER DESIGN BY
KALMAN ANDRASOFSZKY

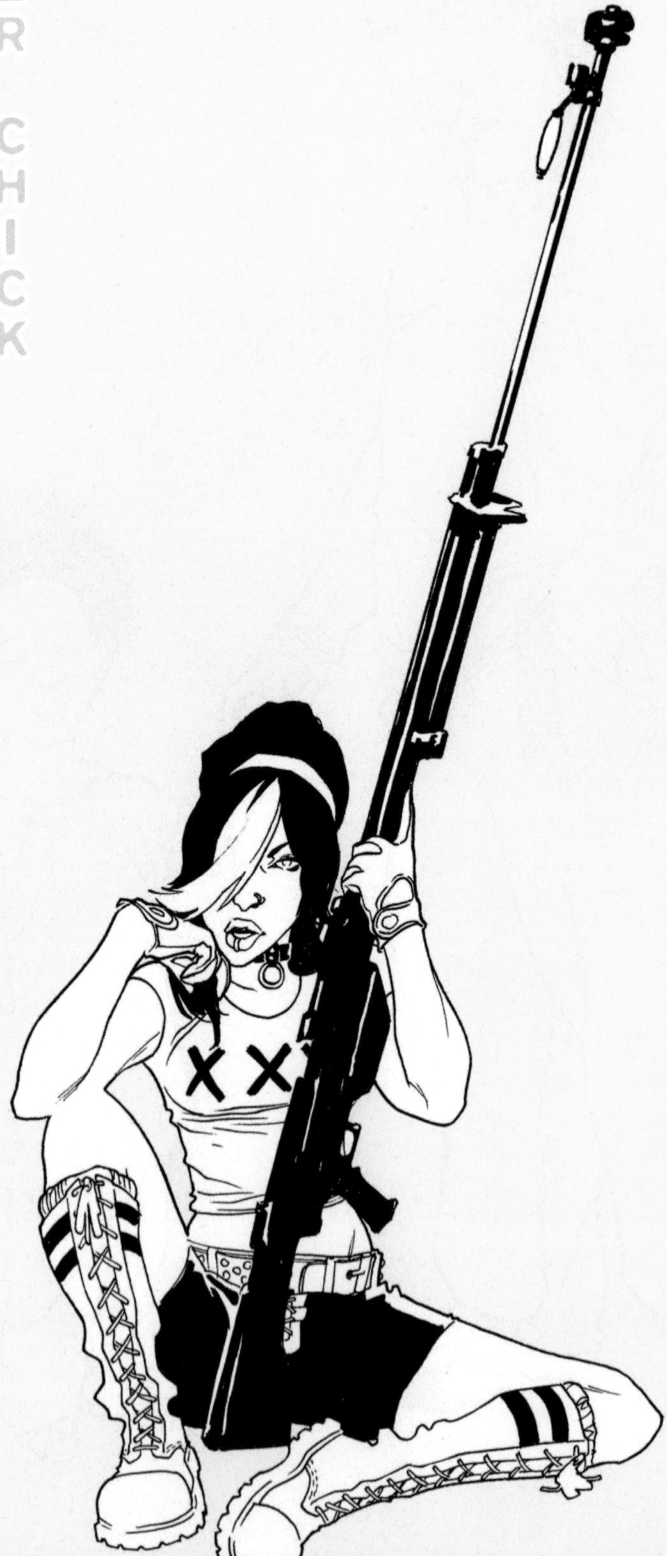

CHARACTER DESIGN BY
KALMAN ANDRASOFSZKY

NICK NIXON

NYX

In the third and final part of their one-on-one conversation, writer Marjorie Liu and Artist Kalman Andrasofszky tell us how the world of NYX has changed since the original series hit over five years ago…and why Kiden's soother just HAD to go.

Kalman: I understand you were a fan of the original series. What serpentine series of events led you to this particular gig? In my case it was a very un-serpentine phone call out of the blue.

Marjorie: How I got this gig...it is, indeed, a twisty tale.

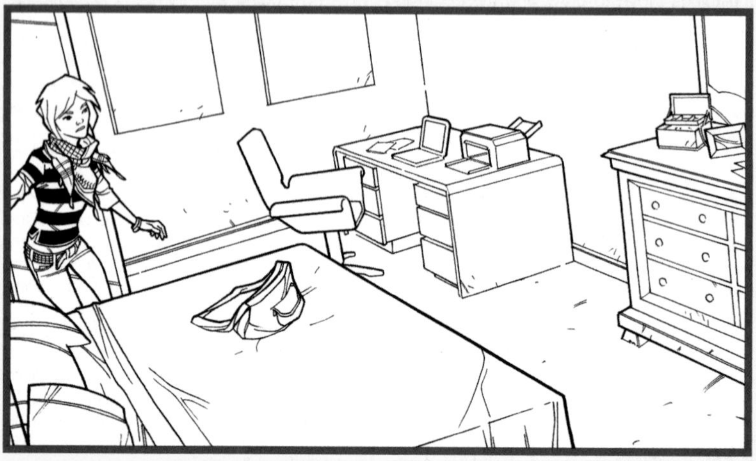

Basically, it began in 2004, when I was having lunch with my agent for the first time. It was Halloween, her son came up to the table dressed as Spiderman, and I said, "Oh, man, he's so cute." Followed by, "I would love to write comics one day." And it just so happened that my agent, Lucienne, knew an editor at Pocket who was acquiring for a new line of prose novels they were publishing in conjunction with Marvel. Long story short, I got a chance to write the first of the X-Men line, called DARK MIRROR, and it was fairly well received by the guys at Marvel. Which gave me the courage at the New York Comic Con the following year to walk up to Ruwan Jayatilleke, VP of Development, and hand him my card. I told him I was interested in doing more for Marvel, he told me to follow up after the conference--which I did--and the rest is history. He was the one who originally suggested relaunching NYX. I was, of course, more than willing to get involved. And even though it took, literally, years to get to this point, better slow than never.

K: Did they give you a starting point for the relaunch or did you pitch cold, and most importantly, how close or far is the story to/from your pitch, and what changes did it go through?

M: There were no rules set on me. I wasn't told to use the same characters, or follow what had come before, though NYX has a certain vibe that I assumed I had to capture.

I really loved the way the characters were introduced--Kiden as this flawed, emotional wreck of a kid, who was also tough as nails, was just so much more fascinating than a lot of characters--plus, I had some unanswered questions that the end of NYX simply left hanging. Like, what was the deal with the dad? And why did he bring all those kids together? It wasn't random, I was certain of that. And that was the big question that I started turning over and over in my mind, and that formed the basis of the original proposal. Which, looking back, was crazy and full of crap. There were demons involved, and predatory old women--but the characters were the same, and the basic idea of them being hunted hasn't changed all that much. I think what got me the job was that the folks in charge had the sense that I knew the characters, that I could write these kids and not have it be totally off the wall.

Anyway, I had a talk with Axel Alonso at Comic Con in San Diego--we went over what would be going on in the Marvel Universe--then I went back to the drawing board. Second proposal wasn't much better--a lot of focus on the Purifiers, so much so that the book didn't really stand out from anything else. But John Barber was on board by that time, and we went back and forth until it was just right.

Had you read the original series

K: Yes and no. I read the first fo issues, the Middleton ones. I or got to read the final three recently research for Vol 2.

M: I'm really curious about ho you felt regarding the art. I thoug Middleton did a fantastic job, but I' not a visual artist, so there may b nuances that you would notice th would totally pass me by.

K: Okay, let's get this out of the w right now...I was and am a HUGE fa of the original NYX, and most of th reason for that is Josh Middleton's a I would crawl through broken glass get a closer look at something he drawn. My interest was really centere on the art. NYX was an event, ar I actually remember anticipating before its release, which is a rare thi for this jaded old warhorse, lemm tell you. So it would be impossib to contemplate something like th without being aware of the massi shadow Josh's visualizations of thes characters casts. But hey, I gotta b free, I gotta be me.

I was working on a series calle iCandy at the time, which I had bee asked to draw and color, much lik Josh had done with NYX, and so I wa really eager to see what he'd do. C course, he blew me out of the wate and really forced me to up my game

M: Was there anything about th NYX concept you could relate to?

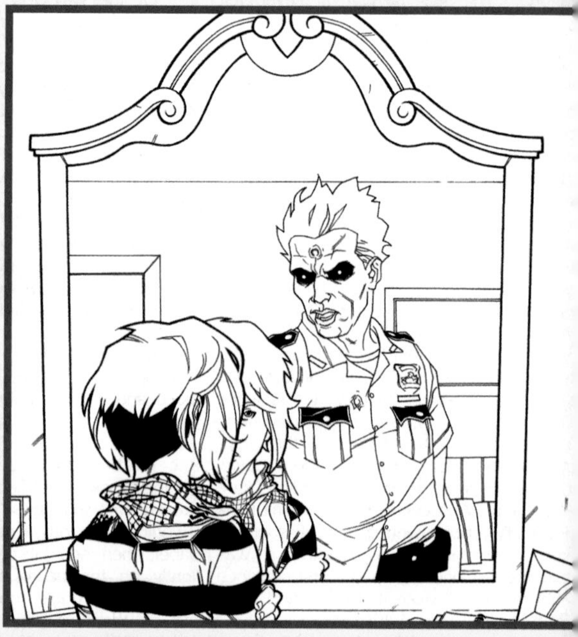

K: Well, right off I loved the fa that it seemed to be set much mo in "our" world than in the Marvel U Opening with a young teen taking "E at a rave, then flowing seamlessly int vomiting, and a broken nose in th

hoolyard, everything in issue 1 was a etty extreme approach. Some people lt that sort of thing has no place comics, or that too many comics

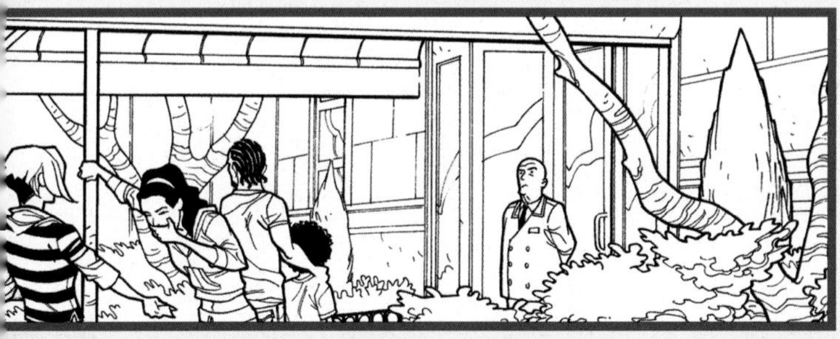

e like "that", but to me, it's a valid d of the storytelling spectrum, and it as refreshing. That aspect of it, the it, the phlegm, is something I think u've been able to capture really well volume 2, without it feeling forced, tacked on.

I really liked the unorthodox story w. If regular Marvel comics can compared to orthodox three act reenplay structure, then this felt ore like an art house film. The two st examples of this that I can think offhand are the six-month jump rward in time that occurs in the first lf of issue 2, and the interest the rrative takes in Cameron Palmer and r story. Looking back, it reminds me Donnie Darko; remember how much tention every character got in that ovie? Not just Donnie and his love erest, but his parents and several of s teachers all had their own storylines at played out.

Your take on the book feels VERY thful to the tone of the original ries, so I'm guessing you dug it.

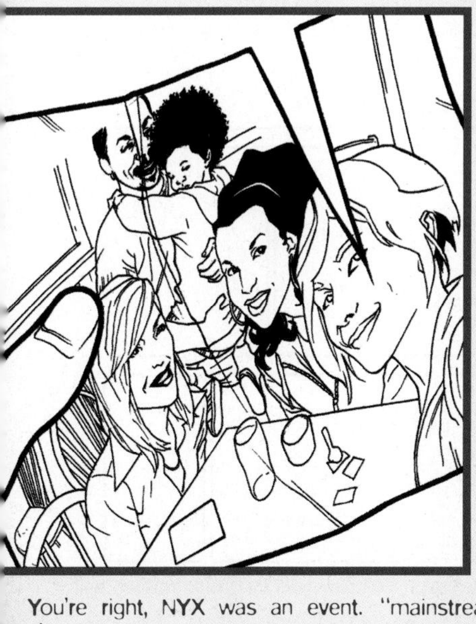

You're right, NYX was an event. didn't think about it that way at the ne, though. And thanks--I have en trying to capture...some kind of ality of the situation, but as a reader, lways hate being knocked over the ad with it. I really loved the way the characters were introduced--Kiden as this flawed, emotional wreck of a kid, who was also tough as nails, was just so much more fascinating than a lot of the characters in the Marvel universe.

And speaking of which, what inspired you during the initial concept design for NYX? I know there was the original series to draw upon, but I wasn't certain how much of a factor that was for you, especially as Kiden and the others have such a unique, distinctive look now. And attitude, man. I love the attitude you've given them.

K: I'm glad to hear you like my re-interpretations, and that they read as distinct. Some days I think they're way too far, and some days way too close.

Kiden is probably the most drastic change, and the one I'm sure to get rocks thrown at me for. Sorry guys, the soother had to go. When NYX came out in 2003 rave culture was pretty much on its last legs, and now in 2008? Well, most people Kiden's age don't even know what a rave is. So I just updated her to the teen hipster look du jour, which is how a rebellious young urchin like Kiden would deck herself out today. And this book takes place today, as in, right NOW.

M: Yeah, the soother definitely had to go.

K: In Tatiana's case I just tried to contrast Kiden's look in some way. She seemed to be a more "mainstream" girl, in her attitude as well as her look, so I made her Sporty Spice, essentially.

Bobby's probably the least revised, at least at first glance. I thought about changing his hair, but ended up sticking with the corn rows. In his case, the real change was to his physical attributes. With the girls, I pretty much stuck with Josh's designs in terms of their facial features and builds, it's who they are to me. But in Bobby's case his looks in the book just didn't work for me. He kind of looked like a white guy colored brown, so I rebuilt his face and buffed him up a bit, not to super-hero proportions or anything, but just to contrast a little better with the girls.

Oh yeah, last but not least, Lil' Bro. Ask yourself this: If you had a near-catatonic child on your hands, would you give him a haircut that requires weekly maintenance, or one you could let slide for a while?

Finally I feel the need to come clean here, in that I've cast people I know in the roles of each of these characters (except Lil' Bro), and use them not only as visual touchstones, but also as models when the need arises. I don't slavishly follow their features or the photos, but sometimes when the panel needs an angle that's aimed right up someone's nose (see pages 14 and 15 of issue one) there's nothing like a digital snap to get you through. So take a bow Matthea, Cristina, and Val, this book wouldn't be the same without you.

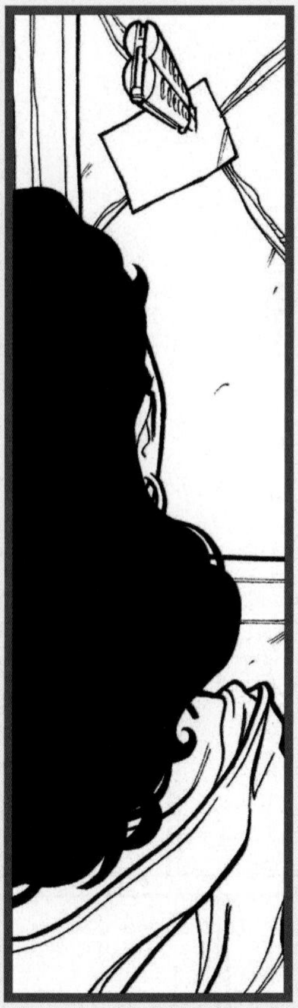

M: No offense to anyone, but I prefer Bobby's new look, which feels much more real--and masculine--compared to his original design. Issue #3 is Bobby-centric, so I'm having fun with him at the moment, really trying to get into his head and figure out what makes him tick.

I have tried to stay faithful to the original because I liked the characters so much, but I see the kids as having matured a lot since the original series. Their issues are more with each other now--trying to figure out what's important when their bonds are tested.

The End.

ISSUE 1 PENCILS BY KALMAN ANDRASOFSZKY

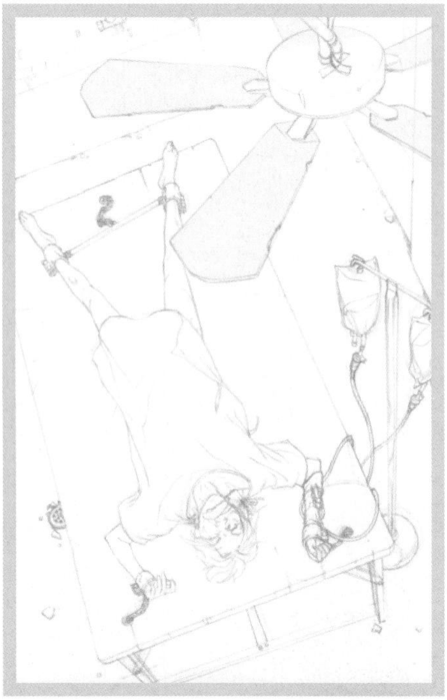

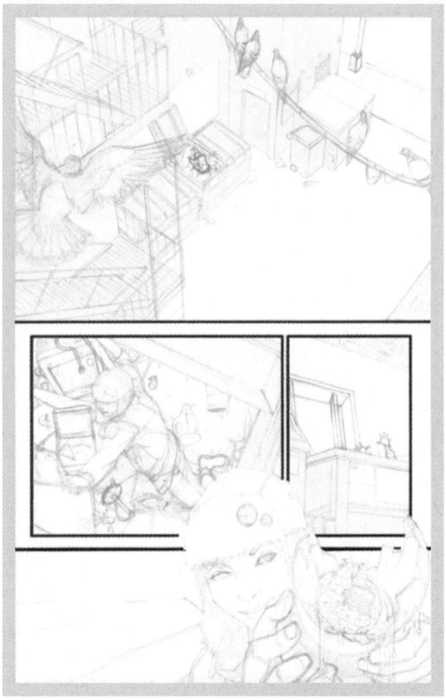

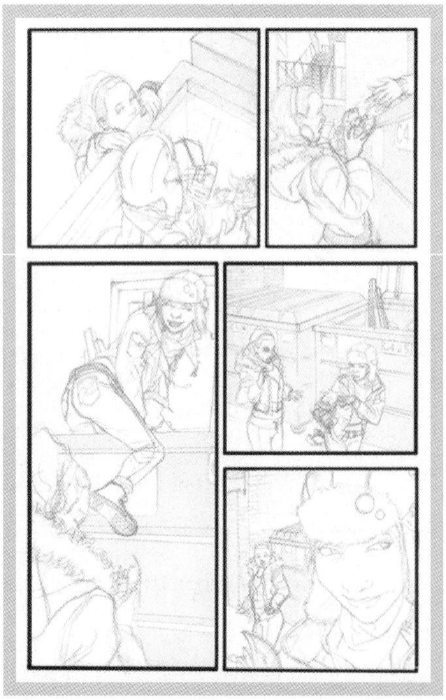

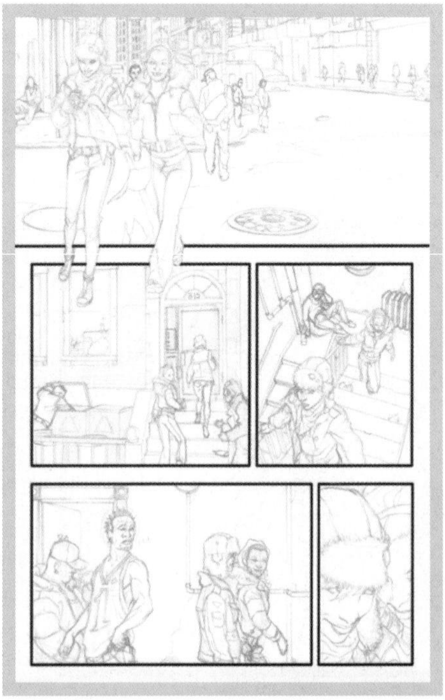

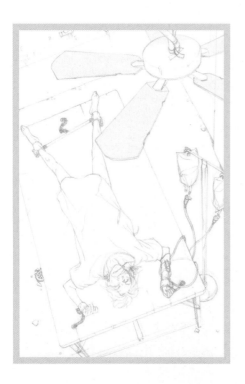

ISSUE 1 PENCILS BY KALMAN ANDRASOFSZKY

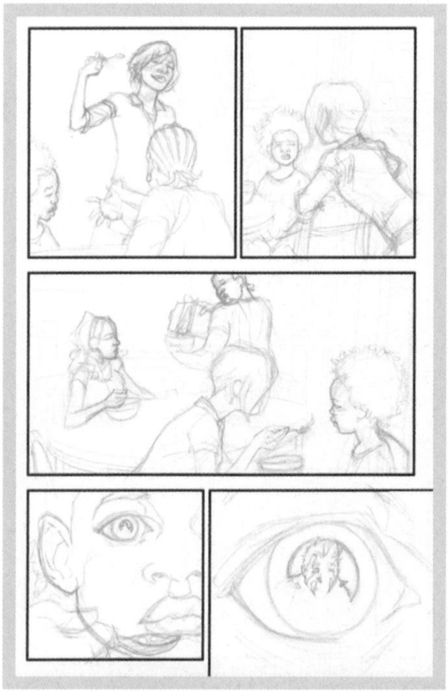

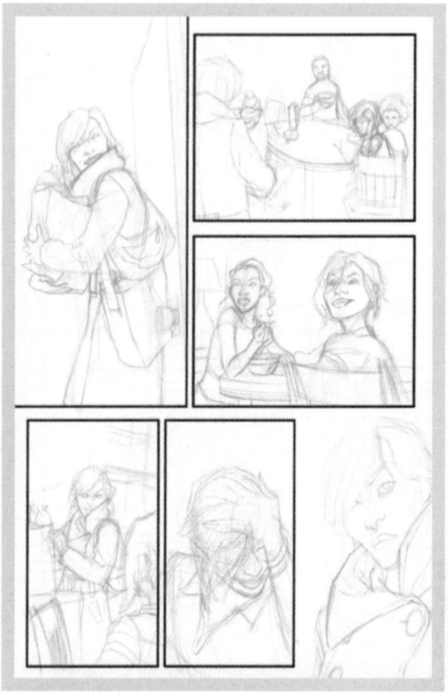

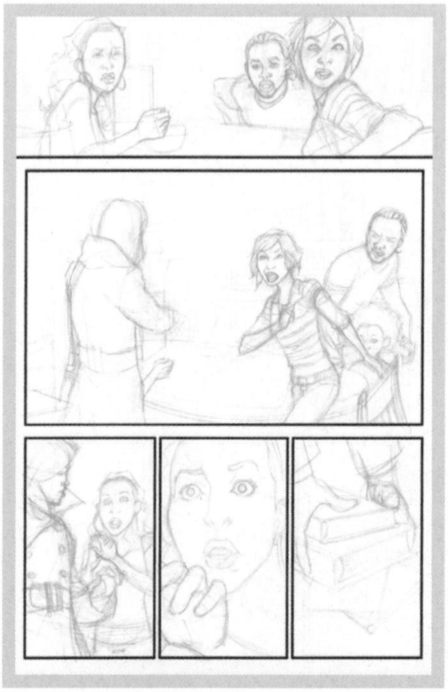

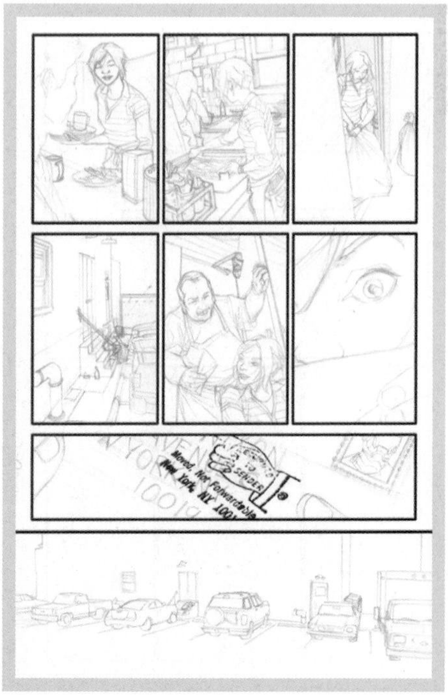
Moved, Not Forwardable
New York, NY 1001

ISSUE 2 PENCILS BY KALMAN ANDRASOFSZKY

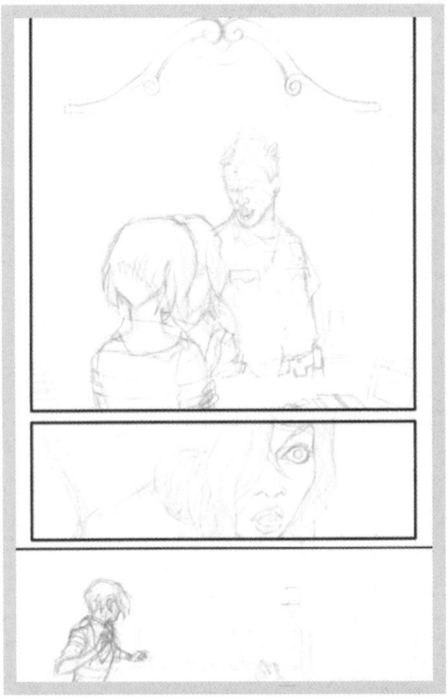

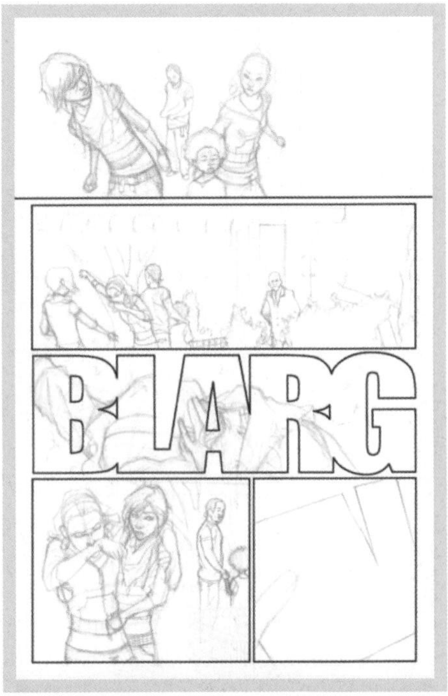
BLARG

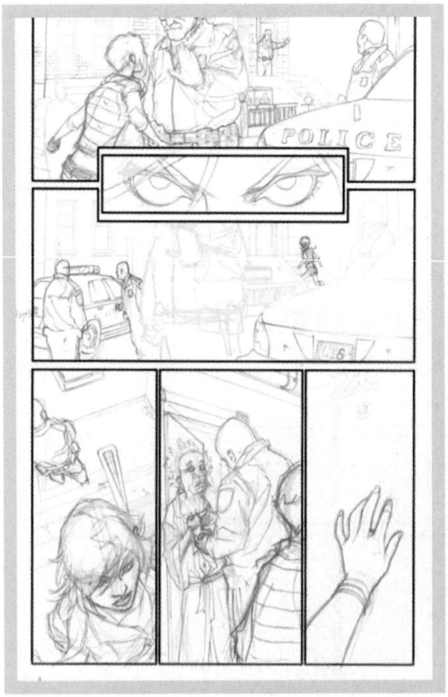
POLICE

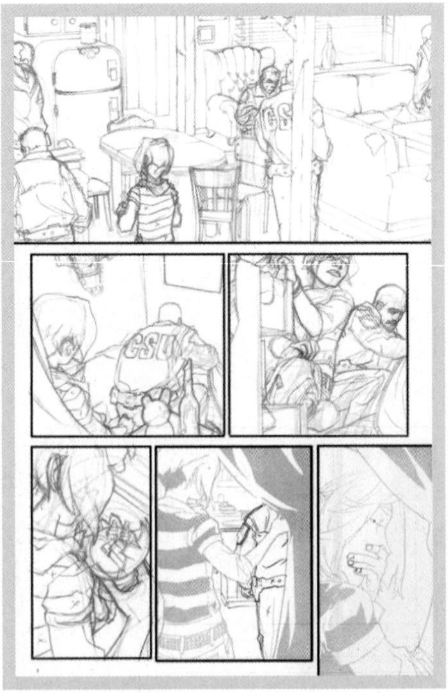
CSU

ISSUE 2 PENCILS BY KALMAN ANDRASOFSZKY

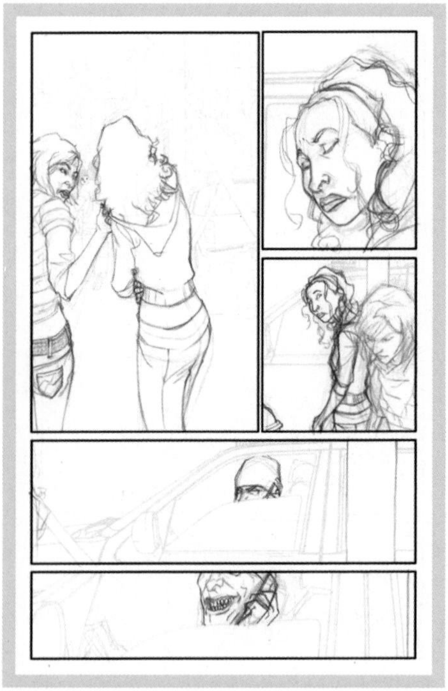

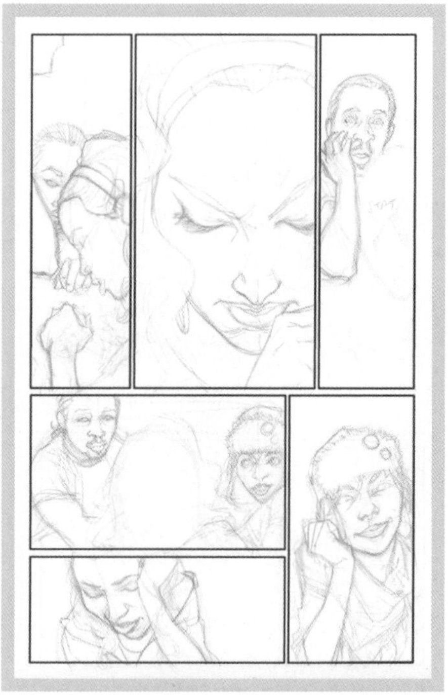

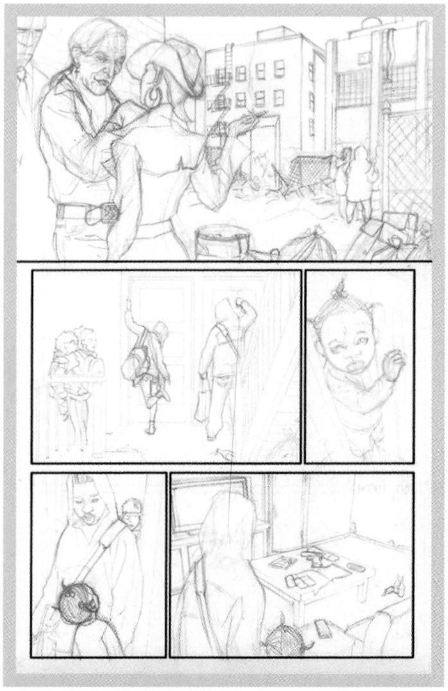

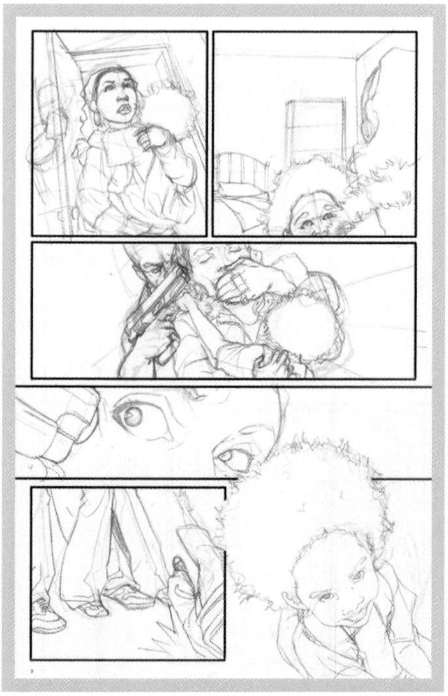

ISSUE 3 PENCILS BY KALMAN ANDRASOFSZKY

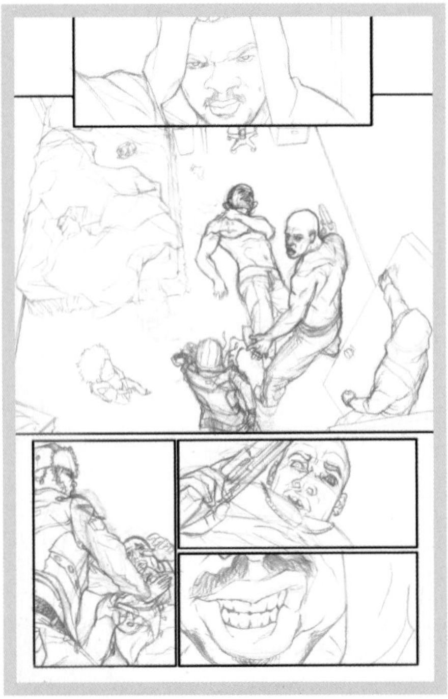

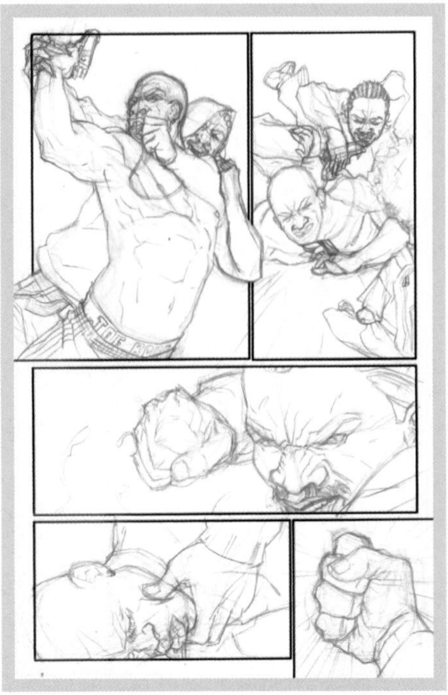

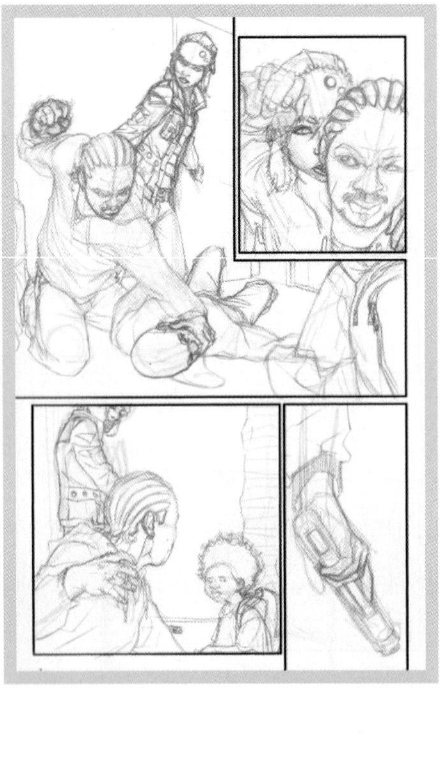

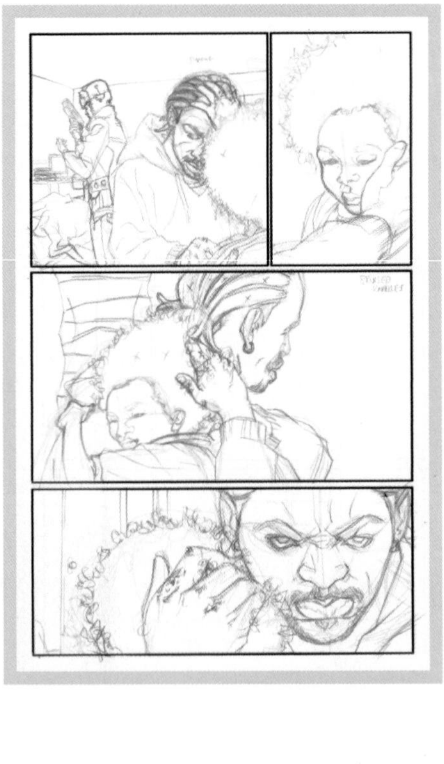

ISSUE 3 PENCILS BY KALMAN ANDRASOFSZKY

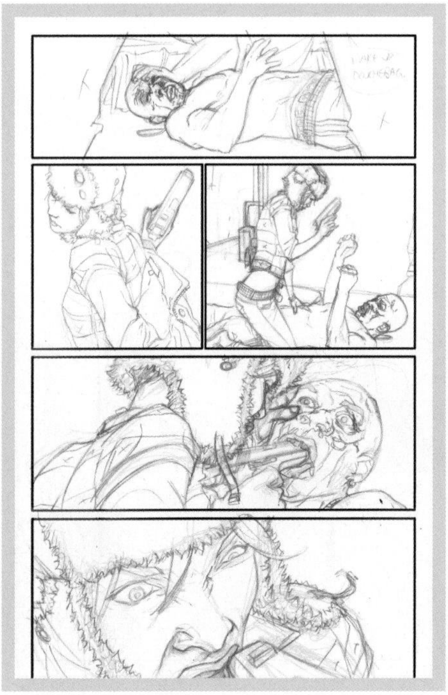

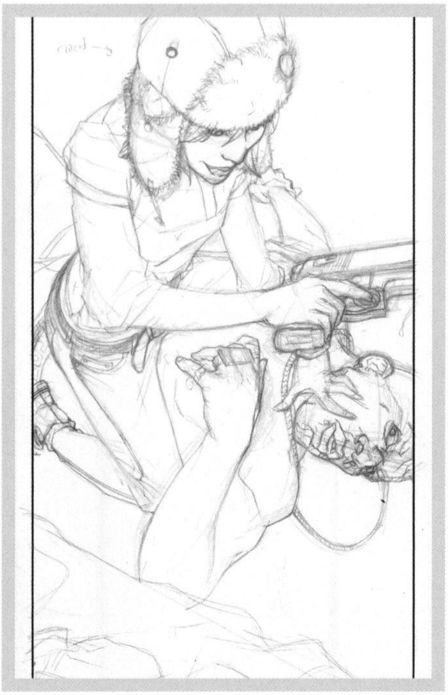

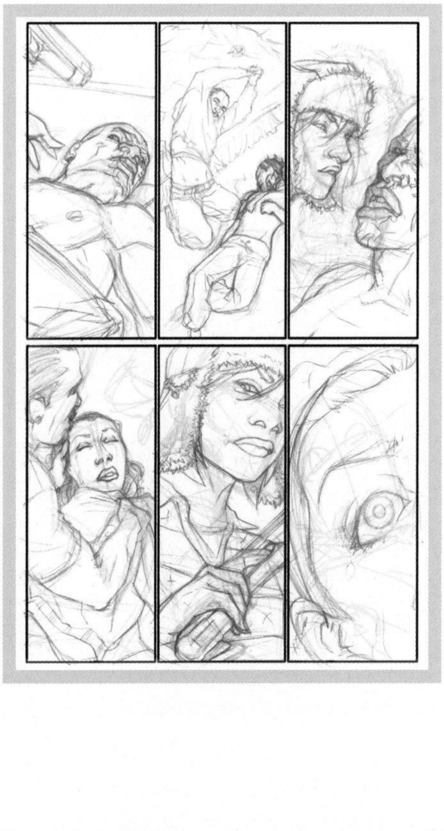

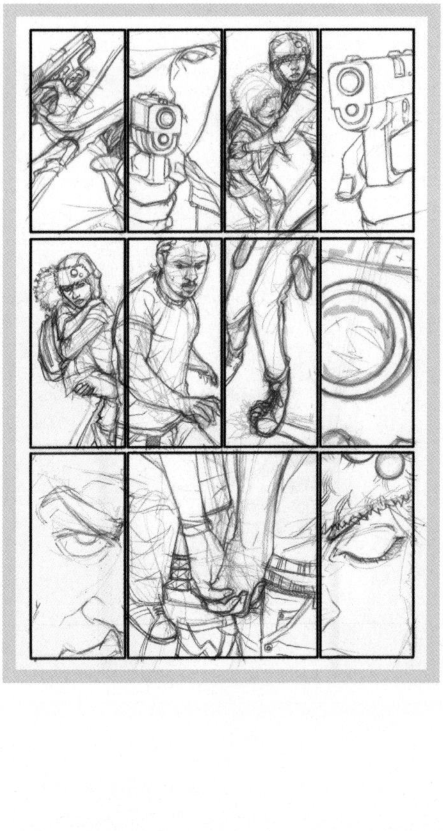

ISSUE 3 PENCILS BY SARA PICHELLI

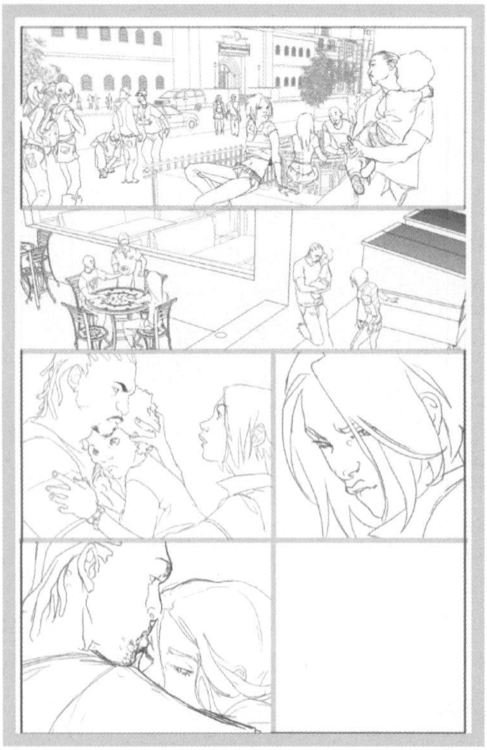

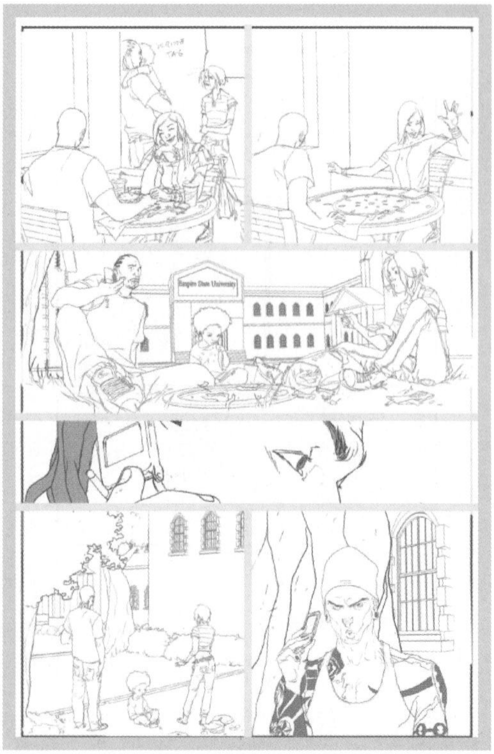

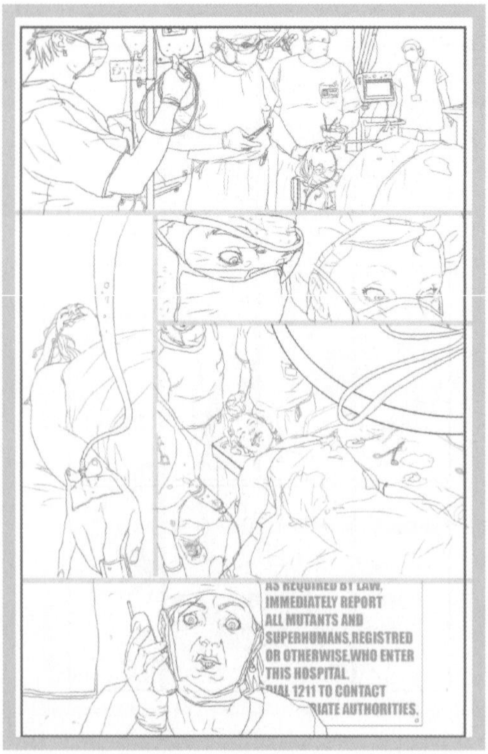
AS REQUIRED BY LAW,
IMMEDIATELY REPORT
ALL MUTANTS AND
SUPERHUMANS,REGISTRED
OR OTHERWISE,WHO ENTER
THIS HOSPITAL.
DIAL 1211 TO CONTACT
RIATE AUTHORITIES.

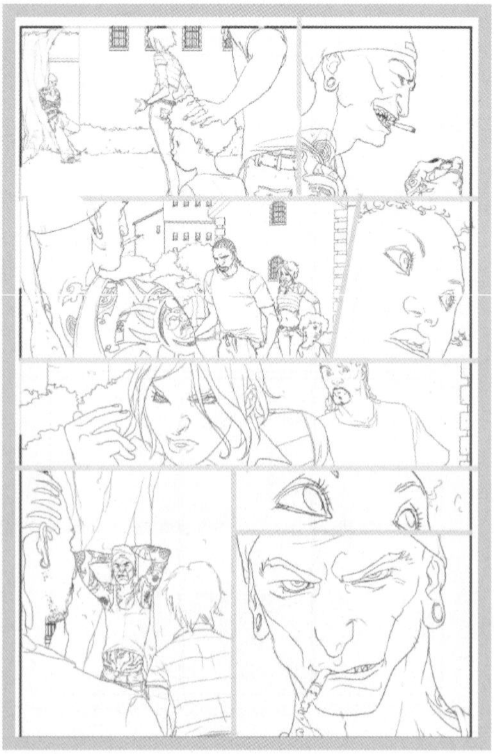

UNUSED SNIPER CHICK PAGES FROM ISSUE 3

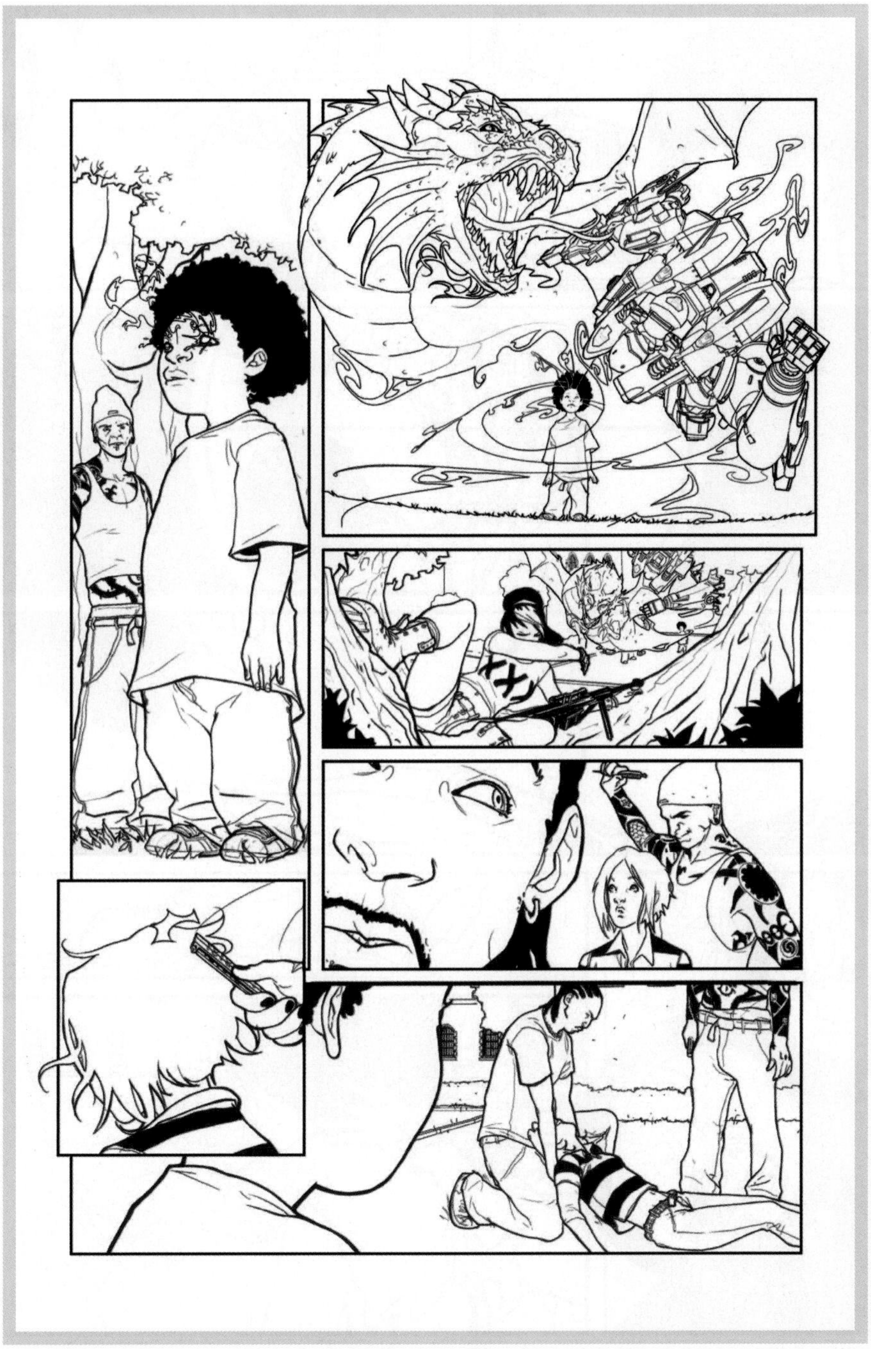

The gun-loving femme fatale with an inexplicable immunity to Kiden's powers makes her debut in issue 4, but initially she was scheduled to appear at the climax of issue 3. Marjorie decided to hold off on premiering this all-new menace, but we've got Sara's art from that explosive cliffhanger's original ending for your viewing pleasure!

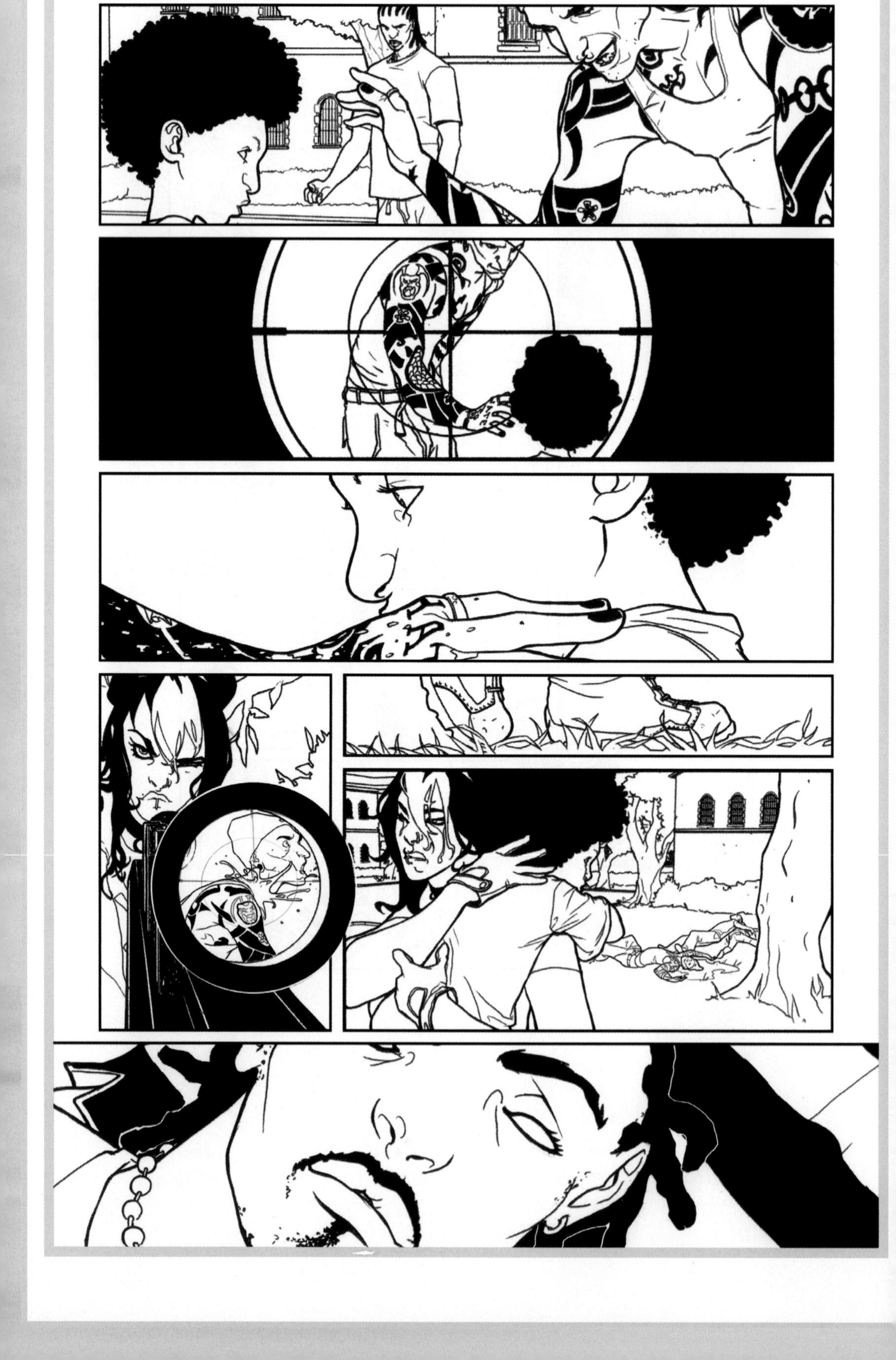

ISSUE 4 PENCILS BY SARA PICHELLI

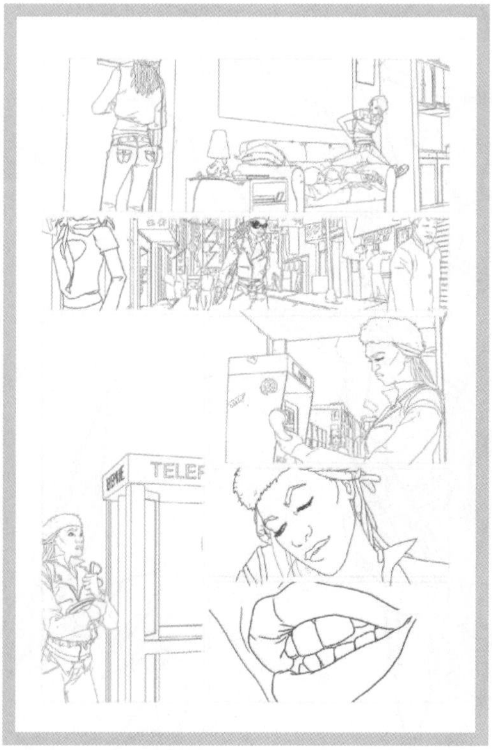

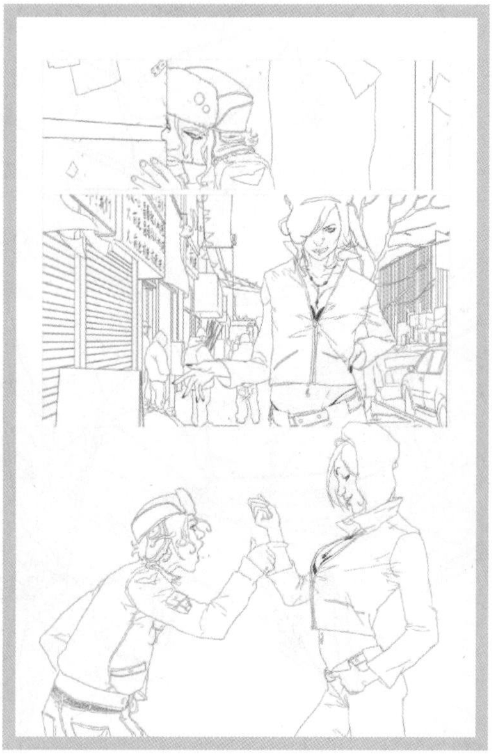

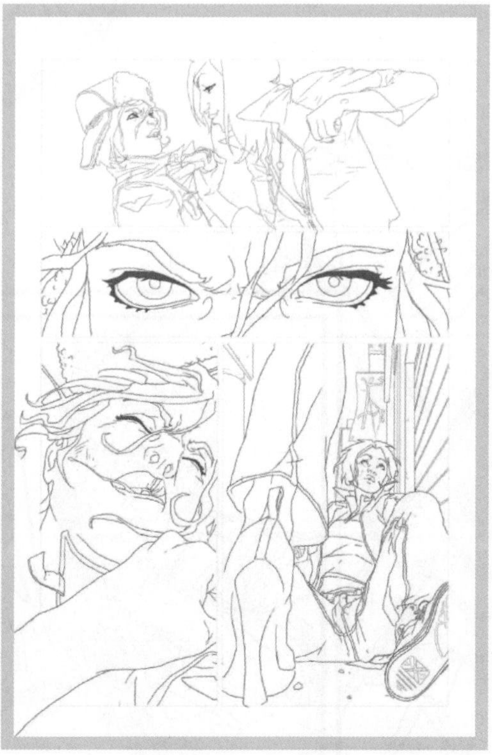

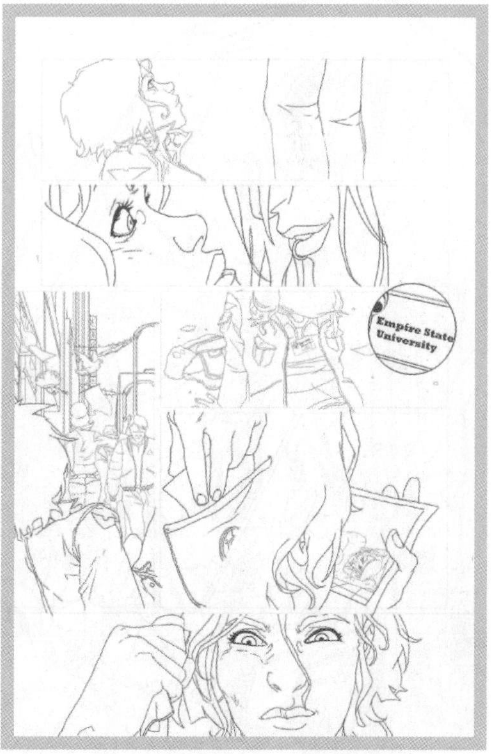
Empire State University

KALMAN PENCILS FOR ISSUE 5, PAGES 2 & 3

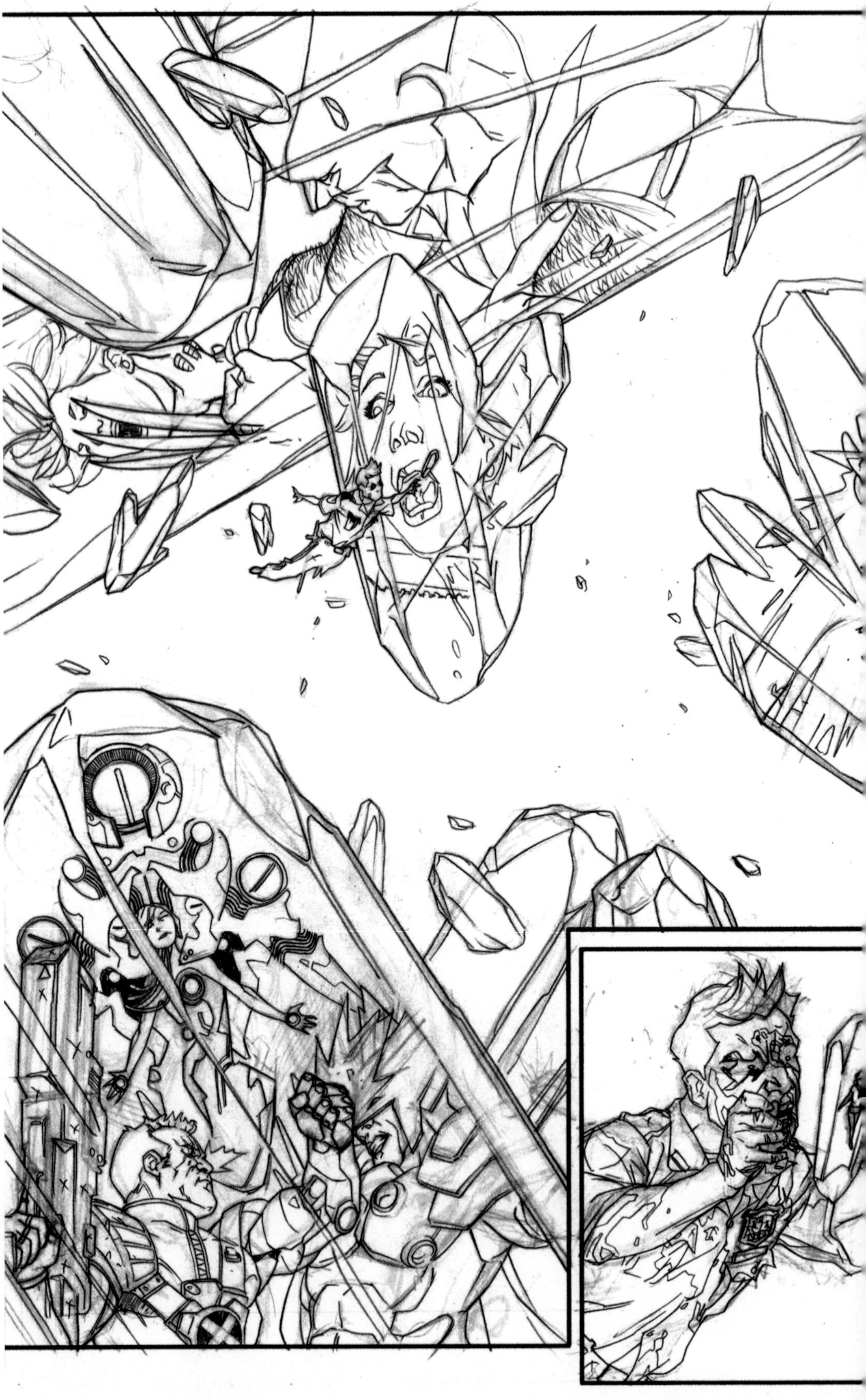

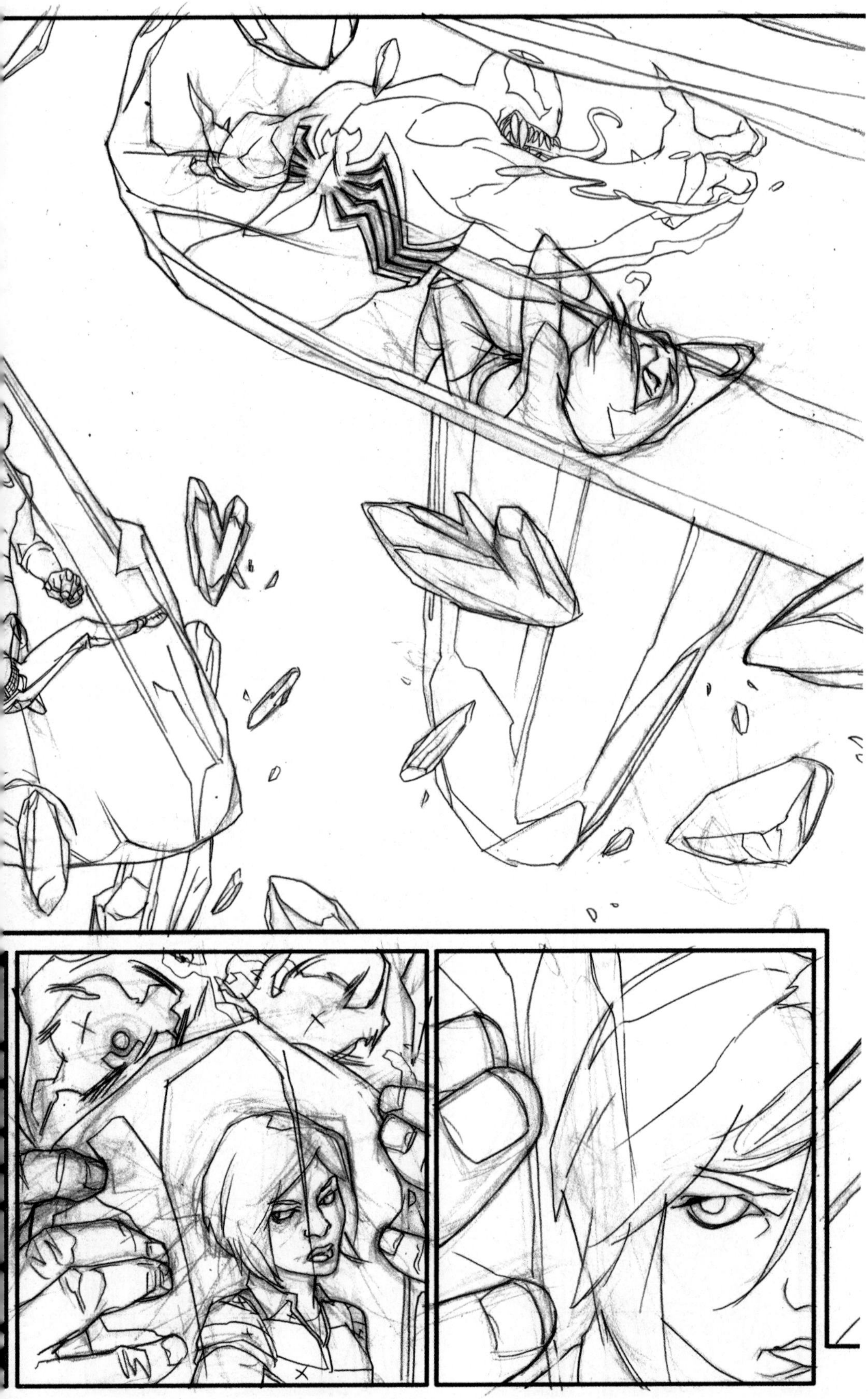

KALMAN PENCILS FOR ISSUE 5, PAGES 11 & 12

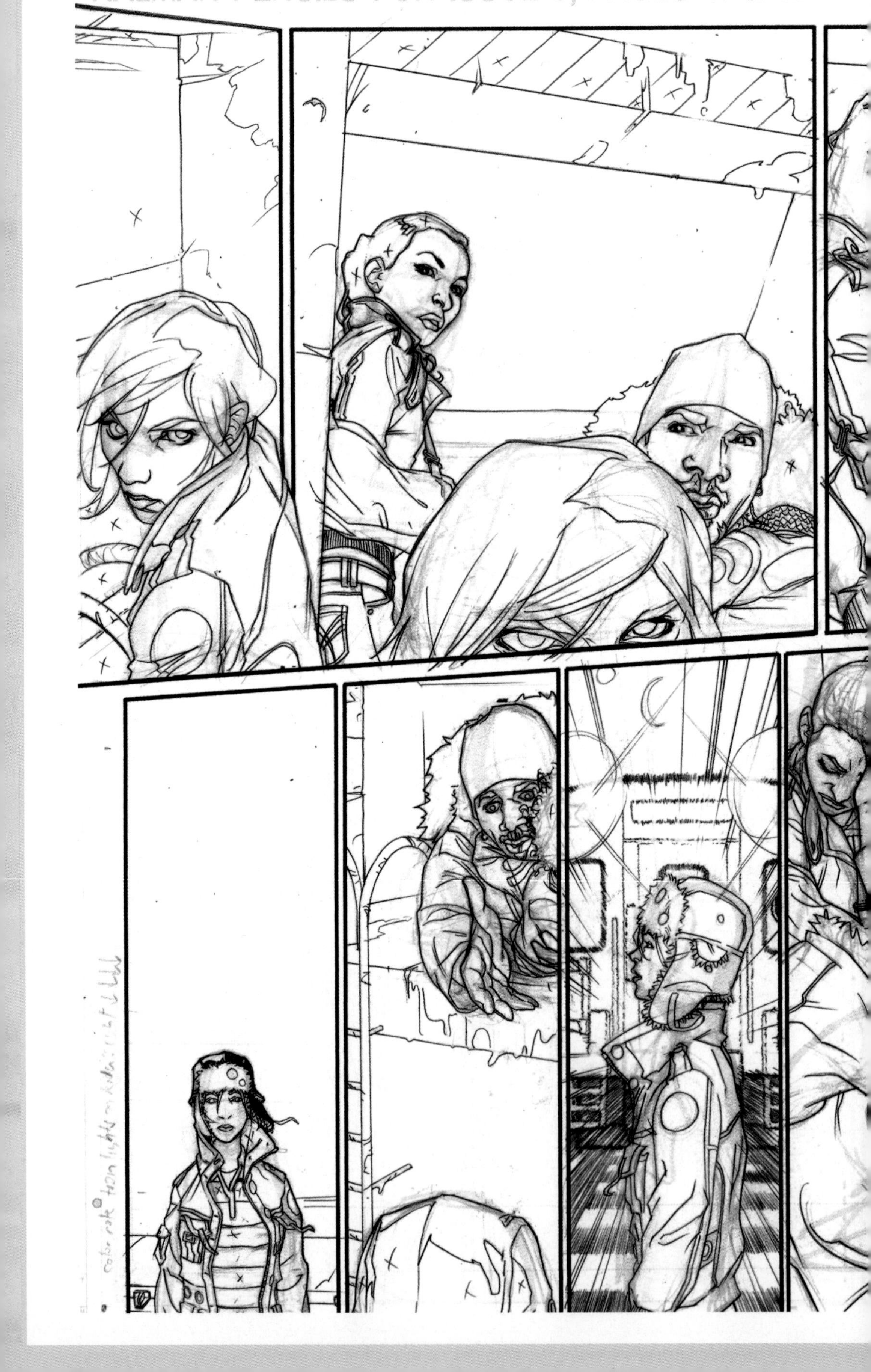

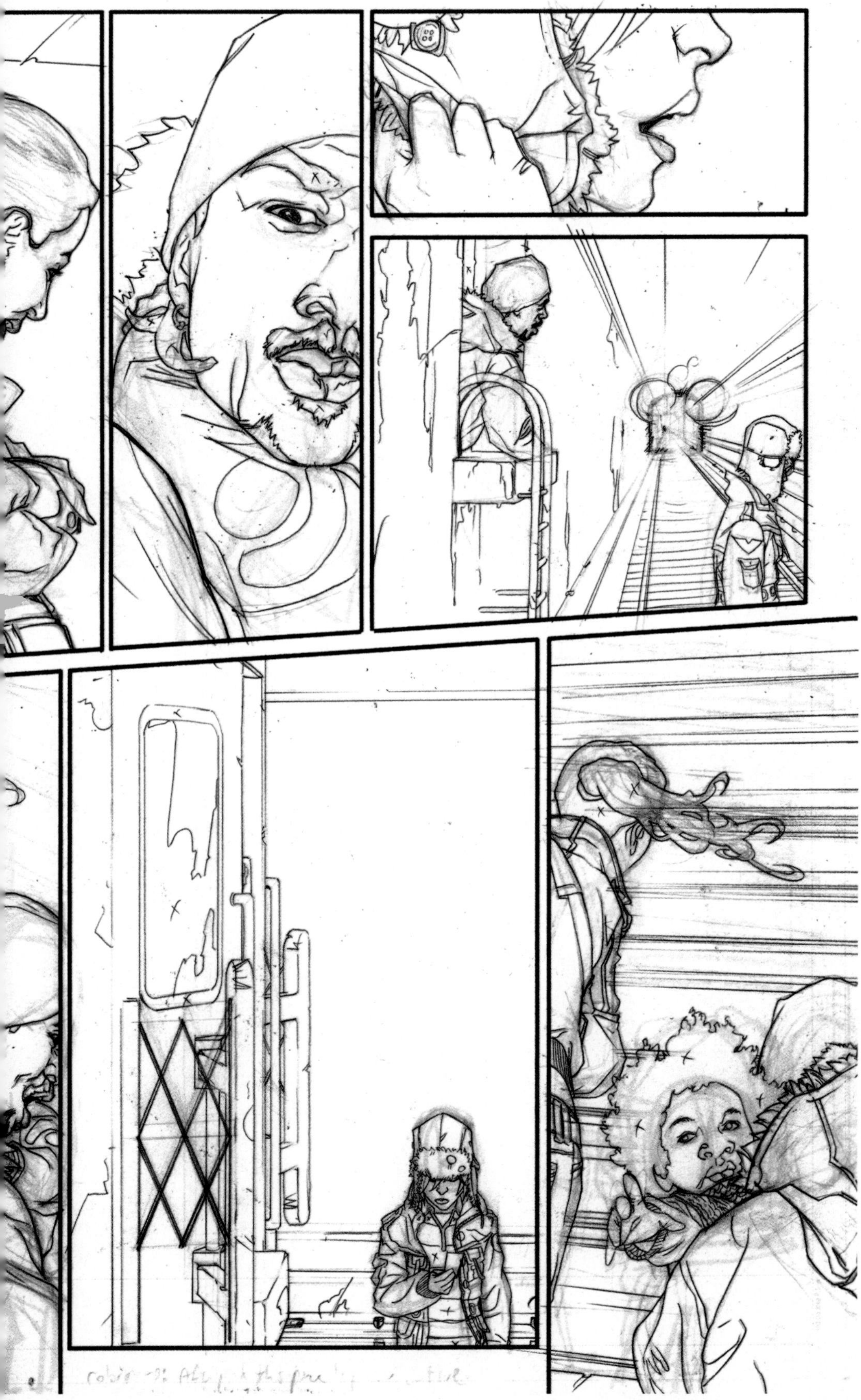

COVER PENCILS BY ALINA URUSOV

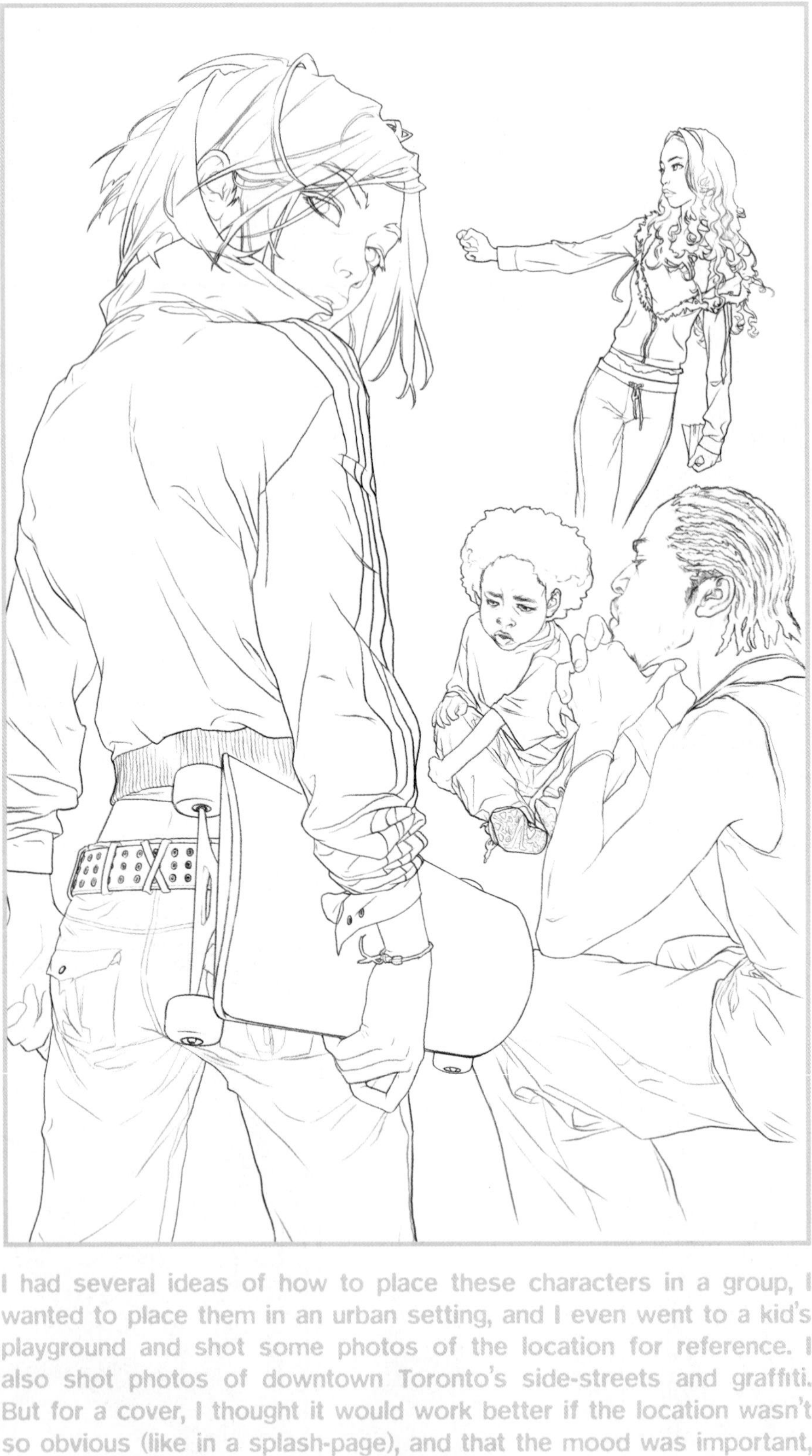

I had several ideas of how to place these characters in a group, I wanted to place them in an urban setting, and I even went to a kid's playground and shot some photos of the location for reference. I also shot photos of downtown Toronto's side-streets and graffiti. But for a cover, I thought it would work better if the location wasn't so obvious (like in a splash-page), and that the mood was important, so I played around with different moods and color-schemes (late-afternoon, dusk, mid-day etc). Generally I only have an approximate idea of what I want, and the rest is experimentation and a feeling of 'what looks right'.

-Alina Urusov

COVER CONCEPTS BY ALINA URUSOV

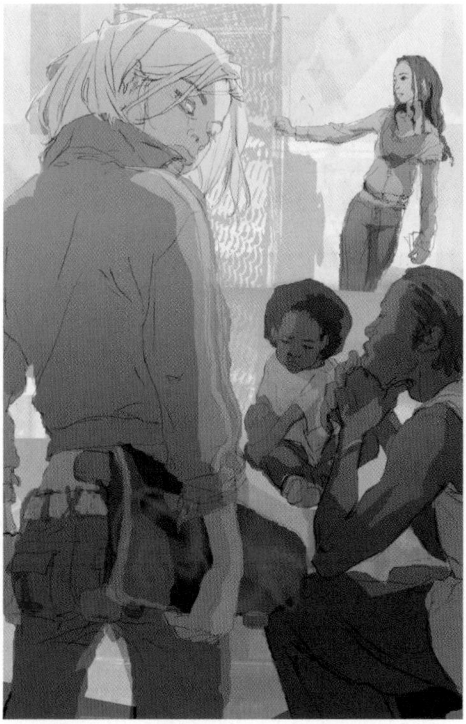

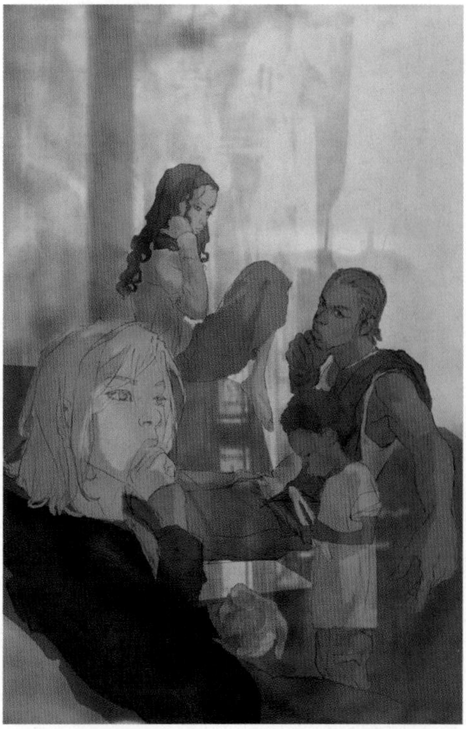

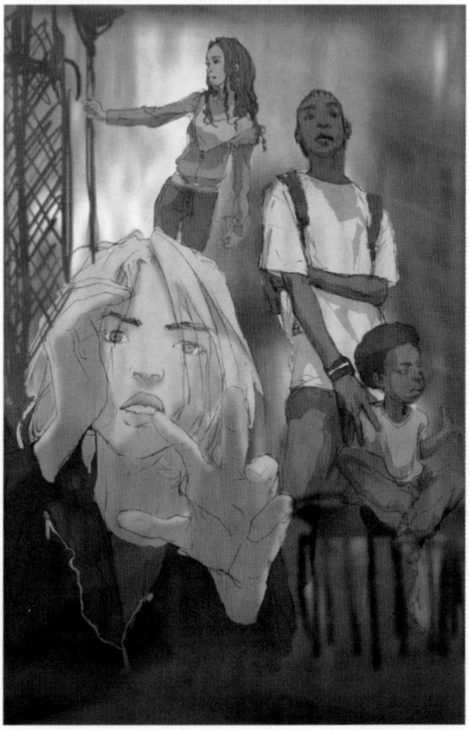

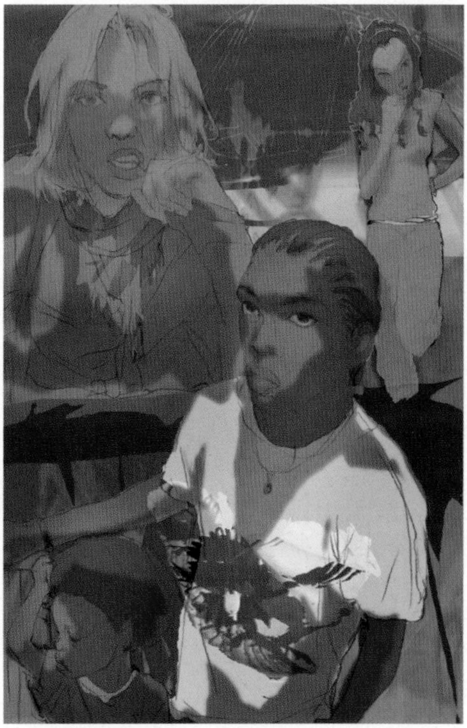

COVER CONCEPTS BY ALINA URUSOV

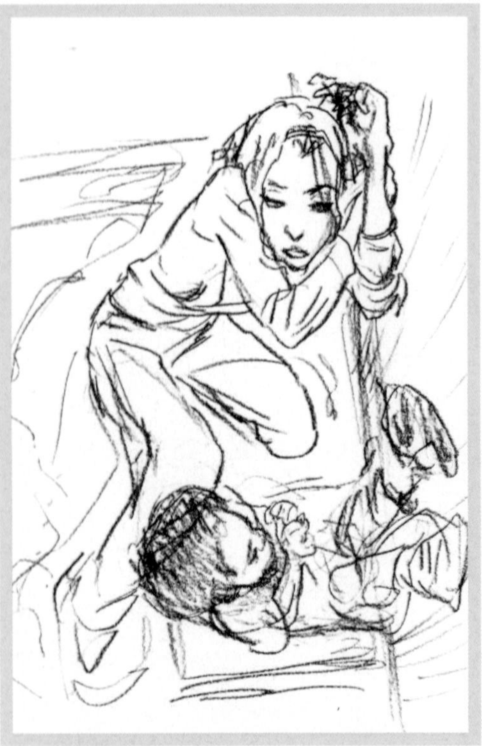

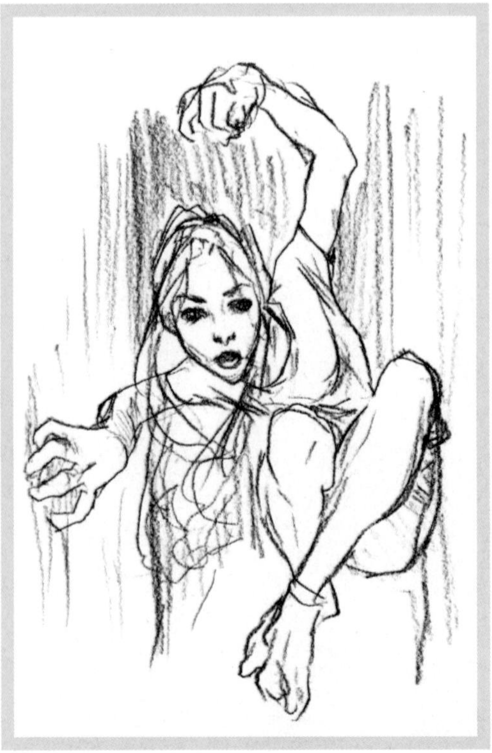

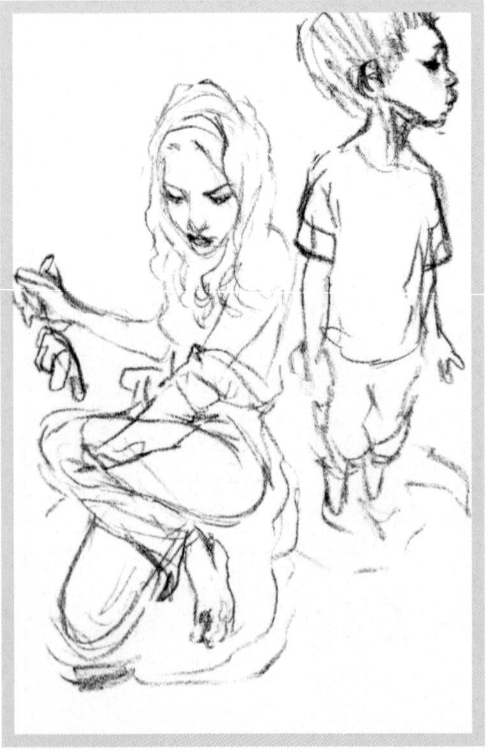

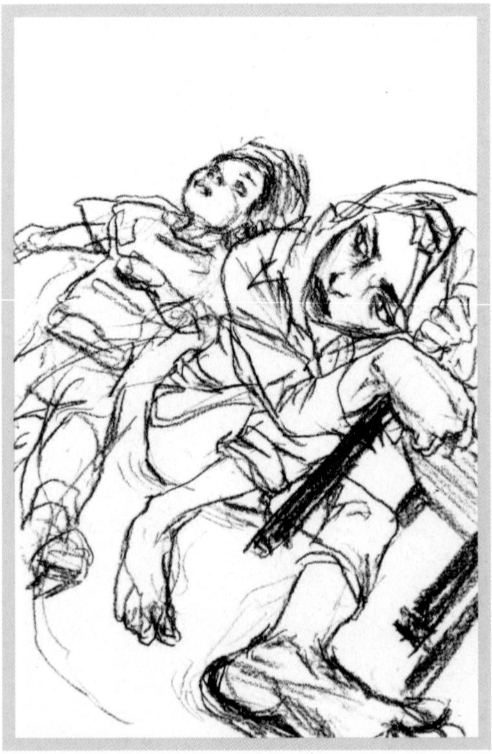

COVER CONCEPTS BY ALINA URUSOV

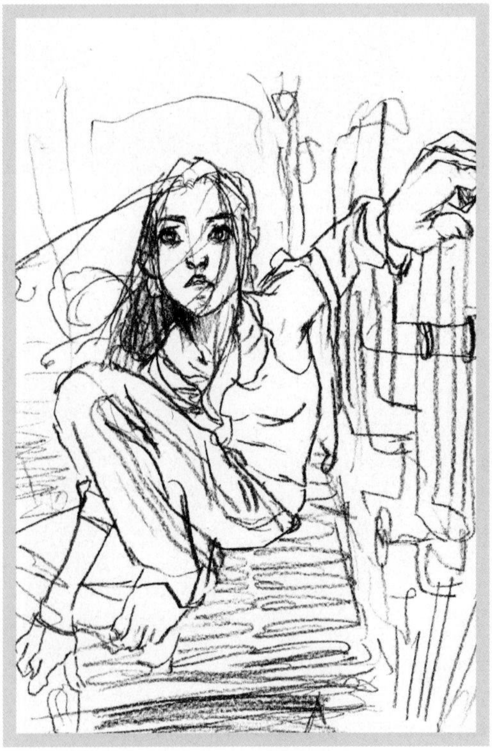

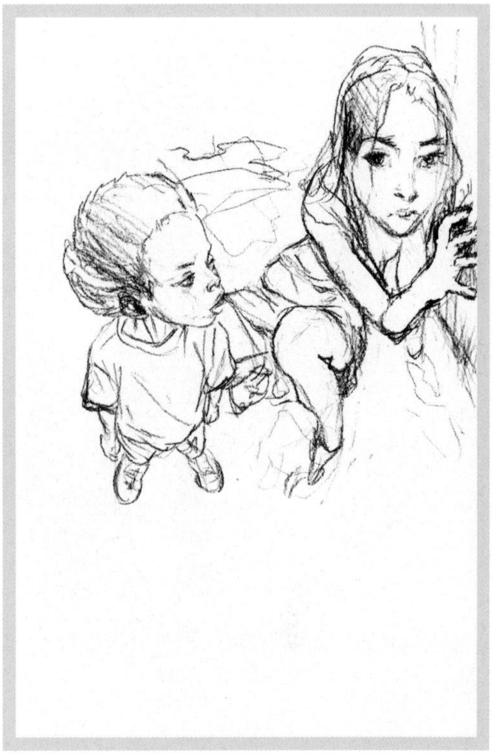

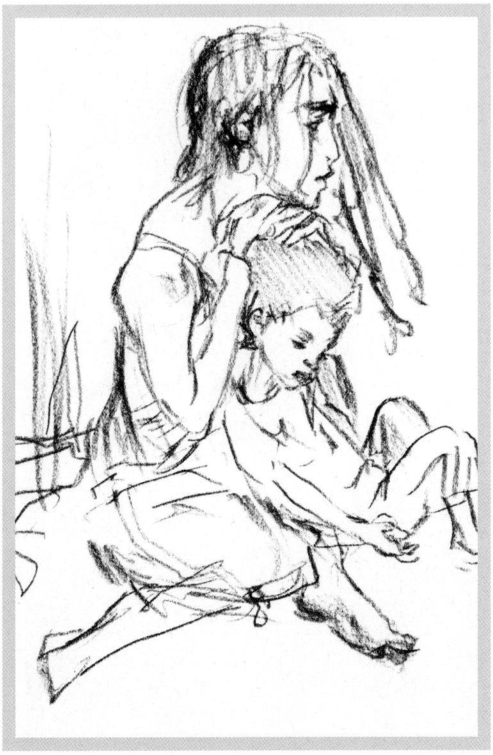

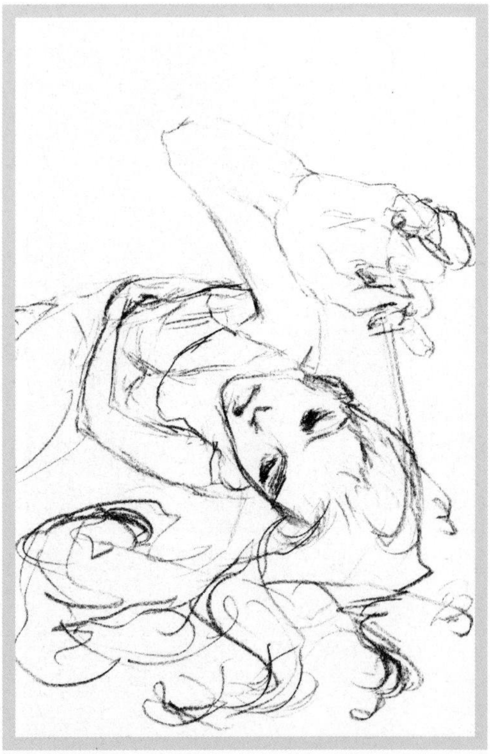

COVER ROUGHS BY ALINA URUSOV

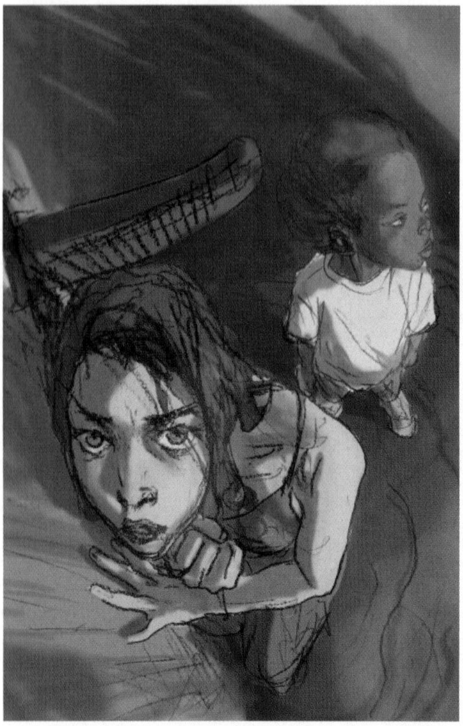

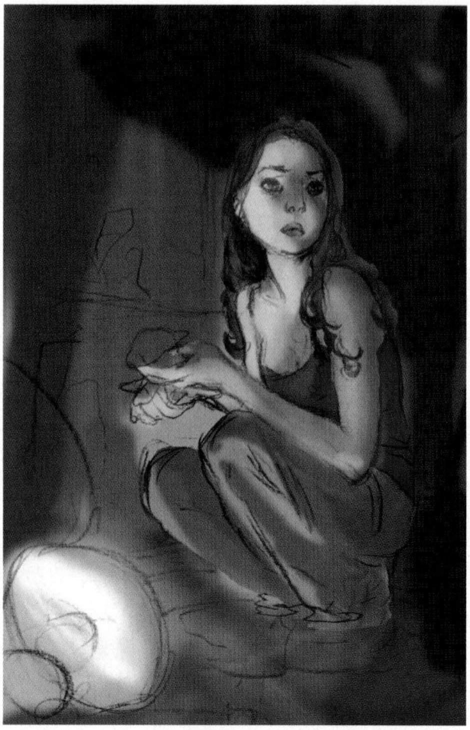

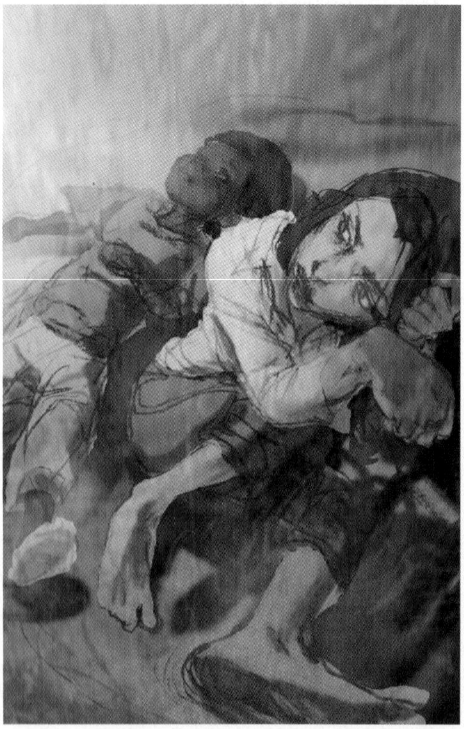

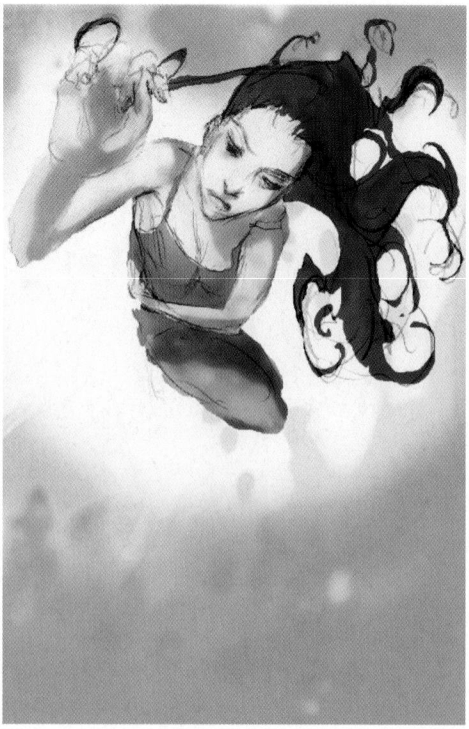

COVER ROUGHS BY ALINA URUSOV

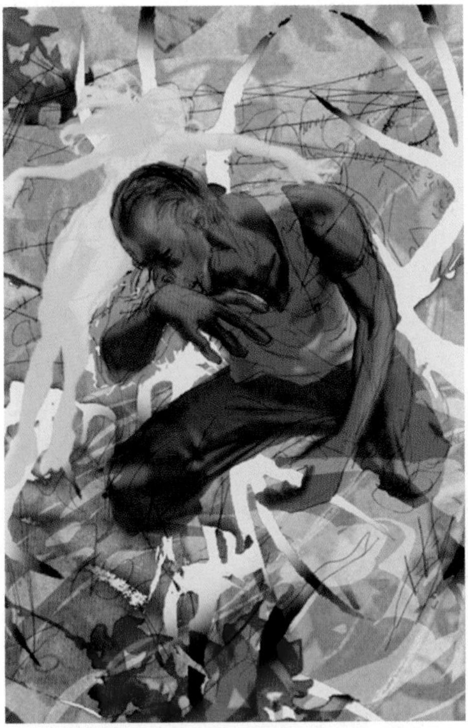

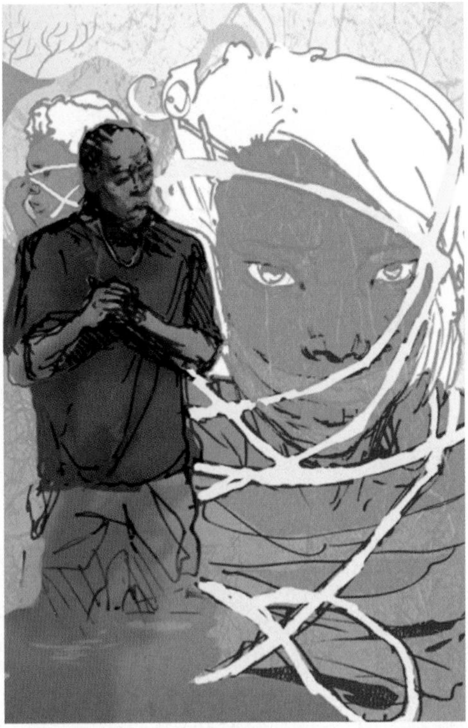

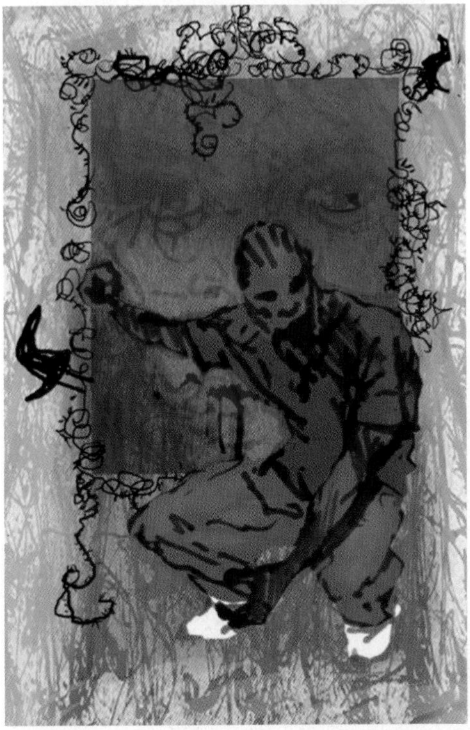

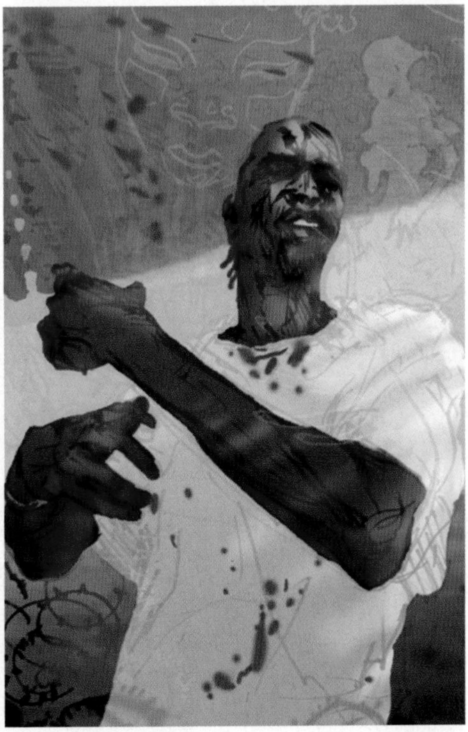

COVER ROUGH BY
ALINA URUSOV

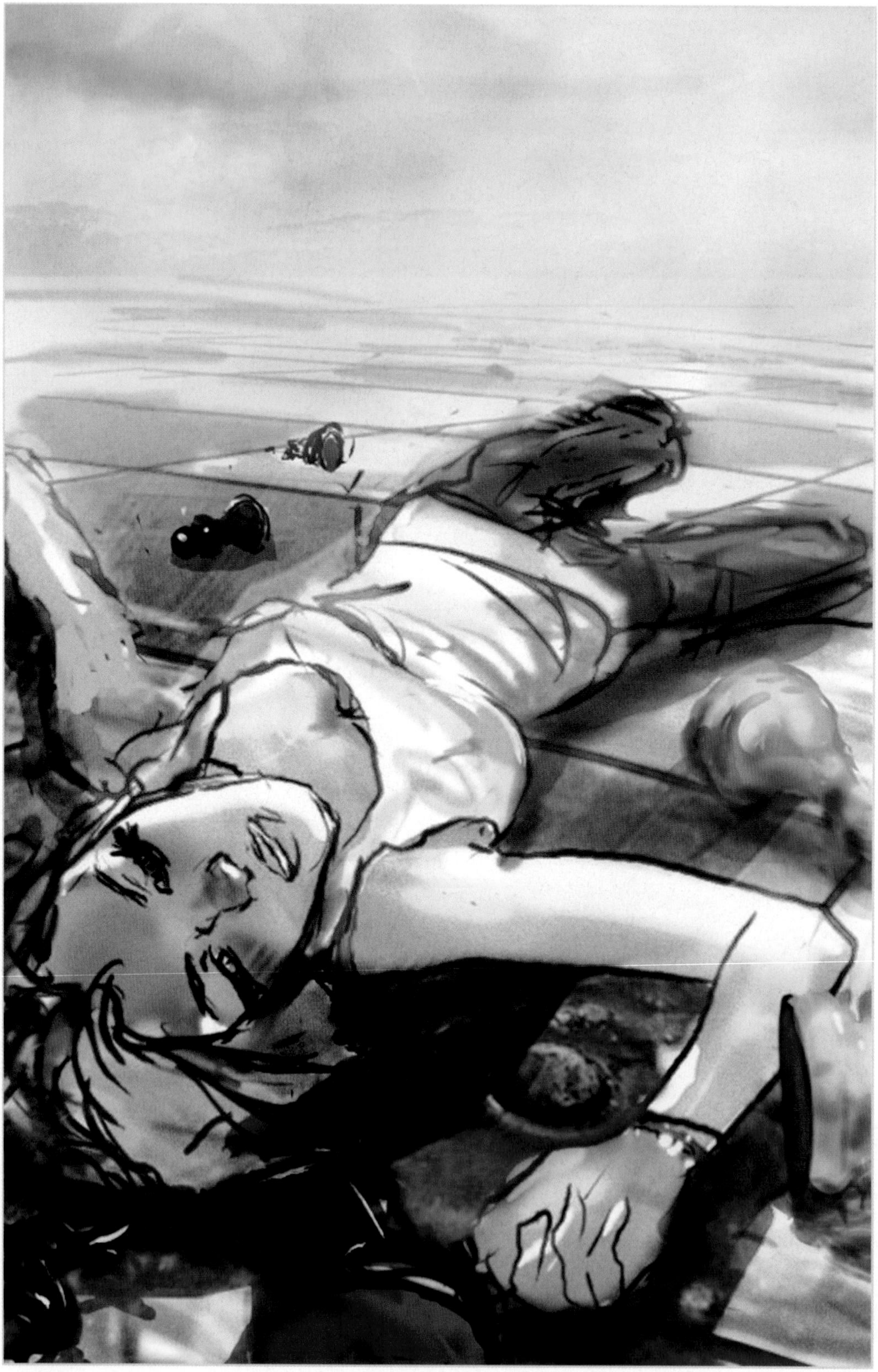

COVER ROUGH BY
ALINA URUSOV

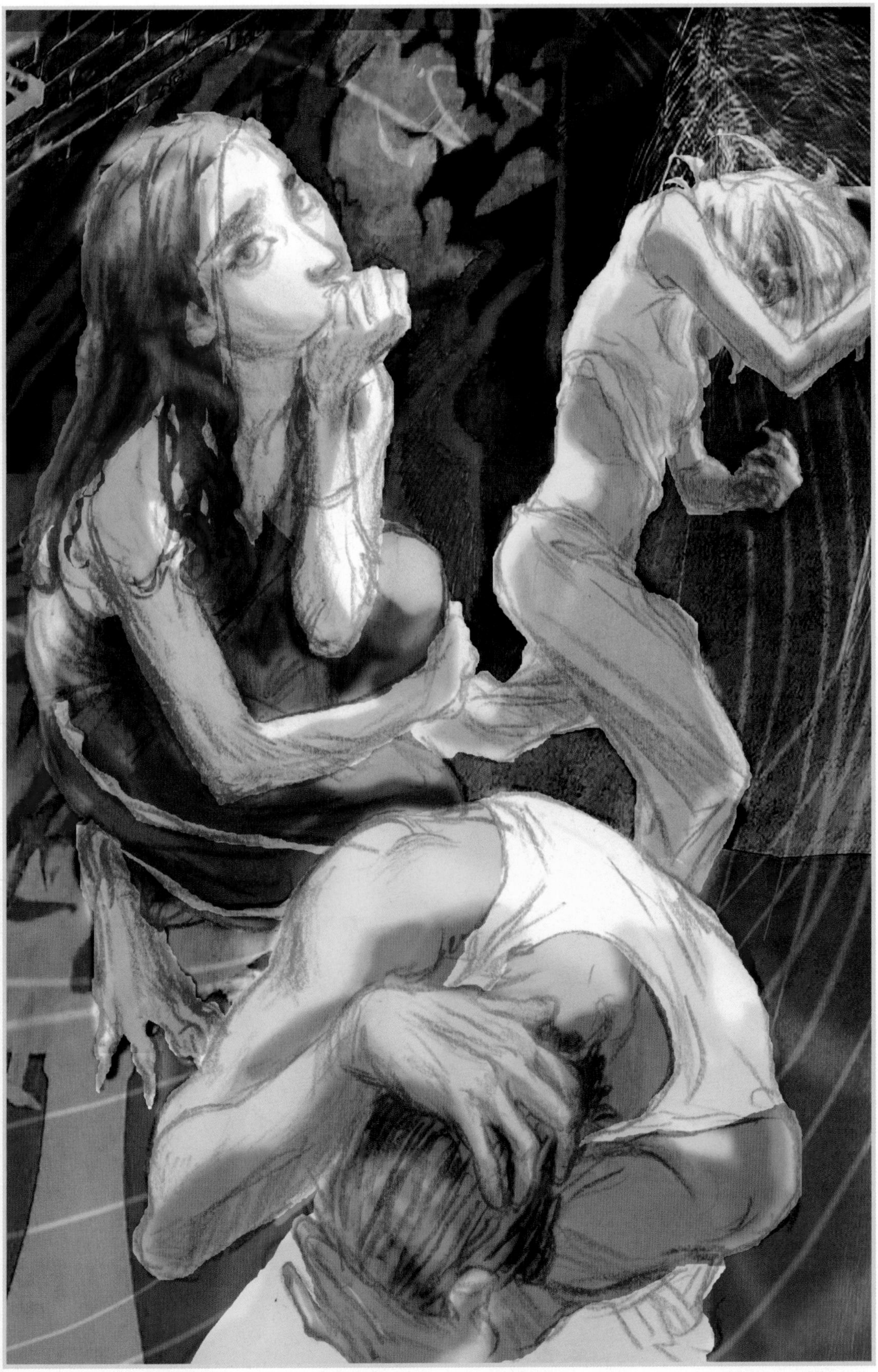

NICK NIXON STUDIES BY ALINA URUSOV

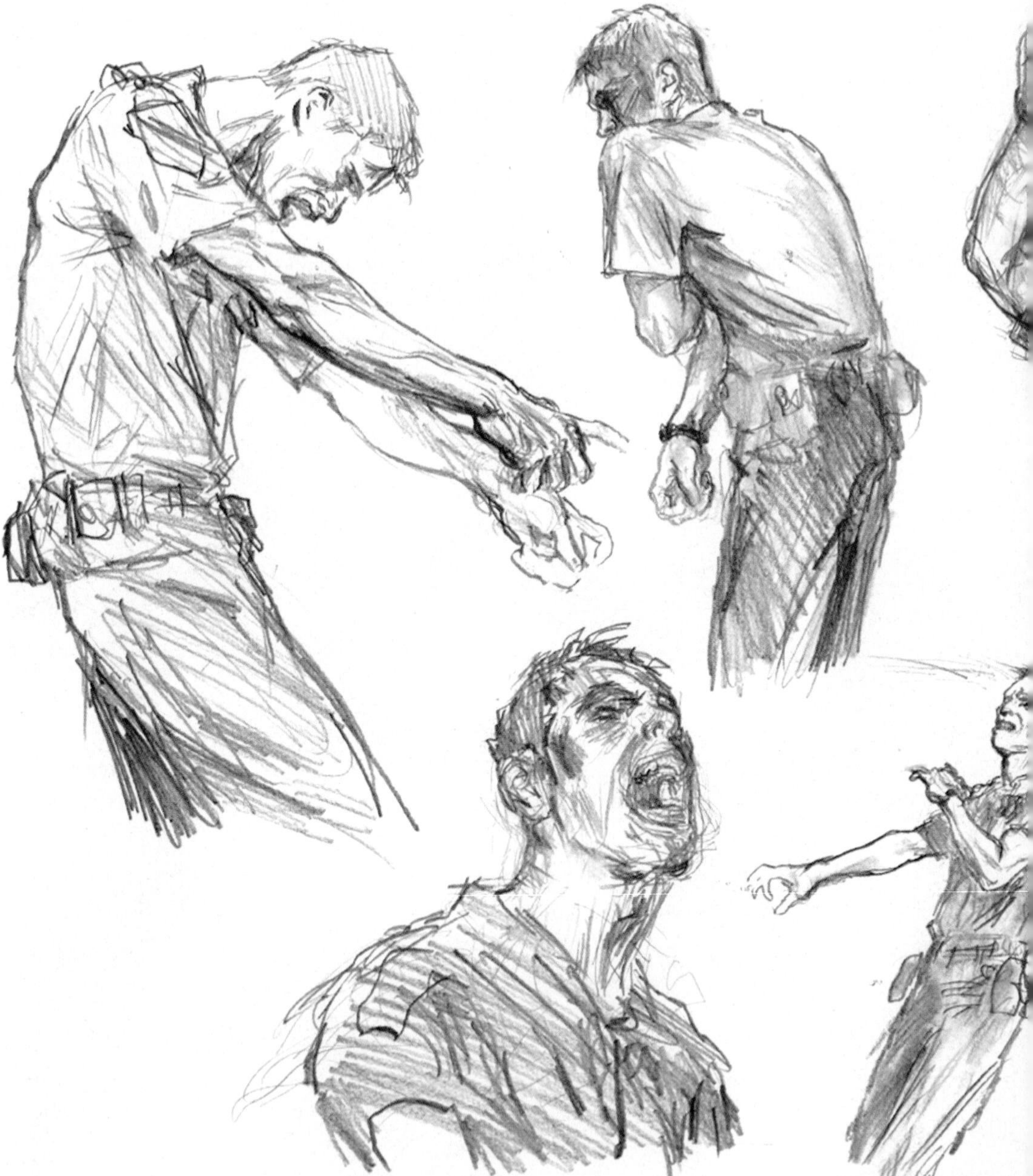

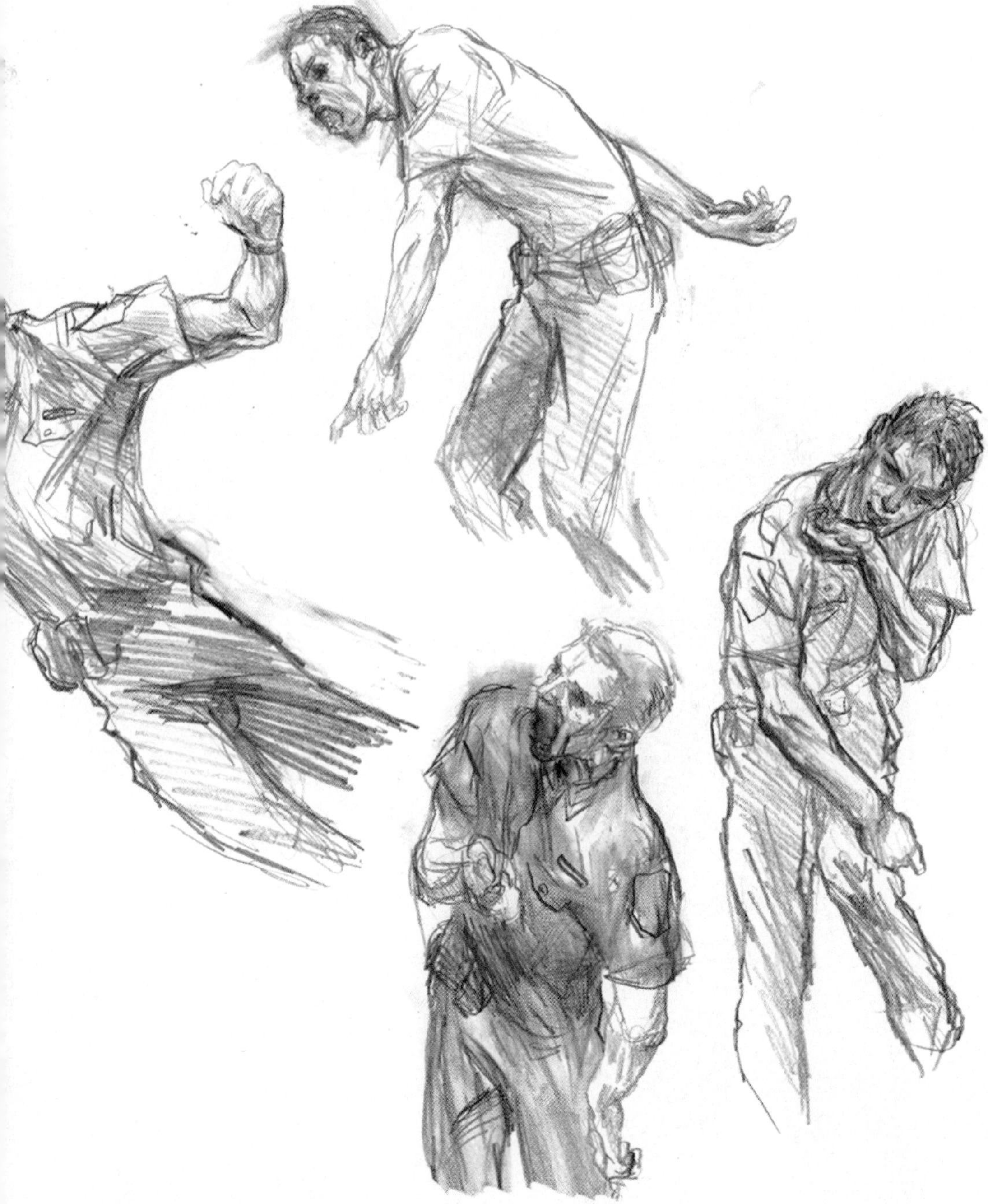

KIDEN STUDIES BY ALINA URUSOV

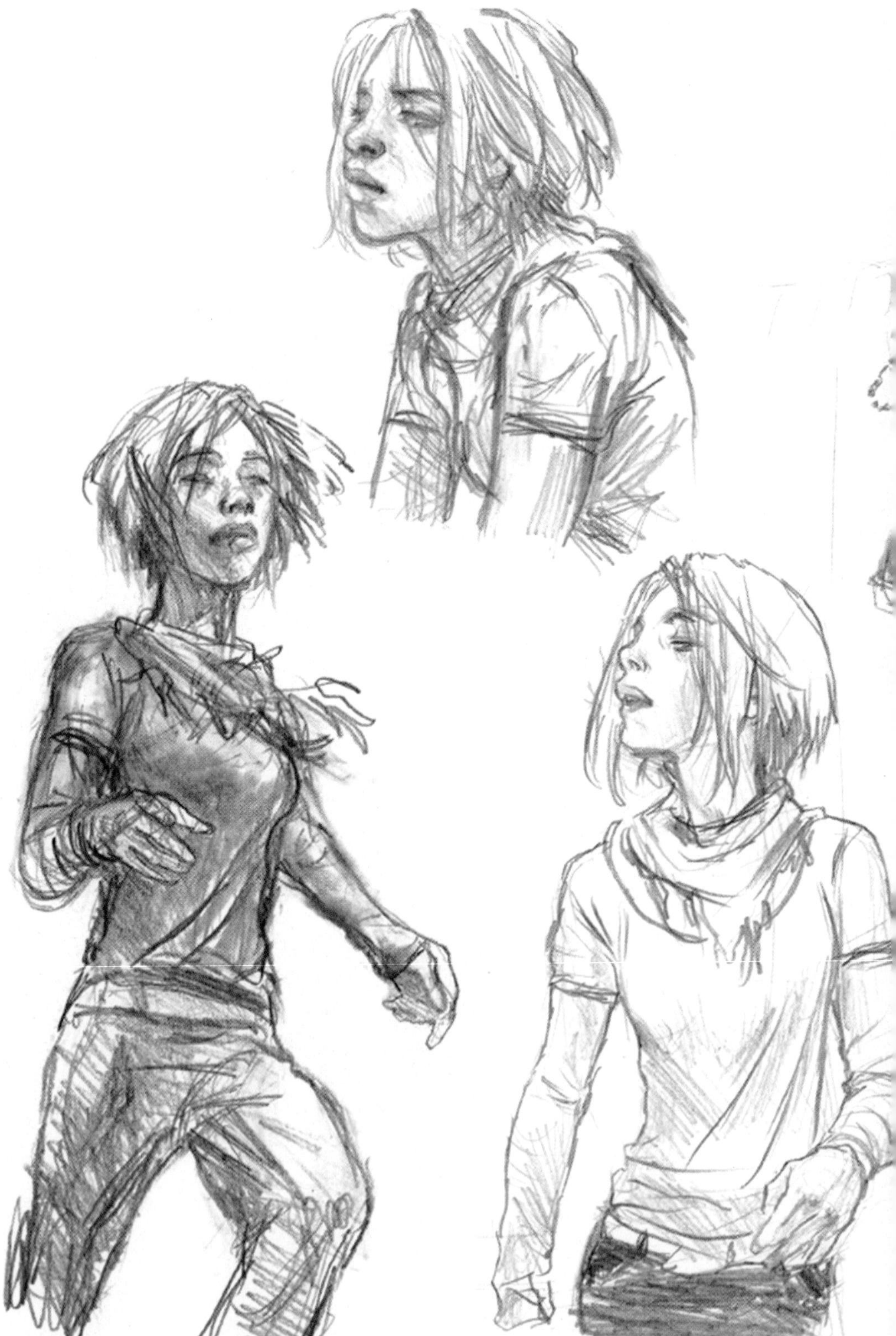

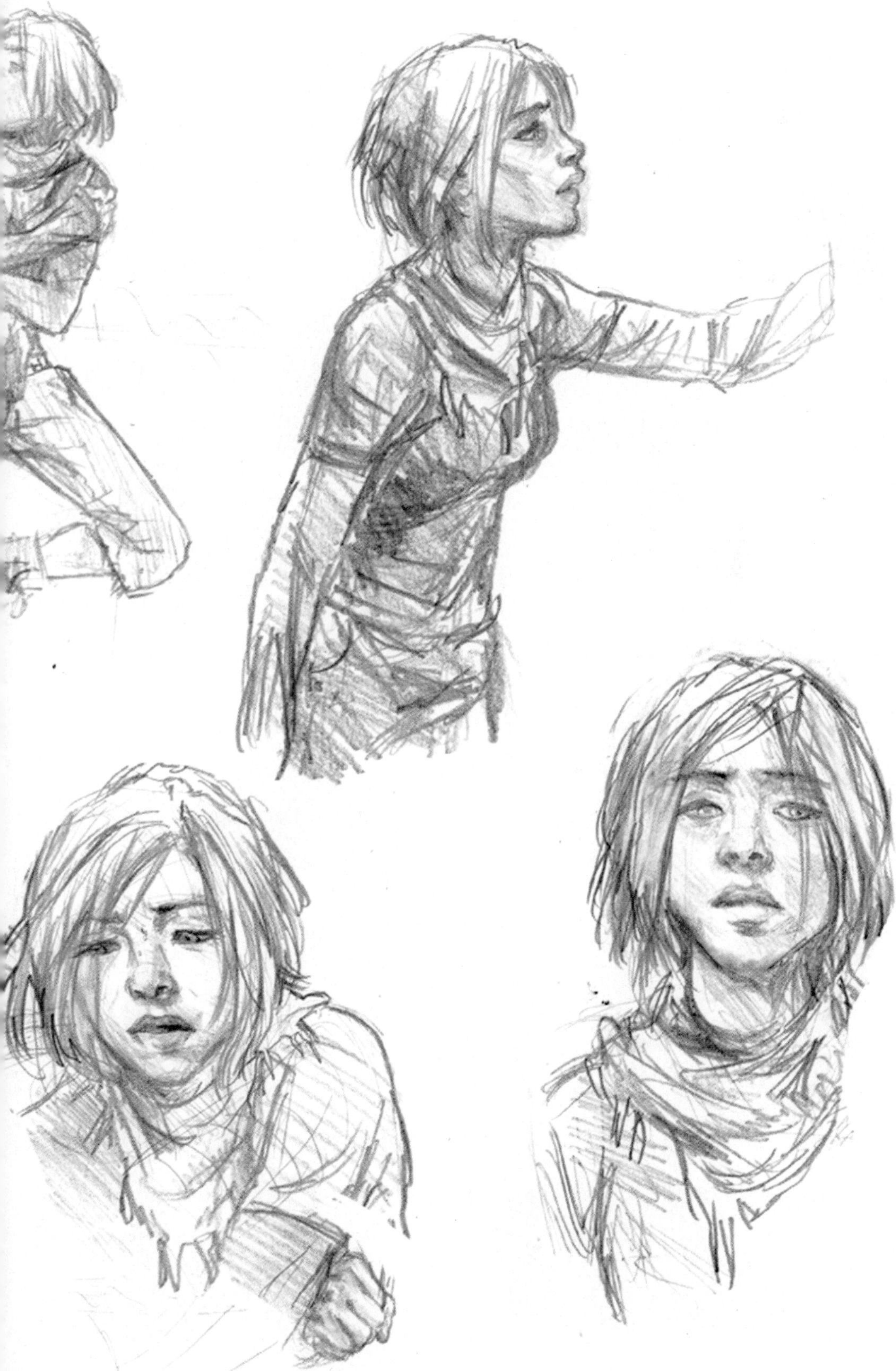

COVER ROUGHS BY ALINA URUSOV

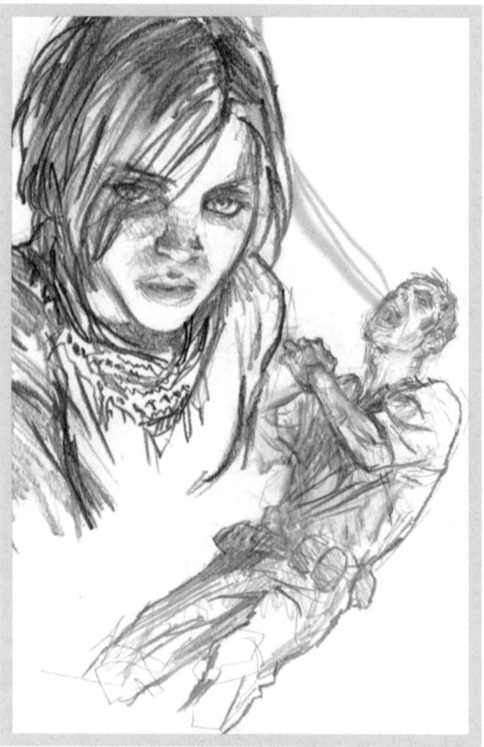

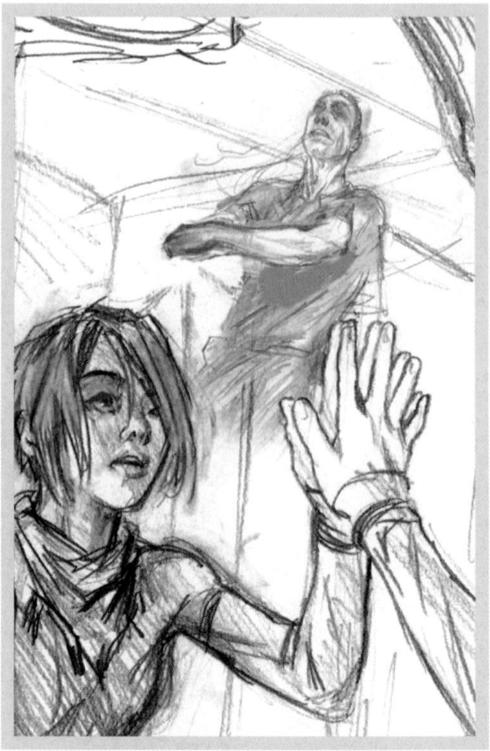

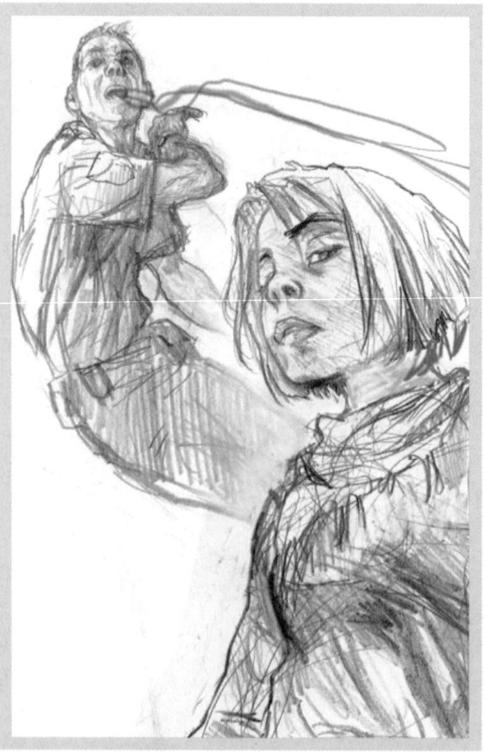

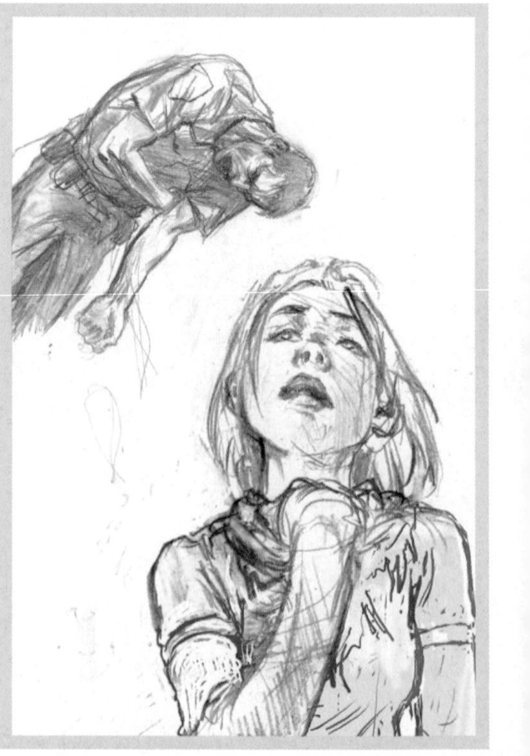